FOR PROPHET AND TSAR

For Prophet and Tsar

ISLAM AND EMPIRE IN RUSSIA AND CENTRAL ASIA

Robert D. Crews

HARVARD UNIVERSITY PRESS
Cambridge, Massachusetts
London, England

2006

Copyright © 2006 by the President and Fellows of Harvard College

ALL RIGHTS RESERVED

PRINTED IN THE UNITED STATES OF AMERICA

Library of Congress Cataloging-in-Publication Data
Crews, Robert D., 1970–
For prophet and tsar : Islam and empire in Russia and
Central Asia / Robert D. Crews.
p.   cm.
Includes bibliographical references and index.
ISBN 0-674-02164-9 (alk. paper)
1. Islam and state—Russia (Federation).   2. Muslims—Russia (Federation)—
Political activity.   3. Islam and state—Asia, Central.   4. Muslims—Asia, Central—
Political activity.   5. Russia (Federation)—Politics and government.   6. Asia,
Central—Politics and government.   I. Title.
BP65.R8C74 2006
322'.10947—dc22   2005056387

CONTENTS

NOTE ON TRANSLITERATION AND SPELLING

The Russian empire was constructed by peoples who, like the descendants of the builders of the Tower of Babel, spoke dozens of different languages and dialects and whose literatures appeared in a dizzying array of alphabets and scripts. The Soviets built on this imperial Babel by changing these writing systems. Post-Soviet elites continue to debate the utility of Cyrillic, Roman, and Arabic orthographies, while scholars disagree about how to transliterate them.

The sources for this study reflect only a small part of this linguistic heterogeneity. In the polyglot world of the empire, words appeared in different forms, depending on the context and the language of the document; the name of one important Muslim religious figure was written as "Muḥammadjān bin al-Ḥusayn" in Tatar using Arabic script, but became "Mukhamedzhan Khusainov" in Russian-language texts. In transliterating such names, I have tried to follow the spellings found in the original sources, while including alternates in parentheses or in the notes that follow the text. For Russian sources, I have followed the Library of Congress system, with some simplifications (like "Kazan" in place of "Kazan'," "Dostoevsky" for

"Dostoevskii"). For others, I have relied on the transliteration charts found in the *International Journal of Middle East Studies* and Edward Allworth's *Nationalities of the Soviet East*; however, I use modified spellings of a number of terms that are already familiar to readers in other forms (as in *mullah* for *mullā*, *'ulama* for *'ulamā*, and *fatwas* for *fatāwa*). Where names and places appear in a variety of spellings even in a single language, I draw on the comprehensive *Islam na territorii byvshei Rossiskoi imperii*. The builders of Babel would understand.

FOR PROPHET AND TSAR

Men belonged to a single community, and God sent them messengers to give them happy tidings and warnings, and sent the Book with them containing the truth to judge between them in matters of dispute; but only those who received it differed after receiving clear proofs, on account of waywardness (and jealousies) among them. Then God by His dispensation showed those who believed the way to the truth about which they were differing; for God shows whom He please the path that is straight.

Qur'an 2:213

We, the below-named, promise and vow before almighty God and the great Prophet Muhammad on four of his most just books, the Gospels, the Torah, Psalms of David, and the Qur'an, that we . . . must serve as loyal subjects of his imperial majesty . . . In concluding this our oath we kiss the Qur'an of our Prophet Muhammad. Amen.

An oath sworn by Muslims of the Russian empire, 1809

INTRODUCTION

The symbols of Orthodox Christianity have long permeated the landscape of modern Russia. In the Russian empire, Orthodox tsars claimed God's blessing in ruling as autocrats. The golden domes of Orthodox cathedrals illuminated Moscow and brightened villages that stretched across a vast empire. Under the icons and banners of Orthodoxy, subjects swore loyalty to the tsars and "Holy Russia." But this mythology of a sacred realm united in Orthodoxy hid a more complex reality and a perennial dilemma for Russian elites: not all of the inhabitants of the empire were Orthodox Christians. The tsars also ruled Jews, Catholics, Protestants, Buddhists, and others. From the fifteenth century, the eastward expansion of Moscow brought Muslims under the dominion of the Orthodox tsars. By the early twentieth century, the empire was home to some twenty million Muslims (15 percent of the total population), forming the largest non-Orthodox group. From St. Petersburg to Central Asia, the minarets of thousands of mosques stood in the glow of Orthodox churches. Alone among non-Muslim states in the modern era, Russia has ruled Muslims for more than five hundred years.

The linchpin of the tsarist regime's management of Islam and other non-Orthodox faiths was forged in the European Enlightenment. Beginning with Catherine the Great (r. 1762–1796), the empire created a religion-centered framework for its subjects to engage with the autocracy. Religious authority in all its varied forms, Catherine concluded, could be useful for the empire. Rather than try to impose religious uniformity on its varied subjects, the empress and her successors devised a policy of toleration to make faiths such as Islam the basic building blocks of the empire. They sought to transform religious authority in each community into an instrument of imperial rule. For millions of tsarist subjects, the state did more than tolerate other confessions; it presented itself as a defender of certain forms of Islam, Judaism, Buddhism, Protestantism, and other faiths. Confessional politics facilitated a kind of civic engagement in a polity that recognized only subjects, not citizens. The tsarist regime competed for the loyalties of its subjects, especially of those with co-religionists across the empire's porous borders. Muslims, Jews, and other non-Orthodox subjects were encouraged to focus their allegiances, along with their complaints and aspirations, on the monarchy and its institutions.

Muslims presented a special challenge to this imperial project. Catholics, Protestants, Jews, and Muslims lived in neighboring empires, but unlike the Jews, who had no foreign king or army on their side, Russia's Muslims could look to the Ottoman sultan, who pledged to protect the faithful on his frontiers. By the twentieth century, Nicholas II (r. 1894–1917) faced competition not only from the Ottomans, but also from the Germans and Japanese, who tried to undermine rival empires with Muslim populations by promising to defend Islam as well. In pursuing toleration, the tsarist government attempted to both seal off the borders of the empire and extend its reach into the local mosque. Law courts and administrative offices penetrated deeply into local communities because they became forums for the arbitration of disputes within the local mosque, synagogue, church, and temple. Millions of Muslims from all walks of life actively participated in these confessional politics. Many of them found common cause with a regime that appeared to back their understanding of the true meaning of the faith. Muslims came to accept the empire as the "House of Islam" *(dar al-Islam)*, a place where they could legally fulfill their religious obligations. In the process, they became the essential intermediaries that permitted the policing, judicial, and administrative organs of the empire to expand and rule at relatively low cost in much of Eurasia. This book shows how Russia became a Muslim power—and how the government made Islam a pillar of imperial society, transforming Muslims into active participants in the daily operation of the autocracy and the local construction and maintenance of the empire.

The story of the making of Russia's "House of Islam" and of the confessional foundations of the Russian past has been obscured by a lengthy historical tradition that has focused on seemingly timeless conflict between Christianity and Islam and between Europe and the East. Violence plays a central role in such narratives. Russia's Chechen wars, like many others from the dissolution of Yugoslavia, are haunted by images of religious violence once consigned to Europe's distant past. They recall Reformation-era riots in which Catholics and Protestants sought to purify their communities of "pollution" by exterminating their "heretical" enemies and desecrating their sacred symbols.[1] Outside of Northern Ireland, most Western Europeans now view such hostilities as anachronistic. But in turning to Europe's frontiers, the Balkans and the Caucasus, observers have arrived at different conclusions. To many politicians, journalists, and scholars, the outbreak of fighting in the 1990s between Christians and Muslims represented a predictable return, after an artificial hiatus under socialism, to a natural state of conflict between these religious traditions. In one oft-repeated formulation, these wars were evidence of a "clash of civilizations" driven by age-old hatreds.

The standard accounts of Russia's past have offered fertile ground for such thinking. The medieval Russian state of Muscovy grew out of a dependency of the Muslim rulers of the Golden Horde. By the mid-sixteenth century, the Muscovite state managed to subjugate its former overlords. Aided by miracle-working icons in their struggle against the "infidels," the Muscovites celebrated this reversal as a victory of Orthodox Christianity over Islam, a wondrous occurrence commemorated by the construction of St. Basil's Cathedral on Red Square—and by the demolition of mosques in the newly conquered territories along the Volga River. As the Russian state expanded in the seventeenth and eighteenth centuries, it faced resistance from Muslim populations along its eastern and southern frontiers. In the nineteenth century, we are often reminded, Russian troops fought a bitter war to dominate the Caucasus. Between the 1820s and the 1860s, mountain communities responded with *jihad*. The tsarist conquest of Central Asia in the second half of the century brought the empire prestige, but with it, the burden of absorbing a vast Muslim population on the distant frontiers of China and British India (see Map 1). By the early twentieth century, the Muslim population of the Romanov empire was larger than that under the Ottoman sultan. With each phase of expansion, Russia had risked confrontation with the Ottomans. In eleven major wars between the late seventeenth and early twentieth centuries, both the Orthodox Christian tsar and the Muslim sultan had to contend with the presence of his enemy's co-religionists within their borders.

Historians of later periods of Russian history have reinforced this vision of nearly continuous antagonism between the Russian state and Islam. By most accounts, Muslims proved no less a challenge to the Soviet regime that inherited the complex legacies of the Rus-

Map 1. The Russian Empire in the Early Twentieth Century

sian empire.[2] Muslims in the Caucasus and Central Asia continued to fight the new authorities after opposition had been crushed
elsewhere. Armed with its ideology of militant atheism, the Soviet
state launched antireligious campaigns that devastated Islamic institutions and personnel. When Hitler's armies advanced along the
southern frontiers of the Soviet Union, they found Muslim volun-
teers, among others, ready to join anti-Soviet forces. Stalin's deportation of the Chechens and neighboring Muslim peoples demonstrated lingering doubts about the loyalty of populations that had
long resisted tsarist, then Soviet, rule.

During the Cold War, Western observers identified Islam as the
Achilles' heel of the Soviet system. It was not just that the faith
seemed to safeguard Muslims against communist ideology; Muslims
also had the highest birthrates in Soviet society. Under this demo-

graphic pressure the future Red Army, experts projected, would have a majority of Muslim conscripts. In the 1980s, the victory of the *mujahidin* over the Soviets in Afghanistan made a deep impression on the Eastern bloc and the West, as well as on its proxy warriors, the nascent jihadist circles. Their success pointed to the possibility of a revolution under the green banner of Islam to roll back the red empire.[3]

That Muslims failed to play the revolutionary role that many Westerners had predicted in the Soviet collapse of 1991 did not entirely diminish the perceived menace. From Moscow to Tashkent, post-Soviet elites have continued to regard Islam as the primary threat to the stability of these new states. They have pointed to dangers emanating from foreign Muslims along the volatile frontiers shared with Turkey, Iran, Afghanistan, Pakistan, and China. The Taliban movement seemed to confirm these elites' sense of alarm about Islam as an aggressive ideological force. Moreover, recent experience has heightened anxieties about their own Muslim citizens. Chechen separatists have taken their struggle to civilian targets such as theaters and rock concerts in Russian cities, while oppositional groups in Central Asia have retreated to a murky underground, agitating against dictatorial regimes on behalf of diverse causes ranging from freedom of conscience and democratic elections to the creation of a single Islamic state for the region's Muslims.[4]

At the same time, the implosion of the Soviet empire yielded a paradox that has gone largely unnoticed. On the one hand, it unleashed diverse forms of violence that models of civilizational conflict purported to explain and even normalize. On the other, it produced opportunities to question understandings of the past upon which such interpretive schemes are based. The opening up of archives and libraries in the region and expanded avenues for intellectual exchange have permitted scholars to explore topics related to Islam that the Soviets had deemed taboo.

This book utilizes many of these new sources to revisit the history of Russia's engagement with Islam. Where other accounts of Russia's relationship with Islam have highlighted confrontation, as in Chechnya, this one examines the historical search for alternatives to such violence in the tsarist empire between the late eighteenth and early twentieth centuries. It aims to demonstrate that the history of Islam in the Russian empire offers a crucial perspective on one of the most central interpretive questions of Russian history and, more broadly, the history of empire. Long concerned with explaining the revolutions of 1917 and judging the legitimacy of the Bolshevik regime, historians have only recently begun to explore how the tsarist empire endured for so long and enjoyed such relative stability, even despite the extraordinary heterogeneity of the empire's population, the vastness of its territory, and the seemingly weak and disordered character of its government. Recent research has underscored the essential role of the autocracy. As Richard Wortman has shown, the Romanov dynasty acted as a dynamic and adaptive force.[5] Other historians have highlighted the regime's reliance on a multiethnic elite that assumed key governmental positions at the center and ruled on its behalf in the heterogeneous borderlands.[6] Scholars have also noted that this elite was multiconfessional and that this religious diversity sometimes gave rise to tensions between the Orthodox Church and the state and between Orthodox Christians and those who did not share the tsar's faith.

What historians have not examined is the tsarist regime's persistent attempts to ground imperial authority in religion. Throughout its three-hundred-year history (1613–1917), the Romanov dynasty drew on Orthodox Christian symbols. Yet from the early eighteenth century, the empire was home to significant numbers of Catholics, Protestants, Jews, Buddhists, Muslims, and various localized faiths. Modern scholars tend to conceptualize this diversity in terms of ethnic or national categories, but tsarist elites consistently viewed the heterogeneous peoples of the empire through the lens of religious affiliation. In this book, I have tried to reconstruct how contemporaries, both Muslims and their rulers, related to the confessional politics that underpinned the empire. The tsarist state's commitment to ruling through religious practices and institutions and the policing of orthodoxy—the *confessionalization* of the population of the empire—allowed the state to govern with less violence, and with a greater degree of consensus, than historians have previously imagined. Religion was central to how both sides engaged in the construction of a shared moral universe. Social estate and rank mattered, of course; and the category of "nationality" grew in importance for some elites in the last years of the empire. Like the historians of other empires, historians of Russia have focused on the rise of nationalism as the key to understanding the unraveling of the empire.[7] Concerned with tracing the origins of national movements that ultimately won out in Europe after the First World War and the collapse of the Romanov, Habsburg, and Ottoman empires, they have tended to exaggerate the appeal of national symbols as well as the secularization of Russian imperial society before 1917; they have neglected the continued viability of the integrative confessional politics that served as the modus operandi of the tsarist regime. For the Russian state, religion seemed to offer a more fundamental basis for allegiance—and discipline. Indeed, tsarist law obliged every subject to belong to a confessional group and, equally important, to submit to the authority of the clerical estate of each confession. According to this scheme, religious conformity enhanced respect for order. It regulated the family and conditioned obedience to temporal authorities. The opposite was also true. Nonconformity and religious heterodoxy seemed to pose threats to established authority. Deviation from the canonical norms, rites, and doctrines of one of the tolerated faiths presented a challenge to the imperial order. Memory of the seventeenth-century schism within the Orthodox Church, and the

rebellions that religious dissenters inspired, placed most tsarist officials firmly on the side of "orthodoxy" within each confession, even
when they regarded these faiths as inferior to Orthodox Christianity.

Like members of other communities, many Muslims initially opposed tsarist conquest. Still, relatively few resisted Russian rule once
it was established. Thus the story told here is not a romantic one of
persecution and resistance. Nor is it about Muslims who ostensibly
lived in a world apart, isolated in their own communities, indifferent or hostile to the empire that surrounded them. Some Muslims
preached avoidance of all things Russian. But this option became
more and more difficult to realize as tsarist institutions penetrated local communities. The prospect of avoiding contact with the state
and its officials proved so difficult for such Muslims precisely because so many of their co-religionists looked to the regime to order
these communities. To whom could pious Muslims turn when their
neighbors refused to attend mosque prayers, drank alcohol, or performed mystical Sufi rites in error? Muslims themselves solicited
state intervention in disputes with other Muslims. As we shall see,
Muslims needed the tsarist state to live according to God's plan, as
they understood it.

The tsarist empire emerged out of wars of conquest, of course. After the fighting ended, however, rulers and ruled had to come to
some peace. Rarely did either side wish for a resumption of hostilities. From the late eighteenth century a peculiar regime of religious
toleration lay at the heart of this quest for civil peace on the territory
of the Russian empire. Though the Orthodox Church retained extensive privileges, Muslims, Catholics, Protestants, Jews, and Buddhists gained official recognition for their faiths. Initially a strategy to
calm the passions that inflamed the persecuted against the regime,
"toleration" became much more than a policy of noninterference, as
the term is commonly understood today. The concept had a different meaning in eighteenth- and nineteenth-century Europe. In Rus-

sia, toleration was a structure for integrating non-Orthodox Christian subjects, whose numbers continuously increased as the empire expanded. This scheme rested on the proposition, elaborated by Enlightenment thinkers throughout Europe, that religions everywhere displayed certain traits in common. Essentially elaborate systems of discipline, tolerated faiths could prove valuable to "enlightened" rulers. Where violence was too blunt an instrument, recourse to religious authority might contribute to the making of loyal and disciplined subjects out of those who might not heed the sovereign's word alone but who could be persuaded to obey God. Toleration was a means of state intervention that Muslim subjects frequently welcomed.

This book seeks to show both how the regime sought to use religion to govern the empire and how Muslim communities utilized the tsarist police and courts for their own aims. The regime instrumentalized Islam, but Muslims captured the state, applying its instruments of coercion to the daily interpretive disputes that divided Muslim men and women. This empire held on to Muslim loyalties in significant measure because it became a fixture in the minds of Muslim intermediaries, an essential lever in diverse locales where Muslims debated, argued, and clashed with one another about the meaning of their faith and their place in this world. The Romanov state drew strength from this alliance with Muslims seeking assistance against their foes, even when it was not clear which ally was exploiting the other. Through such interactions, the empire took shape in the heads of its subjects, though the outcome might prove disappointing for some Muslims. Religion came to depend on the institutions of this state, just as the empire rested upon confessional foundations.

The dilemma for both the tsarist state and its Muslim subjects then was how to make Islam useful as a tolerated confession in the empire. Much as in Europe today, the government saw the recruitment of influential but trustworthy Muslim religious specialists as the key to this strategy. They were to act as intermediaries for the regime, transmitting the state's directives, guarding the morality of the faithful, and symbolizing the tsar's paternal care for Islam. Like Judaism, this faith posed a particular challenge to the Romanov state, however. Whereas other tolerated confessions came with some form of hierarchical organization that the state might co-opt, Islam had evolved historically, as Richard Bulliet observes, "without the benefit, or burden, of an organized ecclesiastical structure or a centralized source of doctrinal authority." Religious authority had been fluid and informal: "local societies of Muslims largely found their own way, nominating their own local religious leaders through their willingness to follow those among them who seemed the most pious or learned."[8] In Russia, the search for what was authoritative in Islam forced the regime to engage Muslims, to draw them into the process of constructing Islamic institutions to receive state patronage—and aid in the disciplining of the tsar's Muslim subjects.

For Muslims, the quest for social peace was no less thorny. Today Muslim political leaders in Moscow are quick to point out that Islam arrived in Russia before Orthodox Christianity; Islam thus is the most "traditional" of Russian faiths.[9] Muslims brought their religion from the Arabian peninsula to the peoples of Eurasia in the first centuries of Islam. By the tenth century, substantial Muslim communities had become established along the Volga River, in Siberia, the Caucasus, and the oases towns of Central Asia. Islam spread throughout the basin formed by the Volga River and Ural Mountains and to the north Caspian steppe. Most of these converts became Sunnis and adopted the Hanafi school of legal interpretation (after the seventh-century jurist Abu Hanifa); smaller numbers became Shi'ites and followed other legal schools in the Caucasus and Central Asia. Conversion to Islam among the peoples inhabiting these varied forest, steppe, and desert regions continued into modern times.[10] From the fifteenth century on, however, more and more of these communities fell under the rule of Russian tsars, who, by tradition, embodied Orthodox Christian piety.

The Muslims of the empire never constituted a homogeneous community. The timing and nature of their incorporation into the empire gave rise to different experiences of imperial rule. By the reign of Catherine the Great, Russian rulers had governed the Muslim peoples settled along the Volga River for more than two centuries. Catherine incorporated new Muslim populations in the Crimea and the steppe regions north of the Caucasus Mountains and Caspian Sea. By the late 1820s, tsarist forces under Alexander I (r. 1801–1825) and Nicholas I (r. 1825–1855) had seized control of the territory south of the Caucasus range, driving the Iranians and Ottomans beyond the Aras River. The Russian military needed another three and a half decades to conquer the Muslim communities that dotted the North Caucasus range extending from the Black Sea to the Caspian. As tsarist forces confronted a formidable resistance movement under the leadership of Imam Shamil between 1834 and 1859 on the territory of Daghestan and Chechnya, Russian administrators simultaneously moved their frontier outposts beyond the Ural River and deeper into the Kazakh steppe. By the end of the nineteenth century, the tsarist state had pushed the borders of the empire to the Amu Darya River and Tien Shan Mountains in Central Asia. In this drive toward the Hindu Kush, the empire seized control of grasslands, deserts, high mountainous terrain, and densely settled oases inhabited by varied populations, including nomads, townspeople, and isolated highland communities.

This pattern of expansion into such heterogeneous regions inhabited by Muslims yielded another paradox of empire. Tsarist elites understood the conquest of the Caucasus, the Kazakh steppe, and Central Asia as an affirmation of Russia's imperial glory and European identity. Yet they also recognized that new borders created new vulnerabilities. Only the Black Sea separated the Crimea from the Ottoman empire. Expansion beyond the Caucasus range created an extended border with both the Ottoman state and Qajar Iran. Lengthy frontiers shared with Afghanistan, British India, and China symbolized Russia's great power status but also heightened official anxieties about projecting imperial power far from Peter the Great's capital. Along the southern edges of the empire stretching from the Crimea to the Pamirs, millions of Muslims lived on both sides of a border far from the imperial center. The tsarist state faced the challenge of severing Muslims' ties with their neighboring co-religionists, including their former masters in Istanbul, Tehran, and the oasis courts of the khans of Transoxiana.

By the late nineteenth century, Muslims resided in eighty-nine provinces and territories of the empire (plus the protectorates of Bukhara and Khiva). The environments they inhabited can be analytically divided into seven distinctive zones of concentrated settlement: the Crimea, the Northern Caucasus, Transcaucasia, the Volga River and Ural Mountains regions, the Kazakh steppe, and Central Asia (Transoxiana). An eighth zone, represented by a northern belt of scattered diaspora-like communities, extended from Poland through St. Petersburg and Moscow to Siberia. In 1897 the first comprehensive empire-wide census officially registered nearly fourteen million Muslims, though census-takers concluded that they had undercounted Muslims and estimated their true number at closer to twenty million. More than three and a half million Muslims lived in the provinces designated as "European Russia." Over three million resided in the Caucasus, and the largest proportion, some seven million, inhabited the Kazakh steppe and Central Asia.

Apart from geographical setting, demography, and historical exposure to Russian administrators and settlers, cultural differences marked the heterogeneity of the tsar's Muslims. According to the 1897 census, Muslims belonged to more than a dozen of the lan-

guage groups counted by the authorities. Over twelve million spoke
a language of the "Turkic-Tatar" group. The two next largest groups
were the "Caucasian mountaineers" (with over one million speakers) and the "eastern Indo-European" (with over a half a million
speakers); more than ten thousand Muslims identified "Russian"
as their "native tongue."[11] Moreover, before tsarist institutions tied
these different communities together under imperial rule, they had
limited contact with one another and probably had only the most
abstract sense of belonging to a single religious community. Once
under the tsar, the regime devised particular administrative arrangements for each locale, perpetuating differences among them. Muslims on the Volga and in the Crimea were subject to civilian administration, but those in the Urals, the Caucasus, and Central Asia
experienced distinctive forms of military rule. The state similarly assigned duties and privileges to these populations on a regional basis,
all the while incorporating them into the broader social estate structure of the empire.

The demographic size, territorial distribution, and geopolitical
significance of these Muslim communities limited the range of policy options available to the Russian state. Beginning in the sixteenth
century, sporadic attempts to proselytize on behalf of the tsar's faith
among Muslims in the Volga and Urals regions yielded few converts
but provoked serious resistance. In the eighteenth century, Muslims
repeatedly took up arms against Christianization campaigns. Just as
these populations could not be converted *en masse* without jeopar-
dizing the stability of the empire, they could not be easily expelled
beyond its borders. Unlike the rulers of medieval Spain who expelled (or converted) Muslims and Jews, the Romanovs never resorted to wholesale expulsions to create a homogeneous population. To be sure, the Muslim populations along the southern rim of
the empire adjoining the Ottoman empire were vulnerable to such
state-sponsored violence. In the course of the tsarist army's brutal

subjugation of the Caucasus, Russian commanders under Nicholas I boasted of putting disloyal Muslims to flight. Several hundred thousand Muslims abandoned their homes in the Caucasus and the Crimea in the wake of the Crimean War (1853–1856) and the defeat of the resistance movement in the Northern Caucasus.[12]

The bloody history of expulsions and flight from this southern frontier zone should not be viewed as the basis for generalizations about the empire's approach to Islam as a whole, however. Russian military strategies had limited, if merciless, goals. Tsarist elites did not imagine cleansing the Northern Caucasus or the Crimea of all Muslims. Russian generals had long promised to answer disloyalty with "extermination," and war with the Ottomans revealed the extent to which these regions—and the loyalties of their inhabitants—may still have been in play. But at no time did such strategies preclude co-optation of loyal elites or even the enlistment of defectors.

Nor was Muslim emigration the result of tsarist violence alone. Muslim commanders such as Imam Shamil, who led the anti-tsarist resistance in Daghestan and Chechnya, forcibly relocated communities who refused to join his jihad against the Russians. Mark Mazower has drawn attention to the problem of establishing intentionality and distinguishing between "expulsion and panic," noting that "the two may be intertwined, as the case of the Germans of East Prussia in 1944–1945 suggests." In the case of the Caucasus and the Crimea, both Ottoman recruitment and Islamic law played a role. Ottoman envoys traveled throughout the region to encourage migration from "infidel" rule in the "House of War" *(dar al-Harb)*—rejecting Russia's status as the "House of Islam" and promising aid in resettling Muslims in the sultan's "well-protected domains." Their appeals confirmed the judgment of Islamic religious authorities who called on fellow Sunni Muslims to flee Christian rule to reside in a state ruled by a Sunni Muslim sovereign. The connection between the geopolitics of these frontier zones and the treatment of Muslims is reflected again in the pattern of in-migration by Muslims during the same period. In the wake of Sunni flight from the Caucasus, Shi'ites crossed the border into Russian territory from Iran, where Shi'ism was the dominant faith. By the 1860s the demographic balance shifted, from rough parity between Sunnis and Shi'ites, to Shi'ites outnumbering Sunnis by a ratio of 2 to 1. With the oil boom in Baku and the construction of the railway in Central Asia, Iranian migrants flocked to the Russian empire. In the late nineteenth and early twentieth centuries, tribes from northern Iran and Afghanistan repeatedly petitioned for permission to become Russian subjects.[13]

Tsarist elites desired secure borders and internal order. They sought domestic stability and, where possible, political advantage vis-à-vis weaker neighbors. Tsarist elites never countenanced the expulsion of the Muslim peasants, merchants, artisans, and soldiers who were so essential to the functioning of the empire in the interior provinces. Indeed, the Romanov empire endured for so long, and managed to rule such a vast and heterogeneous space with relatively modest resources, largely because its elites tended to be cautious. The forces that kept the empire together—the tsar's generals and policemen—had a feel for both the possibilities and the limits of imperial power. In the nineteenth century the path to imperial glory lay in Asia, especially when Russia's position in Europe appeared more vulnerable following defeat in the Crimean War. Further expansion, tsarist elites acknowledged, hinged on some accommodation with Muslims.

Muslims faced very similar constraints in responding to the Russian challenge. The prospect of becoming subjects of the tsarist empire was more attractive—and the costs associated with the alternatives much higher—than nationalist or Islamist rhetoric would suggest. Historians of the Muslims of the empire have, for the most part, treated them as a community affected by the social and economic structures of the empire but largely autonomous in their internal politics. In practice, this isolationist scenario was available to few contemporaries. A seemingly unlikely case given the mythology of Muslim resistance to the Russian presence in the Caucasus, the experience of the Muslims of Daghestan and Chechnya between the late 1820s and 1850s presents an instructive example. In the face of Russian military conquest, the Muslims of these regions failed to formulate a unified answer against tsarist forces, even though historians have long treated it as an era of "jihad" inspired and organized by Muslim Sufi brotherhoods. Muslims fought on both sides of the conflict, for and against the empire. More important, Michael Kemper has shown, the fundamental contours of the resistance drew upon pre-Russian arguments on behalf of Islamic law against indigenous—not tsarist—authorities. By this account, Imam Shamil and his predecessors used the "jihad state" as more than a way to "defend" Muslims against "infidels"; their concern with implementing Islamic law formed a critical strategy against other indigenous rulers and an essential component of state-building at the expense of local elites, some of whom had sided with Russia.[14]

Answering the tsarist regime's offer to act as patron of Islam meant, for Muslims and Christians, forgetting the violent conquests that had preceded it. To build social peace and imperial order, they built on a tradition of looking for common ground, not by ignoring religion but by dwelling on it. From the medieval period, Muslims had sworn oaths on a Qur'an kept for this purpose in the Kremlin. In later periods, Muslims in each conquered region swore oaths of loyalty on the holy book, which the regime recognized as a binding authority. Christians and Muslims remained sensitive to religious differences. But in dealings with one another, they learned to make reference to what they ostensibly shared, submission to one God. This idiom, of monotheism linking rulers and the ruled, established terms for negotiation. It was nonetheless only a starting point. The implications of such claims would be worked out in countless interactions between Muslims and Russian authorities between the late eighteenth and early twentieth centuries, with each side attempting to manage the response of the other. This common reference point did not erase distinctions between Islam and the tsar's faith. Nor did it mask the subordination of Muslim subjects to the coercive instruments of the tsarist state. Rather it established a framework for the search for congruences that would lend solidity to imperial rule, where possible, without resort to force. As in the scenarios of exchange in North America between Indians and whites analyzed by Richard White, each party pursued its own goals but justified "their own actions in terms of what they perceived to be their partner's cultural premises."[15]

The Russians were not alone in pursuing such an approach. Napoleon pledged devotion to the same God worshipped by Muslims during his Egyptian campaign. As a strategic bridge between Christians and Muslims, such appeals, including the construction of parallels between Jesus and Muhammad, informed European diplomatic language in exchanges with the Ottomans. British and French administrators later sought Islamic legitimacy for their rule over colonies in Africa and Asia. In Bosnia and Herzegovina, the Habsburgs created an Islamic hierarchy to administer Muslim affairs—and cut Muslim ties to Istanbul. In the twentieth century, the Japanese claimed a special bond with Islam as part of a broader campaign to subvert European empires in Asia and establish Japanese power in their place. Even the German Kaiser seized upon this strategy. In 1898, Wilhelm II pledged himself the protector of three hundred million Muslims, including those under the British, French, and Russian empires. In the First World War, he dreamed of inciting "the whole Mohammedan world to wild revolt" in a jihad against Germany's enemies.[16]

But in forging its empire the tsarist regime sought out Muslim allies with greater consistency, over a longer period of time, and with greater success than its imperial challengers. Indeed, the notion that Islam had a particular utility for the state, even when it did not sit well with official ideology, outlived the tsars. It persisted in fitful but important ways under the very different conditions of the Soviet environment; it even survived the collapse of the USSR, resurfacing in the young post-Soviet republics intent on domesticating Islam to shore up their claims to political legitimacy.

Like their Ottoman rivals, the multiconfessional tsarist elite found valuable allies in seeking to ground imperial rule in religious authority. The construction of such a confessional state required not only religious elites but, in the tsarist context, the mobilization of laypeople as well.[17] In order to claim benefit from the overlap of temporal and spiritual authority in administering the empire, the regime found itself obliged to reinforce particular religious injunctions, whether Muslim, Catholic, or Jewish. But in such a vast, polyglot empire stretching from the Baltics to the Caucasus and the Pacific Ocean, tsarist officials struggled to gain knowledge about the internal workings of the faiths from which they sought advantage. They looked first to a "clergy" in each community, even in traditions such as Islam that did not historically recognize such sociological categories. Yet in nineteenth-century Russia, as in Europe, an anticlerical spirit impinged upon toleration as well.

Where the tsarist bureaucracy valued the supposed contribution of religion to morality and order but distrusted clerics, it created a space for lay initiative, inviting challenges to clerical authority from below. As in colonial India, suspicion of indigenous religious elites stimulated official interest in the exploration of texts that would allow administrators to overcome their reliance on such mediation. Russian officials engaged different Muslim interlocutors in each region of the empire, but bureaucratic recourse to varying informants and texts meant that official conceptions of Islam shifted over time and space. Tsarist elites often disagreed with one another about their assessment of Islam. They voiced some of their most hostile views where the Orthodox Church and its converts seemed to be at risk. Despite the variety of official opinion, and the heterogeneity of these Muslim communities themselves, imperial elites who argued for Islam's fundamental contribution to the stability of the empire tended to win out, whether they were in St. Petersburg or in the Caucasian or Central Asian borderlands. Where the critics of Islam had an advantage, as in the mid-nineteenth-century Kazakh steppe, their gains were Pyrrhic victories. The state remained weakest where it was least entangled with the affairs of Islam and where Muslims could not utilize its power on behalf of religion.

Drawing on sources from central and local state archives as well as on various sources authored by Muslims, this perspective casts the Russian empire in a new light. Long characterized as an "under-governed" polity, with weak connections between the capital and its far-flung peripheries, the empire in fact loomed large in the minds of Muslim men and women, the subjects of the tsar who typically are depicted, alongside Jews, as among the least likely to be integrated into the imperial environment.[18] Petitions, denunciations, court records, police reports, and numerous Muslim sources reveal how, within the broader framework of tsarist toleration, Muslim men and women came to imagine the imperial state as a potential instrument of God's will. Like historians of law courts and policing institutions in other societies, I read court records, police reports, and other sources for what their language reveals about these actors' identities, how they sought to adapt the law for specific purposes and, in this context, shape the Islamic tradition—and the workings of the tsarist state. Not every issue related to Islam in the empire made its way to the imperial archives. Yet, as I try to show, the tsarist state became an essential forum for the resolution of disputes among Muslims. Some Muslim subjects of the tsar may have preferred to avoid the state, but they could not be guaranteed that other Muslims, including their neighbors or spouses, would not bring them before the court or police. This was an empire in which policing, justice, and piety were simultaneously intimate affairs—and the business of both the community and the institutions of the empire.

Long before modern Muslim thinkers conceived of the "Islamic state" as a bureaucratic instrument to enforce divine law, Muslim subjects of the Romanov dynasty looked to the institutions of the empire to realize the obligations and rights of the faith. Based on familiarity with other colonial environments, readers might expect a story of Muslim resistance to tsarist encroachment, especially in areas like the domestic sphere. Responses varied among the Muslims of the Russian empire. But even sources generated outside of state institutions by Muslim themselves document the varied channels of engagement with the institutions of the regime; Muslim scholars who collected biographies of other notable religious figures made reference to court cases and other interactions, even if they downplayed such contacts to avoid the appearance of corruption.[19]

Where the tsarist regime established administration, Muslims engaged the regime not simply as an instrument of repression, but as a means to advance true religion—to set spouses, children, relatives, and others on the correct path to God, the *shari'a*. Rather than insulate women and the family from police organs, Muslims learned to associate the state with the mediation of family conflicts and the defense of rights based on the shari'a. Thus the state reached deep into the mosque communities of the empire. Historians once saw "undergovernment" where the conventional, secular arm of government had no reach, but this is a misreading of the bonds that linked ruler and ruled. Both shared the conviction, emerging out of the eighteenth century, that the imperial order rested on religious authority, and that the tsar's agents, along with every subject, had a stake in establishing a world pleasing to God. Haunted by anxieties of popular upheaval inspired by religious heterodoxy within their own Church in the seventeenth century, the interests of the Russians converged with those of the Muslim scholars who shielded the tradition against "illicit innovation" *(bid'a)* in religious interpretation. What in hindsight may look like "traditional" religious practices were, in fact, the creations of the state and its Muslim intermediaries.

These convictions did not mean that each side always acted as the other wished, of course. It gave ample room for misunderstandings, miscalculations, and conflict. Catherine the Great first formulated this mode of toleration, but many of her successors remained cool to it. The Orthodox Church remained a staunch opponent and insisted on exclusive state support. It campaigned not only against Muslims whom it suspected of proselytizing among Christians but also against the Orthodox who praised "the moral teaching of the Qur'an and find 'that it is not even inferior to the Gospels'" or who lived by the credo that "it's all the same whether you're a Christian or a Muhammadan, as long as you are an honest person." Moreover, repeated wars with the Ottomans revived and sustained misgivings about Islam both within and beyond government circles. The writer Fyodor Dostoevsky detested accommodationist policies. In 1877, in the midst of yet another Russo-Turkish war, he warned the Russian public against the "extolling of Muslims for monotheism," calling this the "hobby-horse of a great many lovers of the Turks" in society who mistakenly regarded Islam as more enlightened than the polytheism of the icon-worshipping Russian peasant. For Dostoevsky, as for other figures of Russian literature and especially opera, Russians who embraced the national spirit were to celebrate Russia's domination of the Orient.[20] For critics, the confessional politics of the empire were too particularistic. Liberals came to disdain them as an impediment to universally applied law, and conservative nationalists saw them as an obstacle to the consolidation of a more homogeneous empire dominated by Russian culture and ethnic-

ity. Both camps failed to grasp how the empire's systematic investment in particularism had managed to accommodate diversity while
strengthening the regime's hold on these populations. Such champions of a more aggressive approach toward Islam influenced the tenor
of local politics at the regional level but never fully succeeded in reorienting tsarist policy. With extraordinary consistency, the imperative of policing the empire trumped nationalist (and liberal) calls for
conflict.

Institutional interests were also at stake. Having defined the task
of the "preventive police" in "well-ordered states" as "the safeguarding of the rites of religion and the curbing of schisms," tsarist officials
followed the model of the Napoleonic state and established a centralized bureaucratic body for the administration of the tolerated
confessions.[21] Founded in 1810 as the Main Administration of the
Religious Affairs of Foreign Confessions and reconfigured as the
Ministry of Religious Affairs and Education in 1817, this institution became in 1832 a department of the primary organization entrusted with policing the imperial domestic order, the Ministry of
Internal Affairs. This ministry oversaw the officially recognized clerical bodies for the non-Orthodox confessions, including an official
Islamic establishment that Catherine the Great had created on the
eastern steppe frontier in 1788, though it was forced to compete
with other institutions—including the Orthodox Church—in shaping tsarist policy. The Ministry of War administered Muslims in the
Caucasian and steppe borderlands. When the tsarist army assumed
responsibility for the administration of Muslims in areas of the Caspian steppe and Transoxiana that it annexed between the 1860s and
1880s, it managed to wrest control of religious matters from the minister of internal affairs. In 1872, however, the Ministry of Internal Affairs reclaimed some of its power when it established an Islamic hierarchy for the administration of Sunni affairs, and another for Shi'a
communities, in Transcaucasia. Yet another entity, the Ministry of

Foreign Affairs, inserted a voice in the policy debate. Sensitive to the perception of Muslims residing just beyond Russia's borders, its personnel frequently defended broad toleration for Islam as a means to prepare the way for expansion into the Ottoman empire, Persia, Transoxiana, Afghanistan, India, and China. But unlike other ministries, it remained open to the utility of émigré groups whom other Muslims regarded as "unorthodox," including Ismailis and Baha'is, treating them as a wedge against Persia and the British empire. Tsarist policy thus emerged out of an institutional patchwork marked both by competing ministries in the capitals and provincial towns as well as by different officially sponsored Muslim authorities based in the Crimea, the eastern steppe frontier town of Ufa, the Northern Caucasus, and Transcaucasia. Laypeople were another force. In resorting to the tsar's justice and calling for official intervention in disputes with other Muslims, they often directed the local course of tsarist state-building in ways that St. Petersburg could not predict or control.

Such lay activism underscores another little-studied dimension of the tsarist empire. Scholars have long followed Russian intellectuals in identifying Europe as Russia's natural framework for comparison. When they have juxtaposed Russia with the Ottomans or Safavids, the point has been to highlight difference. But the angle pursued in this book also points to similarities between the tsarist and Ottoman regimes. Both states introduced dramatic changes in the lives of their subjects in the nineteenth century, while simultaneously presenting the expanding state as a conservative guardian of Islamic piety. The symmetry of state decrees calling for compulsory mosque attendance is but one example of this common enterprise.[22]

Alliances between Muslim activists and tsarist officials in the name of "orthodox" Islam did not reinforce an unchanging Islam, as some historians have suggested. Rather, these interactions produced novel understandings of the sacred law. Like their contemporaries in the Ottoman empire and Egypt, Russia's Muslims perceived the rapid expansion of state institutions and legislation not as a displacement of the shari'a but instead as a complement to it.[23] While resisting some tsarist legal norms that they took to be in violation of God's law, Muslims responded to the extension of tsarist law and bureaucratic practice by adapting these new resources to local debates about the shari'a. At the same time, the prospect of state backing for legal norms that might shore up the moral foundations of the empire engaged officials and Muslims in attempts to regularize the process. As in British India and the Ottoman empire, local and variable understandings of the shari'a as a divinely ordained path began to give way in many circles to its conception as a uniform and static "law" whose meanings were fixed in texts and codes.[24] Official concern with consistency and uniformity aided particular Muslim actors who argued for a certain vision of orthodoxy based on a narrow selection of Hanafi legal texts. But state backing for the "letter of the law" could also work against Muslims, as when the state seized land held ostensibly in violation of the shari'a. These interactions placed religious authority—and the state-building processes to which it was linked—in flux.

The terms of such contests for influence were not infinitely malleable. Like "customary law" in colonial African societies, the elements of Islamic law that received state backing were likely to be those advanced by parties who presented themselves as the most authoritative arbiters of tradition and whose claims overlapped with the interests and expectations of the tsarist regime. Many of these Islamic legal texts accommodated the possibility of multiple outcomes to legal contests, including citations to authorities justifying a range of positions on a given legal issue. Under the tsars, the power of the state proved essential in tipping the balance in favor of one interpretation over another. Thus in the tsarist empire, as in other societies, Muslims drew the boundaries of "orthodoxy" and community with the institutions of the state, not against it.[25]

This story has not been told before because historians have tended to focus more narrowly on Muslim elites. In valuable research drawing on unpublished manuscript sources in a variety of languages, scholars have shown how Muslim thinkers who advocated the reform of various aspects of the Islamic tradition in the late tsarist empire reflected the adaptability and dynamism of Muslim culture from the second half of the nineteenth century. These elites have attracted attention in part because their renown extended beyond Russia. Most embraced Europe's fascination with nationalism. Unable to realize national political ambitions on the territory of the Russian empire in the early twentieth century, many were forced to pursue them in Europe, Japan, and, above all, in Turkey. There Muslim émigrés from Russia scripted national ideologies not only for the peoples back home, but for the Turks as well.[26] At the end of the twentieth century, the Communist Party bosses who found themselves the rulers of autonomous republics or independent states after the Soviet collapse rediscovered many of their ideas. Eager to manage a Muslim revival and consolidate loyalties toward new nation-states, elites looked back to the reformist heritage. Out of this varied body of thought, they have sought to construct a legitimate past for Islam seen as merely a secular attribute of national culture. A national lens has thus framed the history of Muslim intellectuals in Russia.

But this view has also obscured the wider context and hidden another story. This focus has not only neglected Muslims who rejected the national and secular platforms propagated by elites. It has too often reproduced narratives that celebrated the struggle of the nation against empire, treating all Muslims as outsiders. The reformist agenda of the late nineteenth and early twentieth centuries was not the only controversial theme in the lives of the Muslims of the empire. Nor did it pit progressive reformers against backward-looking obscurantists, as much of this scholarship would suggest. Muslims challenged the authority of clerics well before the onset of print and other mass media that scholars have recently highlighted, following historians of the Reformation, in explaining religious change in Muslim societies. For their part, Muslim men of learning and piety in this context acted as "custodians of change," in Muhammad Qasim Zaman's apt formulation.[27] Though both Muslims and their Christian rulers appealed to "tradition," their engagement with one another unleashed dramatic changes that continually remade the local contours both of the empire and Islam. The story of Islam in the empire is one of dynamic change. We should not assume the presence of a static Islam before the era of reform.

We should also not take Muslim solidarity for granted. Following Rogers Brubaker, this book probes the extent to which one can speak meaningfully of Muslims, even within a single region of the empire, as a bounded and homogeneous "group" at all. For many activists, being Muslim and living according to the shari'a meant to turn to the instruments of the state to seek their aid in compelling others to conform to a particular vision of Islam. Even in the Northern Caucasus, Muslims disagreed about the legitimacy of waging jihad against the Russians.[28] The story of Muslim reformist elites in the empire may offer a usable past for contemporary political agendas, but it contributes little to understanding how these Muslim communities fit into the empire, or how Islamic institutions and practices bound Muslims to the state. To illuminate both this wider perspective on Muslim politics and the Islamic underpinnings of the Orthodox tsar's empire, this book pays particular attention to the everyday controversies that most concerned clerics and laypeople alike, namely those surrounding the shari'a and the rites of the faith, including the Sufi devotions that divided local communities.

The chapters that follow trace efforts pursued by Russian officials and various Muslim actors to sustain social stability in the empire, with each side committed to making the most of the other's convictions for its own purposes. Far from underwriting the status quo, these relationships reshaped Muslim communities and state institutions. These efforts began on the eastern steppe frontier in the late eighteenth century (see Map 2). Chapter 1 traces the establishment of a state-backed Islamic hierarchy in the eastern town of Ufa under Catherine. The relationship forged on the frontier proved paradigmatic for other Muslim regions, though institutions everywhere took on the local cast of officialdom and indigenous intermediaries. Chapter 2 shows how this Islamic hierarchy extended its authority into mosque communities throughout the Volga and Urals regions in the first half of the nineteenth century, transforming local religious life and state institutions in the process. As a microcosm of the imperial order—one to be disciplined by the power of religion—the Muslim family forms the focus of Chapter 3. The remaining chapters chart the fate of official patronage of Islam as the eastern frontier evolved. By the mid-nineteenth century, the conceptions of Islam to which Muslims and tsarist officials appealed had changed dramatically, and Russia had begun to confront formidable Muslim resistance in the Northern Caucasus. Chapter 4 shows how the regime experimented with reworking its treatment of Islam among nomads in the Kazakh steppe. The conquest of Central Asia is the subject of Chapter 5 and reveals the state's efforts to integrate the most populous Muslim region it had yet encountered. Chapter 6 shifts from this eastern frontier to take in a wider view of the empire at a moment when Russian nationalism—and the social and economic change of the turn of the century—prompted both tsarist and Muslim elites to renegotiate the accord, sealed by commitment to Islamic orthodoxy, that had long served both Muslims' quest for piety and the solidity of the empire.

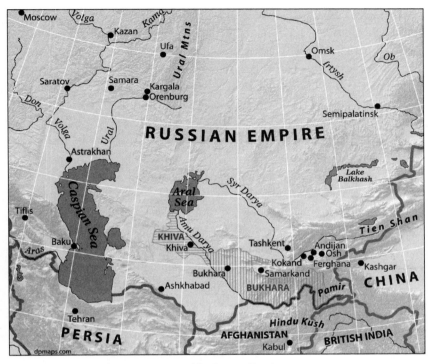

Map 2. The Southeastern Frontier of the Russian Empire

In the end, I want to suggest how the search for that which could be "useful" for the state in Islam was so embedded in the consciousness of so many actors that it survived the collapse of the tsarist regime. The Soviets retained central principles of the tsarist approach for much of the twentieth century, and it has been revived today in Eurasia as well as in Europe and other regions where Muslims form significant minorities. Calls for state involvement in backing certain kinds of religious interpretation on behalf of "moderates" (meaning "good Muslims") now exercise a powerful attraction where nation-states feel threatened by transnational Islam and besieged by the threat of terrorism.[29] The tsarist experience with such practices should alert us to their unintended consequences. The mechanisms of imperial rule were only as effective as their intermediaries. The crisis of tsarist rule in Central Asia during the First World War demonstrates some of the costs of overestimating the prestige of particular local authorities and institutions. Other imperial powers, most notably Germany, faced this challenge during the war when they solicited Islamic backing (including *fatwas*) and mobilized Muslim prisoners of war against their rivals. Poor choice of collaborators has doomed more than one empire.[30] At first glance, the strategy of supporting particular Muslim factions against others appears to be an alternative to the violence that has torn apart Bosnia and Chechnya. But its consequences have been more complicated. Although official patronage of select Islamic authorities was a powerful asset in the policing and integration of Muslim populations in the Russian empire, it also drew Muslims and their rulers together in the common enterprise of curtailing liberty of conscience. Applied more broadly, such strategies tend to promise further conflicts, not between "civilizations," but within modern states that deny their citizens basic legal protections, including respect for fundamental human rights. In Russia itself, the violence visited upon Chechnya since 1994 has formed only one prong of Russian strategy in the Northern Caucasus. The other has been to try to co-opt loyal Muslim authorities. The result remains a state of unrelenting civil war pitting Russians against Chechens, and Muslims against Muslims.

1

A CHURCH FOR ISLAM

In 1802 Fayz Khan (Fayḍ Khān al-Kabūlī) was laid to rest in a shrine at a mosque complex in Kabul. With the passing of this Muslim scholar, an era came to a close. A guide on the path of Islamic mysticism, he had inherited the wisdom of a lengthy chain of Sufi masters. Fayz Khan himself transmitted the teachings of Shaykh Ahmad Sirhindi, who had formulated a critique of Islam in his native India of the late sixteenth and early seventeenth centuries. Celebrated by his followers as the "Renewer of the Second Millennium," Sirhindi argued that "unlawful innovations" had corrupted Islam. He taught that the pursuit of Sufi knowledge, paired with rigorous devotion to the essence of the divine path, the shari'a, showed the way to renewing the faith. Sirhindi's vision inspired the emergence of a new community. Drawn from members of the Naqshbandiyya, a Sufi brotherhood established in the fourteenth century, his devotees formed an offshoot, the Mujaddidi order, which lost one of its most authoritative figures with Fayz Khan's death in Kabul.[1]

Mourning for this holy man spread beyond the local faithful, for

Kabul and Fayz Khan's circle had drawn Muslims from throughout Eurasia. In the second half of the eighteenth century, hundreds of men traveled to Kabul from as far away as the Volga and Kama River valley, a region claimed by the Russians since the mid-sixteenth century. After some initial study with local mullahs, these young men set out across the steppe, retracing ancient caravan routes, to centers of Islamic learning and piety in Transoxiana. The madrasas of Bukhara and Samarkand were revered throughout the world and offered training in the holy law and other religious sciences. Many of these students then traveled on to Kabul. Through Fayz Khan, they earned induction into the brotherhood that linked them to Shaykh Sirhindi and the wider Islamic networks of the subcontinent. These scholars then returned home to the Russian empire to pass on this learning in their own communities.[2]

It was not the death of Fayz Khan alone, however, that brought about a reorientation of this pattern of pilgrimage and study. Recent developments in the north also played a role. Under Catherine the Great, the Russian government had begun to reshape the horizons of its Muslim subjects. By the early nineteenth century, Muslims had recourse to an expanding network of domestic institutions devoted to cultivating Muslim piety and learning within Russia. Muslims still traveled widely to seek religious blessings and wisdom. But now Muslims could construct mosques and madrasas, with government permission, in their own villages and town quarters. Moreover, Russia's Muslims could look to their own authorities in the form of an Islamic establishment empowered by the government to resolve difficult religious questions, oversee appointments to mosques and schools, review disputes based on Islamic law, and issue legal opinions (fatwas) about them.

Catherine had not merely established a legal basis for the existence of these institutions in Russia. She had instead transformed the imperial regime into a patron of Islam. The empress pursued a program of religious toleration in the spirit of the "well-ordered police state" imagined by the jurists of Central Europe. Because tolerated faiths were regulated by the police ordinances of the empire, they held out the promise of reinforcing autocratic power, particularly in restive areas where Muslims had repeatedly risen up against state authorities or joined the rebellions led by their non-Muslim neighbors. The empress hoped to ease tensions among Muslims and Orthodox missionaries, officials, and settlers in the eastern provinces bordering the steppe, but she also viewed Islam through the lens of imperial expansion. Accommodation became a means to win over Muslim intermediaries who might assist the regime in securing this frontier and projecting Russian power into the steppe, and toward the deserts and oases of Central Asia.

Having adopted the role of benefactor, a fundamental question remained: How would the empire discipline a faith whose every believer, in theory, might look to whomever he or she regarded as an authoritative guide to God's will? This chapter examines the Russian state's answer to this dilemma. Tsarist elites reasoned that Islam, like other faiths, would be useful to the empire when it conformed to a strict hierarchy and submitted to a domestic chain of command linked to St. Petersburg. For the multiconfessional architects of tsarist policy, Orthodox Christian and Protestant alike, the structures of the dominant church seemed to offer a model for such organization. Moreover, in looking abroad to the Ottoman empire, these officials concluded that Islam under the sultan conformed to such a hierarchy.

To domesticate Islam in the empire, and to turn Muslims away from alternative sources of authority in Kabul, Istanbul, and elsewhere, Catherine and her officials opted to introduce a churchlike organization among a population that had previously known no such institutions. The process was far from smooth. The state could not simply impose its will from above without the mediation of both

Muslim elites and laypeople. In constructing this church for Islam, moreover, the regime found that its proper functioning depended on a close union between the mosque and the throne. Rather than merely subordinating Muslims to the empire, this institution created interdependence. These new structures of Islamic authority rested on tsarist police power.

Discovering the Turkish Creed

The Catherinian search for an organizational structure for Russia's Muslim communities was a product of Russia's engagement with the Enlightenment. Beginning in the late seventeenth century, Russia's pursuit of European learning furnished a fresh lens on Islam that compelled Muscovites to forget much of what they already knew about that faith. Like the Spaniards before them, Russians turned their backs on a lengthy period of shared experiences.[3] With Europeanization, Russian elites turned abroad to understand their Muslim subjects at home.

For enlightened Europeans, Islam was not a "world religion" but "the religion of the Turks." Indeed, to them conversion to Islam meant "to become a Turk."[4] Even Spanish writers treated the faith as a foreign novelty, apprehended only by studying the Ottomans. The biography of the Prophet, like the practice of polygamy, featured prominently in Italian, French, and Polish treatments of the faith. By the time Muscovites discovered these accounts, European writers had gone beyond mere religious polemic. Focusing on the life of Muhammad and the rites and customs of "the Turks," Christian scholars had begun to systematize knowledge about Islam by focusing on the institutions of their geopolitical rival, the Ottoman state (see Figure 1).

In 1692 Andrei Lyzlov reworked many of these European ideas in

Figure 1 A print depicting a ceremony at which Ottoman forces surrendered the fortress of Kars to the tsarist army during the Crimean War. E. Iakov, *Sdacha goroda i kreposti Karsa 16 noiabria 1855–go goda* (1868). Print Collection, Miriam and Ira D. Wallach Division of Art, Prints and Photographs, The New York Public Library, Astor, Lenox and Tilden Foundations.

a Russian context. His *Scythian History* claimed to relate the past and present condition of the peoples on the eastern and southern frontiers of Muscovy, including the Ottomans and their vassals, the Crimean Tatars. Though Lyzlov had gained firsthand experience during military campaigns against the Crimean khans, he relied chiefly on foreign texts. Closely following these sources, he labeled Muhammad a "cursed charmer" and the "diabolical" son of a Jewish mother. The origins of the faith could be traced, Lyzlov claimed, to "Muhammad's charm" and his devious imagination. Islam was thus "lawlessness" *(bezzakonie)*, the antithesis of a true creed *(zakon)*.[5]

At the same time, European scholars judged Islam against a set of categories that seemed to define religion among all peoples. Christian theology, though, shaped their expectations of other faiths. In this vein, Lyzlov described Muhammad's legacy as a system of ten injunctions:

> 1. on frequent ablutions; 2. on the number of prayers; 3. on respect for parents; 4. on the observation of matrimony; 5. on circumcision; 6. on the assistance of the dead; 7. on war; 8. on charity; 9. on respect for chapels [mosques]; 10. on profession of one God.

Muhammad's devotees, then, had a structure of rites and rules that were intelligible to Christians. Their religion ordered marriage and commanded filial respect. They professed monotheism, even according "Our Lord Jesus Christ" and "the Virgin Mary" a place in their sacred history.[6] Thus observers like Lyzlov sketched a disjointed image of a religion marked by base deceit and disorder, but also resembling the structure of Christian theology.

Besides such scholarly treatises, Europe gave Russia a literary genre devoted to the adventures of Christians, like the writer Cervantes, who found themselves the captives of Muslim pirates and slave-traders. In the southern steppe, Russia had its own Barbary Coast. As Russian power stretched toward the Black Sea in the late seventeenth century, contacts with Muslims—Ottomans, Crimean Tatars, and Nogays—also intensified. Raiding and battle yielded Christian slaves for Muslim merchants. Those who managed to escape retained valuable information about their captors. One of the earliest Russian descriptions of the Ottomans came from the pen of

F. F. Dorokhin, who returned to his native land in 1674 after twelve years of captivity.[7]

Aided by such informants, Peter the Great (r. 1689–1725) drew on other European sources. While leading troops toward Astrakhan and the Caspian Sea, he commissioned a Russian translation of the Qur'an. Based on a mid-seventeenth-century French edition, it appeared in 1716 as *The Al-Koran on Muhammad, or the Turkish Creed.* The emperor also imported expertise supplied by numerous Christian émigrés from the Ottoman empire, who knew a great deal not only about Islam but about the Ottomans' treatment of the Christian populations of their empire. In 1711, Dmitrii Cantemir, a former governor of Ottoman Moldavia, defected to Russia. At Peter's request, he composed *A Book of Rules, or The Condition of the Muhammadan Religion*, published in 1722. With the establishment of diplomatic representation in Istanbul, not only escaped captives, adventurers, and renegades, but Russian diplomats began to supply information about the "Turkish faith." The essential window onto this religion came not from the neighboring Persians or the distant peoples of Arabia or India, but from the Ottomans. Like the Europeans before them, Russian writers applied the adjectives *Turkish* and *Muhammadan* interchangeably in describing Ottoman institutions and rites.[8]

Peter the Great's plans to modernize the empire also included changes in the status of Russia's Muslims. In a departure from Muscovite practice, conversion to Christianity became a prerequisite for membership in the landowning service elite. Tatar nobles who refused to abandon Islam found their estates and Orthodox serfs confiscated by the state and found themselves demoted to the ranks of the peasantry or laborers for the admiralty. Peter subordinated the Church to the interests of secular government and declared toleration for Protestants in a bid to attract foreign specialists. But the emulation of Europe also translated into state backing for figures within the Church and civil bureaucracy who advocated introducing Christianity among non-Christians. Violence accompanied proselytization. In 1743 alone, state officials and churchmen may have destroyed 418 of the 536 mosques in the town and district of Kazan.[9]

The protection of Orthodox Christians, in the empire and in neighboring states alike, was a central priority of tsarist policy. Christian converts from among Turkic and Finnic language groups appeared vulnerable to Islamic influence in areas where Muslims lived alongside them. The empress Anna (r. 1730–1740) tried to assert control over Muslim men of religious learning among the Bashkirs, ordering them to swear oaths that they would not "introduce anyone of other faiths to their religion and not circumcise [them]." Elizabeth (r. 1741–1761) repeated this warning against Muslim proselytizing among "Russians, as well as Kalmyks, Mordvinians, Cheremis, Chuvash and other people of every rank."

Elizabeth's concern with protecting the Orthodox prompted the regulation of mosque construction. She forbade the building of mosques in villages with Orthodox Christian inhabitants and set a minimum population requirement of two hundred males for the existence of a mosque. Even though the empress prohibited mosques in mixed settlements, she opposed the destruction of mosques in other locales. And like her Muscovite predecessors, she recognized the importance of mosques as places where "Tatars of the Muhammadan faith living in Russia are brought to swear oaths [to the state] according to their [own religious] laws."

On this issue, too, Elizabeth focused on the welfare of the Orthodox community as a whole. She pointed to the Ottoman empire and the potential repercussions for Ottoman Christians of tsarist policy. Explaining that the Tatars regarded attacks on their mosques as an "insult," Elizabeth noted the danger that their grievances could reach "those places" where "people of the Greek [Orthodox] confession live in other States, among Muhammadans." She noted the risk of Muslim "oppression" of their churches in retaliation.[10]

Though Elizabeth reiterated earlier bans on forcible conversion to Orthodoxy, Christian proselytizing and the destruction of mosques provoked unrest among Muslims. Moreover, state expansion to the east of the Volga River toward the Ural Mountains led to armed confrontations with local Muslims, the Bashkirs. The influx of Russians and Muslim Tatars to areas of Bashkir migration and settlement increased competition for land and other resources on this steppe frontier. Russian officials blocked the pursuit of Orthodox proselytization and mosque destruction there; all the same, several decades of armed conflict culminated in 1755 in a revolt among the Bashkirs under the leadership of a Muslim leader, Mullah Batyrshah (Bāṭïrshāh). In the following year, St. Petersburg was compelled to reaffirm the right of Muslims in a number of Volga provinces to restore or construct mosques in villages where no Christians were present. This measure afforded new security to mosques such as the one at Sterlibashevo (Istärlibash), built in 1722, and another established in 1745 in Kargala (Seitovskii Posad or Qarghalï), a Muslim merchant settlement outside of Orenburg; both quickly emerged as influential hubs of scholarship and piety.[11]

After seizing the throne in 1762, Catherine tried to restore stability to these restive frontiers. In keeping with her self-representation as an enlightened ruler whose maternal wisdom would bring renovation, harmony, and justice to the empire, the empress inaugurated a new paradigm for the treatment of her Muslim subjects.[12] Redefining the goals of the state, Catherine blocked the bishops' efforts to find new converts among the non-Orthodox. In 1764 she closed the office of the militant proselytizers who had antagonized Muslims and animists in the Volga and Kama River and Urals regions. In 1767 Catherine composed a treatise to demonstrate to both a domestic and an international audience that she was the enlightened sovereign of a "European state" ruled by universal laws. In her *Instruction* to deputies who had been invited to participate in the drafting of a new code of laws, she proclaimed that public order and the general good suffered from religious persecution. "In so vast an Empire which extends its Dominion over such a Variety of People," she announced, "the prohibiting, or not tolerating of their respective Religions would be an evil very detrimental to the Peace and Security of its Subjects." Rejecting an older political maxim that advised rulers to insist on confessional uniformity within their states, the empress drew on European jurists and philosophers who contended that religious persecution only stirred irrational passions. Religious discord harmed the welfare of the population and hindered its increase, which cameralist thinkers regarded as the foundation of a state's wealth. For Catherine, this form of toleration was a pragmatic means to avert confrontation with "Obstinacy, quenching those Contentions which are contrary to the Peace of Government and to the Unity of the Citizens."

But like most contemporary notions of toleration on the Continent, her approach had explicit limits. It did not spell neutrality with regard to different faiths and forms of religious expression. She would not extend toleration to those whom the Church labeled heretics, freethinkers, or atheists. Nor did this conception preclude conversion to Orthodoxy at some future time. "There is no other Method," Catherine advised, "than a wise Toleration of such other Religions as are not repugnant to our own Orthodox Faith and Policy, by which all these wandering Sheep may be reconducted to the true Flock of the Faithful."[13]

Cameralists theorized that proper state direction enhanced the contribution of religion to public order and the general welfare by instilling practical morality and providing ethical training. Johann Heinrich Gottlob von Justi maintained that "faith definitely belongs to the number of elements fortifying a state," even though rulers should not regard it "as the single or most important basis of civil societies." States had the obligation, moreover, to place definite bounds on the forms of religion that were to enjoy toleration. Justi cautioned the "Christian sovereign" against permitting the spread of "dangerous teachings" that might threaten the "tranquility and prosperity of a state." Citing the "dreadful Mexican faith" and the religions of other non-European societies, he argued that "faith may contribute very much to bringing civil arrangements into perfection" but advised that religious excess could lead to "various wild behaviors and absurdities contrary to good morality." He similarly condemned religion that distracted people from work or procreation, or otherwise interfered with the economic priorities of the state. Justi warned that unbounded zeal "may also not only corrupt the morals of state inhabitants but also in various other ways do harm to the general good."[14]

The cameralists had the toleration of Christian confessions foremost in mind, but their lessons on the uses of religion as an instrument of state policy could apply to other faiths as well. Joseph von Sonnenfels recommended that each citizen in a state have a religion that "makes him love his duties." The Viennese cameralist noted approvingly that "wherever the eye of the lawgiver and thus also the punishment of the judge cannot reach," there would be the "exalted principle of God's omnipresence as a witness and judge of all, even the most secret misdeeds" as the "single means to put a stop to evil undertakings." He thus recognized the utility of any religion "that recognizes the judgeship of divinity." Sonnenfels concluded that every religion that promised future "reward for righteousness and virtue" and the "punishment of vice" merited a place in the law of the land. Similarly, Immanuel Kant warned rulers not to mix matters of state and religion except insofar as religion contributes to the formation of "useful citizens, good soldiers, and loyal subjects."[15]

Guided by her own definition of the utility of religion, Catherine carried through the ecclesiastical reform begun by Peter and imposed further limits on the power of the Orthodox Church. Under state direction, Church leaders assimilated the lessons of cameralist thought; they placed new emphasis on education and the value of religion both for personal salvation and the general good. Orthodox elites also had to reconcile themselves to religious pluralism. Catherine's plans for increasing the population of the empire included attracting foreign Catholic and Protestant colonists and annexing neighboring lands.[16] Thus the partitions of Poland absorbed Catholics, Protestants, Uniates, and Jews; and the annexation of the Crimean Peninsula increased the number of Muslims.

Because her *Instruction* was more an abstract statement of philosophical principles than binding legislation, Catherine issued no general statement of toleration. Instead she made ad hoc announcements in various treaties and decrees pledging noninterference or respect for the status quo. This approach was not to be confused with individual freedom of conscience, however; and as even the Orthodox had learned, religious communities would exist only within a framework of hierarchical state regulation.

Valued as a comprehensive system of discipline, toleration became the responsibility of the policing institutions of the regime. Each subject, in turn, was obliged to profess a religion. Backed by the police, the laws governing each religion were binding on the confessional community as a whole, subordinating individual members to communal leaders appointed and supervised by the government. Cameralist theories assigned the state broad discretionary powers in determining which questions of ritual and dogma merited state intervention. Catherine's restructuring of ecclesiastical organization and her claims about which issues belonged to the realm of religion and which to the regime compromised her pledges of noninterference with respect to each of the tolerated faiths.[17]

At the same time, this mode of toleration served as a dynamic means to project imperial power across Russia's frontiers, affording Russia opportunities to gain leverage in neighboring states. From Polish, Ottoman, and Persian lands, dissident Orthodox Christians (and even Polish Protestants) appealed to the empress for protection against religious persecution. A form of policing at home, toleration justified tsarist interventions abroad. Catherine's enthusiasm for toleration in Poland provoked war with the Turks. In July 1768, Orthodox Cossacks, emboldened by tsarist involvement in Polish affairs, took up arms against their religious foes. Their offensive led them onto the territory of the khan of the Crimea, where they massacred local Jews. Despite the protests of the Porte, the Russians refused to break off their operations against Polish forces along the Dnestr River. In October the Ottomans, backed by the French, declared war on Russia.[18]

A number of figures around the empress argued for the seizure not only of the Crimean Peninsula but of Constantinople itself. Cast variously as the liberation of fellow Orthodox Christians, or Russia's reclamation of its classical Greek heritage, the war inspired calls for the expulsion of the Turks from Europe. In a letter to Catherine of November 1771, Voltaire expressed hope that other powers would join her to "exterminate, under your auspices, the two great scourges of the earth—the plague and the Turks." Upon learning that the sultan had hanged a Greek bishop, the *philosophe* advised her to "do the same to the muphti [mufti, a Muslim cleric] at the first opportunity." Similarly, an ode celebrating the birth of the grand prince Konstantin Pavlovich praised him as the "Defender of the faith, glory of the Rus, / Terror and horror of the turban-wearers." Others commemorated the annexation of the Crimea as "the first step toward cleansing Europe of Muhammadans and the conquest of Stambul."[19]

This struggle with the Ottomans made their faith the subject of varied literary genres in Russia. While Russian readers discovered such texts as "The Life of the False Prophet Muhammad in Brief," the court staged Voltaire's play *Muhammad, or Fanaticism,* which sounded the well-worn theme of the founder's deceit. Captivity narratives, too, reworked confessional polemic, now as adventure tales. Appearing in multiple editions, *The Unhappy Adventures of Vasilii Baranshchikov, a Petty Townsman from Nizhnyi Novgorod, in Three Parts of the World* told the story of a sailor who became an Ottoman slave and later an infantryman (Janissary) in Istanbul. Like other such captives, he was forced to undergo the rite of circumcision and become a Muslim. Baranshchikov took a Muslim wife, he maintained, under constant surveillance and pain of punishment. He was nonetheless tormented by memory of his "dear fatherland Russia," his "Christian faith," and his wife and three children back in Nizhnyi Novgorod. The unhappy convert missed "the way of life and morals of the Russians, which are unlike those of the Turks." Even though the Turks had converted the "Christian Greek church," Hagia Sophia, into a mosque, their faith had little to match his "Christian piety." "In their mosques there is no image to bring to mind the Divine grace and wonder," he complained. When an imam instructed him to take a second wife, a notion that increased his "disdain toward the Muhammadan religion," Baranshchikov finally resolved to flee "Tsargrad" for "his fatherland Russia."[20]

The anti-Muslim rhetoric of this sailor's adventure tale and other texts like it did not, however, prompt a shift in how the regime managed the imperial confessional order. Indeed, in the midst of the first Russo-Turkish war (1768–1774) of her reign, Catherine broadened the legal basis for toleration. In June 1773 she qualified the rules prohibiting mosques in mixed settlements for the town of Kazan, where the Orthodox episcopate had protested the existence of two stone mosques in the old Tatar quarter. Catherine supported a governor who had cited her *Instruction* in permitting the construction of the mosques in the presence of churches and Orthodox converts. Though her decree mentioned the "toleration of all confessions," it directly affected only these two mosques and the relations between local Church and state officials. As an explanation for her decree, the empress observed that "since Almighty God tolerates all faiths, languages, and confessions," she would act in accordance with "His Divine will," "wanting only, that among the subjects of Her Majesty love and harmony always reign."[21]

Her caution was well founded. Muslim deputies to the Legislative Commission of 1767–1768 had voiced dissatisfaction with local administration; and a rebellion in the fall of 1773 in the eastern provinces demonstrated its scope. Alongside Orthodox dissenters ("Old Believers"), some Muslims joined the revolt under the banner of the Cossack Emelian Pugachev. Forced to shift her troops from fighting the Ottomans to suppressing Pugachev, Catherine concluded the Treaty of Küçük Kaynarca in 1774. The pact opened up the Black Sea to the Russian navy, strengthened tsarist influence in the Crimea, and made St. Petersburg the guardian of Orthodox communities under Ottoman rule. But in the long term the treaty's ambiguous language clouded Russia's gains by seemingly granting the Porte a say in Muslim affairs beyond its borders. Although fear of Ottoman intervention on behalf of Muslims was not new, Russian expansion had brought these two states into closer contact and increased the number of Russia's Muslims. Anti-Muslim critics such as Prince Mikhail Shcherbatov would warn that all Muslims remained "born enemies of the Christian" who harbored memories of the time when they ruled "over Russia." Tied by faith "with the Turks," they waited for the outbreak of "war between Russia and the Ottoman Porte, at which time these peoples will openly show their loyalty to them."[22]

The empress nonetheless overrode objections from the Church and other critics because Islam seemed useful to her pursuit of enlightened cameralism, a benefit to order and discipline among her subjects. She was aided by a new body of European literature that suggested how Islam fit the criteria laid out by cameralists like Sonnenfels: the "Turkish creed" appeared less alien than it once seemed. These works interpreted Islam for an audience of educated Russians using Christian categories. More didactic than polemical, these authors were concerned with identifying seemingly universal features of religion. To be sure, they argued, Muslims erred by elevating Muhammad to a height that only Christ is worthy of, a fault they highlighted by referring to the religion as "Muhammadanism" (magometanstvo). European commentaries nonetheless highlighted a shared monotheism: "The Turks worship one God, one deity, or entity, the creator of heaven and earth, the rewarder of the good, punisher of the evil, having created Paradise for the former, eternal torments for the latter."

The likenesses between Islam and Christianity did not end there. Though the Turks held Muhammad to be God's greatest prophet, they still believed in "the Ten Commandments of Moses" and "observed its prescriptions." They kept Fridays holy, "like Christians, Sundays." They gathered in "temples" for prayer and celebrated, "as among Christians," a holiday after a month of fasting, calling it not "Easter" but "Bairam." Differences remained, of course. Muslim men could take four wives; for "sacraments," they knew only that of circumcision.[23]

The structure of guides like *An Abridgement of the Muhammadan Faith* (1784), a translation from an anonymous Latin text, invited readers to appreciate theological and moral principles held in common. The *Abridgement* presented Islam as a "Turkish creed," incorporating eight commandments as well as the Seven Deadly Sins known to Christians. The Turkish faith knew rituals, clergy, and final judgment in heaven and hell. Its commandments communicated moral and social lessons, regulating family and community. The first enjoined worship of a single God and his prophet Muhammad. The second instructed the faithful "to do as much as possible to try to preserve loyalty, love, honor, and kindness toward parents, and do nothing against their will." Subject to special instructions on regular mosque prayers, fasting, and charity, Muslims, too, were disciplined by a universal social code. Besides prescribing entry into matrimony and forbidding the taking of human life, the creed taught the Golden Rule. "That which you do not wish on yourself," its third commandment warned, "do not do to others."[24]

Though Russian observers remained sensitive to doctrinal differences between Islam and Orthodox Christianity, they nevertheless identified in Ottoman religious institutions a hierarchy akin to a church. The appearance of new vocabulary in the Russian language reflected these associations. Just as the generic Muscovite term for "non-Christian" (*basurman*) largely gave way to the more specific "Muhammadan" (*magometanin*), the titles of the Ottoman religious establishment entered Russian in the early eighteenth century.[25]

An extensive taxonomy of Muslim offices appeared in Fedor A. Emin's description of the Ottoman empire, published first in 1769 and reprinted in numerous editions thereafter. The author had come to the attention of tsarist authorities under murky circumstances in 1758, introducing himself as "Mahomet Emin" to the Russian ambassador in London. Claiming to be a native of the Russian empire (originally a Pole, by another account), Emin described how he had served the Ottomans for some two decades as a Janissary and a convert to Islam. After settling in Russia, he adopted Orthodoxy, mastered Russian, and became an influential informant on Ottoman life. His was one of the first accounts to translate the titles of Muslim men of religion into Orthodox ecclesiastical language. He rendered the title of the head of the Ottoman religious establishment, *şeyhülislam*, as "patriarch," and likened imams to "priests" and Islamic law court judges, *kadis*, to "archpriests." Muftis were the equals of "priors" in small towns and "bishops" in larger ones; dervishes were no more than "monks." When Russian scholars began to explore their own Muslim peoples, they likened the ranks of mullah and *abyz* to "our priests," while the "*muezzin* corresponds to the post of our sacristan." These terms—and their seeming equivalents in the Orthodox Church—became mainstays of writing about Islam, even while they retained an exotic flavor, as when Russian courtiers dressed up as "muftis" and "Janissaries" at masquerades in St. Petersburg.[26]

"Muhammadans" thus seemed to have a "clergy" as well as a monotheistic creed, derived from a sacred book, with norms resembling canon law. Their "law," complete with concepts of sin and repentance and of heaven and hell, related actions in this world to eternal punishments and rewards. Such images enhanced the value of Islam in the eyes of officials who saw in it a means to make the threat of God's judgment complement the more conventional sanctions of imperial rule. Even Russians who mocked the historical Muhammad as a charlatan often conceded, grudgingly, that Islam shared too much in common with Orthodoxy to be dismissed entirely. Maksim Nevzorov was one such ambivalent critic, who marveled at visiting a mosque in early nineteenth-century Kazan. The faithful prayed with such "extraordinary reverence," he wrote, that it seemed as if "during prayer they feel in a palpable way the presence above them of God, the strong, the powerful, and the fearsome." Muhammadans felt "the power and might of God," though, he regretted, they did not "feel His love" in Christ. The origins of the faith seemed to explain why. The "Muhammadan religion" had been coupled together from "all the faiths then existing, particularly from the Jewish faith," making mosques resemble "the Jewish temple." Despite these faults, comparisons with "the ignorance of pagans and idol-worshippers" showed that

> Muhammad opened in his teaching a sliver of the moon to
> those wandering in the impenetrable night of ignorance and

godlessness; for out of fairness one may say that those who
continually feel above them God the just, almighty and the
avenger of all injustice are less likely to do evil to others
than those not recognizing any supreme authority in the
world at all, or those rejecting His Providence for our well-
being.

Thus while Muhammad himself was a "total cheat" and a seducer of
virgins, who turned sons against fathers, he had advanced his people
beyond primitive paganism and idolatry.[27] As a deterrent against evil
and a warning of divine punishment for earthly sins, Islam appeared
useful, if imperfect. Moreover, the costs of the alternative—repression—had proved too high. The empire thrived on order; and while
toleration dealt a blow to the Church at home, it aided the Orthodox
in Muslim lands and laid the foundations for future expansion.

Throne and Mosque

Russian officials who embraced this vision of the utility of Islam still
faced a number of challenges. It was not enough to declare toleration and leave Muslims and other non-Orthodox Christians to their
own devices. The "well-ordered" European state that Catherine
hoped to construct in Russia assigned all faiths a role in sustaining
the empire. Whereas European administrators had envisioned leaning on generic Christian teachings in support of the state, Russian
officials confronted the task of adapting other doctrines to this task.
Moreover, the tsarist government encountered a fundamental dilemma about linking the presumed usefulness of Islam to the practice of ruling the empire. Unlike the Protestants and Catholics—but
similar to the Jews—of the western borderlands, the Muslims in the
east had no preexisting church structures to incorporate into the bureaucracy in St. Petersburg. In a polity in which even the dominant
faith had been subordinated to secular oversight since Peter, a faith

without hierarchical organization was unthinkable. There could be no throne without an altar, and no altar—or mosque—without the throne.

To realize Islam's potential contribution to the empire, Catherine's administrators set out to find a mode of organization to discipline the faith and its officiants and draw them into state service. They devised a composite institution, drawn first from the model of the contemporary Orthodox Church, but also from the supposed guardians of the Islamic tradition, the Ottomans. Officials did not seek to recreate an exact replica of the Ottoman religious establishment. Yet they aspired to create institutions consonant with what they thought to be the authentic religious norms upheld by their rival. To tsarist administrators, these designations seemed to parallel ecclesiastical ranks in the Church. These likenesses suggested the possibility, indeed the necessity, of organizing a centralized ecclesiastical hierarchy under the direction of the state. The elaboration of this organization drew upon the priorities of clerical discipline and training shared by post-Reformation Protestant, Catholic, and, later, Orthodox Church elites.[28]

The outbreak of a second Russo-Turkish war in 1787, following on Catherine's annexation of the Crimea as well as her expansion of policing into the provinces, focused the regime's attention on the creation of an Islamic establishment under imperial direction. A confrontation with a charismatic Sufi leader, sparked by the Russian burning of his village in Chechnya in 1785, had further highlighted the danger of sedition bred by religious loyalties that ignored state boundaries. Catherine condemned this shaykh Mansur as a "deceiver" and a "false prophet" (lzheprorok), incited by the Ottoman sultan, Selim III.[29] In the context of the war, St. Petersburg sought to deflect the sultan's claims on all of Russia's Muslims. The setting that Catherine's officials chose for the new institution reflected their ambitious aims. They aspired to make use of a domestic source of Is-

lamic leadership in a volatile region still smoldering from Pugachev's rebellion. Located on the eastern stretches of the empire,
some 1760 kilometers from Moscow, the Orenburg territory formed
a borderland north of the Caspian Sea along a mixed forest zone and
the edges of the grassy steppe. Originally fortresses on a defensive
line constructed along the Ural, Belaia, and Samara Rivers and the
Ural range, the towns of Ufa and Orenburg safeguarded Russia from
the turbulent steppe world of raiding horsemen, forming a border
between settled agriculture and the pastures of the nomadic Small
and Middle Hordes of the Kazakhs. These towns also opened up to
the East, serving as entrepots for diplomatic exchanges and trade
with Russia's nomadic neighbors as well as with the peoples of Central Asia, China, and India.

The initiative for a state-sponsored hierarchy for Islam grew out
of this steppe frontier environment where Russian officials had already employed Muslim clerics as intermediaries in dealings with
Muslim Tatars, Mishars, Bashkirs, Kazakhs, and foreign merchants.
Initiated by Bashkir religious scholars in the 1730s, Muslim overtures to the state had sought official recognition for their shari'a
courts and special recognition for esteemed Muslim jurists (ākhūns
or akhunds). In 1754 the government appointed Mullah Batyrshah to
one of these posts, but he proved a liability. In the following year he
led a rebellion against the regime, and the Russian administrator
had to resort to forging letters in the name of another Muslim religious figure to deter the Kazakhs from joining the fray. Batyrshah
nonetheless proclaimed his innocence, avowing that he had always
"enjoined good and forbade evil" for the benefit of society and had
preached loyalty to the authorities, according to the Qur'an: "O Believers [moeminler]! Obey the padishah of our time and his governors."[30]

Russian interest in using such religious precepts only increased.
In 1785 the governor-general of Simbirsk and Ufa petitioned Cath-

erine to elevate a Muslim scholar from Kargala, Mukhamedzhan Khusainov (1756–1824), to the post of "first *akhund* of the region," with a salary of 150 rubles for "border and external missions," a sum that was doubled the following year. Yet it was the new governor-general who arrived from the recently annexed Crimea, Baron Osip A. Igel'strom, a nobleman from a Protestant Baltic German family, who proposed to institutionalize Khusainov's authority as part of a broader strategy of offering state support for the Muslim faith. Drawing on his experience as an administrator in the Crimea and a participant in Russia's diplomatic relations with the Ottomans, the governor-general associated Islam with sedentary agricultural and trading communities. Igel'strom saw schools, courts, mosques, markets, and hostels (caravansaries) as means to promote the settlement of nomadic Bashkirs and Kazakhs and turn them away from raiding. Catherine supported him, drawing on the treasury to commission numerous mosques on the steppe frontier and in Western Siberia. Moreover, to propagate a proper understanding of the faith, Catherine ordered the printing in 1787 in St. Petersburg of the Qur'an, to be distributed to the Kazakhs on the frontier without charge; by the end of the century this press had printed at least another thirty-six hundred Qur'ans for sale to Russia's Muslims.[31]

From the eastern frontier, these institutions faced across the steppe. It was hoped that upon seeing firsthand Catherine's care for the welfare of Islam, the merchants who frequented Orenburg's markets from Persia, Bukhara, India, and beyond would carry word of her patronage along the caravan routes to the East, inducing other "Muhammadan peoples" to seek her enlightened protection. In two decrees of September 1788, Catherine called for the establishment in Ufa of an "Ecclesiastical Assembly of the Muhammadan Creed" (*dukhovnoe sobranie Magometanskogo zakona*). The empress appointed the familiar frontier hand, the thirty-two-year-old Mukhamedzhan Khusainov, to head the institution. Given the title *mufti*, with an annual salary of fifteen hundred rubles, Khusainov was to be aided by "two or three Mullahs chosen from among the Kazan Tatars," a people who had long produced loyal tsarist servitors. The decrees assigned them the task of securing control over "mullahs and other clerical ranks [*dukhovnye chiny*] of the Muhammadan faith" in all provinces of the empire where Muslims lived, with the exception of the Crimea, where Catherine proposed to establish at a later date a separate institution along similar lines.[32]

In 1789 Igel'strom elaborated on the responsibilities of the Assembly, reflecting official concern with imposing order and discipline on Muslim religious life. Igel'strom recommended that the Assembly be subordinated to the provincial administration on an equal footing with other judicial organs. His regulations defined the duty of the Assembly as "the examination of knowledge of the rules and rites of the Muhammadan faith of all who have the desire or are chosen and found worthy to become mullahs and akhunds or another title of an ecclesiastical rank and sent by the provincial administration for testing in this assembly." Before traveling to Ufa, prospective mullahs or akhunds were to attain, with certification from the district police chief, "residents' approval" testifying to their "behavior" and appropriate residence. Candidates were then to appear before the Assembly, which would appraise not only the candidates' knowledge of the faith but also their political reliability and moral qualities. Following the approval or rejection of the candidate, the Assembly was to submit the results in writing for the confirmation of the provincial administration.[33]

Igel'strom added that besides checking the qualifications of those wishing to assume "ecclesiastical ranks," the Assembly would also "hear and decide cases belonging to the religious part of the Muhammadan law, like circumcision, marriage, divorces, and mosque service." This institution would afford a voice to the Muslim laity: "Whoever is not satisfied with the decision of a mullah or akhund is to be free to announce his dissatisfaction to the Ecclesiastical Assembly and request that it take the case under its consideration." He thereby delegated to the Assembly an appellate function with the power to overturn decisions taken at the mosque level. The governor-general thus envisioned this institution as a center of doctrinal authority, assigning it the task "of extending the utmost supervision so that . . . superstition and other abuses that cannot be tolerated do not creep in."[34]

Below the Assembly, Igel'strom called for a closely regulated network of mosque communities, using the Orthodox parish as a standard. His guidelines regularized and integrated these communities, known as *mahallas* in Tatar sources, into a wider framework of bureaucratic supervision. Like Orthodox villages, Muslim settlements would have to meet a minimum population requirement before receiving permission to found a mosque; however, Igel'strom also permitted mosques in smaller communities, "as long as Muhammadans perform the five daily prayers [there]."[35] Placing the Assembly between petitioners and Russian officials, Igel'strom entrusted it with reviewing requests for mosque construction before forwarding them to provincial officials, who had the final authority.

In addition to controlling the number and size of Muslim parishes, the Assembly was charged with monitoring the "mosque servitors" attached to them. Since Peter, Church and state officials had combated the appointment of "excess" clergy, who ostensibly exacerbated clerical poverty and burdened parishioners. In the view of secular officials, such clerics better served the "public good" by taking up more "useful" professions. Permitting only the necessary number of "ecclesiastical officials," Igel'strom eliminated the "superfluous and idle." Igel'strom's rules restricted the legal performance of clerical duties to men licensed by the state, effectively creating an official Muslim clergy where none had existed before. They instructed the

Assembly to take care that no one "appropriate of his own accord the title of *akhund, imam,* or *mullah* for himself." Another set the number of akhunds per district at no more than two, adding that they were to oversee "the mosques, schools, and servitors attached to them." Igel'strom also entrusted the Assembly with supervision of Muslim schools. The schools were confined to mosque complexes, and only instructors who had been examined by the Assembly were allowed to teach in them.[36]

The new institution, first called the Ufa Ecclesiastical Assembly of the Muhammadan Creed, later the Orenburg Muhammadan Ecclesiastical Assembly, soon bore the imprint of its Muslim head as well. The son of an imam from the village of Kargala, Khusainov had studied in local schools before traveling to Bukhara and Kabul, where he studied under Fayz Khan, the figure with whom this chapter began. From the 1770s he had worked closely with imperial officials and acted as their agent on the southeastern frontiers. In the Northern Caucasus, he negotiated Muslim acquiescence to Russian rule. In the steppe east of Orenburg, he lobbied the Kazakhs to pledge loyalty to the tsar, while appealing to them to deepen their devotion to their religious obligations in the community of Islam.[37] Later, he solidified these bonds by marrying his daughter to the head of the Kazakh Inner Horde settled between the Volga and Ural Rivers.

Despite the patronage of Igel'strom and the empress, the initial powers of the office did not match the ambitions of Mufti Khusainov. In 1792 he had requested the right to hold serfs, explaining that his rank made him "the first among Muhammadans" and that he merited the favor, "like those who have rendered service from ancient times until now." He had brought Kazakhs under "the invincible Russian scepter" and mediated conflicts between them and the Russians. Enjoyed only by the nobility and royal family, the privilege of serf ownership befitted his position, he argued, while the religious obligation to enter into a legal marriage according to "the Muhammadan law" made it a practical necessity.[38]

Guided by the enterprising Khusainov, the Assembly boldly asserted its power over the Muslim men of learning and piety in its first decade. By 1800 the mufti and three judges attached to the Assembly, aided by a staff of six secretaries and translators, had administered oral examinations for more than nineteen hundred clerics.[39] Records from 1791 show that these included 527 mullahs, who led mosque prayers and offered instruction, and 339 *azanchis (muezzins)*, who sang the call to prayer; besides various specialized titles related to teaching, seven men bore the title *akhund*, designating seniority in a particular locale. In the early nineteenth century, the reach of the Assembly nonetheless remained weak, and its ties to mosque communities superficial. With a meager staff and budget, the Assembly lacked its own building until midcentury, apparently housing its offices and archive with those of the provincial government. Equipped with these modest resources, the Islamic establishment faced numerous difficulties in imposing clerical discipline and a parish structure on the Muslim communities under its jurisdiction.

Though Catherine backed Igel'strom's project, opposition came from officials in the capitals and, in particular, from provincial authorities. Some regarded the institution as a threat to their power. The civil governor of Orenburg complained that when the Assembly opened on 4 December 1789, local officials did not understand either its "direct duty" or its responsibility to check the qualifications of "ecclesiastical officials of the Muhammadan faith." Governor Frizel advised against giving too much latitude to the mufti and Assembly, pointing to the fragility of local administration and "the fanaticism of a people little-educated but steeped in the coarseness of their ideas."[40]

Frizel insisted that Russian officials retain absolute authority over their Muslim charges. He defended their involvement in disputes among Muslims, especially relating to marriage, for "difficulties in the adjudication of cases concerning [marital] union among Muhammadans are worthy of the regard of higher government." The hierarchy overstepped its powers to such an extent, he charged, that the Assembly considered the provincial government "merely an executive instrument of its decisions." Frizel called for provincial authorities to exercise strict control; otherwise, he warned, "the biased evil and self-interest of ecclesiastical officials of the Muhammadan faith will never be prosecuted." The governor found the mufti over-ambitious, noting Khusainov's proposal that the Assembly in Ufa be replaced by a "College of the Muhammadan Faith" in St. Petersburg, directly under the sovereign. With this, the mufti aspired to become, Frizel argued, "the direct ruler over the faith professed by Muhammadans and simultaneously over this people." He concluded that "the ecclesiastical authority over the local Muhammadan people must in no way be strengthened in its functioning."[41]

Mistrust of this new office was not confined to provincial bureaucrats alone. Muslims, too, had mixed reactions to the new state-appointed head for the empire's Islamic community. The idea of an official muftiate apparently did not by itself provoke significant opposition. Muslims may have adapted to this body because analogous institutions had been known among Muslims in past times; they also existed in contemporary societies, most notably in the form of the Ottoman şeyhülislam and the graded ranks of judges, scholars, and teachers subordinated to him.[42] For critics, the legitimacy of the muftiate suffered from the behavior of Khusainov. Of modest background, he alienated Islamic scholars and laypeople by assuming the role of exclusive arbiter of Islamic orthodoxy for scattered communities that had previously sought guidance from multiple centers of Islamic learning, from Kabul to Cairo. His critics had studied with many of the same teachers who had trained Khusainov. Personal rivalries also played a role. Many of the scholars who loathed Khusainov had vied for his office; some never forgave him for thwarting their aspirations to become the leading Muslim authority in the empire.

Charges of corruption and bias eroded Khusainov's moral authority, though his enemies distinguished his behavior from that of the state and sought to enlist the government against him. Islamic texts that circulated in the Russian empire and Central Asia outlined the codes of behavior and moral qualities required of a mufti.[43] But his opponents did not cite them in their protests. Before an audience of Russian officialdom, they characterized his behavior in terms familiar to opponents of malfeasance in the bureaucracy. They used a vocabulary of venality and favoritism, pointing to both his "corruption" and his association with behaviors that Islamic law had forbidden.

In 1805 a Kazan merchant of the first guild denounced Khusainov in a petition to the tsar. Abdulla Khasamdinov accused the mufti of violating "the order of the liturgy," by which he meant neglect of the appointed times for prayer. The mufti committed further acts against the shari'a, Khasamdinov charged, like wearing silk clothes and using silver spoons. He had even extorted money from candidates who traveled to Ufa to be tested by the Assembly. Those who refused to pay, the merchant claimed, were given questions during the exam "that may not exist at all, and because of this [Khusainov] rejects them as if they were not capable and worthy."[44]

The judges in the Assembly defended Khusainov. Khamza Emangulov explained that he was obliged to recognize and honor him as a "sage mentor." Refuting the first charges, the judges insisted that they all prayed at the same time. When investigators from the provincial administration interviewed mullahs who had passed through the examinations, prayer leaders also attested to his probity: twenty-four in the district of Sviazhsk and forty-three in the district of Mamadyzh in Kazan Province denied being forced to pay bribes.

But others sided with the mufti's accusers. A mullah from Kazan came forward to back Khasamdinov's accusation, as did a mullah from Tsarevokokshaisk and another from Spassk. Several others from the old Tatar suburb of Kazan added that Khusainov "curses them with abusive words, threatens them with exile to Siberia, and takes money from them." An assistant to a local akhund, Salikh Akhmetev, complained that the mufti's "pointless" summons to Ufa cost him fifty rubles. Forty-six villagers from Starye Tigana informed investigators that when the mufti had passed through their village twenty years ago, he had not compensated them for the twenty horses he took. Despite these accusations, investigators remained unconvinced. One official rejected the last charge, noting that "twenty years ago a mufti of the Muhammadan faith had not yet been appointed in Russia." By the autumn of 1805, more than fourteen thousand Muslims from various districts in Kazan Province had testified that the mufti had never abused them "with insults and oppression" nor extorted money from them.[45]

The controversies surrounding the first mufti did not end here. Clerics and laypeople joined provincial officials in raising further charges. When Orenburg authorities accused Khusainov of violating his office in 1811, the case precipitated a broader debate about the authority of the mufti. The resulting legislation elevated the status of the office for Khusainov and his successors by removing the mufti from the provincial Chamber of the Criminal Court. It transferred cases involving the holder of this office to the highest judicial body in the empire, the Ruling Senate in St. Petersburg. Among his co-religionists, Khusainov claimed the power to declare who did—and who did not—belong to the community of the faithful: in reports to officials in 1815, and again in 1818, he asserted that "whoever scorns the decision and fatwa of a mufti should not be considered a Muslim."[46]

Even though Khusainov had now been elevated as the highest Islamic authority in the empire, his power still did not go unchallenged. Lay accusations against his "bias" in marriage and divorce cases prompted officials to refine further the authority of the post. A conflict about the punishment of Muslims for adultery reflected continued uncertainty about the power of the mufti and, more generally, about the relationship between civil and religious authority. Officials recalled that they had responded to complaints against Khusainov's handling of marital disputes by instructing him to review each case together with other members of the Assembly. Following his tenure, the Senate ruled in 1832 that civil authorities were not to execute the "personal decisions" of the mufti—in this case, orders from "religious authorities" to apply corporal punishment to adulterers.[47] Though this decree aimed at delineating more clearly the lines between "civil" and "ecclesiastical" authorities, the two would remain intertwined.

Dissenters from the Church of Islam

Cultivating this mutual dependence, the first mufti ventured to instrumentalize the very regime that sought to make use of Islam in managing the empire. He actively sought out alliances with St. Petersburg to support his authority in the face of opposition from both Muslim notables and provincial officials. In June 1815 he turned to Alexander N. Golitsyn, the director of the Main Administration of the Religious Affairs of Foreign Confessions. Khusainov complained about local authorities who had supplied "Muhammadan clergy" with passports permitting them to leave their parishes for extended periods of time. Some of these officials had even issued permission for the pilgrimage to Mecca. These officials undermined his ability to control the clergy, the mufti protested, even though he had served the state "with zeal," persuading "the Muhammadan people as well as its clergy" to lead tranquil lives and obey established authorities.

Adding that these clerics engaged in "evil affairs," Khusainov felt it his duty to bring this information to Golitsyn's attention. He insisted that he did not want "praise" or reward from St. Petersburg but instead acted out of "devotion to my imperial Russian fatherland [*vserossiiskoe otechestvo*]" and "out of sorrow for my pastorate." Professions of patriotic fervor and episcopal concern helped gain the measured backing of officials in the central government and earned him a place in a wider imperial elite as a member of the Free Economic Society, the Order of St. George, and even the Russian Bible Society.[48]

Khusainov's connections in the capital still did not guarantee the Assembly the degree of ecclesiastical control envisioned by its architects. A conflict between Khusainov and a mullah in Kazan Province highlights key dimensions of the mufti's struggle to project his authority into local religious life over the objections of officials and, most dramatically, his co-religionists. The case sheds light on religious debate and on the interplay of village politics and the official Islamic establishment in shaping local disputes about wider controversies. Argument about Islamic tradition extended beyond a scholarly elite. It linked the competing voices of the lettered and unlettered alike to debates throughout the Islamic world, engaging villagers of different social categories through bonds of patronage and the pursuit of the Sufi path. Such important controversies called for powerful arbiters.

In October 1801, Mufti Khusainov wrote the Ruling Senate in St. Petersburg to communicate disturbing news he had received from a Muslim notable of the old Tatar suburb of Kazan. According to his informant, a lower court had unsealed in the village of Ura (Orï) a mosque that the mufti had ordered closed in the previous year in a ruling confirmed by the Senate. Khusainov emphasized his own role in interpreting for his readers the activities being pursued in this mosque. "It is my office and duty," he explained, "to watch so

that among my fellow countrymen [*edinoplemenniki*] no provocation may arise among the simple folk, especially from ecclesiastical
officials who are ignorant of the law or are schismatics [*raskol'niki*],
which would lead to depravity and disobedience to authority."[49]

The mufti underscored the threat of what he portrayed as the in-
evitable union of religious schism and revolt. He blamed the re-
opening of the mosque on the "intrigues and cunning" of a former mullah, Khäbibulla Khuseinov, whom the mufti had "long ago
found to be an opponent of our law, that is, a schismatic." The
mufti's conflict with this village mullah embroiled him in a complex
dispute rooted in the locale. One kin group's claims to preeminence
in religious affairs had recently split the community. A prosperous
village dotted with small factories and inhabited by artisans and
fishermen, Ura was also home to merchants who traded with Central Asia.[50] Hostility toward Khäbibulla Khuseinov's notions of Islamic piety further intensified the tensions that divided a stratified
community.

The patriarch of the leading family in the village, the Näzirs, had
founded a stone mosque there following his return from study in
Bukhara in 1787. Khäbibulla became the prayer leader, apparently
after one of his female relatives married into this family. Relations
soon soured among these in-laws, however, and several members of
the Näzir clan began to voice their opposition to him. Mömëin b.
Tahir b. Näzir complained to Ufa about the new appointment, protesting, "I built this mosque only for myself and my children, and
none of us are satisfied with mullah Khäbibulla being the imam."[51]
The sources do not reveal whether the mufti formally ordered
Khäbibulla's dismissal. It appears instead that the mullah deflected
pressure exerted by the Näzirs by leaving the mosque that they
claimed as their family patrimony.

When his brother, Fätkhulla b. äl-Khösäen b. Gabdelkärim al-

Öri, took over the imamate at the village's stone mosque in 1799, Khäbibulla moved to found his own mosque.[52] Arguing that the village needed a mosque (perhaps without mentioning the existing mosque), Khäbibulla requested permission to construct another one in Ura in 1800. The Assembly approved his petition, and with the aid of villagers who recognized him as their Sufi guide (*ishan* or *īshān*), Khäbibulla built a new wooden mosque near the older one for his followers. Meanwhile, feuding in the village of Ura continued. The men of influence in the village—the *bāys*—repeatedly appealed to the Assembly seeking assistance against Khäbibulla. The mufti then gave orders for him to be removed from his post and for his mosque to be sealed (or, by one account, burned).[53] Yet, as Khusainov discovered sometime in the latter part of 1801, a local court had reversed his instructions and unsealed the mosque.

Khäbibulla had found a more powerful patron in local government. A petition campaign had apparently met with success. His followers, including a number of Mishars who joined him as he traveled in the region preaching and offering instruction, had submitted petitions to the governor in support of Khäbibulla.[54] In another direct challenge to the power of the office of the mufti, a provincial official granted Khäbibulla permission to return to his position, displacing his brother, Fätkhulla, the replacement approved by Khusainov.

These supporters backed Khäbibulla again when the bāys mobilized their servants and factory workers against him. Armed with cudgels, the two groups came to blows in the village in fierce fighting. Despite the threat of continued violence and the opposition of the mufti and his brother Fätkhulla (who occupied the post of "senior akhund" for the district from 1819), Khäbibulla continued to attract devotees from around the region. He also established a Sufi shaykh's lodge (*khānaqāh*) in the village, where he apparently transmitted the mystical religious knowledge he learned from his guide to the Sufi path, Fayz Khan, from whom he had received a license *(ijāzah)* while studying in Kabul.[55]

Sufism, alone, was not the source of the conflict with Khäbibulla. Mufti Khusainov, too, had studied with Fayz Khan; Fätkhulla apparently shared the sober legalistic outlook of the Mujaddidis as well. Rather, it seems that Khäbibulla's claims to spiritual leadership in both Ura and the region as a whole, based upon a broad following among unlettered Muslims, threatened both Fätkhulla and the mufti. Khäbibulla had even challenged Khusainov for his office, offering himself as a candidate.[56]

Khäbibulla apparently upset scholars like his brother by assuming leadership of a Sufi orientation that appealed to the common people. His charisma radiated beyond the village, drawing Mishars and other recruits from throughout the region. At the same time, Khäbibulla's religion set his followers apart and fractured the local community of the faithful. In perhaps the most telling of his charges against Khäbibulla, Khusainov complained that this mullah had intended to found a "shaykh's home," a place to lead his followers in Sufi rituals and prayers under the pretense of converting the mosque into an orphanage. In criticizing Khäbibulla, the mufti did not condemn Sufi practices in general. He focused his ire instead on the "schismatic rules" introduced among the "simple folk" by Khäbibulla following his travels to Bukhara and especially to Kabul. Khäbibulla's adherents spread word of his teachings from a text entitled *A Lesson for the Ignorant*, the work of a tenth-century jurist. Mishars are said to have associated Khäbibulla's appeal with this text, a collection of brief sayings and admonitions on morality and piety and excerpts from the Qur'an and *hadith* (accounts of the words and deeds of the Prophet and his Companions), which circulated among Muslims elsewhere.[57]

According to Khusainov, Khäbibulla and his followers had even traveled in the steppe and spread his teachings among the Kazakhs. Ordered by Baron Igel'strom to put an end to the "agitation" that this had provoked among them, Khusainov countered Khäbibulla by delivering "exhortations" and "commentary on the rules of the Muslim faith" in the steppe and condemned Khäbibulla's acts as "very contrary to our law." As justification for his campaign against the shaykh, he cited a policy established in 1746 by the former governor of the Orenburg territory, Ivan Nepliuev, which called for the restraining of Muslim leaders who caused "unrest" among the people. In the meantime, Khusainov received word that a Tatar in the district of Petrovsk in Saratov Province, Khamza Aitov, had also begun to carry on "various acts of provocation and agitation among the simple folk," naming himself a follower *(murid)* of Khäbibulla. Moreover, Khusainov claimed, Aitov had "willfully" founded a mosque in the village of Ust' Uziliakh, thereby committing an act of open disobedience to the government. The mufti also persuaded Count Viktor Kochubei, the minister of internal affairs, that Khäbibulla and a companion, Mullah Shaban, had deceived villagers throughout Saratov Province by presenting the former as a "saint and miracle worker" *(ugodnik bozhii i chudotvorets)*. Khusainov accused them of collecting money from the gullible, for which they founded their own "treasury."[58] In the tsarist empire, such a display of unbridled religion was politically suspect, even among the non-Orthodox who were otherwise unaffected by the Church's history of schism and political revolt.

The opponents of Khäbibulla and Shaban cast them as a direct threat to the official Islamic hierarchy. A mullah in the district of Kuznetsk reported to the Assembly that the two had formed a special "judicial chancellery," where Khäbibulla held forth from an expensive chair, which no one else was permitted to occupy. This Sufi guide even dared to hold "daughters of peoples of the Russian-Greek confession" as "hostages." Khäbibulla and Shaban nonetheless continued to travel around gathering followers, the mullah claimed, though such acts violated Islamic and imperial law. Based upon this denunciation, Saratov authorities investigated whether Khäbibulla had acted as a "false prophet" or had committed an "illegal innovation" *(novizna)*. When the criminal court looked into the matter, claims that the shaykh had instructed followers to take Russian wives and concubines could not be substantiated.[59] Muslim feuding had entangled the police, but Islam had still not demonstrated its utility for the empire.

A Faith for the Tsar

Governor Igel'strom and Mufti Khusainov had imagined Islamic institutions sponsored by the regime as means to project the regime's authority on the eastern borderlands and beyond. The Orenburg muftis continued to play an important role both on the frontiers and in Russia's relations with other Muslim states. But in the second quarter of the nineteenth century the Ministry of Internal Affairs devoted more attention to elaborating a role for the Assembly and mufti as instruments of administration within the empire.

St. Petersburg called upon non-Orthodox faiths to aid the secular arm of government, just as they expected the Church to employ its spiritual authority to maintain law and order among its flock. Through the mufti, the government aimed to utilize the authority of Islamic doctrine to compel the acquiescence of its Muslim subjects in temporal affairs as well. Khusainov's insistence upon the binding, rather than merely advisory, character of the fatwa accommodated officials' search for a religious underpinning for the autocracy. The preaching of Islam would instill active regard for the obligation to serve "tsar and fatherland." Thus lawmakers turned to the mufti seeking religious legitimation. His sermons, instructions, and legal opinions became indispensable tools for the transmission and dissemination of state directives, paralleling the role of the Church in communicating tsarist decrees to the Orthodox population.

After Khusainov's death in 1824, subsequent muftis also demonstrated their willingness to employ their interpretation of Islamic writ to legitimize tsarist law. Upon Russian officials' direction, the second mufti, Gabdessaliam Gabdrakhimov (in office 1825–1840), issued a fatwa in 1831 instructing Muslims to send their children to Kazan University for medical training. In the following year, he mobilized citations from the Qur'an, hadith, and a Hanafi legal text to persuade Muslims, as the civil governor of Orenburg Province had requested, that laziness and the shirking of work had no place in religion. Emphasizing the necessity of work in protecting one's family from poverty and avoiding sinful pleasures, the mufti ordered clerics to exhort their parishioners to sow and harvest at the appropriate times.[60]

Like Khusainov, Gabdrakhimov still faced competing sources of Islamic authority whose networks extended through madrasas and Sufi lineages throughout the region. Like so many other scholars, he had studied at a madrasa in Kargala. A controversy in the late 1820s and early 1830s nonetheless demonstrated the limited extent of the mufti's capacity to sway Muslim opinion. Gabdrakhimov clashed with a Muslim scholar in Kazan and with rural mullahs among Bashkir regiments over whether it was permissible for Muslims to obey a decree of February 1827 declaring a three-day waiting period between a person's death and burial. In 1829, St. Petersburg appealed for Gabdrakhimov's help in countering objections to the legislation voiced by the senior akhund of Kazan, Abdulsatar Sagitov. After several years of study in Bukhara (and a close association with the Bukharan amir Haydar), Sagitov had established a reputation as an authoritative jurist and mullah of the "Fifth Cathedral" mosque community in Kazan, where his father and brother also ran a madrasa. The akhund had campaigned for the office of mufti when the post became vacant following Khusainov's death, but his candidacy faltered on the objections of the governor of Orenburg Province. Sagitov again placed his knowledge at the disposal of imperial authorities when he objected to the burial decree.[61]

In asking that Muslims not be subject to the new law, he argued that Muslims must be buried on the day of their deaths or risk violation of the shari'a and pointed to previous legislation establishing "freedom" for the exercise of the Muslim faith in Russia. He complemented his citations of eighteenth-century decrees and charters with one of the hadith that warned, "When one of you dies then do not hold him as in a prison but hasten to put him in the grave."[62] But in November 1829 the mufti countered Sagitov's argument. In constructing his refutation, the mufti built upon the rationale offered by Grigorii I. Kartashevskii, the director of the Ministry of the Religious Affairs of Foreign Faiths. When Kartashevskii requested his input against Sagitov, he reminded Gabdrakhimov that this law was "a general Police measure, that is, strictly speaking not one concerning the faith of any peoples that inhabit Russia." Should this law present "difficulties" in connection with "Muhammadan law," he continued, "then the higher Muhammadan ecclesiastical authorities would render assistance to the government by averting these difficulties in its instructions, for the benefit of Muslims themselves." In complying with this request, the mufti insisted that the shari'a presented no obstacles to this policy, which he regarded as binding for Muslims. Quoting from the original correspondence, Gabdrakhimov added that it would be "welcome for the government to publish [this] law to prevent such unhappy cases" when "people who are actually not dead have been buried alive out of haste in burial."[63]

But some officials remained uneasy about the compatibility of Islamic law and state decrees on burial. This uncertainty arose largely out of distrust of Gabdrakhimov and his dual role as supreme jurisconsult and imperial servitor. When officials consulted with the religious authorities in the Crimea, a mufti appointed by the government for this locale replied that Islamic law definitely commands burial on the same day of death. Citing legal texts establishing this opinion, the mufti asserted that the people regarded this practice as a "doctrine of the faith." One Russian official understood the Crimean cleric's response to pose "definite difficulties" for this legislation. He questioned Gabdrakhimov's consent with the new law, voicing his suspicion that it had been based more on "obedience to the government" than on fidelity to "orthodox" Islamic legal doctrine. Thus tsarist authorities were not content to have the imprimatur of the mufti alone. They insisted on establishing the true meaning of the shari'a, even as state-backed Muslim authorities disagreed about its interpretation.

The approach devised for the Jews of the empire appeared to offer a way out of this impasse. Like Muslims, Jews were bound by religious law to bury their dead on the same day. In a proposal apparently initiated by the future Alexander II (r. 1855–1881), the Jewish Committee recommended that Jews be permitted this "custom" temporarily until "they are prepared by exhortations through their rabbis" to conform to the burial law. The administration thought this solution applicable to Muslims as well, though with the provision that the "Muhammadan parish clergy" notify police authorities before performing burials in cases where there may be "doubt about death." It also attached the condition that, like the rabbis, the "higher Muhammadan ecclesiastical authorities do not cease to take all possible measures at their disposal to persuade Muhammadans of the beneficial goal for themselves of the imperially approved opinion of the State Council."[64]

When the measure came before Nicholas I, it stood out as a departure from policies aimed at standardizing the law and equalizing civic duties, as in the extension in 1827 of military conscription to the Jews. Consistent with his personal involvement in the formulation of policy toward Jews, the tsar rejected the measure in his own hand: "Do not deviate from the general rules, for Jews too will be made subject to them."[65] In this case, concern with application of general legal principles and the wider imposition of civic obligations overrode uncertainty within the Ministry of Internal Affairs about establishing accord between the laws of the empire and the particularistic legal cultures of its subject peoples.

Though the tsar and the Orenburg mufti supported the new burial regulations, many clerics and laypeople remained unconvinced. They still feared that postponing the burial of Muslims would contravene God's command. The legislation threatened communal performance of the ritual and prayer obligations attending the death of a Muslim. It provoked anxiety and alarm among the living about the fates of deceased relatives and about their own standing in God's judgment. The Qur'an and hadith provided the faithful with detailed prescriptions for the washing and shrouding of the body of the deceased, the saying of prayers, the procession to the place of burial, recitation of the Qur'an, and the placement of the body in the grave in the direction of prayer. Death brought the separation of body and soul and, later, their reunion in the grave, where the deceased faced interrogation by the angels Munkar and Nakīr. Depending upon the answers to questions posed by the angels, the deceased might experience "the punishments of the grave" or rewards as a token of God's mercy—until the appointed hour of the resurrection and final judgment.[66]

How the living coped with, or surreptitiously eluded, a law that introduced an unsettling temporal dimension into this eschatological order remains unclear. Spokesmen for these communities nevertheless campaigned for its repeal. In 1831, scholars from Kazan petitioned Nicholas I, who rejected their request; and clerics from other regions continued to protest. To the great displeasure of the Ministry of Internal Affairs, fatwas and "exhortations" from the mufti's pen failed to persuade Muslims that the government's instructions were "useful and even essential" for them. In December 1833, Minister D. N. Bludov urged Gabdrakhimov "to make an effort again toward the eradication among the Orenburg Muhammadans of prejudices and biases that are so harmful for themselves, paying special attention thereby to the clergy, who have a powerful influence on them." Officials nervously watched Bashkirs of the Fifth Canton of Orenburg Province throughout 1834, when rumors circulated hinting at escalating protest against this legislation, reportedly led by an official mullah recently returned from pilgrimage to Mecca, the *hajj*. In conjunction with Governor V. A. Perovskii, the Assembly compelled eleven of these Bashkir scholars to travel to Ufa to sign an oath pledging compliance with Gabdrakhimov's fatwa sanctioning the burial law. Finally, in September the Assembly ordered an "Asiatic printing house" in Orenburg to print thirty-five hundred copies of a fatwa in Tatar directing Muslims to wait three days before burying their dead.[67]

Despite the establishment of a domestic Islamic hierarchy, this controversy—and the anxieties it provoked about pilgrims—shows how international ties persisted as a challenge to attempts to create a Muslim community defined by the borders of the empire. While celebrated madrasas and Sufi guides drew the tsar's Muslims to Bukhara, Istanbul, and elsewhere, pilgrimage brought foreign Muslims to Russia. With the founding of Odessa as a port on the Black Sea in 1796, a new route to Mecca became established by way of Istanbul. For Muslims from neighboring regions, the trade corridors across the steppe and through Russia's south to Astrakhan and then Odessa now also facilitated the hajj. In 1803, Alexander I approved a request from Bukharan merchants to pass through Russia on the way to the Holy Places.

Geopolitical considerations soon gave rise to new concerns. Between 1804 and 1813, Russia was at war with one or both of its southern neighbors. The Ottomans, in particular, retained claims on the loyalties of Muslims on Russia's frontiers. Throughout the nineteenth century, the Sublime Porte dispatched emissaries to the Caucasus. In 1813 they carried decrees instructing communities in Daghestan to celebrate the accession of a new sultan. Invoking the traditional practice of recognizing a Muslim sovereign, the instructions called on preachers to mention the name of the sultan in Friday sermons. When a son was born to Mahmud II, the Ottomans summoned Muslims throughout the Caucasus to offer prayers. Later the Ottomans directed Daghestanis and others to celebrate the liberation of Mecca and Medina from the "false religion" of the Wahhabis (referred to here as "Kharijites") and the return of the Holy Cities to the sultan's guardianship. Just over a decade later, war returned to these unstable frontiers. During the Russo-Turkish War of 1826–1828, a Russian general advised the Adygei people of the Northern Caucasus that "this war does not concern you" and that "the Russian government will not confuse you with the Turks." With Russian control still weak in many places, the Adygei preferred to keep their options open. In the 1830s, Muslim resistance to the Russian advance stiffened, prompting new misgivings about the dangers of Muslim solidarity. By 1843 the Russians learned that Adygei communities had sent a delegation to Istanbul seeking the protection of the sultan.[68]

In the quarter century following Alexander's decree on the hajj, Russian authorities had grown anxious about transimperial contacts from the east. Sufis now appeared as agents of "fanaticism," and not only in the Northern Caucasus, where Russian commanders identified Sufi networks as the backbone of the anti-tsarist resistance movement. In the early 1830s the Asiatic Committee, a coordinating body for policy in the Ministry of Foreign Affairs, proposed to ban *hajjis* from traveling from towns such as Tashkent, Khiva, and Bukhara through Russia to Istanbul and Mecca, "in order to break their ties with our subjects, which from experience have turned out harmful, for these Asiatics, and Dervishes in particular, instead of going to Mecca for worship, have stayed among us in places inhabited by Muhammadans, [and] incited in the latter fanaticism and have engendered all kinds of subversive principles." Unlike the licensed mullahs who retained their utility for the state, "these people have been judged to be not entirely useful by the government."

The Orenburg governor, P. P. Sukhtelen, shared this view, calling them "useless people, whose whole life consists in vagrancy and fraud." For Sukhtelen, such hajjis were a burden not only to the state but to their co-religionists in Russia, for they "have great influence on the minds of our Muhammadans, which they always use for evil, preaching among them hatred toward Christians and against the government itself, so that they gain the trust of their co-religionists and the opportunity to live at their expense." Henceforth, caravans of merchants and hajjis were not to be permitted beyond trading centers. The government warned the governors of Astrakhan, Orenburg, and Western Siberia not to permit these "dervishes" to stay on and become Russian subjects.[69]

Similarly, authorities in the Caucasus began to deny local Muslims permission to go on the hajj. In 1842 the War Ministry secretly ordered the Orenburg governor, V. A. Obruchev, to pursue this same strategy there. Once again, utility and security defined the extent to which the state would accommodate religious practice. Pilgrimage diverted Muslim soldiers and officials from service, the minister argued, and hajjis in general returned with an "influence on their co-religionists [that is] unfavorable to us." But even in announcing this modification in policy the authorities remained sensitive to the charge of violating the principle of toleration. As recently as 1830 the governor-general of New Russia and Bessarabia, M. S. Vorontsov, had discouraged Crimean officials from impeding local pilgrims at all. Invoking Catherine's promise of toleration, he rea-

soned that adherence to this pledge "was and will be one of the primary reasons for the loyalty of conquered peoples, of the greatness
and strength of Our Fatherland." Not only would such interference
be "contrary to the system of our Government," Vorontsov contended, but abandoning "previous experiences and promises" might
increase "fanaticism." All the same, by 1842 the Ministry of War justified interference but cautioned secrecy. Like his peers in the Caucasus, the Orenburg governor was instructed not to reveal these misgivings about the hajj; rather he was to turn down the would-be
pilgrims' travel applications "on various plausible pretexts."[70]

Yet the hajj continued in spite of periodic harassment, and the
next decade brought more danger from the south. In 1844 the war
against the forces of Imam Shamil in Daghestan and Chechnya
was ten years old. Consuming hundreds of thousands of soldiers, it
would drag on for two more decades. Continued resistance had
given rise in official circles to the belief that a "new teaching" had
been brought by "shaykhs from Persia and Turkey." When officials
informed Nicholas I, the tsar secretly directed them "to prohibit
completely the entry across our borders of any figures of Muhammadan ecclesiastical rank," including Russian subjects, if they had
acquired religious training abroad.[71] Thus, in deterring pilgrimage
and study abroad, the regime sought to limit tsarist Muslims' contacts with other centers of piety and learning. This move, in turn,
bolstered the domestic Islamic establishment as the doctrinal pivot
of Islam for Russia's Muslims.

The search for congruences between the muftis' interpretation of the best interests of Muslims and tsarist administrative
demands led to the improvisation of a common moral language.
For Russian authorities, sin formed the basis of a universal moral
order binding the interests of the empire to the moral teachings of

religion. In this, as in other assumptions about Islam, Russians' understanding of Orthodoxy served them as a guide. Since Feofan Prokopovich's "Sermon on Royal Authority and Honor" (1718), the Church had instructed the Orthodox "that he who resists the powers [of government and other authorities] is resisting God and that one must obey not only out of fear of wrath but also out of conscience." The identification of offenses with divine retribution presumed a moral system defined, above all, by the principles of sin and punishment. As Prokopovich explained, "the highest power is established and armed with the sword by God and . . . to oppose it is a sin against God Himself, a sin to be punished by death, not temporary but eternal."[72] A number of officials in the Ministry of Internal Affairs and local administration discerned an analogous moral order in "Muhammadanism": it appeared to confer a concept of moral consequence upon actions that concerned the state.

Russian officials frequently invoked the angry God that they discerned in Muslim theology. Commanders in the Caucasus cast rebels as traitors and threatened them with "destruction" *(istreblenie)*. In 1829 Nicholas I defined the army's mission there as "the pacification for good of the mountain peoples or the extirpation of the recalcitrant."[73] Facing the forces of the shaykh Kazi Mullah, General-Adjutant Pankrat'ev attacked his opponent as an enemy of God and of Islam. In an appeal to the "mountain peoples of Daghestan" in 1831, the general deplored those "who, joining the perfidious and deceitful Kazi Mullah, believe his false words, which are contrary to the will of God, his prophet, and the holy books." Motivated only by self-interest, his jihad had spilled "human blood in vain" and had only harmed "his co-religionists, the inhabitants of these lands." "Oh, Muslims!" Pankrat'ev urged,

> Avoid the consequences and reprimands, to which you are
> subject in this, as in the next life. Here you will be deprived

of all of your property. But there you will have to answer to
God, that you did not execute the will, as stated in the
Qur'an. Don't lead yourself to ruin. This deceiver lies to
you. We favor all faiths and confessions, [and] even encourage peoples' fulfillment of their rites, for we all believe in
one and the same God. Look at the Muslim peoples living
within Russia itself, do they not follow their own confession,
do they encounter an impediment in the fulfillment of rites
and do they not solemnly praise in the mosques the name of
God [and] his prophet?

All those who rejected the general's words risked "complete destruction." In later proclamations, the general warned that it had been the
devil, not God, who had sent this traitor, a patricide and merchant of
vodka and wine, "to spill Muslim blood and bring misfortune to all
of Daghestan."[74]

Tsarist authorities preferred to make such appeals using Muslim
voices. For their part, the Orenburg muftis accommodated their
superiors by stressing those teachings about sin that most approximated Orthodox notions. Their instructions and fatwas paired down
the variegated vocabulary that Islamic scholars had devised to expli-
cate the nature of wrongs and of Muslims' duty to forbid them.[75] Underscoring the Qur'anic injunction to "command right and forbid
wrong," these texts also aimed at harmonization with the theological orientation of the Church. They placed singular emphasis upon
sin as "transgression" of divine command. When his "wrath" was
provoked by such offenses, God rained punishment down upon sin-
ners in this world and the next. Overlooking dissimilarities in doctrine, state authorities and Muslim clerics perceived a common religious idiom focused on sin; they employed it when officials sought
to invoke the cautionary prospect of divine reckoning to reinforce
the prescriptions of imperial law. Cooperation between officials and

Muslim intermediaries grew out of the articulation of this idiom of moral guardianship.

In 1836 Mufti Gabdrakhimov issued "religious instructions" that reflected the convergence of Islamic piety and official notions of patriotic duty under Tsar Nicholas I. The mufti urged Muslims "to be wholeheartedly submissive to Almighty God, follow the path shown by Him, fulfill obligations placed on you, do good, [and] avoid evil." Demonstrating the utility and responsiveness of the Islamic hierarchy to the shifting needs of state administration and ideology, Gabdrakhimov's instructions called for a form of patriotism that the Orthodox Church had only recently espoused. Contemporary Orthodox primers taught that the fifth commandment enjoined obedience not only to parents but to ecclesiastical and temporal superiors: subjects were the "children of the ruler and the fatherland." Whereas earlier catechisms had stressed the Christian duty to sacrifice one's life for the tsar, Metropolitan Filaret's catechism of 1828 (citing John 15:13) extended this obligation to include not only the tsar but the fatherland. Gabdrakhimov echoed this patriotic emphasis, directing Muslims "to be obedient to the Sovereign Emperor Nicholas Pavlovich and obey all commands emanating from him; to serve the Tsar and Fatherland by faith and justice, in accordance with sworn oath and loyal duty, without sparing one's life."[76]

Russian officials backed the proposition that Muslims who refused to embrace this patriotism angered God. Thus the Orenburg governor, O. L. Debu, asked the mufti to assist in the "eradication" of an act that violated both the shari'a and imperial law. He complained that "many Muhammadans avoid state service and, fearing [military] recruitment, commit self-mutilation in its various forms, thereby committing a criminal act." The governor requested "frequent exhortations and sermons of a religious nature" to persuade Muslims that "the goal of each loyal subject is to serve his true, natural Sovereign Emperor faithfully and unhypocritically and with all means available to strive toward the good of service for His Imperial Majesty, zealously guarding the interests of the State against the encroachment of enemies." Taking up the governor's request, Gabdrakhimov ordered clerics to read his instructions to their parishioners, reminding them that "each orthodox Muslim [*pravovernyi musul'manin*] is obliged to obey the authorities and laws, not to commit illegal acts, to be submissive to fate, patient in everything and to put trust in Merciful God . . . [and] to enter willingly and readily into state service." Citing the *Khadimi*, a commentary on a pietistic work by the sixteenth-century Ottoman preacher Birgili, the mufti warned that "self-mutilation is one of the greatest sins, invoking God's anger and punishment."[77]

Gabdrakhimov praised submission to the political and social order of the empire as a religious act. The mufti pointed out that every Muslim "should be content with [his] fate, should bear misfortunes sent by God patiently and without complaining and be grateful to God for all good and pleasure in life, which He sends to him, remembering that acts contrary to this are regarded as great sins and invoke God's anger and punishment." Gabdrakhimov concluded by reminding his co-religionists "that in one of the lines of the Holy Qur'an it says to be obedient to God, the Prophet, and authorities, and [that] the Prophet Muhammad said 'Obey authorities and be submissive, whatever troubles and hardships may stand in the way of fulfillment of this duty.'"[78]

Provincial authorities and the Orenburg mufti cooperated in utilizing the authority of the office, bolstered by reference to Islamic texts, to cast as "sin" behaviors deemed contrary to both Islamic and imperial law. The impact of Gabdrakhimov's instructions remains difficult to gauge, even though reports of mutilation declined in the 1840s.[79] In other instances, the translation of imperial writ into Islamic doctrine proved even more complicated. In the late 1840s and early 1850s, a campaign to utilize the authority of the mufti pointed to the difficulties that state officials and Muslim clerics alike faced in searching for correspondences between different faiths. In October 1849, Vladimir Obruchev, the military governor of Orenburg, turned to the third mufti, Gabdulvakhid Suleimanov (in office 1840–1862). With the approval of Nicholas I and the military, the governor proposed to tackle the spread of venereal diseases among Bashkirs and Mishars. His plan called for medical examinations for brides and grooms, a measure to be introduced not only among these two groups administered by the Department of Military Settlements, but among all Muslims in the region. Governor Obruchev sought out Suleimanov's help because he feared "abuses" on the part of medics and midwives charged with conducting the exams. More importantly, he suspected that these precautions may "be taken by the Bashkirs for oppression and give birth to false understandings," raising the specter of disorder. Obruchev requested that the mufti

> compose, in accordance with the rules of the Qur'an, an exhortation in a religious spirit to the effect that Muhammadans infected with venereal disease must regard entrance into marriage before medical treatment of the disease as the gravest sin and that they should try their utmost to observe cleanliness and neatness in their way of life and avoid all contact with those afflicted by the disease.

The text was meant to dispel "false understandings" and "serve as confirmation of imperial will" and the "solicitude of the government, which endeavors to preserve their health."[80]

In this case, the governor's solicitude extended to the wording of the mufti's "exhortation." Before being distributed to and read by clerics "in mosques at prayers on holidays or outside of them before meetings of the people" in the provinces of Orenburg, Perm, and Viatka, as well as among Muslims serving with the Orenburg and

Ural Cossacks, the text required Obruchev's approval.[81] Under the governor's pen, the mufti's directive went through several drafts.

In the first draft, Mufti Suleimanov, who had also studied in Kargala's madrasas, underscored Muslims' duty to submit to the "most gracious command of the Sovereign Emperor." Outlining the responsibilities of parents, guardians, brides, and grooms, he warned that anyone offering any "falsity" about the health of marriage partners would be regarded as "disobeyers before the Holy Qur'an and the hadith of the Prophet as well as the commands of the Sovereign Emperor." The guilty would be punished by military court. Referring to another hadith, Suleimanov added that each head of household, "father, mother, or guardian," is obliged, "like a shepherd," to watch over those in their charge and to preserve them from "harmful diseases." They were to see that Muslims washed once a week "in warm water" and then put on "clean underwear" and also observed "neatness in your homes with clothes, dishes, and generally in [your] way of life." In case of outbreak of disease, parents and guardians were to ensure that the infected received treatment.

To this formula, Suleimanov added his own diagnosis of the problem. The mufti pointed to "adultery," though Obruchev apparently had not raised this factor as one of the causes of syphilis among these peoples. "Muslims must," Suleimanov instructed,

> repent of adultery and refrain from it because where adultery is committed it is said that Almighty God punishes . . . [the guilty] with wholesale death and harmful diseases, for in the Qur'an it is mentioned in several articles that adultery is a great sin and a depraved path.

In a gesture directed as much to the presumed ecumenicism of his superiors as to his co-religionists, the mufti added that, besides the Qur'an, the "holy books of the Torah, Gospels, and the Psalms of

David" also regard the offense as a "great sin in this world and the next."[82]

A miscalculation soon followed upon this diplomatic move. Though Suleimanov had appealed to the authority of other holy books, he reminded the faithful that the Qur'an prescribed one hundred lashes for "the debauched." Invocations of corporal punishment may not have raised objections in a society where the knout and the lash were the familiar mainstays of justice. But the original guidelines for the Islamic establishment explicitly proscribed the application of Qur'anic punishments as an infringement upon a more "enlightened" imperial law.

Obruchev's response reflected Russian officialdom's conception of the utility of Islam at midcentury. He quickly answered Suleimanov's draft with corrections and additions. But he did not expressly object to its reminder about the penalties that the Qur'an called for in the case of extramarital relations. Rather, in the revision that the governor returned to the mufti for translation into Tatar, he removed all reference to the "command of the Sovereign Emperor," emphasizing instead the authority of the mufti and the threat of God's punishment. In the language that Obruchev inserted into the "exhortation," the mufti spoke to the "most honorable akhunds and mullahs" as "the Head of the Clergy of Muslims appointed by the Government." Referring to these clerics as "my sole collaborators," the mufti was to request their assistance in warning "all the faithful" of the dangers of disease. "What could be a greater sin?" this version of the instruction asked, regarding parents who have rejected treatment and burden children born with the disease. Such a person becomes a "criminal before God as well as the Prophet Muhammad, thereby violating the commands of our Holy Qur'an."[83]

Obruchev's draft differed from Suleimanov's original in that it omitted reference to imperial law. Quoting from a saying attributed to the Prophet, the governor concluded that

> God demands that Muslims observe ablutions and neatness
> in everything and that God has offered medicine for the
> treatment of illness . . . is it not obvious that they [who]
> nonetheless disobey the commands of the Creator and His
> Prophet . . . will be held accountable before God?

Again referring to the Qur'an and hadith, the governor identified cholera as the instrument of God's punishment, saying that God had dispatched the deadly visitor to the region "for our sins." In 1831 cholera had "prematurely swallowed up . . . thousands of Muslims who did not follow God's commands." "Should we not," it continued, "rectify ourselves and ask God with tears of repentance—to have mercy on us."[84]

Though Obruchev incorporated Orthodox language in his appeal for "tears of repentance," he underscored the primacy of narrowly Islamic obligations. His draft studiously avoided mention of government decrees. The wording that he chose for the mufti reminded Muslims that the Qur'an and hadith directed them to follow "those who have authority over you" as an "amir" and recalled the necessity of punishing those "who oppose the command of the Sultan." He emphasized the role of "your Mufti, as father and pastor caring for his flock in the name of God and his Prophet," and equated obedience to God with adherence to measures that the mufti "found necessary" to combat disease. The governor's text also recast the role of the government. Deleting reference to Jewish or Christian texts, it described the state now as a guardian of Islamic orthodoxy. God would bring the guilty to account, and "the government itself will not hesitate to judge you *as disobeyers of God and His Prophet.*" By this account, the regime disciplined not for its own sake, but for Islam.[85]

This formulation of the consequences of transgression only confused further the relationship between Islamic and imperial law.

Like many of his predecessors, the governor once again suggested that the police powers of the regime would be mobilized to reinforce the writ of orthodox Islamic opinion, even in the absence of specific legislation to this effect. This blurring of the boundaries between state and Islamic law became marked, too, in the area of criminal law. According to the criminal code, many crimes entailed moral offenses that required both temporal and religious punishments. In the case of offenders belonging to the Orthodox Church, its jurisdiction often overlapped with that of the state.

The discretion of local officials played a decisive role in determining the availability of police power for such purposes. In 1824, General A. P. Ermolov instructed Islamic authorities in the Caucasus to compel fulfillment of one of the five pillars of Islam; "the people must without fail" give alms *(zakat)*, he ordered, to provide for the maintenance of "holy persons." But he did not specify how such an injunction would be enforced. Similarly, legislation confirming that the "Muhammadan clergy" was subject to corporal punishment called for the quick notification of communities when a cleric was deprived of his rank, to allow new clergymen to be nominated "so that there will not be stoppages in worship." Tsarist officials rejected the corporal punishments prescribed by Islamic law for offenses also punishable by state laws. Some Muslim authorities still ordered these penalties, but officials and Muslim clerics reached a compromise by devising a common vocabulary of repentance. For many Muslim thinkers, repentance *(tawba)* marked one of the first stations of the Sufi path, a turning away from sin and a turning toward God, an obligation achieved, in the words of the great Muslim theologian al-Ghazali, through "knowledge, regret, and renunciation." Muslims could pursue this path as an individual endeavor elsewhere, but not in the Russian empire, where the law prescribed the mediation of an official cleric, as in the Orthodox Church.[86]

In the system formalized under Nicholas, crimes committed by

Muslims frequently called for an Islamic punishment in addition to that imposed by the criminal statutes. A case that began with a simple theft typified this overlap of temporal and religious discipline. In 1856, Abdulnasyr Suleimanov, a Muslim from the village of Ura, had been arrested for theft. In prison with Russian inmates in Kazan, Suleimanov had requested permission, perhaps in hopes of reducing his sentence, to convert to Orthodoxy. But before he went through with the conversion, his jailers transferred him to another cell. There his plans were complicated by the fact that his jail mates were fellow Tatars; he now found himself surrounded by co-religionists, who, moreover, happened to be observing the holy month of Ramadan. By the time a priest arrived to baptize him, Suleimanov had rethought his offer to convert. For refusing the sacrament, the authorities removed him from the cell with the Tatars. They placed him in a room by himself, but his troubles did not end. In solitary confinement, his prosecutors observed, the hapless villager was overwhelmed by "extraordinary boredom and melancholy [and] took it into his head to take his life."[87]

Suleimanov survived the attempt and confessed his crime. In addition to the jail time he was serving for theft, the court ruled that he must now also face a second penalty for his suicide attempt. Citing articles 1944 and 2077 of the criminal code, the court deferred to the Orenburg Assembly, upon whose decision "the measures of punishment" depended. The Assembly ordered that Suleimanov pursue "repentance through the parish imam," whose "exhortations" were to deter the offender from committing such acts in the future by warning him of the grave consequences to be meted out both by temporal law and, in the afterlife, "God's judgment" (sud Bozhii).[88]

Ties between the official representatives of the Islamic and Orthodox Christian traditions went beyond claims of moral guardianship. On behalf of the empire, Muslim and Orthodox clerics not only monopolized the definition of sin and its renunciation through repentance. They also asserted control over the ritual ties that linked these faiths to the state in novel ways. In both traditions, religious symbols and rites had long served as the principal means to affirm or deny a ruler's legitimacy. In the Russian empire, the liturgical calendar of the Orthodox Church fused with the many holidays celebrating the Romanov dynasty. Christmas, Epiphany, Palm Sunday, Easter, and other holidays affirmed "the charisma of otherness and dominance" that elevated the monarchy and underscored its bonds with God and its devoted Christian subjects.[89] Like these holidays, the birthdays and name days of the imperial family brought Orthodox peasants, townspeople, and officials to the local cathedral or chapel to pray for the dynasty. A model of social relations throughout the empire, the image of the royal family prevailed in the day-to-day ritual and ceremonial life of the empire in a variety of settings ranging from the village school to the army regiment.

Prayers for "His Imperial Majesty and Most August Family" claimed a singularly prominent position in the ritual calendar of non-Orthodox subjects as well. For many Muslims this dynastic priority harmonized with the Islamic tradition of mentioning the name of the ruling sovereign before the sermon *(khutba)* preceding Friday communal prayers. The preacher's mention of the ruler and his prayer for God's blessing on him was a marker of legitimacy in Muslim societies. Omission of the ruler's name announced a shift in the political allegiances of the preacher or leading scholars, a signal that might sway mass opinion in times of succession struggles, rebellions, and war.[90]

From the late eighteenth century, preachers prayed for the tsar and royal family from the pulpits of mosques in the Russian empire. With the support of the Orenburg mufti, the regime sought to routinize the practice in all mosques. As with oaths sworn on the Qur'an at legal proceedings and at induction into military or civil service, most Muslim scholars and laypeople adopted these prayers as legitimate religious obligations.[91] Stretching back to the sixteenth century, Muslim noblemen had performed similar demonstrations of loyalty to an Orthodox ruling house. The dynasty esteemed vows pledged upon the presumably indissoluble bonds of religion, even a religion it regarded as "foreign" and otherwise flawed. In the nineteenth century, more and more Muslims of different social backgrounds experienced oath taking. They swore allegiance to the tsar and offered prayers for him the imperial family at the Friday congregational prayers and numerous other Islamic holy days. Remembrance of the Romanov dynasty assumed a central position among the commands of Islamic worship for the community as a whole.

The invocation of God's blessing on the tsar may have enhanced the integrative role of the monarchy by cultivating Muslims' feelings of devotion to the sovereign and patriotism for the empire. The penchant for direct supplication to the tsar among Muslim subjects suggests that, at the very least, most regarded the tsar as an agent of justice and protection who might right the wrongs inflicted upon Muslims by erring bureaucrats as well as by neighbors and relatives. For more skeptical minds, the Orenburg mufti's support for the offering of prayers for the tsar invited critical reflection upon the legal status of the Muslim community under Christian rule. The controversy emerged in the late eighteenth and early nineteenth centuries when a few Islamic jurists voiced conflicting legal opinions about the definition of the Russian empire as the House of Islam. In assuming their posts, Khusainov and the judges who joined him had signaled their conviction that Muslims could fulfill their religious duties in Russia, thereby recognizing it as a land with the status of dar al-Islam. In effect, this position affirmed the tacit consensus achieved by subsequent generations of scholars inhabiting territories conquered by Muscovite rulers in the sixteenth and seventeenth centuries.

Early debates about the loss of Islamic political leadership in these regions remain unclear; however, it appears that these scholars did not believe that the prevailing conditions resembled those faced by the Prophet Muhammad, who led his community from Mecca, where Muslims faced persecution, to a settlement that came to be known as Medina. This migration, the *hijra*, became a model and, according to many sources, an obligation for able-bodied Muslims who possessed the means to flee the "House of War" or "House of Unbelief" and, by some accounts, wage war (jihad) against these lands of infidelity and unbelief.

Disagreements divided legal scholars who analyzed the exemplary behavior of Muhammad and interpreted God's will for the hijra. A few early legal theorists concluded that the obligation to migrate had been confined to the lifetime of the Prophet. Some regarded it as a duty that might be performed by a few members of the community on behalf of the collective, while others concluded that the retention of even a few provisions of the shari'a in a non-Muslim land exempted Muslims from the requirement. Later, important Sufi thinkers would view the hijra as a spiritual and ascetic passage and a command to be performed internally, as a "migration from the land of human beings to the presence of Allah."[92] Debate on the subject intensified in the eighteenth and nineteenth centuries as "reformist" movements in the Hijaz and West Africa took up arms against opponents whose profession of Islam they rejected as "unbelief" and as more and more Muslim rulers were forced to surrender sovereignty over their lands to European colonial powers.

In Russia, as in India, Muslim jurists of the Hanafi school of law confronted similar circumstances. In both settings, a non-Muslim regime curtailed some aspects of Islamic law. Both permitted the functioning of Islamic courts and the administration of the shari'a, but they limited the application of the law to matters concerning personal status, like marriage, divorce, and inheritance. Despite the loss of political power, the Muslim communities of the subcontinent, like their co-religionists to the north, enjoyed the right to construct mosques and schools. Muslims were allowed to announce the call to prayer from the minarets of these mosques, unlike some Muslims under Christian rule elsewhere. They could attend Friday and daily prayers, fast, give alms to the needy, and celebrate religious feasts; they performed the pilgrimage to Mecca, though the regime attempted to regulate the practice. The ability to perform these obligations under British and Russian rule was a crucial factor in the calculations of Muslim jurists. The choice of migration or armed struggle, on the other hand, entailed substantial risks. The majority of Hanafi scholars thus judged the two empires part of dar al-Islam; they even recognized non-Muslim rulers' right to appoint Muslim governors and judges.[93] In both empires, a minority of scholars dissented, though they also cited Hanafi sources in support of their views.

But unlike the British government, the tsarist regime patronized a central body whose head claimed the authority to issue binding legal opinions on such questions. Here, too, the Assembly and its mufti failed to establish a monopoly on religious authority. These efforts faltered even despite the mufti's assertion of the right to issue binding fatwas with the support of the tsarist administration. Other learned men of religion continued to interpret and transmit Islamic knowledge on behalf of local communities throughout the region. A few notable scholars who opposed Mufti Khusainov challenged him on the issue of Russia's legal status for Muslims as well.

At the turn of the nineteenth century, a Muslim scholar spoke out against the saying of Friday congregational prayers in the empire. Following his return in 1798 to the village of Isliaikino after studying in Bukhara, Samarkand, and Kabul, 'Abd ar-Rahim Utiz Imani declared that the shari'a forbade Friday prayers in the dar al-Harb. Russia must be regarded as the "House of War," he argued, because according to Hanafi law Friday prayers may be performed only when a

Muslim governor rules and when a Muslim judge guarantees the application of Islamic law.[94] Word of Utiz Imani's pronouncement spread as his manuscript treatises circulated and his students traveled to other mosques and madrasas to debate the issue with other scholars. The dispute continued to engage jurists and sparked a broader debate about the use of "independent reasoning" *(ijtihad)* versus "imitation" *(taqlid)*, or the following of authorities of the Hanafi school.[95] Yet the judgments of these scholars did not inspire either hijra or an external jihad.

Most scholars negotiated more subtle, intermediary positions. They neither offered unconditional support for the regime nor rejected outright its status as guarantor of the empire as the "House of Islam." When the state did compel Islamic authorities to legitimate policies that Muslim jurists and laypeople rejected as unlawful, the latter typically resorted to strategies of stealth or avoidance. In response to measures like the burial legislation of 1827, Muslims largely tried to evade enforcement rather than assume a wholly oppositional stance that would have led to the momentous undertaking of emigration or rebellion.

More than mere instruments of imperial policy, the muftis Khusainov, Gabdrakhimov, and Suleimanov used the Islamic establishment as well as imperial administrative and police power to advance their interpretation of the best interests of the empire's Muslims. But their vision for the community frequently met with opposition from Islamic scholars and laypeople alike. For the most part, Muslim clerics appear to have understood that the regime maintained an interest in the fulfillment of orthodox Islamic rulings, even if Muslims and state officials had different motivations for seeking their implementation. In 1848, ten imams from the village of Kargala petitioned the Assembly to be relieved of the obligation to say prayers for the tsar on a series of occasions listed by a recent government circular. They did not renounce the principle behind the practice of praying for the emperor, but they expressed the fear that prayers offered on days other than Fridays and Islamic holidays "for an increase in the victories, might, and prosperity of his imperial majesty" would not "be received by God and that through this we would make ourselves sinful before him." The group also submitted citations from texts such as the *Khadimi*, a commentary favored by the mufti, as well as the sura *An-Nur* of the Qur'an in support of their argument. When police investigated, the petitioners denied involvement and laid the blame exclusively on a mullah beyond the reach of the law: the suspect had died during a recent cholera epidemic.[96]

The petitioners backed down in the face of police pressure. But the incident points to a sense of the possibility of arriving at a coincidence of interests between Muslim religious authorities and tsarist officials. The imams calculated that they could gain exemption from the prayers by appealing to textually sound interpretation of God's command. Their petition assumed that the Islamic hierarchy and tsarist authorities would yield to their objection in the name of orthodoxy. The arrival of the police disabused them of this notion, of course. An earlier generation of prayer leaders might have renounced this obligation with impunity, and no superior body would have imposed a settlement upon disputing scholars. But these imams now confronted a centralized hierarchy backed by the police. Through this structure, they had become linked to the state. Their appointments depended upon a license from the mufti in Ufa and the approval of the governor. Once registered in the archive of the Assembly, these imams could not legally move on to a new mosque or school to flee the commands of the hierarchy. The regime regarded resistance to any of its institutions as a political offense, and those who ran afoul of official Islamic authorities and their tsarist backers risked removal from their posts and imprisonment or exile.

The Orenburg Assembly furnished the state with a means to impose clerical discipline and doctrinal uniformity in Muslim parishes. But its capacity to perform this function did not derive from the natural leadership of the Muslim elites chosen by the Ministry of Internal Affairs. It hinged instead on the cooperation of state officials. The scattered mosque communities under the Assembly continued to resort to their own religious guides, and the mufti in Ufa had to depend on the assistance of imperial officials to establish his power there. Aided by a select group of Muslim allies, imperial officials erected a churchlike hierarchy to make this tolerated religion "useful" for the empire. In practice, its utility depended upon the fragile interdependence between Muslims and state authorities; each side pursued its own interests by appealing to the other's religious convictions.

2

THE STATE IN THE MOSQUE

In September 1793, Amirkhan Abyzaev and Abdull-zelil' Sultanov submitted a petition to Catherine the Great on behalf of the Bashkir people on Russia's eastern frontier. Praising "Almighty God, the protector of Russia," they thanked the empress, "first, for the creation, out of your munificence toward your people, of mosques; second, for the establishment of the Ecclesiastical assembly according to our law; [and] third, for the founding of a mufti for our people." They had been given "complete and unshakable freedom to fulfill our law according to our rite and faith," adding that many Bashkir regiments felt grateful for numerous medals and orders earned during campaigns against the Swedes. Pledging to offer "warm prayers to God" for Catherine and "all of Russia," they asked only that they have their duties reduced and land-rights guaranteed, and that "our clerics" be freed of all civil obligations, "so that they may fulfill their service more comfortably."[1]

These Bashkir petitioners pointed to one of the dilemmas of toleration under Catherine's "well-ordered police state." To utilize a domestic source of Islamic authority and turn Muslim subjects away from Kabul, Istanbul, and Cairo, the regime had created a hierarchy with authority over Muslims in the capitals, the Volga and Kama River region, Siberia, the eastern borderlands, and the southern frontier extending to the Crimea. In sponsoring the construction of mosques and permitting communities to establish others, this policy led to their proliferation throughout the empire. With mosques came experts in religion *('ulama)*. Even Holy Moscow received a mosque in 1823, despite long-standing opposition from the Church. At the same time, the expansion of tsarist trade with Asia generated new wealth in Muslim communities, together with an ambitious merchant class eager to parlay their affluence into mosque patronage and spiritual leadership.[2] These changes raised new questions about administrative control.

Officials like Baron Igel'strom had the model of the Church and an Ottoman script on hand to follow in erecting an Islamic hierarchy, but it was not as clear how to root the state in the mosque community. The government had erected a "church" of sorts for Islam but hesitated to confer state support upon a "clergy." Eager to use Islamic authorities to give the state a religious air for its Muslim subjects, the tsarist bureaucracy sought a balance. Too much support for Muslim clerics might undermine the preeminence of Orthodox Christianity or even create a fifth column for the Turks. The empire needed Islam but feared its guardians. From the second quarter of the nineteenth century, encounters with rebellious Poles and with insurgents in the Northern Caucasus heightened official anxiety about non-Orthodox clergy. This chapter shows how the regime backed a church structure for Islam but gradually embraced anti-clericalism when it came to its interpreters. For state officials committed to the support of orthodox religion within each of the confessional communities but increasingly wary of clerical elites, the common people became a crucial link in the chain of imperial order. The regime did not have to resort to force to penetrate Muslim communities. In villages and towns throughout the territory under the jurisdiction of the Orenburg Assembly, laypeople drew the state into the mosque.

 Though principally concerned with elites, imperial policy affected the entire Muslim community. It aimed at both the regulation of a clergy and its separation from laypeople. Before Catherine the Great, religious leaders had been set apart only by a reputation for piety and knowledge of the Islamic religious sciences. They enjoyed their informal status only insofar as other Muslims sought out, and deferred to, their learning and guidance. But since Catherine, Russian officials conceived of this open and diffuse group of scholars, prayer leaders, teachers, judges, and preachers, known in their own communities as 'ulama (or *rukhanilär*), as a clergy (*dukhovenstvo*), a distinct social estate like the servitors of the Orthodox Church. Besides making them subject to examinations and official approval, imperial authorities assigned them a range of duties, including the exercise of moral suasion, the oversight of marital and family discipline, the keeping of official records, and the communication of state directives.

Tsarist officials presumed Islam to be useful to imperial administration as a source of stability and morality. But inhibited by the obligation to maintain the privileged position of the Orthodox Church, they hesitated to confer upon Muslim clerics the rights, privileges, and support enjoyed by Orthodox clergymen; many officials could not overcome suspicion of Muslim clerics as enemies of the state interest. Though the 'ulama were valued by the Ministry of Internal Affairs for their contribution to various administrative tasks, their position remained precarious. The status of the officially licensed men of religion hinged not only upon the approval of the provincial governor and the Orenburg Assembly but also upon the community members who nominated them for these posts. The vulnerability of official clerics, in the face of both the Russian state and Muslim patrons and activists, set the stage for intense conflicts about religious authority.

From the perspective of these mosque communities, neither these men of religious learning and piety nor the official Islamic establishment enjoyed a monopoly on religious leadership or interpretive authority. Historians have tended to follow the lead of sources produced by Muslim elites, viewing Muslim common people, or the "unlettered" *('awamm)*, only as subordinates and followers of learned and charismatic religious leaders. A very different picture emerges, however, from the legal records, petitions, and biographical literature produced in these communities. This evidence shows instead how laymen and women challenged the knowledge and piety of their prayer leaders, preachers, scholars, judges, and teachers.

Recourse to the state became a critical tool for 'ulama and laypeople alike. Frequently unable to compel dissidents by other means, clerics solicited the intervention of courts and police to correct behavior that they judged to be contrary to the shari'a. And learned and unlettered alike used bureaucratic procedures and rhetorical strategies beyond the mosque community to denounce erring prayer leaders and other licensed clerics. Villagers wrote complaints in Tatar or had a scribe take down their oral testimony and translate it into Russian. Many townspeople, as well as a number of 'ulama, could write Russian.[3] They communicated their demands not only to the Orenburg Assembly but also to provincial and central government officials; many sent their supplications to the tsar himself. In lay activists eager to leave their imprint upon the piety of the community, the state found partners willing to aid the common cause of upholding clerical discipline. Thus the regime invited denunciations of immoral or subversive mullahs.

The outcome of such engagements was not always predictable.

Nor was it obvious, as imperial administration reached deeper into the provinces, how to manage a perilous terrain of intracommunal strife. The confrontation with Islam in its local setting multiplied the complexities associated with policing the "orthodox" dogma and practices to be tolerated by the regime. Still largely dependent on European translations on Islam, officials had to rely on Muslim informants and their claims about the tradition. When laypeople connected with tsarist authorities committed to maintaining conformity within each of the officially recognized confessional communities, these interactions redefined orthodoxy and simultaneously amplified the reach of the state into previously inaccessible locales.

The mosque community *(mahalla)* could be a contentious setting. Though rumors of state-sponsored Christianization campaigns swirled throughout the Muslim countryside at various intervals, threats to Islam came more frequently from within the community in the form of neighbors who did not attend communal prayers alongside other villagers or townspeople. Prayer leaders who neglected to perform obligatory rites of passage, especially burial prayers, inflicted a similar harm upon the community, making its members subject to God's judgment. The gravity of these transgressions and omissions led many lay activists to seek mediation from outside.

Though important localized factors gave form to religious controversies, these did not occur in isolation. Networks of scholars and Sufis linked village and small-town mosque communities through trade, study, preaching, pilgrimage, and the circulation of manuscript literature in Tatar, Arabic, and Persian to regional centers of learning, the madrasas, whose number increased in the late eighteenth and early nineteenth centuries. Their ties extended to cosmopolitan hubs of scholarship and piety in Bukhara, Samarkand, Kabul, Istanbul, Baghdad, Cairo, Mecca, and other locales. Through these channels, Russia's Muslims shared in the conflicts and concerns of their co-religionists throughout the community of Islam. How Muslims in the Russian empire experienced and made sense of these broader dialogues and disputes turned on their adaptation of resources from both a cosmopolitan repertoire of Islamic norms and imperatives and the political context of the tsarist empire.[4]

As illustrated in the case of the village of Ura in Chapter 1, social relations between patrons and clients and their recourse to courts, police, and the Islamic hierarchy all structured the contest for the definition of authentic Islamic practices. In such Muslim communities, debate and argument about doctrine, ritual, behavior, and community shaped the tradition. In the communities under the supervision of the Orenburg Assembly, Muslim clerics struggled to establish an incontrovertible domain of orthodoxy.

Islamic authorities in other times and places enjoyed some success in imposing their vision of orthodoxy, by proscribing popular festivals or disallowing polytheistic practices. But several factors hindered a comparable exercise of power by the 'ulama in Russia. Despite the bureaucratic strictures of exams, licenses, and parish record-keeping, religious leadership remained highly variable and informal. The opinion of influential members of mosque communities, not a license from the state, defined the moral standing and authority of would-be religious leaders. "Unlicensed" *(neukaznye)* clerics thrived in a gray religious underground as itinerant preachers, tutors, reciters of the Qur'an, storytellers, poets, and informal mentors and spiritual guides. Supported by patrons and disciples, they continued to elude the police and operate outside the official Islamic establishment, outliving the tsarist regime itself.

Unable to suppress unlicensed clerics, the regime stopped short of fully endorsing the authority of the official ones. It permitted mosque communities to select candidates for nomination as prayer leaders, preachers, teachers, and mosque functionaries. The law aided parishioners when they sought the removal of clerics whose behavior disappointed the patrons who sponsored their nomination. In the provinces, the authorities often harbored suspicions about the social utility or political loyalty of Muslim clerics. Thus the threat of censure or removal from an official post lent further weight to parishioners' demands when disputes arose between them and mullahs whom they judged incompetent, lazy, debauched, or irreligious.

While parishioners might find an ally in the local official, the mullah who felt duty-bound to discipline a villager whose drinking, carousing, or refusal to attend prayers violated the shari'a usually had to rely in some measure on other members of the community to assist him. Clerics who failed to win the backing of the community turned to the Orenburg Assembly. Ufa could be far away, however. Its reach depended almost wholly on the good offices of the local district court. This body had a mixed jurisdiction of judicial and police duties with limited resources. With a staff that in many locales included Tatar notables or bilingual scribes, it acted, in effect, as judge, investigator, witness, and police; it adjudicated disputes, notarized village elections, for example, of mullahs, and enforced decisions from the Assembly and other higher offices.[5]

The 'ulama thus shared the predicament of men of religious learning in other Muslim societies—such as later Iranian clerics, who, Michael Fischer has observed, "spoke for ideals that often transcend the possibilities of practical life" and were "thus always vulnerable to the charges of hypocrisy and pretension." Everyday life in the empire meant that, like the clerics of Ottoman Damascus, they also "produced both the breachers as well as the defenders of the public moral code."[6]

Tsarist legislation made the rites of birth, marriage, divorce, death, and repentance the exclusive domain of a "Muhammadan clergy"; and it held the entire community subject to the legal opinions (fatwas) of the mufti. But the laity was never the passive object of hierarchical control. Muslim parishioners undertook a range of initiatives, often with the conviction that they acted in fulfillment of a collective obligation to "command good and forbid evil."[7] Besides acting as patrons of mosques, schools, and charitable endowments, laypeople devoted themselves to persuading others, including non-Muslims, to adopt their religious values. Heightened by the spread of the pietistic teachings of the Naqshbandiyya, moral expectations and concern with careful fulfillment of the shariʿa eroded confidence in many licensed clerics. Where laymen and women sought to establish a new moral order in a community by challenging the dedication of their mullah, appeals to imperial law and autocratic authority could become essential resources. Charges of immorality, irreligion, and false teaching prompted police intervention and, with it, state support for a new definition of orthodoxy.

A Muslim Clergy?

Though Russians drew parallels between Ottoman ʿulama and an estate of clergymen, tsarist authorities grappled with the juridical definition of a Muslim clergy as a social estate *(soslovie)* with specific privileges and obligations in the imperial legal system.[8] The sole area of consensus and certainty lay in the goal of establishing a measure of clerical discipline. Appointments were to be based upon a system of examinations and licenses certifying minimal educational qualifications and the approval of the provincial governor.

Unlike the Orthodox clergy, however, these men and women of religious learning and piety belonged to a relatively informal and open social category. Centralized states imposed bureaucratic structures on their upper ranks in later periods of Islamic history, as in the Ottoman and Safavid empires and the amirate of Bukhara. But in most parts of the Islamic world, ʿulama formed "not a distinct class, but a category of persons overlapping other classes and social divisions, permeating the whole of society."[9] In Damascus, Aleppo, and

Cairo, for instance, preachers, prayer leaders, Qur'an readers, Sufi shaykhs, teachers, jurists, judges, market inspectors, professional witnesses, overseers of pious endowments, and mosque functionaries had also pursued careers as officials, merchants, artisans, and workers. They offered instruction in Islamic doctrine to the faithful, interpreted the divine law, oversaw education and charity, and administered the broad array of familial, social, and economic affairs under the purview of the shari'a. The 'ulama laid the foundations of associational life and social cohesion in these towns through informal study circles and clienteles surrounding madrasas, mosques, law courts, and Sufi lodges. These elites operated in close, if sometimes strained, association with the temporal regimes upon whom they conferred a degree of legitimacy in exchange for patronage and the defense of the community. In times of crisis, however, religious elites could withdraw their support, using their influence among the population to mobilize crowds in opposition to the government.

In Russia, the 'ulama displayed many of these same characteristics, though their roles were shaped by the changing social context and institutional setting of the empire. The creation of an official Islamic hierarchy in 1788 was by no means the sole determining factor. Four decades after its founding, the Assembly had not yet established a monopoly on clerical appointments. Muslims who had not received authorization from Ufa continued to lead prayers, offer religious instruction, and perform other duties. They assumed these roles alongside—or often in competition with—licensed clerics. The Ministry of Internal Affairs never succeeded in measuring the extent of this unlicensed underground. In 1829, officials claimed to have compiled numbers of "official" versus "unofficial" mullahs, muezzins, judges, and others for the town and district of Kazan. Though it remains unclear how authorities identified those who performed these functions illegally, their study asserted that there were 207 unofficial and 128 official clerics, who together served some 64,000

Muslims in 187 mosques. The biographical dictionaries maintained by Muslim scholars kept records of numerous figures whose activities remained beyond state regulation. Though the village of Tünter traced its first mullahs back to the year 1730, none acquired a license until 1832. Before he died at the age of 75 in 1844, Tulun Khwaja bin Musi acted as a Sufi guide and offered religious instruction without any license (*ukaz* or *manshūr*).[10]

Muslims pursued the Sufi path unencumbered by administrative oversight. Students in search of religious knowledge and spiritual guidance sought out their own teachers and guides. Traveling widely, they studied with scholars renowned for their learning and piety in village madrasas throughout the region and beyond the borders of the empire. A young man might study the foundations of jurisprudence under a scholar in Kazan and hadith under an instructor at a village madrasa in Orenburg Province before traveling on to Bukhara for an education in logic, philosophy, and mysticism; there he might also be initiated into the Sufi path of the Naqshbandi brotherhood before returning to his native village or town, where he would commit himself to instructing others in the knowledge gathered on his travels.

The educational horizons of women appear to have been focused more on the Qur'anic school, the *maktab*, than the madrasa. Parents entrusted girls to the wives of mullahs and imams for religious instruction in the school or in these women's homes. The education of girls did not end following a few months or years under the mullah's wife. Like men who did not pursue education beyond the elementary level, women continued to learn the fundamentals of religion through other social channels; they were able to be in attendance at public preaching and storytelling, as well as recitation of the Qur'an, poetry, and other texts, and they benefited from the circulation and discussion of a wide range of Islamic literature, including commentaries on classical texts of Islamic law and theology. Mullahs' wives led village women in informal readings, discussions of saints' lives, transmission of hadith, and the telling of edifying stories during Ramadan. In 1843 the government identified thirty-eight women among the Muslim "clergy" in the town of Kazan.[11] Yet the Orenburg Assembly did not assign them official status.

Tsarist officials expressed frustration with their own unfamiliarity with the Islamic "ecclesiastical offices" subordinated to the Assembly. The regime discerned in them many attributes of a clergy that might be enrolled in state service, but it hesitated to confer upon them the privileges enjoyed by the clergy of the Orthodox Church. Exemption from corporal punishment, one of the most important privileges in tsarist society, marked a substantial divide between the two groups. In 1785, nobles, officials, and merchants were distinguished from the lower orders of Russian society by their release from the threat of the knout. In 1801, Orthodox priests and deacons received exemption as an "example for the people of respect for the holy office." In 1822, when members of the State Council and Ruling Senate discussed whether "Muhammadan clergymen" should possess the same privilege, they ruled that mullahs under the Orenburg Assembly should remain subject to corporal punishment like other subjects who paid the poll tax.[12]

When the government did grant special rights and privileges, it reconfirmed the hierarchy of the Islamic establishment. Only the mufti and judges (akhunds) enjoyed personal immunity from recruitment and corporal punishment. From 1811 the mufti was to stand not before provincial authorities to answer charges, like the accusations of corruption that dogged Khusainov, but before the Ruling Senate in St. Petersburg.[13] Still, an ecclesiastical rank did not spare those below him from criminal prosecution by provincial authorities.

In 1826 the State Council rejected a proposal from the mufti concerning the criminal prosecution of Muslim clerics by civil authorities. Mufti Gabdrakhimov sought the attachment of deputies from the Assembly to these proceedings. The council ruled that insofar as the Muhammadan clergy "does not have any special privileges related to the office" and remained liable to taxes and other obligations, they should "be punished alongside other villagers." Here, too, the regime distinguished between Muslim and Christian clergies by denying the former ecclesiastical courts. It clarified this position by pointing out that only offenses directly related to "religious duties" would fall under the jurisdiction of the Orenburg Assembly; all others would be subject to standard provincial courts. In 1849 the State Council and Senate reconfirmed the authority of the Assembly to punish clerics by suspending or removing them from their official posts and depriving them of "ecclesiastical rank" for violating their "religious duties." However, St. Petersburg made the exercise of this power dependent upon provincial authorities. These officials were to perform "mediation" on behalf of the Assembly, though this measure prohibited them from rescinding its judgments.[14]

Despite the efforts of the Bashkirs who petitioned Catherine in 1793, clerics enjoyed freedom from duties and obligations only at the discretion of the laity. Exemptions required a formal voluntary agreement by the mahalla to assume responsibility for these burdens. Some mosque communities relieved mullahs from the obligation to serve in the military by offering others as recruits in their place, but they also dispatched to the army clerics who displayed "bad behavior."[15]

Devised in an ad hoc fashion by the government of Nicholas I, legislation of the 1820s and 1830s left unanswered many questions about the status and functions of clerics. In May 1834, D. N. Bludov, the minister of internal affairs, wrote to Ufa requesting information about Muslims serving at mosques and schools. Lacking an accurate statistical portrait of this group, the Ministry was uninformed about the "rights and obligations accompanying these offices, in what relations they stand to one another and to the Assembly, and in what way and on what basis they are appointed to and removed from their offices."[16]

Bludov's inquiries met with sketchy replies; Mufti Gabdulvakhid Suleimanov offered a detailed response to the Ministry only in December 1840. He confirmed official doubts about the organization of Muslim clerics. He pointed out that under the first two muftis, district judges had lacked direction. Seemingly beyond the control of the Assembly and provincial officials, their responsibilities were ill-defined. Many had been involved in "groundless" litigation, and the number of cases presented before the Assembly had swelled, contributing to "disorder" and "slowness" in adjudicating them.[17]

Suleimanov tried to clarify for his superiors the function and duties of the 'ulama. Parish imams issued names to infants, performed marriages and divorces, and buried the dead. From 1829 they recorded these events in the parish registers they maintained on behalf of the state. Imams also acted as mediators. They persuaded parishioners to seek "reconciliation" (primirenie) in cases of "marital dissatisfaction."[18] Imams issued "divorce certificates" and entered agreements in the parish register. When such mediation failed to lead to a settlement, the imams referred the litigants to the district judge, the akhund or kazi (qāżī, kadi).

These judges, too, had received orders to strive for "reconciliation and voluntary settlement." Failure to reach an agreement "according to the rules of Muhammadan law" at this stage obliged the litigants to seek out mediators and witnesses to present evidence for each side. Judges then issued a ruling and submitted a report on the case to the Orenburg Assembly for review. They also supervised the distribution of inheritance to orphans. Because they did not receive compensation from the state, Suleimanov added, judges were permitted to claim a portion of the inheritance in accordance with the shari'a. These figures had been given restrictions by the Assembly in the past. They were prohibited from traveling around settlements to hear cases "of their own accord." Given "the simple folk's esteem and respect for them," they were also expected to exhibit "good behavior and morality" and obey the commands of their superiors or risk removal. Finally, the mufti reported, these judges were expected to forward women's complaints about marital abuse to civil authorities.[19]

How did Muslim clerics respond to the redefinition of their status and responsibilities under the centralized authority of the official Islamic hierarchy? Many continued to pursue Islamic learning but declined to submit to the examinations in Ufa and the scrutiny of the governor that were required to obtain a license. Others objected to the broad powers claimed by the mufti or questioned the legitimacy of scholars who identified the Russian empire as dar al-Islam. Like Jewish communities who maintained official rabbis to perform administrative tasks alongside others who avoided such duties, some mosque communities relied on licensed clerics as well as unlicensed figures whose piety earned them the regard of their neighbors.[20]

Reputation and shared sources of learning and mystical knowledge contributed as much to the creation of bonds between men of religious learning as subordination to a common authority or the vague legal status that came with it. Many scholars had studied under the same mentors in Bukhara, where they often bonded themselves to a spiritual guide of the Naqshbandi order. Contact with Sufi masters such as Fayz Khan in Kabul forged a connection between scholars scattered throughout Eurasia. In the village of Ura (Orï), for example, the brothers Khäbibulla and Fätkhulla received gift-bearing visitors like "the ishan of the district of Ufa" whose pilgrimage to their village honored their reputation. This Jäg'fär b.

Gabid b. Iskhak b. Kotlïgmökhämmäd b. Näriman äs-Safari (d. 1831) may also have shared Khäbibulla's opposition to Mufti Khusainov, though all three shared a link to the Sufi Fayz Khan. Despite the feud that separated these two brothers, their contacts with scholars and Sufis overlapped. Pilgrimage and the circulation of texts complemented these ties.[21]

Funerals were especially important in dramatizing bonds between men of religion. Biographical dictionaries frequently recounted the identity of those who recited prayers at a notable's funeral. Fätkhulla, for example, read the prayers at the funeral of one of Khäbibulla's students in Ashit (who had also studied there and in the village of Urbar) and for another mullah in the village of Kïshkar.[22]

The social and legal context of the Russian empire provided additional markers of group identity. Even in the eighteenth century, Muslim clerics sought parity with the Orthodox clergy when seeking rights and privileges from the regime. In a meeting with Igel'strom in February 1789, Bashkir and Mishar elders of the district of Verkhneural'sk argued for the right to travel freely in the region. They pointed out that Christian "ecclesiastical officials travel around settlements and look after the orderly performance of service in churches, so that their clergymen are allowed to travel around . . . to instruct the people in the necessary commentaries on the faith."[23] As the privileges of the Orthodox clergy became more distinct, and as the regime increasingly assigned Muslim clerics analogous duties, Muslims pushed for a legal status roughly paralleling that of Orthodox clergymen. Thus the 'ulama themselves began to think of themselves as constituting a distinctive estate, a "Muslim clergy."

In 1841, 'ulama in the provinces of Orenburg, Kazan, Viatka, and Perm organized a petition campaign to request from Mufti Suleimanov the legal recognition of corporate privileges. In this, as in other coordinated appeals on behalf of Muslims in this region, the thirty-one petitions from scholars in these four provinces expressed the same content, if not in identical language. The product of networks of communication and association established by ties of Islamic learning, kinship, and trade, this petition was an attempt to acquire privileged status. They likened themselves to Orthodox clergymen in that they fulfilled the same obligations to the state, including prayer for the emperor and the royal family. The petitioners also sought personal exemption from military recruitment and from the payment of state obligations, just as the regime had relieved Christian clergies and even rabbis of these duties.[24]

According to the petitions, Muslim clerics enjoyed no privileges and parishioners rarely assumed responsibility for clerics' obligations. Parishioners shunned these duties even though a decree of 31 August 1826 "obliged" them to fulfill them. In neglecting their imams, members of mosque communities also violated Islamic law, forcing imams to find other means to support themselves. These other occupations detracted from imams' religious obligations and brought little benefit, as the same 1826 law prohibited them from engaging in any form of trade. When clerics did take up other economic activities, parishioners denounced them and called for their dismissal. As a result, these petitions lamented, clerics and their families endured dire poverty and were unable even to pay taxes. One mullah serving in an Orenburg Cossack regiment complained that he had to pay taxes "like a simple Cossack," even though he performed other duties like "guardianship of the Kazakhs," to whom he gave "exhortations" and administered oaths.[25]

The Orenburg Assembly supported these requests and appealed to St. Petersburg for the extension of privileges to all ranks of the Muslim clergy. It asked that parish akhunds, imams, and azanchis be exempted by their parishioners from recruitment and village taxes and that an agreement be reached between clerics and parishioners confirming their mutual obligations at the time of appointment. The Assembly also lobbied for the continuity of clerical families. The sons of "licensed parish ecclesiastical officials" should be able to study the fundamentals of the religion "freely," exempt from recruitment until the age of twenty-three. If they should prove worthy of the position, the Assembly argued, communities should invite them to fill any vacancies. Clerics who did not have to struggle to make a living could better serve the spiritual needs of the parish, by devoting more time to such activities as teaching Muslim children "the rules of the faith." Finally, the Assembly requested that "ecclesiastical officials" who had served "irreproachably" for twelve years be freed from corporal punishment.[26]

The State Council acted on these recommendations to improve the position of Muslim clerics only in February 1850. It offered personal exemption from both conscription and corporal punishment for parish mullahs and imams who had been confirmed in their posts before the introduction of a "permanent status."[27] Yet further legal clarification of this status was not to be forthcoming.

On one level, this legislation elevated the status of Muslim clerics by freeing them from the humiliations of corporal punishment and the threat of conscription into the tsarist army. Like Orthodox clergymen, however, Muslim clerics found no relief from material hardships. Prayer leaders, judges, and others assigned to Muslim regiments received regular state salaries, but parish clerics had to make do with irregular incomes that depended heavily upon the local resources of their parishioners. Moreover, with the 1826 prohibition against clerics' engaging in commerce and trade, the regime criminalized a major occupation of 'ulama in the region. The Senate asserted that these practices had been proscribed "according to their law" and that "Muhammadan Ecclesiastical Authorities" had responded to parishioners' complaints against clerics involved in such affairs by revoking their licenses. Muslims could enter into the official trading ranks only after renouncing their clerical status.[28] Though many continued to pursue the life of both merchant and scholar, this prohibition increased Muslim clerics' insecurity. As the regime assigned more and more responsibilities to these offices, the men who filled these ranks became more vulnerable. Economic survival forced many mullahs to neglect duties they owed to the state or the mahalla.

In some communities, this dependence upon an income derived from the mosque community enhanced the leverage of well-to-do parishioners in debates with imams or other opponents. The exigencies of the parish economy also colored religious disputes by sharpening conflicts between clerics serving a single community. In other mahallas, by contrast, clerics' search for independence from parish incomes left many mosques with no one to perform the communal rites whose fulfillment Muslim villagers and townspeople demanded.

Lay Religion

Lay patrons took on the construction and upkeep of mosques and schools, which often bore the names of their sponsors. These activities formed a crucial dimension of lay piety. It was believed that some deeds would bring particularly generous rewards for the laypeople who undertook them, as Ghazali taught: "The Prophet, upon him be peace, said: 'If a man builds a Mosque for God's sake, be it no bigger than the hollow where a sand grouse lays her eggs, God will build him a palace in Paradise.'"[29] Affluent merchant families underwrote local religious institutions on behalf of the faithful in larger towns and villages. In less prosperous settlements, care for the building and maintenance of a mosque, or a school, and a stipend for a prayer leader and teacher, devolved upon the entire community. Patrons built mosques like the one in Figure 2 in the baroque and neoclassical styles of contemporary Russian architecture, often according to officially approved plans. They used wood, brick, and

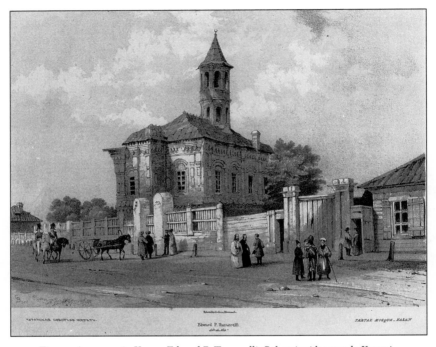

Figure 2 A mosque in Kazan. Edward P. Turnerelli, *Sobranie vidov goroda Kazani* (1839). Print Collection, Miriam and Ira D. Wallach Division of Art, Prints and Photographs, The New York Public Library, Astor, Lenox and Tilden Foundations.

stone and imported carpets, lamps, and books to adorn the space where the community gathered to say prayers, hear sermons, break fasts, discuss communal affairs, and negotiate the resolution of disputes.

Like patronage, charity stood outside the regulatory structures associated with the Orenburg Assembly and the Ministry of Internal Affairs. The offering of alms (zakat), one of the five pillars of Islam, did not receive legislative attention, though various officials adopted conflicting positions concerning their role in enjoining or deterring its collection. Organized aid for the Muslim poor developed extensively in larger towns, especially Kazan. There Muslim charity often resembled more the projects undertaken by Russian civic and church organizations than the traditional charitable institutions like the hostels, soup kitchens, and hospitals of Muslim cities elsewhere. In 1844, for example, members of the Iunusov family founded Kazan's third orphanage, one providing for religious instruction and medical care for Muslim boys.[30]

Muslim institutions like the Iunusov orphanage would expand, and in many ways parallel, the civic work of Russian voluntary organizations in the latter half of the century; however, they differed from the projects sponsored by other activists in that their revenues derived from sources of income endowed, in accordance with Islamic law, for purposes pleasing to God. Converted into a pious endowment (waqf), a building or parcel of land would generate revenue for a religious or charitable aim but be immune from confiscation or partition as inheritance. For the support of their orphanage, the Iunusovs endowed the incomes from fourteen stores. Funds bequeathed by the Usmanovs and Apanaevs (in the form of rent and revenues from stores) maintained the "Second Cathedral mosque" of Kazan. Similarly, Mukhametvali Apanaev willed four thousand rubles from his bank account for the upkeep of the mosque and madrasa of the second parish in Kazan.[31]

The endowment of mosques and schools gave local notables broad opportunities to mold the character of religious life. A merchant of the first guild, Gabdulla Gabdulsaliamovich Utiamyshev, built a two-story stone mosque in the village of Maskara in Kazan Province in 1791. The act added to his fame as "the greatest entrepreneur of the region," celebrated for "his wealth, generosity, and love for religion and the sciences." Under Utiamyshev's patronage, the Maskara madrasa attracted scholars from Kazan as well as from Viatka and Ufa provinces. In 1800 his son, Musa Utiamyshev, formed a second parish in Maskara. Musa had studied the religious sciences in Bukhara and earned a reputation as an accomplished theologian and merchant. After his return to Maskara, he apparently persuaded some sixty animist Udmurts residing in the village to adopt Islam and constructed a wooden mosque for them.[32]

Imperial legislation granted mosque communities the right to choose their own candidates to be tested and confirmed by the Orenburg Assembly and the governor of the province as preachers, prayer leaders, teachers, and mosque functionaries. In some communities a wealthy dynasty like the Utiamyshevs might dominate this process informally by influencing the votes of dependent wage laborers or immiserated clients. A family might also exercise more formal control as a condition of the original deed establishing the endowment for a mosque or school. Contrary to the letter of tsarist law, many of these deeds named the administrators of these endowments, typically family members, as the persons responsible for choosing those who would staff the institutions supported by the waqf.[33]

As in the realms of education and Sufism, such endowments did not figure into the regulatory mechanisms established by tsarist legislation, except in the Crimea, where the administration confronted vast properties held as waqf. In the Muslim communities in the Volga and Urals regions, by contrast, such endowments appear to have been much more limited, likely as a consequence of the Muscovite conquest and the extensive Slavic colonization of the region. But in the nineteenth century, trading and entrepreneurial families renewed the establishment of pious endowments.[34]

A few wealthy families in the town of Kazan supported the construction of village mosques throughout the region; in most settlements, local merchants and peasants financed mosques and schools themselves. In a petition to Alexander II on behalf of the village of Kullarovo in Kazan Province, a peasant named Zaineev requested permission in 1864 to found a second parish. The petition explained that Zaineev and a woman from the village, Feizulla Rakhmetullina, wished to pay for the construction of a new Friday mosque. Of the parish's 578 members, 242 had voluntarily elected to form a new parish, and Zaineev and Rakhmetullina had offered to take on full responsibility for the funding. To counter opposition from officials who might plead against overburdening peasants with such expenditures, the petition underscored that the mosque would be built "without any donations on the part of parishioners."[35]

Such patrons emerged when residents concluded that the mahalla had grown too large for the existing mosque. Petitioning the Orenburg Assembly and government for permission to establish a second parish centered around a new mosque provided notables with an opportunity to claim distinction in their roles as guardians of the spiritual and temporal lives of their neighbors. As many of these petitions argued, the founding of a second mosque in a populous parish encompassing settlements scattered across a wide geographic area could ease the burden of Muslims who had to travel great distances to perform their duties in a mosque.[36]

Such a gift from a wealthy village notable *(bāy)* might alter the tenor of local devotional life by enabling villagers to turn more frequently from their fields, workshops, and homes to join their neighbors in the five daily prayers. In villages divided by conflicting loyalties to opposed religious leaders and differing conceptions of Islamic piety, approval for a new mosque or madrasa could allow one faction to separate itself from its opponents. Though a formal separation of rival groups might bring civil peace to a strife-weary locale, it might also entail the recruitment of an imam to be enlisted in a more intense struggle in support of the theological or legal positions shared with his sponsor.

The authority and status of men of religion, like the one in Figure 3, ultimately depended upon their reputation for learning, piety,

Figure 3 A senior Tatar Muslim cleric *(akhund)*. Karl von Rechberg und Rothenlöwen, *Les peuples de la Russie*, vol. 1 (Paris, 1812). Courtesy of the Library of Congress.

and moral conduct. One village chronicle praised the character of a respected imam, who "in all his zeal . . . was . . . a smiling person with a youthful body, with a broad character, graceful, obliging, and abundant with kindness. His speech was mostly expressed with pleasantries and he would please those assembled." Another was "an extremely temperate person, intelligent, but pretending to be negligent, clever, but feigning to be unmindful." Others cured the sick.[37] The fame of esteemed scholars and shaykhs spread beyond their native mosques and madrasas; the most learned and pious among them attracted students and devotees from neighboring districts and provinces. These figures received invitations from patrons to assume the duties of imam and teacher.

Most ʿulama appear to have operated under more constraining conditions of patronage. The biographical dictionaries document village mullahs giving up their posts because parishes could not or would not support them. After passing his exams under Mufti Khusainov in 1802, Sökhan Gabdelbakïy abandoned his position as village imam and took up trade "in order to earn a living."[38] Those who enjoyed the patronage of a well-to-do bāy could also find it a mixed blessing. As the client of the local notable who sponsored the construction and upkeep of the mosque, a scholar might be discouraged from undertaking the sober "reform" of a local habit (like a village festival enlivened by wine and dance) or encouraged to help his patron's daughter secure a divorce from a disappointing son-in-law. The same cleric might also have been compelled to balance the interests of the bāy with those of an influential faction upon whose approval his official position (and standard of living) might also have depended.

This is not to suggest that, as historians of the Orthodox parish have assumed, the clergy's economic dependence on the laity made them hostages to their patrons. ʿUlama differed from Orthodox priests in that they did not wield the leverage that came with a monopoly on sacraments. Nonetheless, scholars and prayer leaders who embodied piety and integrity in the eyes of the community commanded authority. Their mastery of Islamic learning and moral probity served as an example to their contemporaries and to later generations. A license to transmit religious knowledge from revered scholars in Bukhara, Cairo, Istanbul, or Mecca elevated some over locally trained figures. Like many other such imams, Muhammad al-Amin bin Sayifallah of the village of Nilase in Kazan Province would be remembered in local chronicles as "one of the most exceptional scholars of this country." In roughly 1831, at the age of forty-two, he embarked on pilgrimage (hajj) to Mecca and then to Egypt, where he encountered the Ottoman notable Ibrahim Pasha.[39] The honorific *hajji* distinguished figures like Amin bin Sayifallah from commoners and scholars alike.

But such titles did not guarantee immunity against the wrath of the common people. Laypeople could challenge hajjis and Sufis alike by invoking the aid of imperial institutions. Mustafa bin Musi earned renown as a pious figure who had committed the Qur'an to memory. Having studied in Bukhara as well as in Kabul under Fayz Khan, he served a Kazan village as imam before setting off on the hajj. Though he had appointed a replacement to lead prayers in his absence, the people of the village turned against Mustafa. When they denounced the imam to the Orenburg Assembly, the hierarchy replaced him with a new prayer leader.[40]

In October 1837 the government of Nicholas I further strengthened the hand of nonclerical notables in local contests for religious leadership. When the Ruling Senate and State Council took up the issue of the selection of mullahs and clerics of other ranks in mosque communities, they agreed that such figures should be chosen by "at least two-thirds of persons in the parish who are regarded as the elders of the families." They also mandated that township chiefs and rural police attend the vote among civilian Muslims and that canton heads or other superiors be present when Muslims belonging to military estates gathered for their voting. At the same time, the government sought to exclude the participation of "people who do not belong to the voting society, as well as younger members of the family, that is, sons who do not live apart from fathers, younger brothers, nephews, and the like."[41] Final confirmation of those elected to fill these posts lay, the decree emphasized, with the provincial administration (or appropriate military department).

As in the village of Ura, where the selection of Khäbibulla Khuseinov introduced enormous social and religious conflict, this procedure for the election of local religious leaders left many communities divided. The relatively privileged status of the 'ulama, including possible exemption from taxation (dependent upon the community's offer to adopt this burden) and personal immunity from conscription and corporal punishment for superior ranks, helped make these positions the object of competition among parents eager to secure some advantage for their sons. 'Ulama families thus staked hereditary claims on these positions. Before retirement, mullahs tried to ensure their sons an appointment as their successors. They also married their daughters into other clerical families.[42]

The son did not always inherit his father's reputation, however. Laypeople might object to such nepotism, even when their own sons did not aspire to compete for such positions.[43] In the eyes of the minority in many of these communities, family connections or the social weight of the bāy might unjustly determine who assumed the roles of teacher and prayer leader more than a candidate's personal character, piety, knowledge of the Islamic religious sciences, and dedication to fulfillment of the shari'a.

Parish discord weighed most heavily on the faithful when clerics or laypeople neglected, obstructed, or otherwise poisoned occasions when the community was bound to gather together at the mosque or gravesite for communal prayer. Caught up in disputes about commercial transactions or marriage contracts, Muslim litigants knew too well the ways in which discordant social relations could distract believers from their moral and legal obligations. The tensions that resulted from feuding between prayer leaders and their parishioners challenged the Islamic imperative to live as a community. Daily prayers and the communal Friday prayers, in particular, dramatized such strife.

Most conflicts derived from parishioners' insistence on the correctness of their own understanding of the shari'a. Muslims who aired their grievances before tsarist officials and the Islamic establishment regarded individual prayer as an inferior substitute for collective prayer in the mosque. Neglect of prayer and fasting imperiled the community as a whole, as it invited retribution from God in the form of terrible human suffering. Controversies also centered on a legalistic understanding of rites of passage, such as assigning a Muslim name to a child. Different notions of the legal obligations surrounding death and burial appear to have provoked the most intense clashes, as family members struggled with clerics over rites that could affect the eternal punishments and rewards experienced by their deceased loved ones. Villagers and town residents reasoned that the gravity of the problems in their mosque communities warranted mediation at a higher level. Some attempted to bring cases of injustice and moral failure in their villages to the attention of the tsar himself; many others regularly sought the disciplining of their prayer leaders by soliciting the intervention of local courts and officials.[44]

In the eyes of laymen and -women, Muslim scholars and prayer leaders bore a special burden. Parishioners expected them to cultivate, both in their teaching and personal conduct, a form of piety consonant with the values of the community. A village chronicle preserved a scathing portrait of a mullah named Sharafaddīn who did not live up to these standards: "With his twirled beard he is imam, but finds no time for the madrasa, nor for the prayer of the

community. He is completely occupied with a great many occupations and with his two wives, they are merry in their occupation, and
there is still a third one." As villagers from Verkhniaia Iadygeria in
the district of Kazan pointed out to local officials and the Orenburg
Assembly in 1832, the failings of a licensed mullah could have grave
consequences. In their petition, thirty-nine male residents of the
village expressed their extreme disappointment with Lupman Fatkullin, whom they regretted having chosen as their mullah eight
years earlier. Fatkullin, they charged, failed to appear at the mosque
to lead them in their five daily prayers. Without a mullah to lead
them in prayer at the mosque, villagers were forced to offer prayers
on their own at their homes or at work. Meanwhile, the mosque remained empty and "without collective prayer."[45]

To underscore the seriousness of this omission, the petition added
that this situation deprived villagers of the opportunity to pray together "for the salvation of our Most Gracious Sovereign and for
all concerning the common good [obshchee blago]." Fatkullin neglected the religious education of the children of the village, who
went without knowledge of the tenets of the faith. He harassed "the
parishioners among us who especially want to perform prayers,"
subjecting men and "even women" to "indecent profanity." The
petitioners objected to Fatkullin's refusal to permit Muslims from
a neighboring village to attend prayers in Verkhniaia Iadygeria.[46]
Moreover, the mullah displayed disregard for the rites of death:
though the government had proclaimed a three-day waiting period
between the time of death and burial, the petition noted, Fatkullin
waited up to fifteen days to commit the deceased to their graves.

The petitioners also claimed that he failed in his responsibility
to prevent marriage agreements that created the unnecessary burden of an excessive bride-price (kalym). He nonetheless managed to
help himself to a portion of these inflated payments in performing
marriages as well as divorces. Finally, his opponents alleged that

Fatkullin disappeared from the village from time to time without a word of explanation to his parishioners. All of these shortcomings affected relations not only between members of the parish and their prayer leader and teacher but between these parishioners and God. Unable to perform communal prayer because of Fatkullin's personal failings, they explained, they felt "the shudder of divine punishment [*Bozhee nakazanie*]" in the form of "the recent [appearance of] the dangerous disease of cholera near our village."[47]

Of course, clerics also made use of petitions and denunciations to defend themselves and condemn others. In launching such a defense (or accusation), men of religion claimed the authority that was presumed to accompany the acquisition of knowledge of God's law. Fatkullin responded that some parishioners had initiated their complaint out of "dislike" for him and had acted "in violation of the rules of the Muhammadan faith" by inviting Khasan Ramstullin from the village of Urnashbash to assume the duties of mullah and deprive Fatkullin of the parish register. In this, as in other disputes between clerics and parishioners, the Orenburg Assembly insisted upon its exclusive authority to judge disputes about Islamic law and the behavior of the official bearers of religious law and morality. In 1836 it substantiated the complaint made by Fatkullin's critics and issued an order removing him from his "clerical rank."[48]

Like the residents of Verkhniaia Iadygeria, Muslims elsewhere demanded respect both for the legal obligations of the faith and for the honor of laypeople. In June 1819, villagers turned to the Belebei land court to report mullah Baiazit Kutlukaev's "illegal acts and insults." The mullah's refusal to answer summonses to say funeral prayers for residents moved them to appeal to this court and seek the intervention of the Assembly and the appointment of a new mullah for them. Similarly, in 1831, villagers from Bazitamak in the district of Birsk in Orenburg Province accused their imam, Sharafutdin Mukhamet Rakhimov, of neglecting their needs. In a petition in the name of

Tsar Nicholas, they complained that the imam absented himself from the village without any explanation and left villagers without anyone to lead them in prayer. Rakhimov earned the resentment of residents who had suffered in particular from his refusal to say the funeral rites for their loved ones. In one case cited by a petitioner, relatives had to summon an imam from another village to perform the burial. Abdulvakhit Rysemiatov charged him with misappropriating funds intended for a village school, while Feizulla Ishekeev complained that this imam had beaten him so badly on two different occasions "without any reason" that he had begun to feel "a great ill-health from his blows." The Assembly shared in this condemnation of Rakhimov, labeling his acts "contrary to [not only] the Muhammadan religion but also imperial statutes." It ordered the land court to dismiss him from his position and rejected his many appeals, which continued until 1836.[49]

In 1849 Mukhamet Useinov reported to the Assembly that the licensed imam of his village, Iakub Kuliametev, had stopped leading his parishioners in prayer at their mosque in the province of Tobol'sk. While Kuliametev was traveling around the region, Useinov asserted, "without the offering of prayers, the Muhammadan people has almost begun to forget its faith." This state of affairs particularly affected youth, who strayed toward criminality "without reproof from the imam about fear of God (*strakh bozhii*) and gracious sentiments." Adding accusations of the misuse of funds intended for the mosque and of performing a marriage involving a pregnant girl, the parishioners petitioned to have their imam removed from his post. In another case of this type, a village assembly in the district of Menzelinsk in Orenburg Province drafted a resolution in February 1863 requesting that the Orenburg Assembly dismiss their licensed mullah due to his "inconstant way of life." Accused of drunkenness and other offenses, this mullah lost his post—but only for a year or so. He apparently appealed the Assembly's verdict to the

governor and returned to his official duties by order of the administration in the summer of 1866.[50]

From his village in Kazan Province in 1862, Khasan Ishmukhametev petitioned Tsar Alexander II with a complaint that the local mullah, Mukhametin Amiev, had "forgotten his direct duty, to
which he devoted himself, and has begun to interfere in worldly
affairs." Ishmukhametev charged the mullah with interfering in a
land dispute and accused him of inciting inhabitants of their village
to beat the petitioner's brother. Because of this mullah's "illegal
acts," Ishmukhametev refused to attend Friday prayers in the local
mosque. Though this peasant was able to travel to a neighboring
village to perform Friday prayers, his other needs went unmet due
to his poor relationship with Amiev. Ishmukhametev's complaint
pointed out that the mullah refused to visit his newborn son to issue
him a name or to pray for his sick daughter. When his daughter died
of her illness, Amiev was away from the village in Kazan, and someone else had to bury her. In addition to these slights, Ishmukhametev noted, Amiev had snubbed him in front of other villagers at the
holiday ending the month of Ramadan *(Kurban bayram)*.[51]

In villages served by more than one cleric, rivalries arose between mullahs who competed for the modest income afforded by
the mosque community. In such settings, the parish register became
the object of intense struggle. The performance of Islamic rites accompanying births, marriages, divorces, and deaths, and their documentation in the register, brought its holder small payments from
parishioners. In 1860 a Russian ethnographer recounted an episode
between two mullahs who competed for the control of revenues associated with a saint's tomb that lay between their parishes. The mullah whose parish faced the inscription on the tomb apparently won
the right to claim it in his jurisdiction, though both mullahs agreed
to read the Qur'an there for men and women who made pilgrimage
(ziyaret) to the site.[52] Clerics might work in the fields or engage in

trade. But many who devoted more of their time to a village life of learning and piety depended heavily upon a regular stipend from a wealthy sponsor, in the form of a portion of the harvest or a few rubles, to avoid the demeaning state of poverty. When adversaries did face off over control of the register, the dispute could embroil the entire community. Such tensions might become intertwined, in turn, with antagonisms between feuding village factions and extended kin groups.

Imams turned to provincial officials to secure the removal of their rivals. Rezuvan Utiagolov of the village of Isanbaeva in Viatka Province complained to the authorities about the arrival in 1815 of a Bashkir from the district of Birsk in Orenburg Province who claimed to be a licensed mullah and *muhtasib* (a term used in other societies for an inspector of markets and public morals). According to Utiagolov's complaint, the newcomer, Kagarman Gabdulmennekov, had taken over his position "by force" (by subjecting him to "blows") and had monopolized the duties of leading prayers at funerals, births, and marriage ceremonies.[53]

In the district of Bugul'minsk in Samara Province, a feud between two mullahs over the sharing of the parish register and other duties spilled into the mosque during Friday prayers in June 1865. As one prayer leader read the sermon from the pulpit, the other burst into the mosque shouting protests, denying his opponent's right to perform this duty. Similarly, in January 1848 a licensed mullah from a village in the district of Mamadysh in Kazan Province turned to the Assembly with a complaint against a Muslim from Viatka Province who had recently taken up residence in his village. It was not the first time that this mullah had written to the Assembly about the new arrival, Mukhamet Rakhimov, who had begun to teach his parishioners' children and lead them in daily prayers, for which he accepted their donations. Though a district police officer had communicated an order from the Assembly for Rakhimov to stop performing these duties for which he had no license, Rakhimov continued to lead prayers. The conflict between the official mullah and Rakhimov worsened when both attempted to say prayers at the same burials. According to the denunciation, Rakhimov provoked an "indecent quarrel" with the official mullah, whom Rakhimov also insulted. Finally, Mufti Suleimanov ordered the district land court to enforce compliance with the original order issued by the Assembly against Rakhimov.[54] Thus the tsarist police intervened to put an end to clerical strife.

Another struggle from a village in the district of Sviazhsk in Kazan Province suggests how competition between men of religion might amplify generational and intrafamilial conflict. At the same time, it shows how the resolution of such disputes might prompt the involvement of other actors in the community and, more generally, spark debate about the nature of religious authority. In 1863 Mullah Nazmutdin Rakhmankulov filed a complaint with the Assembly against the second imam in the village—his son, Kamalledin Nazmutdinov. When the district land court initiated the investigation ordered by Ufa, Nazmutdinov rejected his father's accusations, explaining that their dispute had arisen over maintenance of the parish register. Refusing to drop his claims against his son, Rakhmankulov pointed out that this imam had violated an order from the Assembly requiring all ecclesiastical figures attached to a mosque to be present at marriages and divorces. At last, the father brought his son's "conceited morality" to the attention of the Assembly, adding that Nazmutdinov seemed more concerned with selling cattle away from the village than in attending to his official duties.[55]

Several months later, in May 1864, the Orenburg Assembly ordered the son to be removed from his post. It faulted Nazmutdinov's "frequent absences" and his disobedience to his father, "in spite of the fact that on the basis of the shari'a he is obliged to respect his parents and submit himself to them." This ruling did not bring the dispute to an end, however, as residents of the village, including a number of those recognized as "elders" and "frequent mosque-goers," eventually intervened to challenge this outcome. In March 1869, several of them petitioned the Orenburg Assembly requesting that Nazmutdinov be permitted to return as their imam. The petitioners charged his father with falsely accusing him. They also insisted that the son's behavior had always been "excellent," that he had been "gentle and gracious" in his dealings with others. He had "the most mild and quiet character," was "pious and devout," and "always performs religious rites meticulously." In a word, these villagers argued, Nazmutdinov "serves for all of us as a model of a pure and serene life."[56] The community (or perhaps its most influential or articulate members) recast this intrafamilial dispute as a confrontation between competing views of the relationship between moral conduct and religious authority.

This case also demonstrates that even though clerical posts may have become hereditary in many locales, allowing one family to dominate leadership positions for decades, mosque communities might prefer the younger descendants of these lines. In a notable incident in Kazan, members of the Barudiyä mosque dismissed their imam, Shämsetdin b. Bäshir b. Morad äl-Kazanïy Khaji. The community turned against him not long after he assumed the post in 1835, even though he had previously enjoyed a distinguished reputation that allowed him to occupy one of the three judgeships at the Orenburg Assembly. In his place, they elected his son, Säg'detdin.[57]

Working from the complaints of lay activists, the Orenburg Assembly disciplined mullahs for failing to perform required religious duties. A Bashkir commander informed the Assembly that in July 1848, when cholera struck the region, more than forty inhabitants of one village had been buried "without any rite of the Muhammadan faith [*zakon*]." Upon investigation, the mullah accused of refusing his parishioners' requests to say prayers at burials claimed that he

had also been sick during the epidemic and had been unable to perform the necessary rites. Nonetheless, the Assembly concluded that
Mullah Timerbaev "did not render the appropriate diligence in the
performance of his duties at a time when it was especially needed
for the calming of the inhabitants [of the village]." The Assembly
also considered removing him from his post, as his superior, General Major Zhukovskii, had recommended. After thirty-four villagers
contradicted Timerbaev's testimony, the Assembly decided to leave
him in his post but ordered him imprisoned in Orenburg for two
weeks "as an example to others."[58]

In another kind of case, 'ulama disciplined the religion of the folk.
Village prayer leaders denounced their parishioners, accusing them
of "various immoral acts." They combated drunkenness and disregard for attending prayers at the mosque. In monitoring public morality, mullahs complained to Ufa as well as to provincial authorities
about the excesses of an annual village holiday, jïen. Many came to
view it as "un-Islamic," as drinking and mixing of the sexes often led
youth to "immorality" and "debauchery." The complaint became
more frequent in the late nineteenth and early twentieth centuries.[59]

To achieve success, such campaigns commonly required support
from beyond the mahalla. In 1866 a mullah named Akhmetov from
the village of Puskan in the district of Kazan informed the Orenburg
Assembly that all of his parishioners avoided the mosque. The residents of Puskan countered that they "always go [to the mosque], but
it is only Akhmetov himself who is rarely there, because he is more
often away on various trips and does not perform his obligations."
The Assembly sided with the parishioners and resolved "to take no
action on the complaint." Clerics like Mukhamet Valitov of Kargala
attempted to limit the roles of laypeople in religious disputes. In 1833
he complained to the Orenburg Assembly that litigants chose as mediators "the most ignorant [laypeople] who do not understand the

duties of the Muhammadan religion." It rejected his request that only clerics assume these positions. Thus neither moral persuasion from the village imam nor pressure from other members of the community inevitably succeeded in correcting behavior that neighbors regarded as "un-Islamic."[60]

Like disgruntled parishioners, clerics relied upon authorities outside the community to restore orthodox behavior and morality. When residents of the village of Satym in the district of Mamadysh in Kazan Province failed to persuade a man named Tokhvetulin to desist from his disruptive behavior, the mullah turned to the Orenburg Assembly for assistance in 1864. He informed the Assembly that this Tokhvetulin "does not go to the mosque for worship, is constantly drunk, and sells wine from his home without [other] residents' permission." The mullah requested that an "order" be given to compel his "fulfillment of the rules of religion," thereby putting an end to his drunken behavior, a "corruption" that had threatened the community as a whole.[61]

The Assembly ordered a cleric from a neighboring village to investigate. It instructed this muhtasib to confer with the inhabitants to corroborate the imam's claim that this Tokhvetulin's behavior had strayed from that commanded by the shari'a to such an extent that he "may no longer be considered a Muslim."[62] We do not know the outcome of the muhtasib's inquiry, though presumably he would have sought to find out not only whether Tokhvetulin deserved to be regarded as a "Muslim." He might also have looked into who was buying the wine from Tokhvetulin's home—were they Russians from a neighboring settlement, or did the wine drinkers include the Muslim residents of Satym? Did his neighbors object to his domestic winery because they would not tolerate alcohol in the village or because he had not sought their permission to peddle his wine, as the mullah's complaint intimated?

Religious Heterodoxy and Imperial Disorder

From the mufti in Ufa to village residents along the Volga, lettered and unlettered Muslims utilized bureaucratic channels and rhetorical strategies beyond the mosque community to advance particular arguments about Islamic behavior, ritual, and legal interpretation. Indeed, the horizons of many of these communities extended to the offices of the district court, the chancellery of the provincial governor, and even to the imperial ministries and palaces in St. Petersburg as much as to the court of the Orenburg Assembly. Through the mediation of the lower officials who aided petitioners in transcribing and translating testimony for correspondence, Muslims became adept at translating opinions about theology and morality into a vocabulary that had meaning for Russian bureaucrats. Litigants who solicited the backing of these authorities in conflicts with co-religionists learned to cast the personal rivalries and community tensions that accompanied such differences into the familiar terms of schism, heterodoxy, subversion, and disloyalty associated with the polemical vocabulary of the Church.

Disputes between 'ulama and laypeople frequently entailed charges of some form of doctrinal "innovation," "unbelief," or "straying" (bid'a, kufr, and dāll).[63] But in the tsarist context, denunciations of opponents' behavior proved more effective when depicted as "false teaching" in a language drawn from Orthodoxy. Thus in November 1862 Abdul-Aziz Bagamshin, an akhund from a village in Simbirsk Province, charged two brothers in his village with corrupting his parishioners. One, a licensed mullah, Iakup Abdushaev, led prayers, though he had not been appointed for that duty by the Assembly. The other, Iskakh Abdushaev, had no official permission to perform any religious tasks. Nonetheless, Bagamshin informed the Assembly, Iskakh Abdushaev "calls to his home my parishioners, male and female, like Khisametdin Bikbavov with his wife and others, every Friday and instructs them in what one must assume is a false teaching that is unknown to them." Akhund Bagamshin regarded this practice as a "deviation from the liturgy in our religion" and "considered it [his] duty to persuade those being led astray not to listen to the teachings of Iskakh Abdushaev." When he admonished the parishioner Bikbavov for not visiting the parish mosque and for going to Abdushaev's home on Fridays, Bikbavov responded that "it is none of your business." He told Bagamshin that he did not want to listen to him and then cursed him with "foul words."[64]

In his denunciation to the Orenburg Assembly, Bagamshin asked for an investigation of his charges. He also requested that the Assembly "compel Khisametdin Bikbavov and the others whom I point out in the investigation not to abandon the religious rules and go to the mosque for prayer." In March of the following year the Assembly took up Bagamshin's report, but it stopped short of meeting all of his requests. It forwarded the report to the Buinsk district court and asked that it oblige Iskakh Abdushaev to swear that he would not interfere in the affairs of ecclesiastical figures. Yet it issued no orders for the other members of the mosque community who had taken to joining Abdushaev instead of attending Friday prayers led by Bagamshin in the village mosque.[65]

An "innovation" in the way Muslims offered prayers divided another village in the district of Kuznetsk in Saratov Province. In late 1860 one of the two licensed mullahs attached to the Friday mosque began to instruct members of the community in a new form of prayer. The second mullah rejected this change and fought to dissuade villagers from these new teachings. When he failed to convince his co-religionists of the other prayer leader's error, this mullah turned to the land court to seek assistance in curbing what he claimed was an unorthodox practice. In his communication of April 1861, Mullah Baibekov charged the other mullah with leading their parishioners in prayers in a manner that violated the teachings of the Qur'an. "Since long ago," Baibekov explained, "according to the rite of the Muhammadan faith, worship has been performed in mosques in the proper manner [according to which] prayers have been read and are read by each of the parishioners to himself and aloud by the licensed mullah."[66] Six months before, however, a mullah named Abdreshitov had begun to lead a number of the residents of Tatarskie Kanadi in a loud singing of prayers "in one voice" immediately following the regular prayers in the mosque.

The controversy surrounding Abdreshitov's "singing" heightened tensions in a community already strained by a vigorous competition for religious leadership. In his complaint, Baibekov referred to many members of the community who took up this singing as "my" parishioners. In joining "his [Abdreshitov's] parishioners," a village faction formerly loyal to Baibekov apparently had shifted its allegiances to the religious authority of the "singing" mullah. According to his opponent, this move was the latest in a series of conflicts between the two mullahs. It was also, Baibekov lamented, another example of the disputes and "illegal acts" unbefitting "an establishment of God" that Abdreshitov had dragged into the mosque. Baibekov ultimately appealed to the police and asked them to confer with the Orenburg Assembly, because neither he nor the parishioners who remained opposed to the new practice could persuade Abdreshitov and his followers to give it up or even to explain on what authority they justified the performance of this "innovation that is contrary to our law."[67]

When local authorities investigated this conflict on behalf of the Assembly, they discovered a community eager to deflect responsibility from themselves onto the quarreling mullahs, Baibekov and Abdreshitov. Though many admitted to singing prayers, villagers asserted their ignorance of such matters in their collective testimony. These residents pointed out that "whether or not his [Abdreshitov's] teaching is right we do not know, although some of us know how to read the Muhammadan language [*po magometanskomu iazyku*], but since mullahs are appointed among us after testing by the Orenburg Assembly, we must then obey their instructions as people who know the law better than us." They also claimed that disagreement between the village's two functionaries, who had long led prayers separately in the mosque, had left many in the community alienated and confused, so that "some peasants [had] even given up attending prayers."[68]

Whereas the inhabitants of Tatarskie Kanadi pointed to their feuding prayer leaders, Abdreshitov defended the legitimacy of this new form of prayer, though he pointed out that this new "order" had not been his idea but had instead been introduced by a visitor, Khusein Mamabeev, from Kokand, a town in the Ferghana Valley in Transoxiana. For the first time in this investigation, Abdreshitov referred to this collective singing as *zikr*, or remembrance of the name of God. Throughout the Islamic world, remembrance of God lay at the heart of the Sufi path. Manuals of piety established specific rules for the comportment of the Sufi whose invocation of the Divine Name aimed at bringing the mystic closer to God. Though members of various Sufi brotherhoods practiced zikr, they disagreed about performing the rite silently or vocally. Under the fourteenth-century master of the Naqshbandi order, silent zikr became normative. Disputes about the ideal mode of concentration on God still divided the brotherhood, even though many Sufis associated silent zikr with the "sobriety, rigor, and restraint" of an order that stressed firm attachment to the shari'a and the sayings and deeds of the Prophet.[69]

In defense of this Naqshbandi position, the Orenburg Assembly under Suleimanov judged that this "order of pronouncing prayers aloud" stood "in total opposition to the shari'a." It labeled those who would not give up the rite "apostates from the shari'a." Moreover, it instructed the authorities to bar such people from "daring" to enter the mosque to say prayers.

The guardians of the law did not always gain state backing for their efforts to extirpate a "false teaching." In 1843 the senior akhund of the Cathedral mosque of the town of Orenburg wrote the governor to denounce his parishioners. Abdrauf Abdulsalimov complained that merchants from the province of Penzensk, together with local Muslims, had been gathering throughout the month of Ramadan in a home occupied by one of these merchants. There, Abdulsalimov contended, a man claiming to be a licensed mullah from Penzensk had been leading members of Abdulsalimov's parish in communal prayer. These parishioners had also contrived to compose a resolution naming this stranger as Abdulsalimov's "assistant" without the akhund's knowledge or consent. Abdulsalimov also charged that, in the meantime, these parishioners and the strangers from Penzensk had refused to attend prayers in the Cathedral mosque, thereby neglecting the obligations incumbent upon every believer. Finally, to these accusations of religious nonconformity, the senior akhund added an allegation intended to provoke alarm: their avoidance of the mosque also had overtones of political disloyalty. These erring Muslims had neglected to attend "prayers of thanksgiving" at the invitation of the Orenburg military governor at news of the birth of a son to the tsarevna, Maria Aleksandrovna (the wife of the future tsar Alexander II).[70]

Despite the soundness of Abdulsalimov's political instincts in addressing the administration with this line of argument, the authorities received his denunciation more as a petty nuisance than a call to panic about Muslim attitudes toward the dynasty. This reaction may have been uncharacteristically sedate for tsarist officialdom. Yet their behavior appears to have reflected skepticism earned through experience with a form of denunciation that may have been becoming a formulaic commonplace: a note from a provincial official warned the akhund not to "burden the administration with such reports."[71] The office of the governor did not dismiss the accusation entirely, however. Instead it identified the Orenburg Assembly as the institution responsible for handling the investigation of analogous claims.

During the Assembly's investigation, the mullah accused of leading illegal communal prayers in a private home, Nigametulla Abdrakhimov, submitted a rebuttal to Abdulsalimov's "denunciation" *(donos)*. As it turned out, Abdrakhimov explained, he indeed was a licensed mullah from a village in the district of Kasimov in Penzensk Province, though he had not led others in prayers at the merchant's home, "knowing the law that strictly forbids such things." He and others had gathered there during several evenings in Ramadan to hear the Qur'an recited by a visiting Bukharan who had memorized the sacred text by heart (earning the title *hafiz*). Abdrakhimov's defense of himself and others who had attended the recitations was buoyed by the revelation that the military governor had since dismissed the akhund from his post for transgressions apparently unrelated to his recent accusations: the Orenburg police chief's report cited Abdulsalimov's "drunken life and impetuous acts." Another petition from merchants who had been present at the Qur'anic recitations noted that Abdulsalimov had never invited them to attend the prayers on behalf of the royal family. Indeed, they charged, Abdulsalimov rarely led or performed the five daily prayers himself, "delegating this [instead] to other persons unworthy of the calling." These members of the Cathedral mosque community also pointed out that, since early youth, Abdulsalimov's behavior had been marked by "improper conduct" and "inadequate education." He came by his position, they added, only through the intervention of his father, the late Orenburg mufti Gabdrakhimov.[72]

Even lower officials in the tsarist bureaucracy struggled to have supposedly unorthodox practices banned by the Islamic establishment. In 1847 a military chief in charge of the village of Sterlitamakovo appealed to the mufti to prohibit the practice of walking around the village after evening prayers singing "hymns to God *(takbir)* [*Allahu Akbar*]." Suleimanov declined, explaining that "the goal of these hymns lies in disposing the heart of those singing and listening for zealous prayer to God for mercy . . . and repentance of their unlawful acts."[73]

Other attempts at soliciting state intervention to correct an opponent's religious style appealed more directly to the rhetorical conventions and official attitudes of the tsarist context. In September 1858 the mullah and senior muhtasib of the district of Tetiush' in Kazan Province, Tazitdin Mazitov, petitioned the minister of internal affairs, S. S. Lanskoi. He warned of a "pretender" whose "false teaching" he had uncovered. He sought Lanskoi's aid in correcting the error of the "schismatics" who surrounded him. At the same time, he appealed for protection from the pretender's relatives and followers who leveled false accusations against Mazitov solely because of his devotion to the faith, his office, and the laws of the empire.

In his petition to Lanskoi, Mazitov explained that he initiated his investigation when he discovered in 1857 that Muslims from his district were being drawn to the town and surrounding district of Buinsk by "some Muhammadans who perform their religion contrary to the law." An official from the district of Spassk also ordered Mazitov to look into news that a mullah had been presenting himself as a "saint" and had been spreading his "teaching" among the local population. Upon investigation, Mazitov identified the "pretender" as an azanchi (one who performs the call to prayer, *azan*), Abdullatif Alkin, from a village in the district of Sviazhsk. Alkin had been traveling "without any document [of permission] around to various places apparently for holy water in the village[s] of Biliarskoe and Perevo." Mullahs from Perevo and another village had also invited Alkin to their parishes.[74]

To Mazitov's mind, this behavior warranted the intervention of his office—and of the police. He persuaded a local bailiff to take Alkin under surveillance, apparently without consulting with Ufa or any other authorities, after accusing him of "posing as a holy man." Mazitov then compelled clerics in the locale to sign a statement pledging that, in the future, "they will perform their five prayers in the mosques every day, [and] act strictly on the basis of the imperial decree of 25 February 1796, praying for the health of the most August Monarch and the entire Ruling House, for the army, and the whole world." In turn, these same clerics complained to Mazitov that "the number of the devout and those who follow the teaching of the Qur'an had significantly decreased." They, too, pointed to a Tatar who presented himself as a holy man and who had led people away from the mosques "to such an extent that, having forgotten their obligation to religion, they even leave their homes, farming duties, and families." They abandoned all of this, Mazitov charged, to follow this Tatar "in crowds" from one village to the next and even to other districts in neighboring provinces. He later submitted a list of 183 of Alkin's "followers" to provincial authorities.[75]

With these accusations, the muhtasib had outlined a number of religious offenses that, in the Russian context, also bore important political implications. Besides hinting at Alkin's followers' disloyalty to the dynasty, as evidenced by their supposed refusal to pray for the tsar, Mazitov aimed at alarming the forces of law and order about a self-styled holy man's campaign to draw to his following Muslims from surrounding districts and provinces. Mazitov calculated well in directing official attention to the rebellious potential that might adhere to a man boasting sacred authority. The criminal code of 1845 reserved several articles for those claiming to be "gifted with some kind of supernatural, miraculous power, or holiness," particularly when such a person deceived the folk and spawned "disquiet, unrest, or despondency" or provoked "disobedience toward established authorities." Another section of the criminal code devoted to "the false appearance of miracles and other deceptions of this kind" also detailed punishments for the "Muhammadan, Jew, or pagan" who might "through delusion, incitement, and suggestion or by way of the open propagation of his false teaching [*lzheuchenie*]" convert a member of a non-Christian indigenous people *(inorodtsy)* to another non-Christian faith. A first offense of this kind brought a jail term ranging from three to six months. Second offenses deprived the convicted of certain rights and privileges and called for a one- or two-year sentence in a reformatory. In addition to these punishments, exile and the birch awaited those who employed any kind of force in the conversion process.[76]

Mazitov likely reckoned that these charges alone might not have persuaded state officials to intervene against Alkin. He appears to have taken particular care to present himself as a loyal upholder of tsarist law rather than a mere partisan of the faith. To this end, his denunciation elaborated on the political implications of Alkin's transgressions by highlighting the involvement of the "pretender" in the conversion of animist and Christian peoples to Islam at the expense of the "preeminent faith" of the realm, Orthodox Christianity.

His strategy played upon tsarist authorities' commitment, enshrined in the *Fundamental Laws*, to act as defenders of the tsar's faith. Mazitov pointed out that Alkin's "false teaching" had even reached pagan Chuvash in Simbirsk and Kazan provinces. These pagans, Mazitov argued, "having no understanding of either the Christian or the Muhammadan religions, quickly turned to his teaching, [and] regarding him as a prophet, are thereby deterred from Christianity, which is [also] being offered them." Echoing the language of state and Church officials who had battled against the repeated apostasy of converts in the region in the nineteenth century, he added that the deception had spread to "even baptized peoples, who not only themselves but whose ancestors had been enlightened by knowledge of the Orthodox faith." Whole communities had "again" become Muslims and had turned to authorities seeking permission to "remain as of old in Muhammadanism," a phenomenon unknown before the appearance of this "provocateur." Now mullahs and azanchis who followed Alkin performed "Muhammadan rites" over children and gave them Muslim names.[77]

Having warned local authorities of Alkin's dangerous activities in five separate reports, Mazitov now turned to St. Petersburg, he pointed out, not only because persistent denials on the part of Alkin's supporters had brought local police investigations to a close. He also sought protection from Alkin's relatives and followers. In complaints to local authorities, they maintained that Mazitov himself had violated the shari'a by leading musicians into a mosque and forcing them to play there. Thus Mazitov, too, faced investigation. In the meantime, Alkin continued to travel "triumphantly around all districts, [and] gathering followers around himself, [he] strengthens in them the core of his teachings." Mazitov concluded his petition by requesting that Alkin be arrested and his "crimes" punished, adding that investigators should then ask "all Christians among the Tatars how and from whom they received their Tatar [Muslim] names."[78]

As Mazitov looked to the capital, Alkin appealed to provincial authorities for protection from his accuser. Alkin accused Mazitov of insulting his wife. Mazitov was also charged with abusing two men named Saidashev and Sagitov "with indecent words," of beating the latter, and more generally of demonstrating a "wild and obstinate character." Moreover, Alkin countered Mazitov's allegations by asserting that visits to relatives had taken him around the region. He denied allowing himself to interpret *(tolkovat')* the Qur'an and insisted that officials had approved absences from his place of residence. Responding to the charge that he had traded in "holy water," Alkin conceded that he had traveled three times a year to the district of Chistopol'sk to pray at tombs there, but he rejected the claim that he had collected water and given it to others. Finally, he rebuffed Mazitov's claim that he had engaged in proselytizing for the faith and maintained that a number of witnesses could testify in his defense.

Police gathered testimony from parishioners, mullahs, and Orthodox priests in several districts in the province; however, none of them could confirm that Alkin had claimed to be a saint or had spread a false interpretation of Islam. As far as these authorities could conclude, the only crime involved had been a violation of Islamic law, which Mazitov committed when he gathered people together in a mosque in the town of Tetiush' and made musicians from an Odessa infantry regiment quartered in the town play there. Declaring that such an act would not be in keeping with his rank of muhtasib, Mazitov deflected this accusation by fingering a mullah named Biktash Bikhmukhametev, "a fervent follower of Alkin's false teaching." Based on the testimony of the commander of the regiment, the Orenburg Assembly concluded that both Bikhmukhametev and Mazitov had approached him seeking musicians but that the latter bore particular responsibility. As the muhtasib, "that is, a guardian of the fulfillment of Muhammadan law," Mazitov should have prohibited music in the mosque.[79]

The Assembly also judged that Alkin had not violated the sacred law. Some villagers stated that they knew (or had heard rumors to the effect) that Alkin had gathered Muslims in various villages to hear him preach from the testament of Negametulla Gubeidullin, a deceased mullah from the village of Al'metevo. Thirty-four followers from nine villages admitted their affiliation with Alkin and explained that they followed the teachings transmitted from Gubeidullin. For its part, the Assembly expressed no opposition to what Gubeidullin had taught them. A report to provincial authorities explained

> that they sit for prayer in a small circle, joining hands, read
> prayers to themselves with the invocation of repentance
> [tawba], do not do anything wrong, for example, do not

drink wine, do not steal, do not indulge in debauchery and
the like, [but] do help [their] neighbors, not at all in opposition to the Qur'an, for according to the Muhammadan faith,
such teaching, as Alkin's allies show, is followed only by
Sufis, that is, monks . . . those Muhammadans who, having
completely removed themselves from all worldly sins, direct
their path on the way of truth according to the Qur'an.[80]

In its defense of Alkin, the Assembly thus offered a general endorse-
ment of this form of Sufi devotion. Its investigation also revealed,
however, that a number of Muslims in these communities did not
share its opinion about the orthodoxy of such practices. Some persisted in naming Alkin and his followers "schismatics," though they
could not clarify the error to the satisfaction of the authorities.

These feelings of mistrust and suspicion likely arose from the appearance in these village communities of a new chain of religious
authority and perhaps new Sufi rites as well. Because Mazitov and
others failed to persuade tsarist authorities of the threat of "schism"
represented by Alkin and his disciples, Mazitov continued to press
the case against him by emphasizing his role in corrupting Christians. He also positioned himself as a loyal servant of the imperial regime who had sacrificed his material well-being in rooting out a subversive, a task the Assembly had neglected. "Taking advantage of
such indulgence on the part of the Orenburg Muhammadan Ecclesiastical Assembly," he complained in a petition to the tsar in October 1861, "the azanchi Alkin even now continues his false teaching,
which is contrary to the Qur'an, and is finding himself followers not
only in peasants who do not fully understand religion but even in
the mullahs in whose parishes he carries on his teaching." Mazitov
accented the obligation accompanying his rank "to fulfill to the
letter the rules commanded by our religion and the Decree of Her
Imperial Majesty the Empress Catherine II of 25 February 1796."

Though he had "discovered the false teachings of the azanchi Alkin, which are contrary to the aforementioned decree," the Assembly had punished him by imposing a "penalty of 55 rubles, 54 kopecks silver," about which he said, "I am not in a condition to pay, because, in revealing the schismatics I let my domestic and field activities go, through which I have arrived at utter ruin and can hardly pay state taxes and other duties."[81]

Mazitov was not alone in experiencing frustration with the arduous task of setting his co-religionists on the true path in their religion. Other clerics and laypeople had similar reactions to religious styles that seemed to breed divisiveness or make claims to exclusivity. There is little evidence that such Muslims opposed mysticism generally, but practices that distracted neighbors from communal prayer in the mosque consistently prompted controversy and accusations that such acts were contrary to the duties incumbent upon the entire community. These critics saw the rites of the Sufi lodge as detracting from the religion of the wider mosque community. Similarly, neglect of such obligations as fasting, Friday prayers, and the rites of burial heightened social tensions. Muslims in these communities held to the conviction that disregard for the faith and its law invited collective retribution and imperiled the salvation of their loved ones and themselves.

But men of religion like Mazitov faced a particularly thorny dilemma in correcting others' religion. The structure of the parish and its subordination to the Orenburg Assembly and the Ministry of Internal Affairs weakened their authority to claim exclusive religious knowledge and piety. The regime assigned them a number of bureaucratic obligations, yet it denied them the salaries and other privileges or powers that might have bolstered their local standing. Throughout the territory under the jurisdiction of the Orenburg Assembly, Muslim laypeople maintained their own understandings of religion and expectations about their leaders. Lay initiative became a valuable asset for Russian officials, who by midcentury were increasingly drawn to an anticlerical view of the 'ulama, especially in light of Russia's ongoing struggle with Muslim guerillas in the Northern Caucasus, a movement that Russian authorities had begun to associate with Sufi leaders.

State policies had still other unanticipated consequences. In the often raucous world of debate and conflict among patrons, parishioners, and mullahs, the ability to translate dispute and contention into terms that had resonance for tsarist functionaries made imperial law and institutions crucial resources in the struggle to establish Islamic orthodoxy. Tsarist bureaucrats did not have an interest in every issue that Muslims debated at the parish level, and a few alarmist cries, such as those regarding some varieties of Sufi devotion, fell on deaf ears. But such claims proved more effective in triggering intervention when they raised the specter of Christians converting to Islam, or when they appealed to officials' deeply held assumptions about the union of religious conformity and political loyalty, notions derived from the recent history of the Orthodox Church in Russia.

The regime became entangled in Islamic affairs in areas where it sought to derive benefit from the presumed contribution of Islam to the imperial social order. Officials of the Ministry of Internal Affairs were concerned with the regulation of ecclesiastical authorities and the maintenance of hierarchies among Christians, Jews, Buddhists, and Muslims. In the case of Islam, state officials tried to impose a parish structure, complete with the separation of a Muslim clergy from a laity. They sought to enlist the clergy in the performance of various administrative and bureaucratic tasks, in addition to their more conventional and informal roles as prayer leaders, scholars, and teachers. They aimed at creating a state-regulated clergy that would monopolize the performance of Islamic religious activities but stopped short of elevating this group to a position of parity with the clergy of the Orthodox Church, despite calls from the 'ulama themselves for further distinctions to make them a separate estate in tsarist society.

At the same time, provincial and central government officials checked their licensed Muslim clergy by receiving denunciations and complaints from laypeople. Thus, laymen and women unwittingly found common cause with the anticlericalism of officials determined to impose discipline upon this clergy. They became auxiliaries of the Orenburg Assembly and tsarist authorities in policing the activities of the clergy and reporting on them to organs of government. Rather than achieve the imposition of control, state intervention precipitated questioning, debate, and most important, a complex relationship of mutual dependence between Muslims and state officials, binding the quotidian reworking of Islamic identity and tradition to the more prosaic functions of imperial rule. While the clergy's vulnerability facilitated state efforts to regulate and control them, it simultaneously inhibited tsarist officials' ability to maximize the presumed utility of Islam in the governing of the empire. As we shall see in Chapter 3, regulation of the family put Russia's approach to Islam to the test.

3

AN IMPERIAL FAMILY

The tsarist regime did not rest with the construction of a church hierarchy and parish structure for Islam. To maximize the benefit that the empire might derive from religious toleration, the bureaucracy also intervened in the realm that Russian administrators regarded as the most basic building block of tsarist society, the family. As in Europe, the metaphor of a universal hierarchy linking the power of the sovereign to all fathers and husbands sustained the *ancien régime*. From the pulpit and the throne, the authorities declared that each family contributed to the moral foundation of the empire by reproducing this order. In 1827 a Russian scholar summed up this view, declaring, "The family is a representation of the State!"[1]

Russian elites maintained that if the empire was constituted by the family, the domestic order depended on the authority of religion. For its part, the Orthodox establishment embraced this role. Metropolitan Platon (Levshin) instructed the faithful in his *Short Catechism* of 1775 that the fifth commandment "demands that we render our parents, and under their name, in the first place, the great Sovereign, ecclesiastical and civil government, teachers and benefactors, masters and elders the appropriate respect and obedience, and to every person sincere love."[2] The dominion of God, tsars, fathers, and masters defined the family, and the larger society to which it gave shape, as a relationship formed by mutual obligations and duties commanded in the teachings of the Church.

At the pinnacle of this hierarchy, emperors and their families projected models of Christian piety and familial devotion. Jurists and churchmen made this notion of the Christian family the centerpiece of imperial and Church law. "One could not better conceive of the essence of an Autocratic Christian Empire," wrote the author of an 1833 commentary on newly codified imperial law, "than by comparing it with a large family: the father of the family has no goal other than the prosperity of the children entrusted to him by Divine Providence, and the children cannot repay him for the works undertaken for them but with love and loyalty."[3]

Such visions of the imperial order failed, however, to take account of the many children who remained outside the Orthodox Church. In the southern and eastern borderlands in particular, populations recognized neither the Orthodox sacrament of marriage nor the teachings of the Church. What would become of subjects who grew up without a foundation in Christian morality? How could these sons and daughters become useful, loyal, and patriotic subjects beyond the horizons of the Orthodox parish?

St. Petersburg responded to this challenge by treating the tolerated confessions as adjuncts of state authority charged with safeguarding family discipline as the basic pillar of the imperial order. Among Catholics, Protestants, Jews, Buddhists, and others, they looked to the authority of religion to regulate marriage and divorce, to discipline morality, and to ensure the subordination of family members to the authorities. In the case of Islam, Orthodox critics pointed to polygamy and the supposedly debased treatment of women in Islamic marriages and noted that Muslim states were in poor condition because they were "deprived of a public and familial order."[4] But the tsarist police nonetheless assumed that Islamic law would guarantee domestic order and harmony among Muslims, much as canon law regulated the Christian family.

The conviction that religious norms should govern the family was not confined to tsarist officials. The French and British brought analogous views about Islam as a system of control to their colonies. Nor were Russian authorities alone in defining an interventionist role for the state in family matters. Muslim subjects shared this perspective; they looked to the state to support a family order rooted in the sacred way of the shari'a. Yet if the fractious character of life in the mahalla resulted from feuds among families and kin groups, these same factions confronted their own internal tensions.

The litigiousness of the mosque did not stop at the door of the household. Muslim men and women—like the Tatars pictured in Figure 4—who faced off in family disputes generally agreed that the shari'a, backed by tsarist law, supplied the framework for the mediation of these conflicts. But they clashed over the definition of the rights that the shari'a accorded pious men and women as spouses and parents.

Accounts of family disputes preserved in state archives and in Muslim sources reveal that the regime valued the opportunities presented by these disputes. In search of a stable domestic order for its non-Orthodox subjects, officials regarded overtures to intervene in family matters as a sign of Muslim submission to the paternal authority of the state, even as they complained about Muslim litigiousness and regretted the bureaucracy's lack of knowledge about Islamic law. Here, too, they interpreted their mission as the defense of the Muslim sacred law against deviants.

But common expectations often yielded unanticipated outcomes. Tsarist statutes backed the power of state-sanctioned religious au-

Figure 4 Kazan Tatars. F. K. Pauli, *Description ethnographique des peuples de la Russe* (St. Petersburg, 1862). Courtesy of the Library of Congress.

thorities to regulate marriage and related matters in each confession. Engagement with Muslim family disputes made clear, however, that the authorities lacked expertise about the religious laws they were supposed to be enforcing at a moment when the British in India and French in Algeria were arming their administrators with the latest Oriental studies scholarship.[5] Moreover, administrators in the Caucasus, the Crimea, and the eastern provinces learned that even Muslim clerics disagreed about the correct interpretation of the shari'a. Officials discovered that Muslims nonetheless expected them to fulfill their pledge to render justice on behalf of all, by backing their arguments about the proper understanding of the sacred law. Laypeople petitioned to authorities as far away as the capital, seeking leverage not only against spouses, parents, and in-laws but also against the clerics whom the state had entrusted with the task of regulating the Muslim family.

Though committed to preserving a tranquil and patriarchal domestic order useful to local administration, officials unwittingly gave license to wide-ranging changes that subverted these goals. Their mediation of Muslim family conflicts contributed to new strategies of interpreting the divine law and novel ways of seeing the state. Unlike colonial administrators elsewhere, Russian authorities did not make the cause of women's emancipation a major focus of the empire's approach toward Islam in the nineteenth century and did not adopt the reformist language of their European contemporaries. They backed rights for women in Muslim marriages that they did not sanction for other women, but in doing so they claimed to be following the textual tradition of Islam itself, not "liberating" women from it. Thus while Orthodox women found legal release from marriage nearly impossible to attain, Muslim women found a receptive audience in officials who regularly backed their views about the rights to divorce, property, maintenance, and physical safety that they claimed the shari'a afforded them. Sanction for such an understanding allowed Muslim women, frequently aided by their relatives, to appeal to various institutions to initiate divorce, sue for property or alimony, and seek police restraint of abusive husbands and in-laws.

In the second quarter of the nineteenth century, the government of Nicholas I faced a vast and increasing number of such appeals from Muslim men and women who defined guardianship of the shari'a as a central aspect of the tsar's justice. Concerned with systematizing a legal order for the family, officials worked with Muslim scholars eager to advance new understandings of Islamic orthodoxy to produce a coherent legislative response to initiatives from below. Bureaucrats faulted some practices common to the region, like polygamy, bride abduction, and marriage without parental consent. Yet instead of intervening directly against such customs, officials cautiously sought out the cooperation of Muslim notables. In nearly every case, officials found Muslim intermediaries willing to support their views and validate changes by making reference to Islamic textual authorities.

Tracing state involvement in Muslim family disputes reveals the extent to which both Russian officials and Muslim scholars struggled to manage overtures from laypeople for state intervention. Both sides looked for convergences between state and Islamic law for their own purposes. For their part, Muslim scholars viewed the power of the state as a means to advance the systematic application of a particular reading of the Hanafi legal school, glossing the interpretations that emerged from this coincidence of interests as "traditional."

As in other areas of policy toward Islam, measures designed to bolster the authority of the 'ulama instead generated intense contestation. Most importantly, they produced an elaborate system for appealing Islamic legal judgments related to the family. In the first decades of the nineteenth century, Muslim engagement with this appellate structure solidified the role of tsarist institutions as venues for Muslims' pursuit of God's will in the most intimate of disputes.

By the 1850s, however, official unease with this dependence upon Muslim jurists prompted an important shift. Animated by the new anticlerical spirit directed against the ʿulama, tsarist officials began to turn to their own non-Muslim scholars trained in the young European sciences of Oriental studies. In this view, texts, not Muslim intermediaries, offered the key to understanding the norms that bound Muslim families to the imperial order. Experts in these disciplines reconfigured the contest over Islamic legal interpretation, which Russian authorities, like their British peers in India, increasingly regarded as a question of identifying the most authentic "codes." Basic continuities in the tsarist approach persisted, nevertheless. Within the Ministry of Internal Affairs, the goal remained the ordering of the Muslim family according to the shariʿa, even when Muslims themselves contested its proper interpretation.

The Pillar of Empire

Though medieval Russian princes had been parties to the marital politics of the neighboring Muslim khanates, it was only in the eighteenth century that the government focused on the domestic order of its Muslim subjects. In 1744 it attempted to establish minimum ages for marriage. In Ufa and Orenburg provinces, officials sought to regulate marriages between Muslim subjects who belonged to different administrative categories. The Russians feared that marriages among Kazakhs, Bashkirs, and Tatar migrants from Kazan might yield threatening political alliances or clandestine religious conversion.[6]

But Muslims, too, drew attention to what they claimed was a state of disorder. Men solicited assistance against unruly women, even while deflecting official interference from other aspects of their lives. In 1746 a Russian official in Ufa reported that he received frequent denunciations from husbands complaining about wives who committed all manner of "indecencies," including abandoning their spouses. Petitions from the district of Sviazhsk in Kazan Province to Catherine's Legislative Assembly of 1767–1768 reveal that Muslim men saw the regime as a guarantor of a particular idea of marriage. The cause of many disputes lay in the fact, the petitioners claimed, that women acted against the will of their husbands. They accepted money and other household possessions as payment of the nuptial gift *(kalym)* from a fiancé or spouse but then jilted their betrothed or married another man without returning the gift. The problem continued, they complained, because Muslim authorities lacked enforcement power. When women refused to give back the kalym, "we are compelled to ask for this in chancelleries by means of the court; but since there are no imperial Russian [*Rossiiskie*] laws on this, we are referred by the working of the courts to our clerics [*abyzy*] to sort this out." The petitioners added that many women were even "baptized in the Russian faith" to avoid repayment, and that "from this, we Tatars suffer unnecessary losses and ruin." They asked that the women be bound by legislation to repay their debts, even while insisting that men be able to seek repayment "according to our law through our clerics," and that officials "not judge us Tatars in Russian judicial seats." They conceded that women who retained the bride-money by converting to Orthodoxy should be called to account in government courts but requested that the authorities then turn these women over "to us without fail."[7]

As this network of state courts expanded throughout the provinces after 1775, more Muslims came to see them as a source of leverage against spouses and rivals. Often perceived as corrupt, expensive, and time-consuming, the courts did not immediately displace more informal mechanisms for mediating disputes in the mahallas. Nevertheless, they still attracted litigants who had recourse to venues outside state control. Catherine and her successors allowed many peoples to adjudicate a wide range of matters according to "custom."

Thus, to safeguard "native peoples" from the abuses of the imperial legal system, legislation of 1822 reaffirmed the right of subjects under the administrative category of *inorodtsy* to remain indefinitely under the jurisdiction of "customary law."[8] Lawmakers envisioned this concession as a temporary measure, anticipating the evolution of popular understandings of law and the gradual acceptance of European legal principles.

In the meantime, the regime reserved for itself the power to define the realm of custom. Provisions for judicial appeal blurred the boundaries between customary and tsarist law. Russian autocrats expressed disdain for legal codification, an independent judiciary, and lawyers, generally. But rulers from Peter the Great onward projected their sovereignty as guardians of justice, the fount of the "well-being" and "happiness" of their subjects. Thus when Muslim Mishars and Teptiars in Orenburg Province complained in 1802 about "oppression, brutalities, and ruin" at the hands of the local land court *(zemskii sud)*, the tsar commanded the military governor, N. N. Bakhmetev, to uncover and put an end to these "abuses," "so that this voiceless and remote people is not estranged from the force and protection of the general laws."[9] The emperor thereby shielded all of his "children" from injustice.

Lawmakers were guided by this promise but nonetheless formulated policies in a largely ad hoc fashion in response to specific Muslim requests for intervention. Despite lengthy experience ruling Muslims, officials knew little about Islamic law. As in other Islamic matters, they looked to the Ottomans for guidance. Russian diplomats and travelers offered clues, while European texts mediated between the tsarist and Ottoman worlds. *An Abridgement of the Muhammadan Faith* (1784) presented an image of a religion that regulated the family in ways that approximated basic Christian doctrines, even if the Turks erred in their theology. The "Turkish creed" frowned on sexual immorality and obliged Muslims to "enter into matrimony" and "as much as possible, to try to maintain loyalty, love, honor, [and] veneration toward parents, and to do nothing against their will."[10]

The search for resemblances between Orthodoxy and Islam extended to officials' understanding of the role of the "Muhammadan clergy" in overseeing the rites and commandments of the faith. From 1788 the Islamic establishment in Ufa assumed responsibility for the regulation of Muslim family matters. Over the objections of some provincial officials, the governor-general of Ufa Province supported the transfer of family-related cases from the civil courts to the new institution, in part because it relieved them of the "great difficulty and vast number" of such cases, which "their clerical figures could judge better and to the greater satisfaction of [these] peoples."[11]

The original architect of the Orenburg Assembly, Osip A. Igel'strom, worked to introduce a discipline to the Muslim family that would accord with norms inspired by Orthodox canon law. He assigned Muslim "ecclesiastical officials" a state-backed monopoly on the oversight of marriage and divorce. The mandate that clerics participate in each of these areas marked a departure from previous practice, whereby people without any special status as 'ulama might conclude marital contracts, conduct the rites of marriage, witness divorces, and conduct various kinds of mediation. In the case of divorce, Igel'strom stipulated that dissolution should occur "by agreement of both sides." Arguing that "fairness and the law" were rarely observed in these proceedings, the governor proposed that each "official" who presided over a divorce be obliged to present a report detailing the grounds justifying it to the Orenburg Assembly, which retained the power "to abolish his ruling."

Igel'strom also envisioned an appellate role for this body. He empowered "whoever is not satisfied with the ruling of a mullah or akhund [a Muslim judge appointed to oversee clerics in a given district] to announce his dissatisfaction to the Ecclesiastical Assembly and to request that a hearing of the case be carried out." As Muslims turned to representatives of the state, the regime confronted the challenge of issuing rulings that conformed both to secular law and to the Muslim "creed." The resulting legislation created precedents that guided subsequent policies as well as the interpretation of the shari'a in these communities.[12]

The first such act concerned the status of widows but had broader implications for the regulation of the Muslim family. It examined the applicability for Muslims of a 1731 decree regarding widows' right to inheritance. In 1804 the Senate ruled that this decree applied only to "those standing in the law of the Greek [Orthodox] confession, having in matrimony only one wife, while contrary to this, Tatars and other people of the Muhammadan creed living in Russia in various provinces have from two to four wives." After consulting with several provincial governors, the Orenburg Assembly, and other Islamic authorities, the Senate determined that the decree securing a widow one-seventh of her husband's immovable and one-fourth of his movable property must be amended "in accordance with their [Muslim] religion and rite." In inheritance cases involving more than one widow, the Senate concluded, "all the remaining wives generally must be given from the movable and immovable estate one-eighth part, which each should enjoy equally, provided that children remain after the deceased; and if upon the death of the husband no children remain, then all wives should receive one-fourth of the estate, with the remainder to be given to the kin of the deceased."[13]

Like British law in India, this measure insisted on the division of property according to Islamic inheritance law. This not only ensured that female heirs acquired a share prescribed by the Qur'an but also indirectly sanctioned polygamy, even though Russian educated opinion remained critical of it.[14] With this decision, the Senate established a critical precedent: it committed St. Petersburg to backing the uniform enforcement of particular shari'a norms derived from the holy book. Henceforth the state would be obliged to underwrite many practices that the bureaucracy found consistent with what particular Muslim informants insisted was orthodox Islamic interpretation grounded in the Qur'an or in a small number of Hanafi legal manuals.

The state's Muslim interlocutors saw opportunity in the regime's search for order. This partnership between Russian officials and the guardians of Islamic orthodoxy targeted customs that Muslim scholars deemed incompatible with the sacred law. Like husbands seeking assistance in disciplining wayward wives, fathers and fiancés solicited police power to prevent bride abduction and secret marriage. Abduction took various forms, but the problem of parental consent lay at its core. In many cases, men and their relatives kidnapped, and sometimes raped, women from other villages whose fathers would not consent to give them over in marriage. In other cases, women may have colluded with their captors to bypass parents who would not permit daughters to marry men of their choice or to escape arranged marriages.[15] To put an end to this "evil," Igel'strom had called for the Assembly to institute "the same procedure that is observed among European peoples and that cannot be at all contrary to Muhammadan law" whereby marriages were announced before the "liturgy" each Friday for three weeks preceding the ceremony. The Assembly then had the right to nullify marriages not conducted according to this rule.[16]

Bride abduction and other "disorders" in Muslim marriage persisted. In 1822, complaints about clerics' handling of marital disputes prompted an investigation by Prince Alexander Golitsyn, the minister of religious affairs and education, and overprocurator of the Holy Synod of the Orthodox Church. The civil governor of Orenburg Province, G. V. Nelidov, reported "on the disorder in the present state of Muhammadan marital affairs and on the harmful results of this disorder for Muhammadans" and presented a proposal "on the measures which may help to avert the[se] evils."[17]

From the perspective of local officials, the "confusion" surrounding Muslim family life resulted from the very informality and flexibility of Muslim recourse to multiple venues. The military governor of Orenburg Province, P. K. Essen, reported that some Muslims took their marital disputes to local clerics, others appealed to the Orenburg Assembly, while the rest petitioned the mufti directly. Ultimately, the governor reported, "there is no exact decree on where they should seek justice in such cases, and they always turn to the governors of the province." To resolve this confusion, the minister of religious affairs and education engaged Muslim elites to formulate new rules. Golitsyn consulted with the mufti of the Crimea, "as the closest to Turkey and Persia, in which the Muhammadan religion prevails." Taking into account the possibility that "[even though] the Tatars of Orenburg Province have the same Muhammadan law, they might have other customs," the minister also consulted with the Orenburg mufti and the local governor "about the propriety of the rules for these Tatars."[18]

Golitsyn focused on the relationship between imperial and Islamic legal jurisdictions. The source of the chaos, he determined, lay not in Russian interference but in the Muslim practice of appealing to various agents of local government. The minister complained that "Muhammadans dissatisfied with the decisions of their ecclesiastical ranks turn with complaints to the civil administration." In an attempt to reverse established practice, he commanded civil authorities "not [to] consider any petitions or complaints [from Muslim litigants]."[19]

At the same time, other provisions undermined his attempt to separate ecclesiastical and secular jurisdictions. Golitsyn proposed to shore up the authority of licensed ʻulama vis-à-vis "commoners," reflecting the consensus of an emerging body of licensed Muslim specialists and Russian officialdom. Both held that the institution of marriage should be subject to the norms and sanctions of religion. In 1821 the Ministry of Religious Affairs pointed to the varied threats posed by unions undisciplined by clerical supervision, noting reports "that Muhammadans marry their brothers to Christians, and that according to their customs, instead of a mullah even their laymen [*miriane*] perform this rite."[20] One issue appeared certain: lay Muslims were to be subject to clerical authority. "Muhammadans' marital affairs related to religion," his proposal declared, "like the performance of marriage rites, the scrutiny of the legality or illegality of marriages, divorces, and every case expressed in accordance with their teachings, and not having civil consequences, are left to Muhammadans, *who [must] honor their ecclesiastical authorities.*"[21] "Muhammadan commoners, that is, those not having received an ecclesiastical rank in the appropriate manner," it warned, "may not perform wedding rites nor examine marital matters." Mullahs were to take care that both the parents of the bride and the bride herself had offered their consent to marriage. Previously married women were another concern: mullahs were to confirm that a divorce had been executed "in agreement with Muhammadan law" before permitting a woman to enter into another marriage. Moreover, clerics were to record agreements about "the nuptial gift and mutual obligations" of the future spouses.[22]

Golitsyn and his Muslim scholars devised a more formal structure for the mediation of disputes. Mullahs and imams were to serve as the mediators of first instance. If a grievance consisted of "an insignificant complaint of dissatisfaction," the proposal instructed, "then local mullahs and imams are obliged to use all means of persuasion available to reconcile the spouses." In cases when women complained against their husbands solely about "discordant life together," then "the mullah must reconcile them"; however, he cautioned, "when a husband subjects her to beatings and this is proven by other people, then the mullah is to send the husband directly away to the provincial administration for restraint." Mediators chosen by each side should try to reestablish "accord" between the two spouses before a party sought divorce.

When peacemaking failed, the parties were to turn to "Muslim ecclesiastical officials having judicial authority." 'Ulama were to oversee cases when "a woman brings a complaint personally or through another to local Muhammadan ecclesiastical officials that the husband beats her, and [if] the necessary number of reliable witnesses confirms this, then they present the case further . . . to Muhammadan ecclesiastical authorities and inform civil authorities." According to Islamic law, the proposal asserted, a husband's "cruel treatment" of his wife gave her the right to seek divorce. Such cases were the purview of Muslim judicial figures. But "beatings or other cruel acts" also fell under the "general laws" of the empire "with which in this case Muhammadan doctrine is in agreement." Muslim authorities should report such husbands to provincial authorities "to be restrained by appropriate measures."[23]

In imposing this structure on the disputing process, the Ministry of Religious Affairs and Education outlined a hierarchy of judicial ranks and a procedure for appeal. Litigants were allowed to present complaints orally to mullahs and imams. If reconciliation did not succeed, these clerics were to forward the case in writing to the nearest kadis or akhunds, whose decisions were to be final and not subject to further review "if their ruling is in agreement with Muhammadan doctrine." Litigants were also to have the option, should both sides agree, to present their case to another kadi or akhund in place of the one nearest to them. In this case, too, the decisions made by these judges were to be "decisive and not subject to further consideration." Should these judges encounter "any doubt in the case," they were to turn, again in writing with all relevant documentation, to "their higher ecclesiastical authority," the mufti.

In the past, officials complained, litigants and their families perpetuated cases by turning directly to superior clerics despite the "unfoundedness" of their cases. The prolonged pursuit of these cases ruined their "familial and domestic well-being." Though muftis had received appeals directly from lay Muslims in the past, they would in the future look into cases only when they had been previously dealt with by the lower ranks, and only on the basis of "reasonable complaints against kadis or akhunds about their decisions that are not in agreement with the laws" or when these judges themselves sought guidance. After consulting with members of the Orenburg Assembly, the mufti was to issue his ruling as a fatwa. The case would then be "considered settled."[24]

Lay Muslims, too, faced obligations. Before marriage they were to present evidence of parental consent, of a previously married woman's right to remarry, and of agreements concerning kalym and other responsibilities. In the event of disputes, Muslims were to turn first to their prayer leaders. A woman who brought a complaint against her husband was to remain in his home until the case had been considered by the appropriate authorities. Neither single women nor married women were permitted to leave their homes for marriage "on a whim." The proposal added that "[if] a husband treats his wife severely, then she may leave him and go to her relatives, but she is obligated to inform the local mullah immediately about this personally or through another."

Taking aim at abductions, Golitsyn prohibited the aiding of "abductors or abductees." The proposal asserted that women actively collaborated in this practice: "Unmarried and married women themselves secretly leave their homes in order to marry as they are inclined." Such schemes were the handiwork of meddling kinfolk who "out of selfishness and from friendship or hatred, incite wives to flight or carry them away themselves and marry them off to others." "Muhammadan marriages are upset," it asserted, "far more by such actions on the part of relatives than by discord itself between spouses." According to the mufti of the Tauride in the Crimea, these cases of abduction and flight violated Islamic law because "unmarried women are not allowed to enter marriage without the permission of their parents."[25]

Golitsyn's rules retained the interpenetration of imperial and Islamic law, and in many cases violators were subject to punishments by both Muslim and secular authorities. Violations by the mufti were judged by the Ruling Senate, but negligent 'ulama were subject to the court of the Muhammadan Assembly. They faced removal from their posts and punishment in a civil court, for example, for performing the rite of marriage for an already married woman or for an unmarried woman who had left her home secretly or had been abducted. Women faced the punishment meted out to "vagrants" for abandoning the home of their husbands or parents "for arbitrary marriage." Those who carried away women or assisted those who did were regarded as "violators of civil order." All marriages that did not conform to these rules were "invalid." If, however, a father "forgave" his daughter and her husband for marrying without his approval, the marriage would be valid, and only the mullah or imam who married them would be prosecuted.[26]

In December 1826 the State Council approved an opinion from the Senate expressing general agreement with the views of Golitsyn and the Orenburg military governor on Muslim marriage, despite criticism from the Orenburg civil governor, Nelidov, and others who questioned their dependence upon Muslim clerics. The Senate affirmed that these matters concerning religion belonged to "the court of Muhammadan ecclesiastical authority." But the State Council's resolution still retained Golitsyn's reliance on mutually reinforcing state and Islamic laws, adding that many issues tied to marital disputes, like "the theft of property, personal offense, and others," remained subject to "civil authority."[27]

Under Nicholas I, the regime developed a more systematic approach to its handling of Muslim appeals to tsarist justice and its mediation of family conflicts. Alongside various ad hoc responses to individual cases, the Ministry of Internal Affairs (which absorbed Golitsyn's Ministry of Religious Affairs and Education in 1832) asked the Orenburg mufti to revisit efforts begun by Igel'strom and Golitsyn to formulate systematic rules for the Muslim family. In January 1841, Mufti Gabdulvakhid Suleimanov refined these obligations. Applying recently established state norms to Muslims, Suleimanov sought to impose regularity in place of the often heterogeneous marital practices of local communities. Backed by police power, his regulations bound clerics and laypeople alike, creating norms for disciplining the Muslim domestic order that remained in effect until the collapse of the regime.[28]

The new regulations reflected the mufti's interpretation of Hanafi jurisprudence under unprecedented clerical and bureaucratic control. Restating the minimum marrying age established by imperial law, forbidding guardians (*valis*) and imams from marrying bridegrooms younger than eighteen years of age and brides younger than sixteen, Suleimanov also repeated the ban on lay conduct of marriage. Imams were to make certain, moreover, that the bride consented to the marriage, by questioning not only the vali but also other "legally capable witnesses" and the bride herself.[29]

The mufti addressed contractual conflicts as well. He ordered guardians to join spouses in accord with the Hanafi emphasis on parity of birth: "Valis should match a bride with her agreement with an equal in social standing and for kalym fitting her condition." He prohibited the bride's vali from taking a portion of the kalym, money or property that the shari'a assigned exclusively to the bride. The rules also regulated how installments of the nuptial gift were paid. They enjoined brides not "to refuse conjugal life" with their new spouses in the hopes of receiving the second half of the nuptial gift after the marriage ceremony. "The final payment of kalym, the *moadzhal* (the second half)," the mufti added, "may result only in case of divorce of the spouses by the husband's irrevocable declaration of divorce [*talak*] or their death."[30]

Affirming the imam's obligation to seek reconciliation, Suleimanov erected new obstacles to the informal and unilateral dissolution of marriage. When spouses reconciled by agreeing on a contract, the imam from the husband's parish was to record its conditions in the presence of witnesses, together with the signatures of the contracting parties and witnesses. Imams were also to oversee divorce by *khul'*, an act by which a woman may terminate the marriage by paying compensation to her husband. Moreover, imams were now to perform before witnesses the rite in which a husband divorces a wife unilaterally. Only after paying his wife the remainder of the kalym and maintenance for the waiting period and presenting her with the rights accompanying divorce (including that of remarriage) was a husband permitted to pronounce such a divorce, which would then be recorded by the imam. Clerics were to ensure that divorced spouses no longer lived together, whether voluntarily or out of compulsion, and to report to the Assembly "in case of their stubbornness." Like Golitsyn's proposal, Suleimanov's rules concluded by threatening violators with the cudgel of the state: "[Should] Muslims and their imams act according to stubbornness against the points sketched above, then the guilty will be taken to court on the basis of the general criminal laws."[31]

To fulfill these new obligations, Suleimanov secured greater powers for the state-licensed "Muhammadan clergy." As the guardian of the well-ordered family disciplined by Islamic orthodoxy, the mullah gained enforcement tools drawn from the modernizing bureaucratic state. Early in the reign of Nicholas I, the regime had taken steps to redefine the status of official clerics of all confessions. Legislation reflected continued ambivalence about amplifying clerical power to apply Islamic law to its fullest extent. But despite some provincial commentators' unease about entrusting the 'ulama with greater authority, the Senate ruled in September 1828 to issue parish registers to Muslim clerics for the recording of births, deaths, marriages, and divorces. First introduced in the Orthodox Church by Peter the Great, the parish register had become a means of systematic church record-keeping by the late eighteenth century. Providing church officials with a new instrument to monitor the laity and to expose violations of canons and statutes on marriage and divorce, registers had extended the reach of ecclesiastical power into Orthodox parishes.[32]

Officials proposed their use among Muslims to gather information about these subjects. The army and police lacked records of the ages of recruits and criminals. Moreover, in delegating this authority to Muslim clerics, the Senate noted that the lack of information had resulted in a situation in which "Muhammadans themselves may be deprived of the fair protection of the laws in their suits."[33] Maintaining one copy of the registers in the mosque, mullahs forwarded another to the provincial administration. The records were then stored in the archive of the Orenburg Assembly and made available to statistical committees within the bureaucracy.

The registers became instruments of standardization, yielding an archive that enabled the authorities to check compliance with new regulations in each mahalla. From June 1849, marrying underage spouses earned mullahs a six-month prison sentence. Closer attention to the documentation of Islamic rites also assisted in the Assembly's attempts to limit the practice of polygamy. Suleimanov ruled that a man could have more than one wife, but no more than four, only when local authorities could verify that such a husband "has [good] cause, can support the wives irreproachably and fairly, and that he did not [thereby] insult his first wife."[34] These new record-keeping practices enhanced the capacity of Muslim clerics to extinguish bride abduction, extramarital cohabitation, lay usurpation of clerical authority, and other practices inconsistent with evolving notions of Hanafi orthodoxy.

The instruments of the modernizing Nicholaevan state could also be appropriated by laypeople. In the expanding institutions of the empire, commoners found novel venues to assert religious claims. Muslim parents looked to secular settings to assert their authority over children. In 1830 the government reviewed the jurisdiction of state courts over disputes between Muslim parents and children. The issue came to the attention of St. Petersburg when a Turkmen woman named Dzhuman Niazova from Astrakhan Province filed a complaint with a "court of conscience" (*sovestnyi sud*) against two daughters who had married without her permission. The Senate observed that such cases normally belonged to the jurisdiction of this court, a civil forum in which parents could call their children to account; however, it argued that it would not be an appropriate venue for the dispute involving Niazova and her daughters, alleging that the litigants "do not understand Russian laws." The Senate's ruling established throughout the empire that "the examination and resolution of matters among Muhammadans concerning the disobedience of children to their parents are to be left to the Muhammadan Ecclesiastical authority, according to the rites and laws of this Clergy."[35]

Such jurisdictional disputes over the family raised broader questions about Islamic authority. In 1833 the minister of justice sought to clarify the purview of the Islamic establishments in the Crimea and Ufa upon discovery that a court in Daghestan in the Northern Caucasus had turned directly to these bodies for opinions on cases involving Muslims. Officials were alarmed that a local court would seek direction from these authorities, without consulting other state institutions, about the legality of marriages between Sunni and Shi'ite Muslims. Fearing that the hierarchies in the Crimea and Ufa might take on independent legislative authority, the Senate forbade local courts from communicating directly with them "in such affairs in which existing laws turn out to be insufficient for resolution of the cases." The same decree established state officials, not the muftis, as the arbiters of disputes that fell in areas where the government's ad hoc approach to legislation on Islam had not yet reached.[36]

Tsarist officials' guarded support for Muslim clerical authority over the family also informed their approach to the sphere of Islamic law that details punishments for crimes against religion (the *hudud*). Igel'strom's project outlining the competence of the Orenburg Assembly had banned Muslim authorities from applying corporal punishment for religious offenses.[37] Yet the issue repeatedly arose in relation to "unlawful intercourse" *(zina)*. Among the Orthodox, criminal and Church law shared jurisdiction over the punishment of adultery, but officials faced a grave dilemma with Islamic law—though they had a strong interest in supporting Islamic prohibitions on sexual relations outside of marriage, they recoiled at the idea of clerics' applying penalties such as stoning or flogging.

The conflict received serious attention in 1832 when the mufti of the Tauride ordered a man found guilty of adultery and a companion who aided him in the abduction of a married woman to be punished with ninety-nine lashes and thirty-nine lashes, respectively. The woman received a public beating with birch rods and was made to perform penance.[38] Provincial officials disapproved of his judgment and sought guidance from the Ministry of Internal Affairs and the Senate. The government focused on the nature of the punishment, which, as one governor argued, deprived one of an "honest name" and thus could only be ordered by a civil court. "According to the general laws, the hearing of cases involving adultery and punishment for it belong to ecclesiastical authorities," the head of the Department of Religious Affairs of Foreign Confessions explained, "but because of their cruelty, the rules of the Muhammadans in this case are not in agreement with the laws of the State." He proposed to resolve the conflict by preserving Muslim jurisdiction over adultery cases at a preliminary stage; but "corrective punishment," administered by civil courts, would substitute for Qur'anic punishments.[39] In support of his proposal, the official cited laws dating to Catherine the Great, noting that "the Police Authorities are obligated to have care for the preservation of public morality and themselves, without the participation of Ecclesiastical Authorities, to punish those guilty of adultery and the seduction of unmarried women."[40]

The Ministry of Internal Affairs thus reaffirmed the status of the local police as the defenders of religious morality among Muslims as well. Clerics were to bring cases involving "sinful relations" between men and women to the attention of the police; but the police did not have to depend on denunciations to investigate suspects. Acknowledging that Islamic law recognized degrees of guilt in "unlawful intercourse" and did not employ the category of "adultery" as broadly as did Orthodox Church law, the Department of Religious Affairs called for consultation with the Islamic establishment to determine the degree of guilt of the parties in each case. Only then would a local court determine the punishment: either police confinement or time in a reformatory or prison with labor obligations for one to four months.[41]

All the same, Muslim communities continued to see local authorities as agents of a shari'a to be realized in its entirety. In 1833 the Orenburg Assembly learned that Gabdrakhim Mendiiarov, a Bashkir, and Margavafa Khabibulina, a Tatar woman, lived together outside of matrimony. Despite the prohibition on corporal punishment of the previous year, the Assembly sentenced the couple to two hundred blows with a lash and local authorities carried out the judgment. In 1837 the Senate repeated its ban, instructing clerics to apply only "religious penance and correction." Where these measures proved inadequate, the decree instructed Muslim clerics to refer the offenders to civil authorities, who would sentence them to temporary confinement ranging from three to fourteen days. The 1845 criminal code reiterated this sentence, calling for "spiritual penance and correction" for "adulterous" Muslims and Christians alike.[42]

The punishment of Muslim adulterers brought state and clerical officials together in the common enterprise of disciplining the morality of Muslim subjects, even though much of the legislation of the Nicholaevan era aimed at the separation of the secular and ecclesiastical realms. The ecclesiastical hierarchies representing each of the "tolerated faiths" gained new powers over family matters within the communities subordinated to them. As the treatment of adultery reveals, religious and state law remained interdependent. Indeed, Russian officials' attempts to detach the secular administration of Muslim regions from the conflicts of the mahalla became increasingly difficult in the second quarter of the nineteenth century.

Intimate Bonds

The reform projects of Igel'strom, Golitsyn, and Mufti Suleimanov expanded the roles of both the regime and Hanafi legal norms in the construction of an imperial family order for the tsar's Muslim subjects. But the more standardized rules of procedure introduced by these regulations simultaneously transformed how Muslims thought about law, and in ways that neither state nor clerical authorities could entirely contain. They created a new linkage between the mahalla and the tsarist bureaucracy, permitting laypeople to advance novel arguments about the divine law. Challenging the monopoly of the licensed clerics, they turned tsarist law and institutions into essential resources in the pious struggle to order their lives in accordance with Islamic law.

From the early nineteenth century, the appellate function of the Orenburg Assembly substantially broadened lay opportunities to engage in controversies about Islamic interpretation. Men and women in the village and town mahallas in the eastern provinces began to look beyond the local 'ulama to resolve their conflicts. The strategies of laypeople reflected both confidence in their knowledge of the Islamic legal tradition and openness to incorporating tsarist institutions and laws into their pursuit of piety and justice. With the expansion of the Nicholaevan state apparatus, Muslims encountered a bureaucratic culture of decrees, petitions, registers, and archives. These forms of documentation presented new types of written evidence to counter the oral testimony and witnessing esteemed by Islamic law. Of equal importance, they offered novel rhetorical resources in conflicts that divided Muslims. Litigants wielded these tools in controversies between Muslims about the definition of Islamic tradition in a context transformed by the possibility of appeal. The institutional environment facilitated maneuvering that challenged religious scholars' claims to an exclusive monopoly of religious knowledge and enabled a more dynamic contest about the definition of Islamic norms.

Women actively participated in this contestation. Although tsarist law defined the licensed "Muhammadan clergy" as an essentially male estate, mullahs' wives and other women studied and transmitted the sacred law in schools for girls and in other settings. Women read and memorized Turkish, Tatar, and Persian legal texts and commentaries on Islamic jurisprudence. In addition to the knowledge of what God had revealed as forbidden, allowed, and required for the people of Islam, they valued familiarity with state courts and laws.[43]

Muslim overtures to police and judicial officials made the tsarist authorities part of the fabric of mosque community life. Disputes about the shari'a began and ended with district authorities, who oversaw judicial inquiries and secured the implementation of the rulings of the Assembly and other institutions. A dispute from Simbirsk Province recorded in a Muslim biographical dictionary illustrates the central role of police authorities at every stage of the disputing process. In 1820 a villager named Sayyid abrogated a marriage contract with his future son-in-law, Mecid. When Sayyid refused to permit his daughter Bibi Habibe to marry Mecid, her fiancé charged him with violating an agreement sanctioned by the shari'a and turned to the district police chief to restore justice. The police chief organized an investigation and gathered testimony from the villagers. After consulting with the Assembly, the official solicited mullahs to help determine the legality of the contract on the basis of Islamic law. Although mullahs likely tried to reconcile the families of the betrothed, mediation failed, and the mufti Khusainov ruled that Sayyid was obliged to turn his daughter over to Mecid—a judgment to be delivered to the litigants and carried out jointly by the mullahs and the agents of the police.[44]

These disputing practices afforded women novel opportunities. Like women in other Muslim societies, in the Russian empire women played a central role, often joined by their guardians and relatives, in litigating before Islamic law courts.[45] From the 1820s they embraced resort to Islamic courts, the Orenburg Assembly, provincial governors, and the tsar as means to advance the argument that Islam afforded them specific protections and rights. Complaints ranged from nonpayment of kalym to "incapacity for marital life." In 1820, for example, Bibi Kiz Bike petitioned the mufti to secure maintenance from her husband. In 1838, after the death of her father, Mukmina Urmametova secured the backing of the Islamic hierarchy in a suit against her brothers for her share of the inheritance. Even women on the frontier, including Kazakhs and Bukharans, turned to the Orenburg mufti to curb abusive husbands and initiate divorce.[46]

The charge of abuse (zhestokoe obrashchenie) was the most common grievance. The victims of such violence, like a woman who was kidnapped and placed in a grain bin for twelve days to coerce her into marrying her captor, might complain to the tsar himself. More often transmitted through police or courts, as in a case brought by a woman in Perm Province in 1819, this charge usually prompted an investigation and attempts at reconciliation by a mullah. When Alina Karinova from a village in the district of Krasnoufa complained to the Assembly about being expelled from her home by her husband, the Assembly instructed the nearest akhund, Akhmetshakir Nizapetdinov Vaisov, "to undertake a fair hearing on the circumstances [of the complaint]." Instructions ordered him to "reconcile them by voluntary agreement, and if they do not agree to this, then to decide on a judgment on the basis of the shari'a and communicate this to them through local officials."[47]

The tsarist criminal code also prohibited husbands' "cruel treatment" of their wives. But what constituted "injury" and "abuse" remained ill defined, as liberal critics pointed out. Muslim wives' complaints might contain references to article 2075 of the law code. But they also maintained that Islamic law afforded their physical persons and honor protection against beatings and insults. Mufti Suleimanov's description of a judge's duties supported part of this understanding when he noted that "according to Islamic law, men are not permitted to subject their wives to beatings leading to the drawing of blood and the breaking of bones and pulling of their hair." Such offenses merited corporal punishment, though civil police authorities, not clerics, were expected to carry this out.[48]

The inability or unwillingness of mullahs to safeguard such protections did not deter many of these women. In 1842 Khamida Salikhova from the Bashkir village of Novoe Baltachevo in Orenburg Province petitioned Nicholas I about her husband's abusive behavior. Her petition explained that she had married her husband fourteen years ago "with her voluntary consent and that of her parents," had led a "mutual life with him," and had given birth to four children. Salikhova's life changed in 1837 when, she pointed out, her husband succumbed to "drunkenness" and "began to cause me oppression." Salikhova then managed to persuade a local akhund to divorce them. But her husband sought reconciliation. He vowed to bring an end to his "drunkenness, unruliness, and other unlawful acts," and Salikhova agreed, "out of pity for my children," to remarry her husband "in accordance with the Qur'anic obligation [*po dolgu Alkorana*]." But this time she concluded a marriage contract with him. It included a provision calling for an automatic divorce, "conditional repudiation" *(ta'lik al-talak)*, should her husband not keep his word.[49]

Nonetheless, her husband's life became even more "depraved," Salikhova complained, and he began to beat her with "slicing blows" and then ran her out of their house. Her petition asked that her case be heard "in accordance with the Muhammadan faith through an ecclesiastical official," again citing her contract and an oath on the Qur'an. The same cleric who had divorced Salikhova and her husband the first time honored her request for a second divorce, though it remains unclear what role her marriage contract, her petition, and instructions from Ufa or St. Petersburg came to play in his decision. In his follow-up report, the akhund, Akhmetchi Abzitarov, cited only "her husband's causing her intolerably severe beatings"; the Orenburg Assembly expressed agreement with his decision to grant her another divorce.[50]

Similarly, a woman from the town of Sterlitamak petitioned Mufti Suleimanov in the late 1840s requesting an investigation of her husband, who, she maintained, had subjected her to "various insults [and] blows" and had refused to pay the remainder of the kalym owed to her. In February 1849 Suleimanov ordered the local akhund "to carry out a fair investigation on the basis of Islamic law between the petitioner and her husband in the presence of mediators chosen by each of them in the Tatar dialect." He directed the judge to "try to incline them toward reconciliation and voluntary agreement" and to impart to them the understanding "that further litigation will not bring them any advantage but will only involve unrecoverable losses."[51]

The sheer volume of demands for divorce made by Muslims to authorities in Ufa and St. Petersburg suggests that this appellate process enabled many women to end, or at least renegotiate, unhappy marriages. Even unsuccessful appeals could involve a third party in mediation of the conflict. Moreover, negotiations mediated by third parties often led to divorce by *khul'*, when the wife paid the husband a compensation (or gave up claim to financial obligations owed her). The frequency of Muslim divorce in the Russian empire was exceeded only by divorce rates among Jews. In 1857 the Orenburg Assembly recorded 27,275 marriages and 3,483 divorces, or 127 divorces per 1,000 marriages.[52] Of 1,581 divorces in Ufa Province in 1866, the husband repudiated his wife in 268 cases (by *talak*), and the spouses came to some kind of agreement in 1,313 cases (by *khul'*).[53] In one such case from the town of Troitsk in Orenburg Province in 1854, a Kazakh woman appealed to Mufti Suleimanov seeking adjudication of a dispute with her husband, who had subjected her to "various insults." Suleimanov ordered the town imam to hear the case "between the spouses on the basis of Muhammadan rules in the presence of mediators chosen by them and . . . to incline them toward reconciliation and voluntary agreement." The imam reported back to the Assembly that the husband agreed to divorce his wife in exchange for five horses.[54]

Many women successfully appealed to Islamic authorities to discipline abusive husbands, defend their honor, and initiate divorce. Aspects of state law sometimes complicated these efforts, however, even as Russian officials grew more aware of debates about Muslim women's rights in the late nineteenth century. Bibilatifa Temirneeva, a woman from Kargala in the district of Orenburg, petitioned the Assembly about her husband, whom the local community and district court had convicted of horse stealing and exiled to Siberia. She asked the Assembly to "dissolve" her marriage because of her husband's "abuse" and issue her permission "to enter into a new marriage, with whomever she pleases." But because her husband had not been deprived of civil status, the Assembly ruled that "it is not permissible to dissolve her marriage with him," though she was not compelled to join him in exile.[55]

Both laymen and women utilized these new state resources designed to order the Muslim family to discipline Muslim clerics. As Golitsyn and later Suleimanov's instructions made clear, the violation of rules established in St. Petersburg and Ufa on marriage and divorce could cost prayer leaders their positions and make them subject to criminal prosecution. Given the seriousness of offenses like colluding in bride abduction or marrying underage or otherwise ineligible Muslims, an accusation filed against a mullah charging him with transgressing these directives became another powerful weapon in the hands of those seeking to unseat rivals. Muslims seem to have been hardest on imams and mullahs who performed marriages involving pregnant women or who covered up illegitimate births. In the province of Tobol'sk in 1849, a denunciation accused the imam Iakub Kuliametev of presiding over the marriage of a pregnant girl. Another case from Viatka Province involved a villager's charge that a mullah had performed marriage rites for a pregnant girl and then recorded the child born three months later as "legitimate."[56]

Mosque communities also selectively denounced their prayer leaders for performing marriages for Muslims before they reached the minimum ages (eighteen for grooms, sixteen for brides) set in 1841. Throughout the nineteenth century, the Assembly received reports that imams and relatives still arranged marriages for underage children.[57] As in Christian and Jewish communities, many Muslims refused to accept the minimum age established by tsarist bureaucrats; and like these other groups, they found sympathetic clerics willing to risk denunciation and criminal prosecution to perform the ceremony.

Parental control was also a controversial issue. Asserting rights they believed were accorded them by the shari'a and reaffirmed by Islamic scholars who collaborated on Golitsyn's proposal of the 1820s and imperial legislation of 1834, parents appealed to Islamic courts and the Assembly to discipline children. In turn, children petitioned for the right to choose their own marriage partners, a view that could be supported with reference to Mufti Suleimanov's instructions requiring only the consent of the bride. Zuleikha Akhtiamova wrote to the Assembly in 1843 from the village of Sibaevo to protest the "most disastrous situation" of an arranged marriage between her and a Muslim official, Iadmir Churamanov. In 1857 Mar'iam Zubairova, too, sought out its protection from her father and the groom he had arranged for her, even traveling to Ufa with her chosen fiancé, Salimgarei Ibragimov, to appear before the members of the Assembly. In both cases, the Islamic hierarchy overrode the will of the parents and upheld the right of these women to marry the men of their choice. The Assembly sided again with a Kazakh woman living near the town of Petropavlovsk who had petitioned the Orenburg Assembly in 1849 complaining that, even though she had concluded a marital contract with her fiancé, her father planned to marry her to another man. A woman from a Bashkir village in the district of Ufa, Gainifura Suleimanova, requested the intervention of the Assembly against a mullah who refused to marry her to her "chosen bridegroom, Ziatdin Sharafutdinov." Suleimanova managed to persuade the mullah to perform the marriage despite the opposition of her father, who appeared in person at the Assembly in Ufa to protest the mullah's having performed the marriage against the father's will and, in his view, "contrary to the shari'a and the law."[58]

Such parents believed that God's law, together with the laws of the empire, granted them absolute control over marriage in their families. Laypeople proclaimed this conviction in various institutional settings. But Islamic scholars in the Orenburg Assembly countered with references to Hanafi doctrine. In such cases, the Orenburg Assembly privileged the mutual consent of the spouses over parental authority, even though article 2057 of the criminal code otherwise prohibited marriage without parental approval. In reviewing the complaint from Suleimanova's father, an assessor of the Orenburg Assembly explained that the school of Abu Hanifa regarded "marriage as valid even without parental consent." However, in this case a different Hanafi principle supported the unhappy father's objection. Because the groom, Sharafutdinov, had acquired a reputation as a horse thief and burglar, the Assembly concluded that "according to the shari'a, in the event of the marrying parties' inequality in behavior and status, the father of the bride has not only the right not to consent to such a marriage but even the right to request [her] divorce." It instructed the imam to deal with this father's complaint and to dissolve Suleimanova's marriage. The judgment also asked the Ufa provincial administration to prosecute the mullah who had married Suleimanova and remove him from his position, claiming that his actions had been "absolutely contrary both to the shari'a and to the laws of the empire."[59]

Conflicts surrounding sexual relations outside of marriage also divided Muslims; resort to the police in such matters became a central feature of community life and persisted into the twentieth century. Like their Orthodox counterparts, Muslim villagers and townspeople closely monitored the intimate lives of community members. Reports of illicit behavior reached the Islamic hierarchy almost exclusively by way of denunciations from neighbors and relatives. In 1888 the hierarchy discovered that Minlibai Abdukaev lived out of wedlock with a Russian soldier's widow, Anisei Iakovleva, in the town of Eniseisk when Bagrashei Bakiev notified the Assembly of Abdukaev's "adulterous association." When a mullah investigated, Fetkhulla Abdullin and Akhmetkhan Safiianov, along with nineteen other Muslims from the town, testified that "he goes together [with Iakovleva] in the bath and sleeps in the same bed [with her]," swearing three times "in the name of God" that their accusations were true. The Assembly ordered Abdukaev to undergo a three-week fast under the direction of a mullah.[60]

Muslims also brought accusations to the attention of civil officials, as in a case brought to the Orenburg Frontier Commission in 1849. During the course of an investigation into an attack by one Muslim against another, a Kazakh woman Aiziarykova confessed to having a "love affair" with one of them. The commission sought instructions from the Orenburg Assembly, which responded that according to the criminal code, this Aiziarykova must undergo "penance" under the supervision of her imam for her offense. The Assembly ordered her to "fast for two weeks in the home of her parents or relatives and then before the imam and her parents or relatives, to bring forth repentance." Her lover Altaev received the same punishment. In 1854 the Kazan district court notified the Assembly of a similar case involving a woman named Salgeeva who also had admitted to "fornication." The Assembly ordered the same penalty of penance but added that the local imam must also direct Salgeeva's parents or relatives to prevent her in the future from "allowing herself such an act."[61]

In many villages, the power of imams to bring alleged adulterers to account on their own was limited. Moreover, the charge of adultery could be very difficult to prove, as a muezzin in Ufa Province discovered. When the mufti ignored his denunciation, the muezzin filed a complaint with the governor in 1879 about "akhund Amirov's frequent visiting of the home of my neighbor Bagaman Iskakov, without any need, and at night, when Iskakov himself is not at home, [and] when only Iskakov's wife and twenty-five-year-old daughter

Fakhrizemala remain at home." The Ministry of Internal Affairs rejected his denunciation, adding that Amirov was entitled to take his
accuser to court for subjecting him to "insult" and that the de-
nouncer was subject to prosecution for submitting a false denunciation. In 1871 two imams from the district of Spassk in Kazan Province reported to the Assembly that Fatima Valiullina had moved in
with Minlibai Ishtuganov, an apostate from Islam. The imams complained that they lived "like man and wife" and requested that the
Assembly "restrain them from such illegality." The Assembly ordered the local police to investigate the charge and "separate them
from cohabitation" should the accusation prove true.[62]

Unsatisfied with such measures, some men of religion disregarded
the punishment of penance designated by the penal code and continued to impose corporal punishment, ostensibly on the basis of the
shari'a. Reports occasionally surfaced about Muslims like the imam
accused by the district court of Verkhneural'sk in 1871 of lashing a
woman with birch rods.[63] Clerics' ability to confine sexual relations
to the family apparently declined further in the second half of the
century. In 1889 a Crimean newspaper claimed that the phenomenon of sexual relations outside the family had been unknown until
the late 1860s or early 1870s, when Muslim prostitutes appeared in
cities such as Kazan, Orenburg, Baku, and Tashkent.[64]

Islamic Law and Imperial Order

This pattern of lay-initiated litigation created diverse opportunities
for men and women to advance their own understandings of the
sacred law against the claims of the Muslim authorities of the community. With the aid of the police assigned to implement official
rulings on the shari'a, women and their relatives gained crucial ad-
vantages over husbands and their kinfolk. Lay men, too, benefited
from the state-backed enforcement of marital contracts against fi-

ancés, wives, and in-laws. At the same time, such overtures also prompted official responses that gradually placed limits on the range of Islamic debate and the variety of possible outcomes from local disputes. Muslim appeals to state institutions revealed vast gaps in officials' knowledge of the nature and content of Islamic law and its role in overseeing the family. By consulting with the muftis of the Crimean and Orenburg hierarchies, the central government adjudicated many cases that local authorities could not resolve. These individual rulings resulted in legislative acts that directed Islamic authorities to issue judgments that conformed to these standards in all related cases.

With time, legislation and the rulings of the Assembly introduced changes to local Islamic judicial practices by imposing binding precedents. As in "Anglo-Muhammadan law" in British India, these new legal principles curtailed the latitude of clerics and judges to attune the dispute-resolution process to local circumstances. The application of standardized rulings removed many cases from the social context of the village or town-quarter mahalla, where mediation had hinged on kinship networks, community factions, and the collective assessment of the reputation and standing of litigants and witnesses.[65]

By the end of Nicholas I's reign in 1855, though, the government had established fixed standards for the determination and application of shari'a norms in only a small number of specific cases. Russian authorities remained dependent upon Muslims, from village mullahs to the mufti, to offer judgments consistent with orthodox interpretation of Islamic law in a wide range of disputed cases. To minimize this reliance on Muslim authorities, state officials intensified their search for independent sources of knowledge about Islam. Beginning with the first Russian translation of the Qur'an from Latin, the 1716 *The Alkoran on Muhammad, or The Turkish Creed*, the regime supported the collection and study of texts related to the "Orient" and the faith of its Muslim subjects. Russia's contributions to the new European discipline of Oriental studies expanded rapidly in the early nineteenth century when the government sponsored institutes and university departments to train scholars and bureaucrats in the languages, literatures, history, and philosophy of the East. By the 1830s and 1840s scholars emerged from these institutions to claim a mastery of Islamic texts superior to that of the 'ulama. Some of them aggressively promoted their own professional qualifications, wielding trenchant critiques of Muslim religious scholars. They offered themselves to the administration as reliable alternatives to the "fanatical" and self-interested Muslim clergy, highlighting their mastery of the sacred texts that supposedly dictated every facet of Muslim life.[66]

Mirza Alexander Kazem-Bek (1802–1870), the son of a Shi'ite notable family harkening from northern Iran, assumed an unparalleled role in interpreting Islam for the state. After converting to Christianity at the hands of Scottish missionaries in Astrakhan in 1821, Kazem-Bek achieved prominence as a language instructor and scholar at one of the most important Russian institutions devoted to Oriental studies, Kazan University. Capitalizing on his childhood Islamic training and linguistic skills, the professor combined his previous life experience with the acquisition of European knowledge. In the *Journal of the Ministry of Education* in 1836, he lamented the "deplorable condition of learning in Asia." He expressed hope that European achievements in these and all other affairs would "wake the sleeping minds" of the East, though "representatives of the Muhammadan faith prohibited and still prohibit [other Muslims] from having any kind of relations with nonbelievers, studying their languages and following in their footsteps, because they believe that Satan rules their deeds and minds." Likening this "fanaticism" to that of Europe in the eighth or ninth century, he enjoined Russian Orientalists to "wake the curiosity of Asia, for only their brilliant achievements in the field of Orientalism [*vostokoznanie*] will attract the thirsting attention of the Asiatics."[67]

Despite his enthusiasm for Oriental studies in Russia, Kazem-Bek and his colleagues struggled to awaken the minds of Russian officials to the ways such knowledge might benefit the empire. For the practitioners of this new international science, "Muslim jurisprudence" stood out as the practical key to all aspects of these subjects' lives. In *An Exposition of the Principles of Muslim Jurisprudence* of 1850, Nikolai Tornau, a former official in the Caucasus, noted growing scholarly interest in the subject in Europe. He alerted his readers, including Nicholas I, to whom the book was dedicated, to "the care with which the governments of Western powers possessing colonies in Muslim countries are seeking to discover and study in detail the basic principles of this jurisprudence." "Experience in the administration of these colonies," he continued, "has shown them all of the practical importance of an element encompassing the secret way of life of the followers of Islam and forming the basis of their public, social, and domestic life." Tornau's service in the administration of the Caucasus had convinced him

> of the extreme necessity of having complete and reliable information on the religious and civil laws of the Muslims, of the laws that govern the entire social and private way of life of the followers of Islam and according to which, on the basis of the *Digest of Russian Laws*, they not only adjudicate among themselves, but that should be, in other cases, judged and administered by government institutions and personnel.

Tornau thus envisioned the *Exposition* as a practical reference guide to the "civil laws" of Islam for administrators in the Caucasus and in other Muslim regions. While Tornau acknowledged his considerable debts to Muslim scholars in the Caspian region, he intended the guidebook as a Russian-language compendium of positive law to free local officials from the mediation of Muslim informants when litigants brought cases before tsarist police and courts.[68]

Tornau joined Kazem-Bek in calling for closer administrative and scholarly scrutiny of Islamic law courts in the Caucasus. A proposal co-authored by these scholars criticized the official neglect that gave Muslim clerics broad autonomy in the administration of Islamic law. "The government is obliged to know those statutes," they argued, "by which several million of its subjects are administered in the religious sphere." Deflecting charges that their proposed oversight violated principles of toleration, they countered, "The desire to know these laws is not interference in religious matters, and if the government has heretofore not considered such knowledge necessary, then we consider this a political mistake on its part."[69]

St. Petersburg never implemented the specific recommendations of this proposal, but officials in the Ministry of Internal Affairs soon adopted Kazem-Bek's wider view of the significance of Islamic law for the state. Following his transfer from a teaching post in Kazan to one at St. Petersburg University in late 1849, Kazem-Bek worked behind the scenes at the Ministry to review Islamic law cases sent to the capital on appeal. In both his scholarship and his reports to the minister of internal affairs, he repeatedly criticized the disarray and arbitrariness that marred the legal reasoning of Muslim scholars and, by extension, of the officials who oversaw their work. In 1845 his first major publication had identified the proliferation of inconsistencies in legal texts as one of the primary causes of this disorder. In preparing an edition of a well-known treatise based on the *Hidaya*, a twelfth-century compendium of Hanafi law, Kazem-Bek had extraordinary difficulty finding "the most authentic" manuscript copy. Noting the "delicacy of the undertaking" and fearing the "curses of the 'ulama and legal scholars," he labored to construct "the most authentic edition, purged of significant additions and gaps, without which, as local 'ulama openly admitted to me, they have not seen a single manuscript." Printing the text proved a challenge as well, because, he asserted, the poor state of Muslim printing in Kazan had produced numerous works with "crude mistakes and significant omissions."[70]

Kazem-Bek's preparation of this treatise reflected both his disdain for what he saw as the incompetence of Muslim scholars and his commitment to providing the Russian administration with guides to Islamic law comparable to those utilized by other European powers. Questioning the scholarly qualifications of the 'ulama of the age, Kazem-Bek redefined the task of determining the proper application of the shari'a as a responsibility of the state. "Every lawgiver," he noted, "always considers the customs of the region, the spirit and inclinations of the people, its faith and even superstition[s]; otherwise he would not be able to advance those ideas on which he wishes to construct his policy for the well-being of the people."[71] In this view, Muslims themselves had betrayed this principle by deviating from the rigors of their own religious law. He thus advocated that tsarist officials and scholars directly consult some of the foundational texts of Islamic jurisprudence.

In St. Petersburg, Kazem-Bek devoted the greater part of his scholarly work to the selection and clarification of Islamic texts on civil law matters like inheritance. His work would allow Russian administrators themselves "to derive the desired truth from them" on behalf of Muslim litigants seeking justice from the state. Yet the "desired truth" that Kazem-Bek elicited from these texts in the libraries of the capital differed in key respects from local practices and understandings of the shari'a and the broad discretion of judges rooted in communities. Kazem-Bek's understanding of these works closely resembled that of British contemporaries who, as Michael Anderson has shown, took them to be "authoritative codes rather than as discrete statements within a larger spectrum of scholarly debate."[72]

Like earlier Russian interpreters of Islam, Kazem-Bek viewed the Ottoman treatment of Islamic law as normative for Sunni Muslims everywhere. Tornau's *Exposition* had compiled positive law on subjects like divorce and inheritance using European Orientalist literature, as well as Islamic sources. Tornau noted his heavy reliance on the more readily available Shi'ite sources from the Caucasus but presented his work as being universally applicable for Muslims in other regions and even other lands.[73] Kazem-Bek insisted instead on strict adherence to the Hanafi school of law that predominated in the Ottoman empire, as the preferred school of the sultans and of Sunnis in the Russian empire. Yet his conception of the obligations of adherence to the foundational authorities of the Hanafi school set him in conflict with Muslim scholars both inside and outside the state-sponsored Islamic establishment.

In the 1850s and 1860s a consultative role in the Ministry of Internal Affairs provided Kazem-Bek unprecedented opportunities to leave his imprint on Islamic legal interpretation. From behind the scenes, through the offices of the Ministry, he sought to impose his vision of a standardized and uniform Hanafi orthodoxy. His secret review of cases from the hierarchies in Ufa and the Crimea confirmed the views he formed during his previous research: Muslim scholars and laypeople alike deviated from the norms established by authoritative Hanafi texts. 'Ulama and local officials violated the rules of procedure and evidence established by the shari'a, and even the muftis and other scholars offered judgments filled with errors of interpretation. Inconsistencies were pervasive. The Orenburg Assembly had failed to distinguish between Islamic law court judges and other official positions. Scholars with the title *akhund* adjudicated Islamic law cases, whereas in the Crimea, he noted, kadis per-

formed this function. Diverging from Ottoman practice, other scholars—not the secular rulers of the land—chose these judges. The
jurisdictions of state law and religious law were unclear, and the
Orenburg Assembly had failed to define the basic functions of Islamic personnel.

Kazem-Bek criticized an environment in which various kinds of
informal mediation persisted, and in which the discretion of local
judges and other notables yielded rulings that differed from place to
place. Customs that seemed to deviate from his vision of Hanafi orthodoxy further contributed to these discrepancies. Petitions from
women revealed how clerics colluded with husbands and in-laws to
deprive wives and heirs of property and other rights afforded by Islamic law. And as a guardian of the state's interest in the proper application of the shari'a, Kazem-Bek scrutinized rulings issued by the
official Islamic establishment to ensure their conformity with imperial law.

A paternity suit from the city of Kazan illustrates how this pursuit
of more uniform interpretation based on a narrow canon of Hanafi
guidebooks in the capital shaped the daily lives of Muslim subjects.
In 1849 Khabib-Zamala Musina petitioned the Orenburg Assembly
seeking its intervention in a paternity suit. She asked that her daughter born the previous year be recognized as the legitimate child and
heir of Galii Munasypov. When a senior cleric investigated, Musina
asserted that in the presence of two witnesses she had been married
to Munasypov, who, she claimed, had set her up in an apartment,
"led her into the bath," and then sent her twenty kopecks for the vac-
cination of the baby that appeared not long after. Investigators also
questioned a muezzin who had recorded the birth in the register but
did not know the identity of the father or if Musina had been married. Munasypov refused to recognize the testimony of four witnesses who corroborated Musina's story, citing tsarist law against offering false evidence. Nonetheless, the Orenburg Assembly ruled

that a form of marriage had occurred; it ordered the Kazan police to communicate to the two parties its judgment that the child should be recognized as Munasypov's legitimate daughter and heir.[74]

Still insisting that he had not fathered the girl, Munasypov appealed to the Ministry of Internal Affairs and filed a complaint against the Assembly. When the Ministry solicited an opinion from Kazem-Bek, he strongly criticized the mufti's ruling. First, he claimed, the mufti's references to collections of Islamic legal decisions, the *Fatawa al-Hindiyya* and *Kazy-Khan*, did not correspond to this type of dispute. Second, the Assembly deviated from Islamic law in its careless investigation of the case and its reliance upon the inconsistent and incomplete testimony of witnesses. Some of them struck him as unreliable, others the Assembly had failed to locate.[75]

In a review of Kazem-Bek's commentary and the details of the case, Minister S. S. Lanskoi agreed with the scholar and concluded that the Assembly had violated not just imperial law. The minister explained in a memo to the Assembly in March 1857 that "the legality of Muhammadan marriage, like marriages of other confessions, is made conditional upon [its] registration in a parish register by an ecclesiastical representative according to the established form." He also reminded the Assembly that, according to Mufti Suleimanov's rules, "the performance of marriage without parish imams is strictly prohibited." Moreover, he warned, this form of marriage, especially when not put in written form "is inadequate for legal marriage by general state decrees and the rules of Muhammadan law itself." Lanskoi concluded that the Assembly had reached this decision "with clear deviations not only from the rules of Muhammadan law, but also from general state decrees, where the conditions for the legality of marriage and offspring are outlined in all clarity."[76]

In other cases, Kazem-Bek's authority on marriage and divorce could prove decisive in limiting lay initiative and bolstering state-backed Islamic authority. He frequently reinforced the rulings of the

Orenburg mufti and Assembly against laypeople who claimed that these authorities had erred in their interpretation of the shari'a. At a moment when many jurists sought the reform of the patriarchal Russian family, and Europeans devised plans to "civilize" family relations among colonial subjects, Kazem-Bek and his supporters in the Ministry of Internal Affairs blunted departures from an emergent Hanafi orthodoxy, even when they may have benefited women.

A case from the Crimea dramatically demonstrated this consistency. In 1859 a Muslim villager named Bariuch abandoned his home in the district of Feodosiia, severing all ties with his pregnant wife. He disappeared for nine years but returned in 1868 only to discover that his wife, Kendzhe-khan, had taken a new husband. Unable to persuade her to return to him, Bariuch turned to an Islamic law court judge (kadi) demanding the return of his wife and the dissolution of her marriage with Zevria Adzhi Mambet-oglu. The kadi ruled that according to the shari'a the return of Bariuch made Kendzhe-khan's second marriage invalid, and he ordered her to return to her first husband. She refused and appealed to the Muslim ecclesiastical administration of the Tauride to reverse the kadi's ruling.

When this body sided with the kadi and rejected her appeal, she turned to the Russian provincial governor, Grigorii Zhukovskii. But he hesitated to confirm or nullify the decision of the state-sponsored Muslim authorities.[77] The circumstances of the case left him uncertain about sanctioning this interpretation of Islamic law with the authority of an imperial decree. Kendzhe-khan nevertheless persisted in her refusal to accept the kadi's judgment.

In July 1868 she even resolved to petition Alexander II. In the petition, which a notary translated (from Tatar into Russian) and transcribed from her spoken statement, she explained why she refused to accept the order to return to her first husband. "Having completely lost hope for the return of [my] husband Bariuch and being left by him with a child without means for existence, [and] in order not to die a death of hunger," she had decided to remarry. She refused to renew the marital bond with her first husband not solely because he had abandoned her and her child to a life of poverty. She argued that, following the birth of two children with her new husband, it would "now be hard to give [my] heart, matrimonial love, and tenderness to that which I hate and which could not value my loyalty and disposition toward him [who] left me without care." Though the Islamic hierarchy had ordered her "to be taken away in accordance with the shari'a," she continued, "I do not know, but it seems to me that in a matter of this kind the main role is played by the *law of nature*, which is hard to overcome and because of all these circumstances and also due to the fact that in the report of the Feodosiia District kadi to the Muslim Ecclesiastical Administration, not a word was said about my testimony, otherwise I assume that the Ecclesiastical Administration would not have decided to give such an instruction." She concluded her petition by warning that if this instruction were not revoked (and since "I definitely do not want to go to him"), "I will not answer for the consequences in case I am taken away."[78]

By highlighting "the law of nature" and "matrimonial love," likely with the aid of the notary or others experienced in the courts, Kendzhe-khan may have crafted her petition to appeal to the novel reformist sensibilities of those Russian officials concerned with elevating the status of women in marriage. But such a strategy did not persuade Professor Kazem-Bek. In the case of Kendzhe-khan and many others, this scholar attempted to test judgments against the strict orthodoxy that he discerned in these legal manuals and collections—not against a more "humane" civil law or concepts like "equity and good conscience" that guided British judges in Anglo-Muhammadan courts. Islamic law, he concluded, permitted a woman to marry a second husband only when honest witnesses testified that the first husband had died: "The Tatar woman Kendzhe-khan must be returned to her first husband." The Ministry of Internal Affairs committed Russian police to enforce Kazem-Bek's notion of Islamic orthodoxy, issuing orders to take Kendzhe-khan (and her children) away from Mambet-oglu and escort her to the home of Bariuch, where she would be obliged to resume married life with him.[79]

In a similar case from the district of Ufa, a Bashkir woman requested in December 1860 that the Assembly dissolve her marriage. Shagimardanova complained that her husband Gabdulvaliev had not paid the nuptial gift. Moreover, she asserted, he "reproached her with a dissolute life" and had "cursed her mother with impermissibly foul language." Taken together, she and her family asserted, these facts provided grounds for their divorce according to Islamic law. Following an investigation by the land court, the Orenburg Assembly ordered the commander of the Tenth Bashkir Canton to return Shagimardanova to her husband. It concluded that "according to the shari'a and article 103 of volume 10 [of the *Digest of Laws*], spouses must live together." It added that the wife's charges did not present sufficient grounds for dissolution of the marriage, noting that the allegation of nonpayment of kalym should be investigated, according to article 1211 of volume 11 of the *Digest of Laws*, by "parish clergy," while the appropriate local court should handle accusations concerning "personal insults." It ordered Gabdulvaliev to pay the remainder of the kalym owed to her and instructed him to live "peaceably" with her and to refrain from "oppression," "under danger otherwise of responsibility according to the shari'a."[80]

But Shagimardanova and her relatives refused to accept this judgment and appealed to the Orenburg governor. When he sought direction from the Department of Religious Affairs of Foreign Confessions, the director solicited an opinion from Kazem-Bek. The professor explained that according to Islamic law a woman does not have the right to demand a divorce from her husband because of nonpayment of kalym, because he cursed her or her mother, or because he accused her of leading a dissolute life. He noted, however, that she may seek satisfaction according to the shari'a in case of non-payment of the nuptial gift. If the husband has called her an "adulteress," Kazem-Bek continued, she has the right to complain against him before local authorities. He added that such a complaint may be heard on the basis of the penal code "for false accusation," or, according to Islamic law, on the basis of "the code of *li'an*, that is, a mutual oath determined by the shari'a taken five times between a man and a woman, after which the dissolution of the marriage ensues forever."[81] Given the circumstances of the case, Kazem-Bek concluded that the Assembly had acted in accordance with Islamic law. In July 1864 the minister of internal affairs, P. A. Valuev, drafted a letter using language drawn directly from Kazem-Bek's report to confirm the judgment of the Assembly as "completely correct" in Shagimardanova's case.

The woman's father still rejected this ruling. In a petition to Valuev of August 1865, Shagimardan Abdushakhmanov explained that his son-in-law had subjected his wife to abuse and had accused his daughter of leading an immoral life, which "according to the law of our religion dissolved the marriage itself in accordance with the meaning of the Qur'an in the sura *An-Nur*." He maintained that this chapter established that

> if someone uses insulting words in relation to his wife and
> moreover about her behavior, then the marriage is dissolved.
> The words of the holy sura *An-Nur* are confirmed also when
> someone has dared to defame her mother . . . These words
> of the Holy Law on the insulting [things said] in relation to
> my wife and daughter give me the boldness to ask Your Ex-
> cellency to order the investigation of this case and to give
> my daughter a divorce according to our religion.[82]

The father's expansive interpretation of this passage of the Qur'an as a defense of the honor of his wife and daughter faltered in a tsarist chancellery where a new European "science" of interpreting Islamic texts had prevailed.

Abdushakhmanov's claims about the "words of the Holy Law" proved no match for the prestige enjoyed by the discipline of Oriental studies. In Kazem-Bek and other scholars, the state had gained another means to monitor and correct the activities of the official Islamic establishment. Scientific knowledge presented an alternative to Islamic scholars whose probity tsarist bureaucrats questioned, while providing a guarantee, Russian officials believed, of the orthodoxy of Islamic interpretation in the empire.

Although Shagimardanova and her father failed to gain state backing for their views about the role of Islamic tradition in sanctifying the honor of their family, others continued to resort to the multiple channels of appeal available to lay Muslims in the pursuit of competing claims about Islamic law and tradition. The Ministry of Internal Affairs remained committed to seeking that which was useful in the Hanafi orthodoxy of family law, even when, in the second half of the nineteenth century, the Church and others within the bureaucracy would intensify their attacks on the entanglement of the state with Muslim family and ecclesiastical affairs.[83]

As a realm of common expectations and an arena of state intervention solicited by Muslims themselves, the family illuminates crucial connections between tsarist state building and religious conflict. The search for the resolution of disputes within these communities linked intimate antagonisms among family members and their neighbors to the workings of the state. Litigants played a vital role in the emergence of an appellate procedure, a significant innovation in the region's Islamic legal traditions. This hierarchical system of appeal linked family disputes to local courts, central ministries, and the tsar. Through it, the struggle for the shari'a made Muslim subjects more dependent upon the regime than ever before.

The state and its Muslim subjects were drawn together by the challenge of establishing a Muslim family order that would be both useful to the empire and pleasing to God. These arrangements contributed to the integration of Muslim peoples into the institutional life of the empire, though they did not impose the order envisioned by tsarist or Muslim elites. The appellate mechanisms established by the regime in the name of protecting lay Muslims against clerical abuses made state institutions novel arenas for debate about orthodox Islam and key actors in its definition. For Muslim subjects, the institutions of this empire became indispensable resources in the continual redefinition and reinterpretation of Islamic tradition and identity. The search for leverage in the resolution of family disputes gave rise to tactical coalitions in the name of "orthodox" Islam.

There was a certain unpredictability, however, about the outcomes produced by such alliances. Muslim disputes drew tsarist officials and institutions into the mediation of these conflicts. They implicated Russian officialdom in Muslim religious and family affairs, even though the state had proclaimed the goal of separating civil and Islamic jurisdictions. These interactions yielded shifting alliances with clerics and laypeople, bringing legal victories for some but state penetration of the mahalla for all. While the regime gained a foothold in these communities through the adjudication of such disputes, these processes showed that the capacity to intervene in family life among this population hinged on Islamic law.

At midcentury, laypeople represented an indispensable part of the imperial contest over Islamic authority, but they were now joined by a new set of actors. The guarding of Islamic morality rested on police power in villages and towns where Muslims lived. At the same time, ultimate authority in mediating Islamic legal controversies increasingly resided in St. Petersburg. This arrangement sometimes undermined the Orenburg Assembly and local Islamic leaders, though it offered litigants defeated in the locales a fresh venue.

By the 1850s the Ministry of Internal Affairs and its Oriental studies scholars regularly intervened in family conflicts and overturned judgments of the Orenburg Assembly. In the next decade, they succeeded in having appointed as Orenburg mufti a Muslim nobleman, Salimgarei Tevkelev (in office 1865–1885), rather than an esteemed Islamic scholar.[84] This choice was the culmination of the anticlerical turn in policy toward Islam and further weakened the power of the Islamic establishment to meet the challenge of experts in St. Petersburg. In ruling this vast empire, the scholarly analysis of texts—preferably by non-Muslim specialists—seemed to offer a more authentic guide to Islam's ostensibly fixed codes than Muslim intermediaries, who, after all, had trouble agreeing with one another. The regime thereby remained wedded to Islamic law as the necessary form of discipline for the Muslim family. The shari'a remained an indispensable pillar of the empire, even if best veiled from Europe's view.

4

NOMADS INTO MUSLIMS

Through regulation of the Muslim family, the tsarist regime gave impetus to novel understandings of the Islamic tradition. Unsatisfied with contradictory pronouncements from various intermediaries, the bureaucracy sought out sources that revealed the shari'a, not as a malleable system of ethics and moral injunctions, but as a rigid code of law that Russian officials could administer without the aid of Muslim informants. Emerging out of interactions between litigants and the bureaucracy, a more uniform and disciplined Hanafi legalism derived by Oriental studies experts from a narrow set of texts channeled police power into the mosque community on behalf of clerics and litigants who succeeded in appealing to such visions of law. This new emphasis on the certainty of scriptural norms yielded unsettling effects. The redefinition of what was authentically "Islamic" in terms of a limited selection of texts and fixed rules raised questions about the religiosity of tsarist subjects who understood the faith differently, and even called into question Catherine the Great's original vision for the unruly eastern frontier.

This chapter explores the conquest of the steppe east of the Orenburg frontier as a turning point in imperial policy toward Islam. Beginning in the 1730s a number of elites from the three Kazakh tribal
confederations, or hordes, inhabiting the north Caspian steppe had
sworn oaths of loyalty to Russia based on the Islamic faith. From the
late eighteenth century, the regime had supported the spread of Islam among these nomads. Catherine recognized that the Kazakhs
had not embraced Islam in the same manner as the Tatars on the
Volga River but was convinced that, with regular access to mosques
and Islamic schools and with the assistance of the Tatars, they might
adopt a more "civilized" way of life, turning to trade, agriculture,
and a disciplined monotheism.[1] Catherine had wagered that her patronage of Islam would ultimately transform the steppe, turning pastoralists into farmers and raiders into loyal artisans and merchants.
However, the cultivation of Islam was a central element of steppe
frontier policy only before the tsars came to fully control the region.
Seen through the lens of the emergent Hanafi orthodoxy, the peoples of the steppe now appeared in a different light. Their religion, to
the extent that one could be identified according to the new criteria,
scarcely resembled the faith of the other Muslim peoples of the empire. Here the regime confronted yet another difficulty. Like the
Uniate Church, which the emperor Paul (r. 1796–1801) is said to
have dismissed as "neither fish nor fowl," the religion of the Kazakh
nomads did not fit easily into the classificatory schemes of the Russian authorities. Was the regime bound to tolerate a faith that was
alien to this people? Had toleration in the steppe amounted to trea-
sonous conversion of would-be Christians to Islam?

Tsarist expansion in the nineteenth century lent a new cast to
Russia's centuries-old encounter with the steppe. As tsarist forces extended a line of fortresses from Orenburg and Omsk toward the Syr
Darya river in Transoxiana in the 1840s and 1850s, the state began to
assume responsibility for the administration of the nomadic peoples

Figure 5 A Russian official and his family with Kazakh elders. Courtesy of George Kennan Papers, Manuscript Division, Library of Congress, LC-USZ62-128111.

of the steppe. The extension of tsarist rule over the grazing lands of the Kazakhs brought into the steppe Cossacks, soldiers, Slavic colonists, and administrators like the Russian official shown in Figure 5 with his family and an assembly of Kazakh notables in front of a nomadic tent. Once divided into three confederations, the Kazakhs now found themselves ruled from the Orenburg governor-generalship, Siberia, and the khanate of Kokand, which expanded north from the densely populated Ferghana and Syr Darya valleys. In the 1860s, further Russian offensives brought some two and a half million Kazakhs under tsarist rule. The arrival of the Russian administrators and settlers initiated a period of turmoil in the steppe. Natural disasters—such as droughts and apocalyptic storms—heightened competition for access to grazing lands. Kazakhs struggled to survive these harsh conditions; many of them were forced to give up herding to settle permanently. Relations with the Russians were also tense. Colonization, a chaotic affair managed haphazardly by administrators, put many Kazakhs at risk for survival. Elite families adapted better than others, and the sons of notables gained access to Russian educational institutions. At the same time, for many Kazakhs, more was at stake than their herds and pastures. Disputes about religion became yet another feature of the steppe world turned upside down by incorporation in the empire.[2]

Officials rethought their approach toward Islam in the steppe as they took on the direct administration of this space. In the second quarter of the nineteenth century, they began questioning the fundamental assumptions behind Catherine's policies. First, Russian ethnographers and Kazakh informants cast doubt on the nomads' affiliation with Islam. They claimed that the state had erred in introducing the faith among a people who lacked any understanding of religion or who had only little sympathy for Islam. Many of these same observers called on the state to support the conversion of Kazakhs to Christianity rather than Islam. Second, officials who had been involved with both the Kazakhs and Muslims from the Orenburg and Volga regions now concluded that Catherine's policy had been mistaken in treating Islam as a bulwark of the state.

Without abandoning support for Islamic institutions elsewhere in the empire, tsarist authorities revised their policies of religious toleration for the steppe. They opted to treat the Kazakhs as a special case, distinguishing them from both Muslims in the neighboring Orenburg region and the settled Muslim populations of Central Asia. Once convinced that the Kazakhs were not truly Muslims, Russians looked to Kazakh customary law (*adat*) and the clan elders who administered it to perform many of the same tasks that they had elsewhere assigned the shari'a and Muslim clerics. These new administrative ideas also found resonance in the Northern Caucasus, where in the 1860s the Russians finally overcame the mountaineers and established administrative control. There, too, officials seized upon the possibility of using ostensibly secular custom in place of the shari'a to link local communities to tsarist administration.[3]

In the steppe, officials confronted communities deeply divided by questions of religious identity. Kazakhs identified themselves as Muslims in some contexts, but 'ulama from beyond the steppe and even some Kazakhs themselves faulted the migratory lifestyle that kept these nomads from constructing their own mosques and schools. In the eyes of their critics, they neglected prayers, education, fasting, pilgrimage, and other Islamic duties. Many mullahs viewed the Kazakhs as a people badly in need of instruction about the strict fulfillment of the shari'a norms deemed orthodox in the madrasas of the Volga region and Transoxiana.

Faced with competing claims from the Kazakhs themselves about their religious identities, tsarist officials aligned themselves with like-minded Kazakhs who shared their goal of directing the Kazakhs away from Islam. From midcentury, the state became a central actor in a struggle already under way among the Kazakhs between proponents of the shari'a and guardians of custom, adat. Some Russophone Kazakhs defended Islam as an instrument to bring "enlightenment" to the steppe; others questioned Catherine's use of Tatar teachers and missionaries to pursue her goal of civilizing these nomads. Kazakhs who rejected Islam and Tatar influence became the allies of administrators who sought to establish their own authority in the regulation of everyday life in the steppe. In conjunction with these native informants and the factions of Kazakh elders who backed them, regional governors advocated state support for secular customary law, in place of the shari'a, as a more reliable and useful alternative to government reliance on Muslim men of religion. At the same time, the regime assumed a role in shaping customary law by linking the office of the judge (biy) to government administration. Officials supervised elections and appointments to the position and confirmed or overturned their judgments. From the 1860s, officials became deeply involved in the affairs of these communities. They frequently shaped the outcome of these struggles by endorsing elders who opposed mullahs and their calls for submission to Islamic law.

The incorporation of the Kazakhs into the empire redrew the boundaries of religious toleration. Tsarist law granted non-Orthodox communities "freedom of religion," including the right to arrange marriage and family matters according to the rules of their faiths. In the steppe, however, local officials challenged Kazakh recourse to Islamic law and severely restricted access to mullahs and holy men from the Volga and Urals regions as well as from Transoxiana. Between the 1850s and 1890s, officials tried to suppress transregional religious contacts without publicly renouncing the basic principles of toleration, which they continued to value as a means to gain leverage in neighboring Muslim lands. For the sake of imperial order, moreover, the Russians feared the confrontations that an open abandonment of toleration might incite.

Governors undermined the general statutes on toleration with administrative decrees that closed mosques and schools. But in doing so, they deprived themselves of the regulatory apparatus that accompanied toleration throughout the rest of the empire. Their treatment of religious institutions and Muslim networks in the territory impeded the formation of links between Muslims and the state. At the turn of the century, these administrative measures alienated Kazakh elites and commoners alike. Joined by Muslims throughout the empire, they responded with increasing demands for legal rights, including access to mosques, Islamic schools, and the ability to live in accordance with the shari'a. Together with the colonization of their pasture lands by Slavic settlers, such policies weakened the local presence of the regime, making its hold on the steppe increasingly precarious.[4] Fearing unrest and the unsupervised activities of Muslim clerics, at the turn of the century the government responded by returning, but only partially, to pairing toleration with hierarchical oversight.

Russia's challenges in the steppe resembled those of other modernizing states confronting nomadic populations. Between the late eighteenth and mid-nineteenth centuries, the tsarist state acted much like its Muslim rivals. In the Ottoman empire and later in Afghanistan, centralizing regimes limited the autonomy of mobile communities. They imposed taxes and military duties, and promoted sedentary agriculture. The expansion of officially sponsored religious institutions—what the Ottoman administrator Osman Nuri Paşa called the "civilizing fold of the Şeriat [Islamic law]"—was critical to the penetration of the state into autonomous tribal areas.[5]

The imposition of legal norms elaborated by official religious establishments in these states, as in the north Caspian steppe, rested on claims about religious orthodoxy and authenticity. Like the Kabyle in North Africa, Kazakhs were regarded by neighboring Muslims (and in modern ethnographic literature, by themselves) as imperfect Muslims.[6] Such thinking shaped French, British, and Russian colonial policies on behalf of the secular "custom" of the tribe and against Islamic law, but they should not be taken at face value as evidence of Kazakh irreligiosity or impiety.[7] The controversies surrounding Kazakh religion reveal instead the ascendance of a more exclusive understanding of Islamic orthodoxy in the minds of ethnographers, officials, imperial informants, and intermediaries. In practice, such normative notions did not always gain state backing. Nor did they preclude religious change and the continual elaboration of distinctively Kazakh Muslim identities. As Allen Frank has shown, Kazakhs experienced a kind of "Islamic transformation" under Russian rule in the nineteenth century.[8] Kazakh notables initiated contacts with neighboring Muslim scholars, recruiting them to train their children. Kazakh parents sent their children to regional centers of Islamic learning and piety, such as Semipalatinsk and Petropavlovsk, or to madrasas in Kargala, Astrakhan, and Troitsk. They consumed Islamic literature, including poetic works relating the lives of major Islamic figures, printed in inexpensive editions in Kazan and Orenburg. Many even began to rework their ancestral affiliations, remembering Muslim ancestors in place of others. Despite contentious disputes among tsarist officials and shifts in policy, in the late nineteenth and early twentieth centuries the Pax Russica continued to sustain conditions that fostered the spread of new forms of Islamic piety in the steppe.

Civilization through Islam

Under Catherine, state elites associated Islam with civility. As part of her plans for the pacification of the southeastern borderlands, the state sponsored the construction of mosques and Islamic schools staffed by Tatar teachers.[9] The establishment of institutions rooted in a monotheistic and cosmopolitan religion appeared to offer an economical and enlightened way to settle and civilize the Kazakhs. Besides blocking the influence of the Ottoman sultan, the cultivation of Islam would turn the Kazakhs away from cattle-stealing and slaving raids on other restive frontier subjects, including the Bashkirs, Kalmyks, and Russians.

Through the mosque and the school, imperial rule was to "instill in [the Kazakhs] humanity and better manners."[10] The agents of imperial rule were to include men of religion recruited from the towns and villages of the Volga region and the Orenburg territory, including the first mufti of the Orenburg Assembly. The regime called on its Muslim subjects to show the Kazakhs the benefits of an industrious and moral life under tsarist protection. But Kazakhs were not simply the passive objects of this imperial strategy of Islamicization. From the late eighteenth century, they petitioned Russian authorities to permit Muslims from the Volga and Orenburg regions to live among them as religious scholars.[11]

Catherine expressed certainty that new mosques would "attract other nomads inhabiting [the area] near our borders." She suggested that the cultivation of Islam "might with time be more effective in imposing discipline than more severe measures." The empress also proposed the construction of "Tatar schools on the example of those in Kazan" and caravansaries alongside mosques, which were to take on a "decorous" appearance with the construction of stone fences around them. According to this plan, future mosques were to be built in the most accessible locations to accommodate up to fifteen hundred people. The local governor, Osip Igel'strom, called for the appointment of mullahs "from among the loyal people of the Kazan Tatars" to "various Kazakh clans [rody]" as a means to inculcate "loyalty to us and to dissuade them from raiding and pillaging on our borders." In the following year, Catherine called "very useful and necessary" the division of the steppe into three parts, with towns to be constructed in each, together with "mosques for their main clans, schools, and markets."[12]

Alexander I continued Catherine's policy of treating Islam as a means to transform Kazakhs into imperial subjects. Licensed mullahs and other official men of religious learning and piety played a pivotal role. Scholars and merchants from Kargala, the Tatar village near Orenburg, supplied the imperial regime with a host of intermediaries. At frontier trading posts and in the mobile Kazakh encampments, these Tatars translated for Russian officials, recorded various transactions, arbitrated disputes among Kazakhs and Russians, and negotiated diplomatic agreements.[13] From Ufa, the Orenburg mufti issued roughly a dozen fatwas enjoining Muslims to take up agriculture. Most important for tsarist authorities, licensed imams like Mukhammed Mukhamedov administered oaths on the Qur'an to Kazakh elders, binding them as "loyal subjects" to the tsar.[14]

Tsarist strategy bore fruit at the beginning of the nineteenth century when a Chingisid khan named Bukei fled one of the Kazakh tribal confederacies, the Small Horde, with several thousand tents and settled between the lower tributaries of the Volga and Ural rivers, where many took up "useful" trades like commerce and agriculture. Though the government divided supervision of these communities between the military governor of Astrakhan and the Orenburg Frontier Commission, St. Petersburg accorded the khan broad autonomy in organizing the internal affairs of the communities, which later came to be known as the "Bukei" or "Inner Horde." There the founding of Islamic institutions accompanied patronage of agriculture, artisanry, and trade as well as the development of a bureaucratic administrative structure. Muslims from outside the horde contributed to this process, and the khan devoted special attention to the recruitment of Tatar mullahs. In 1811 Bukei petitioned the foreign minister, Count N. P. Rumiantsev, seeking legal status for three Tatar clerics. Having escaped captivity at the hands of other Kazakhs in the region of Bukhara and having married Kazakh women, Tatars had taken up posts as mullahs among Bukei's Kazakhs. The numbers of such mullahs rose to 126 by the late 1840s.[15]

Bukei's son Dzhangir founded a hierarchical organization of 'ulama patterned on the Orenburg Assembly, an institution to which the khan was connected by marriage to the daughter of the first mufti.[16] The tsarist government confirmed one of these clerics as an akhund to head this institution. Besides examining the qualifications of candidates who aspired to positions as licensed mullahs, the akhund propagated religious knowledge among the Kazakhs. Patents bearing the stamp of Dzhangir and the chief akhund instructed mullahs to "build mosques and schools" and "celebrate weekly and annual holidays." Dzhangir's directives emphasized the importance of literacy and enjoined the daily performance of prayer and the keeping of fasts. The khan ordered these official mullahs to lead the people in prayer and to deliver "exhortations to the simple Kazakhs" in accordance with a model to be given them by the akhund. They were to instruct the "simple and ignorant Kazakhs in all rules of our religion," assign Muslim names to newborns, and perform circumcisions, marriages, and burials.

Marriage practices were to come under particular scrutiny. The khan directed his mullahs to challenge customary practices like that of bridegrooms going "to their fiancées before the wedding, according to the former Kazakh custom." Dzhangir's new rules governed exchange of kalym and the remarriage of widows (now made dependent upon the consent of both mother and father). In the same spirit, the mullahs of the Inner Horde were to persuade the wealthy to pay alms (zakat). They were to dissuade the "simple and ignorant" from committing violence and theft and urge them "to honor, respect and always be loyal to the Sovereign Emperor and his officials."[17] Like the Orenburg mufti, the khan and his akhund were to cultivate Islam as an institution of social discipline and as a way to keep order in the family and sanctify Kazakh ties to the Russian tsar.

Though the Inner Horde was settled on Russian imperial territory, Dzhangir ruled like a Muslim sovereign. The ceremony marking his elevation to the position of khan of the Inner Horde in 1824 in the town of Ural'sk was orchestrated by tsarist authorities but consecrated by the swearing of an official religious oath and the kissing of the Qur'an under the supervision of a Muslim cleric. When he issued rules in 1836 regulating market behavior, Dzhangir warned that "drunkenness cannot be tolerated among Muslims according to our religious law," advising Russians and others to "behave themselves decently, without allowing insults, quarrels, and fights" arising from this vice. His officials even collected an Islamic tax (zakat), though it did not meet with universal approval. Mullahs complained to Dzhangir that elders resisted all charity, and that "the simple people, due to the ignorance characteristic of the Kazakh, do not obey."[18] The khan also cultivated ties to the Russian bureaucracy and university. He sent the children of elites to Russian schools, though he also promoted Islamic education for these students. In 1842 Dzhangir proposed the appointment of a scholar from Kargala, Sadreddin Aminov, to provide young Kazakhs selected for study in the gymnasiums of the imperial capital with a preparatory education at the headquarters of the khan in "Arabic, Persian, Tatar, and Russian" as well as in "elementary sciences and the Muslim law." Dzhangir himself acted as patron of book publishing. On a trip through Kazan in 1844, he persuaded Professor Kazem-Bek to publish a Hanafi legal text (the *Mukhtasar al-vikayet*), a publication that the khan hoped to distribute among the Kazakhs and Kazem-Bek intended to make "useful for the Orientalists of Europe." The Inner Horde became both a consumer and a supplier of Kazem-Bek's renowned publications and other books from the printing presses of Kazan University, while Dzhangir collected dozens of Turkic, Persian, and Arabic manuscripts for the library of the university, where he was awarded the title "honored member." By 1840 the elite surrounding the khan included figures like twenty-eight-year-old Kubbulsyn-khodzha Karaulov. Claiming descent from a saintly lineage, Karaulov represented a new generation formed by an imperial military education under Nicholas. At the Nepliuev Military Institute he had studied "French, German, Russian, Arabic, Persian, and Tatar; sciences—history, geography, arithmetic, Russian literature, the basic principles of mathematics, physics, and natural history."[19]

Nicholas I, too, encouraged the Kazakhs to adopt the orthodox norms championed by the regime's Islamic institutions. Orthodox Christian missionaries and some local officials objected to state involvement in the promotion of Islam among the Kazakhs, but central government officials remained convinced of the connection between the development of sedentary life and the cultivation of what they believed to be normative Islamic practices. In 1851, A. Evreinov, a tsarist official, showered praise upon Dzhangir for promoting the transition from pastoralism to farming and trade.[20]

Muslims, Manichaeans, and Pagans

The extension of tsarist administration across the southeastern frontier and the incorporation of the Kazakhs confronted the state with complex challenges to arrangements worked out in St. Petersburg and Ufa for the organization of Islam. Not only did officials face the difficulty of integrating a vast population of clan-oriented pastoralists, but the religion of these newest subjects unsettled the conceptual certainties that underlay the hierarchical structures of religious toleration. Tsarist officials faced conflicting theories about the Kazakhs' religion, which they understood to be closely tied to the nomadic way of life.

Judging Kazakh society against impressions of Islam formed in the emergent centers of orthodoxy like Istanbul and Kazan, officials and experts under Nicholas I and Alexander II searched in vain for the conventional markers of Islam as they knew it. The Kazakhs seemed to lack both mosque and clergy. Ethnographers applied comparative schemes that relied on normative and objectified notions of religion.[21] Most of them even rejected the self-identification of many Kazakhs as Muslims, regarding them instead as a people indifferent to religion. Local officials seized on what they supposed to be the absence of religion among the Kazakhs as evidence that this people stood ready for a form of state-directed transformation unthinkable among other subjects in the grip of "Muhammadanism." Some scholars argued that they differed from pagans only because Catherine's steppe policy had exposed them to Islam. From midcentury, local officials joined bishops in the Orenburg region in lobbying for a rejection of the policies inherited from the empress. They argued that her patronage of Islam had outlived its day as a strategy to pacify the southeastern frontiers. In the meantime, provincial officials moved closer to the position of Orthodox prelates, who disparaged Islam as a force that opposed state interests.

Early in the reign of Nicholas I, provincial officials had reacted with alarm to mass renunciation of Orthodox Christianity and the flight to Islam among baptized inhabitants (or their descendants) in Turkic and Finno-Ugric language communities.[22] Officials prohibited any confessional change, other than baptism into the "preeminent and predominant" Orthodox Church, which enjoyed the exclusive right to proselytize, and they accused the "Muhammadan clergy" and the Orenburg Assembly of inciting this religious change. They were confirmed in their attitudes in the 1830s when news of Shamil's war against tsarist rule in the Northern Caucasus reached the Volga and Urals regions.

From the 1850s, relations with the Ottoman empire and developments elsewhere in the Islamic world figured into arguments against continued Russian state patronage of Muslim institutions.[23] The experiences of European powers reinforced tsarist elites' anxieties about "fanaticism" and "hatred of Christians" as the forces animating Muslim rebellion and misrule everywhere. Resistance to French rule in Algeria, the 1857 "mutiny" in British India, and Muslim rebellion in the Qing empire all attracted the attention of the reading public. At the same time, Pan-Slav intellectuals depicted conflicts with the Ottomans, as in the Crimean War of 1853–1856 and the Russo-Turkish War of 1877–1878, as symptoms of a universal struggle between Orthodox Christianity and Islam.

Within Russia, the development of new academic disciplines came to play a role in the reformulation of religious policies. Ethnographers and geographers built upon the work of their forerunners in the natural sciences. The proliferation of classificatory descriptions of the lands, peoples, flora, and fauna of the empire in the 1830s and 1840s differed from earlier projects not only in their range and scope but also, more importantly, in their orientation. Often sponsored by the Ministry of Internal Affairs, the authors of such studies believed that scholarly knowledge would facilitate more systematic and efficient forms of police administration and economic development.[24] Institutionalized in the Imperial Russian Geographical Society in the 1840s, ethnography cast the heterogeneous confessions of the empire in a new light. Ethnographers offered their studies to administrators, but ethnographic description was susceptible to reinterpretation in the tsarist chancelleries. Ethnographic knowledge was only one of several variables available to policymakers. The perspective of imperial informants and, above all, police concern with order were more frequently decisive in shaping policies. ⌐

The first major study devoted exclusively to the Kazakhs appeared in 1832 and became the primary point of reference for imperial administrators. Aleksei Levshin's *Description of the Kirgiz-Kazakh, or the Kirgiz-Kasak Hordes and the Steppes* expressed skepticism about the true character of Kazakh religion. "What is your religion?" Levshin recounted asking two Kazakh informants. "We do not know," they replied. He claimed that "the majority of their compatriots" offered the same response, leading him to conclude that it was indeed difficult "to decide what the Kazakhs are: Muhammadans, Manichaeans, or pagans?" The Kazakhs had an understanding of a "Supreme Being," he observed, and many of them "worship according to the Qur'an," but "others mix the teaching of *Islam* [*Islamizm*] with the remnants of ancient idolatry." Still others believed that human life is overseen by a "good deity" named "*Khudai*" and an "evil spirit" known as "*Shaitan,* the source of evil."[25]

Despite the confused amalgamation of three distinct religious sys-

tems in these beliefs, for Levshin the true measure of Kazakh religious ignorance lay in their resort to various "spirits," "sorcerers,"
and "fortune-tellers." Observers of Kazakh life in earlier periods, like
the German naturalist Peter Simon Pallas, had recorded the prominence among the Kazakhs of men who worked cures and predicted
the future. But observers had not portrayed these individuals as central to Kazakh religion. Indeed, in Pallas's account they largely stood
outside Kazakh religion; they enjoyed their position in the steppe
only due to the paucity of "Muhammadan clergy" there.[26] For Levshin, however, Kazakh belief in magical forces represented a contamination of religion generally. Just as he maintained that no legitimate religion should bear traces of "magic" or "superstition,"
Levshin refused to recognize as anything other than "Manichaean"
his informants' reference to *Khudai* (perhaps from *Khodā*, "God" in
Persian) and *Shaitan* ("Satan").

Levshin nonetheless decided that the "Muhammadan religion"
was the most important element in this "mixing up of various confessions." Though he saw Kazakhs as lacking the "fanaticism" that he
identified with Muslims elsewhere, he believed that traces of Islam
among the Kazakhs accounted for their hostility toward "unbelievers," including Christians, Buddhists, and Shi'ites (even though he
claimed the Kazakhs had only a dim understanding of the differences separating Sunnis and Shi'ites). Discounting the concern of
many Kazakhs for daily prayers and fasting, Levshin focused instead
on polygamy as the essential tenet of Islam that Kazakhs had embraced most fully.[27]

Having cast doubt on the coherence and seriousness of Kazakh religious convictions, Levshin's contradictory but influential *Description* bolstered critics of tsarist policy. Given the scarcity of "zealous
Muslims" among them, he reasoned, "*Islam* might completely die
out," were it not for the "clerics" who acted as its sole proponents.
He stressed that these clerics were outsiders to Kazakh society. Some

came from the towns of Bukhara, Khiva, and Turkestan. Others held appointments sponsored by the Russian government as scribes for khans and clan chieftains. Levshin's assertions about Kazakh indifference to religion in general and Islam in particular outlived the author; and his portrayal of itinerant and state-sanctioned mullahs as the treacherous purveyors of an alien—and politically subversive— tradition among credulous pastoralists had a lasting impact. Imperial officials and Orthodox churchmen used his claims as empirical evidence against state support for Islam. Under Nicholas I, Levshin's work became paradigmatic in academic circles. Yet claims based on ethnography alone failed to displace established administrative practices.

More important than ethnographers were Kazakh informants. With the establishment in the early 1840s of Russian schools in frontier settlements and the entry of Kazakhs into the regular ranks of the military, sons of notables emerged as both intermediaries and allies of Russian proponents of an activist state role in the transformation of the steppe. In mediating interactions between indigenous elites and officialdom, some informants presented evidence of local customs and mores that made Islam appear foreign to the Kazakhs. But this society and the informants who spoke for them were divided. Even Kazakhs who had advanced through the ranks of Russian education and military service were split on the question of Islam. Some portrayed the religion as a danger to tsarist rule; others championed the link between the spread of Islam and the development of Kazakh society. Whereas military officer and ethnographer Chokan Valikhanov insisted on the irreligiosity of his people, Mukhammad-Salikh Babadzhanov focused on the Inner Horde and the leadership of Dzhangir to chart the parallel advance of "progress" and Islamic education.

In a letter of December 1860 published in the *Northern Bee*, a St. Petersburg daily, Babadzhanov, an advisor to the administration of the Inner Horde, avowed that "in the soul of every Kazakh is a Muhammadan of the Sunni sect." This fact went unnoticed, he said, because of his co-religionists' "shaky knowledge of the rules of religion, which they combined with popular habits." Tatar mullahs had been importing literacy and knowledge since the 1830s, but Babadzhanov criticized as "brutality" the pedagogy of these mullahs, whom he treated as interlopers. He reserved his praise for Dzhangir and the school that the khan established at his headquarters. There, in addition to the "rules of the Muhammadan religion," Kazakh children studied the Russian language. For the improvement of the "moral life"' of the horde and the "development of their mental capabilities," he credited its khans: Bukei had resolved to lead "our Kazakhs" from the steppe to the territory of Astrakhan, "where they acquired a gentle disposition," and Dzhangir, "by his own example of zeal and fervor for the study of Tatar reading and writing, the rules of Islam, and the Russian tongue and script, demonstrated to the Kazakhs that study is degrading to no one and is never too late." Islam, Babadzhanov argued, brought "enlightenment" to the Kazakhs and made them better Russian subjects.[28]

While Babadzhanov defended Islam among the Kazakhs in the press of the capitals, officials in Orenburg challenged the claim that Islam had advanced the cause of enlightenment in the steppe. The ambitious Vasilii V. Grigor'ev sought to make his mark by reorienting policy away from its reliance upon Islam. A newcomer to the frontier, Grigor'ev arrived in Orenburg in 1852 after training as an Orientalist in Odessa and St. Petersburg. He had served in the Department of Religious Affairs of Foreign Confessions within the Ministry of Internal Affairs before assuming other ministerial posts; he also served as one of the principal figures in the Imperial Russian Geographical Society.[29] Upon arrival in Orenburg, Grigor'ev received orders to investigate charges of corruption leveled against the leadership of the Bukei Horde. When authorities in St. Petersburg directed him to investigate Dzhangir's family after the khan's death in 1845, Grigor'ev distinguished himself as a vigilant guardian of the state's interest against figures in local government whom he dismissed as neglectful in their supervision of the horde.

The scholar had not served long in his new assignment before he managed, despite the khan's reputation as a "loyal agent of civilization and defender of Russian principles in the horde," to uncover the damage caused by him and his family, who, in the words of Grigor'ev's biographer, constituted "an evil" inflicted upon Russia that surpassed the damage wrought by all of their predecessors put together. "Vestiges of immorality" were Dzhangir's legacy. Worse than laying personal claim to the more than one million acres occupied by the horde, Grigor'ev maintained, Dzhangir had served "his own interests" in converting the Kazakhs to "Muhammadanism, about which they had no idea before him." He had succeeded in "impregnating" the "upper class" with "the ignorant Muslim pride that is hostile to Christianity and enlightenment." In pursuit of this end, Grigor'ev charged, Dzhangir had cultivated "a whole army of mullahs," "the class of the population of the horde, which is the most immoral and hostile to the Russian government." Combining self-interest and "fanaticism," the "cunning" Dzhangir had been the first of the Kazakh khans to compel the collection of the Islamic zakat in addition to the formerly voluntary Kazakh tax, the *sugum*.[30]

Grigor'ev's contribution to frontier administration lay in his assertion that some good could come of Dzhangir's "evil." Disillusioned by the khan's misrule, Kazakhs had come to rely on "conscientious Russian bureaucrats." This development led Grigor'ev to infer, according to his biographer, that "the horde would be capable of quietly accepting any transformation, all possible rapprochement [*sblizhenie*] with the imperial system, as long as it is carried out carefully and with skill."[31]

A Kazakh informant reinforced Grigor'ev's argument. Chokan

Valikhanov combined his linguistic skills and Russian military cadet education to become the most prominent interpreter of Kazakh society in the 1860s. He earned the confidence of the writer Fyodor Dostoevsky, who praised him as "the first Kazakh with a fully European education" and expressed his "love" for him. The son of a notable from the Inner Horde who had entered imperial service in the 1830s, Valikhanov collected intelligence and produced ethnographic knowledge about the peoples of the steppe and oasis towns of Central Asia for the military and Asiatic Department of the Ministry of Foreign Affairs. He seems to have regarded Alexander Kazem-Bek as a rival; his colleague Khusain Faizkhanov complained in a letter to Valikhanov from the capital in 1863 that "Kazembek is translating the canons of Muhammad and making himself out to be an aristocrat."[32] He used his status as both a claimant to the line of Chingiz Khan and a scholar of the European discipline of ethnography to argue for a wholesale reorientation of tsarist policy toward the nomads.

Valikhanov called for direct state intervention in the steppe and official commitment to the active "spread of European enlightenment." In a memorandum composed in late 1863 or early 1864, he warned against support for Islamic institutions and personnel among the Kazakhs: "Islam cannot help the Russian or any other Christian government, [and] one cannot count on the loyalty of a mercenary Tatar clergy." Drawing on his recent study "Traces of Shamanism among the Kazakhs," Valikhanov maintained that Islam remained an alien and marginal force that "has still not eaten into our flesh and blood." Though Islam threatened "the division of the people in the future," he explained, a "period of dual faith [*dvoeverie*]" still prevailed in the steppe, "like that in Rus' during the time of the venerable Nestor." Resembling Russians in ancient times, the Kazakhs remained pagans at heart.[33]

Valikhanov's rise coincided with the fundamental restructuring of imperial institutions in the "Great Reforms" after Russian defeat in the Crimean War. Following the abolition of serfdom, the government of Alexander II planned major judicial reforms.[34] These included the establishment of courts that would expand the reach of imperial law on a more uniform basis throughout the empire. Valikhanov opposed the encroachment of imperial law, however, by appealing to a long-standing principle in the restive borderlands. He suggested that the practice of administration through "customary law" might be a pragmatic alternative to the state promotion of Islam and a promising vehicle for the gradual integration of the Kazakhs into mainstream life in the empire.

The officially sanctioned practice of customary law had a lengthy history in the administration both of Orthodox peasant communities and of indigenous groups inhabiting the borderlands. As early as the second quarter of the eighteenth century, tsarist authorities had directed the tribute-paying peoples of Siberia to adjudicate disputes among themselves before their "elders." Lawmakers later concluded that peoples who differed so much from Orthodox peasants in their beliefs, manners, appearance, and general way of life must have distinctive legal norms as well. The state conferred the right to live according to customary law upon peoples who seemed to occupy a lower level of social organization and who appeared to need protection from more cunning human predators, like Russian colonists and administrators. A decree of 1783 awarded the various peoples inhabiting Irkutsk Province "the freedom to settle civil affairs among themselves orally" before their "elders or elected [people]."[35] Of course, the state maintained its monopoly on the administration of judicial affairs in which it had an interest, and it defended its prerogative to define crimes punishable by the general laws.

In practice, local officials became deeply embroiled in determining which form customary law took in each community. Like their contemporaries in the British East India Company, Russian authorities sought out those indigenous notables and texts that appeared to preserve knowledge about local "laws and customs." In Bengal, administrators translated and compiled texts in search of a compendium of rule-based "Hindoo" and "Muhammadan" law to aid British colonials in policing indigenous legal personnel.[36] Tsarist bureaucrats pursued similar sources. In Siberia, they solicited authoritative texts from indigenous contacts. Russians hoped these records would help them sort out appeals and the conflicting assertions advanced by "dissatisfied" interpreters of customary legal norms. Tsarist officials were from the outset implicated in the elaboration of customary law. By entertaining petitions from dissatisfied litigants, they created an appellate mechanism, making governors and police key actors in the definition and implementation of customary legal norms.[37]

Mikhail Speranskii's Siberian statute of 1822 made the discovery of these legal norms a collaborative project between bureaucrats and indigenous informants.[38] Officials collected information from "distinguished natives," and a state committee sifted through them to ascertain which of the "laws and customs" seemed most appropriate for the administrative purposes of the regime. Finally, at a stage three steps removed from the native assembly, the governor-general confirmed or rejected the committee's selection of legal materials. The laws "characteristic to each tribe" were then to be administered by "elders" and others chosen by the community. Tsarist officials oversaw their work and applied the rules derived from this joint effort.

Among the Kazakhs, Valikhanov acted as a key protagonist in defining the "customary law" that emerged from fierce competition among elders and other Kazakhs. In the early 1860s the central ministries discussed introducing a new system, a form of mixed court, the "justice of the peace court" (*mirovoi sud*). Originally intended for peasants and townspeople following the abolition of serfdom, it consisted of an elected justice of the peace who presided over civil suits and tried petty criminal cases on the basis of the imperial law or customary legal norm that he judged most appropriate. But in 1864 Valikhanov composed a memorandum arguing for the retention of the Kazakh court of elders based on customary law, instead of the mixed court. Invoking John Stuart Mill, Valikhanov urged caution in the pursuit of reform and advised attention to the study of the "mental, moral, and political qualities" of the people to be affected. "The conditions of the tribal organism, of environment, climate, and soil should always be at the forefront," he insisted, "for all human inducements and motives are conditioned by the combined influence of physical and social factors."[39]

Recent European history had illustrated the perils of applying theories that ran contrary to the spirit of a people. Russian history, too, had produced its negative models of this kind of reform: "It is not without reason that our contemporary historians attribute all of our social ills and anomalies to the shattering and anti-national spirit of the Petrine reform." But Valikhanov dissociated himself from a "narrow [theory] of nationality [*narodnost'*]" that celebrated particularism for its own sake. He argued instead that "the acquisition of European, universal enlightenment and the energetic struggle with obstacles that hinder attainment of this goal should form the end goal of every people capable of development and culture."[40]

An avid student of ethnographic theory, Valikhanov was sensitive to the complex interdependence of culture and biology. He maintained that "culture can change the organism of a person for the better, like cultured nurturing improves the stock of domestic animals." "In order to make the Kazakhs capable of the apprehension of European ideas of change," Valikhanov advised, "one must first develop his skull and nervous system by means of education." Introduced in the Kazakh steppe in 1824, Speranskii's reforms had lacked such an understanding, according to Valikhanov. The most recent committee established in 1852 to solicit "popular opinion" from "distinguished" Kazakhs as the basis for judicial reform among Siberian Kazakhs risked producing an equally harmful outcome. "Popular opinion" he dismissed as "nothing other than the babble of foolish children."[41]

Valikhanov denounced as self-interested the assertions made to the committee by "a privileged class of the Kazakh people." First, he explained that the campaign to solicit information from Kazakhs had been severely flawed. "Indifference," "ignorance and incomprehension of their interests," and mistrust of the government had all combined to taint responses to the committee's questions about Kazakh legal customs. Second, not all respondents agreed. The "popular masses" wanted their "court of biys" to remain in its "ancient popular form," while "the office-holding, titled, and wealthy Kazakhs" clamored for recognition as "justices of the peace" or "judicial officials." Although Russian officials on the investigating committee welcomed the elders' appeals for the "reform" of Kazakh judicial life, Valikhanov rejected their responses to official queries as "intrigues" founded on "base motives."[42]

Valikhanov offered instead "statistical and historical facts" about Kazakh legal institutions with the aim of protecting the interests of the largest group of *inorodtsy* in the empire (numbering nearly eight hundred thousand as subjects and another two hundred thousand who had not yet pledged allegiance to St. Petersburg). He concluded that the "most ancient" court of biys "fully corresponds to the present [stage of] development of the Kazakh people." Despite forty years of Russian influence, Valikhanov noted, the court of biys had remained "as it was for hundreds, maybe for a thousand, years before us." The Kazakhs rarely complained about the decisions of these courts or appealed to Russian law, he claimed. The few cases involving complaints against the rulings of biys and resort to imperial courts had involved elites who were "stamped with popular disdain, completely immoral people, who hoped through Russian bureaucrats to rectify by illegal means a case lost in a popular court." More-over, Valikhanov claimed, even Russian litigants and defendants of-ten preferred the court of biys to Russian judicial procedure; in that year alone, dozens of such cases had been handled in this manner in the district of Kokchetav.[43]

He argued that the justice of the peace court proposed by reform-ers for the Kazakh steppe was not the equivalent of the court of biys, as many officials (and some Kazakh elites) had alleged. Unlike these justices, biys were not elected or appointed by anyone and did not receive a fixed salary, meet official qualifications, or serve in a fixed jurisdiction for a set term. Rather, Kazakhs assumed the title *biy* on an informal basis.

The Kazakh scholar likened their authority to that of "poets, scholars, and lawyers" in Europe. There the people regarded Shake-speare and Goethe as great poets, basing their judgment on informal popular opinion, "not on the decrees of governments or on the for-mal elections of the people." A biy acted as a judge only when liti-gants freely turned to him because he enjoyed a "good reputation" *(khoroshee renommée)*. The court of biys differed further from the projected justice of the peace court in that it convened only irregu-larly. In contrast to the new courts, Valikhanov noted, a biy offered an individual ruling only when litigants belonged to his clan *(rod)* and consented to this procedure. The main virtue of the court of biys was the "absence of formality and all official routine." Valik-hanov contended that its informality precluded various kinds of "in-trigue." Litigants were free to choose their own biys, without the burden of official elections that could be manipulated by clan alle-giances and the greed of Russian officials. "Formalism and bureau-cratic routine," he maintained, would bring only "stagnation" to a people for whom these strange laws were still ill-suited. Reform should instead correspond to the "material needs" and "national character" of the population whose improvement was at stake.[44]

He charged previous lawmakers with violating this principle in assigning Muslim mullahs the management of cases involving Kazakh marriage and divorce. In all but the district of Kokchetav, Valikhanov asserted, Kazakhs had responded to inquiries about customary law with the request that "cases about marriages and divorces, now in the charge of the mullahs, be returned as previously to the court of biys." He repeated his contention that the Kazakhs had been Muslims "in name alone" and had formed a "particular Sunni schism [*sunnitskii raskol*] in the Muhammadan world" before becoming subjects of the Russian empire. They had never accepted "Muslim laws," which "were introduced to the steppe by government initiative."[45]

Valikhanov expressed dismay at a policy of "affirming Islam, where it was not fully accepted by the people itself." He accused "the great Speranskii" of acting as the "apostle of Muhammad" in the Siberian steppe because he named mullahs and proposed the construction of mosques and Tatar schools. Marveling at how such a figure had become the "disseminator of such an ignorant and savage teaching," Valikhanov surmised that the only possible explanation lay in the fact that it had been unseemly in Speranskii's day to recognize as Russian subjects a people that had "no religion" or to acknowledge officially a group of "schismatics, even if Muslim." He lamented that Speranskii had judged support for their conversion to Christianity impolitic.

In the meantime, Valikhanov pointed out, the Orenburg frontier administration had begun to take measures to counter the "development of Islam" and had prohibited Tatars from acting as mullahs or residing there for extended periods of time. In Siberia, by contrast, local administration had perpetuated Speranskii's "protective system" in relation to Islam, thanks to which the religion had made "gigantic steps" among the Kazakhs of the region. He believed that "half-literate mullahs from among the Tatars and fanatic emigrants from Central Asia, who present themselves as saints," had engaged in "our moral corruption" with the support of the government. "We must know," Valikhanov warned, "what kind of people among us in the steppe occupy priestly offices, to whom is entrusted the moral state of the Kazakh people and [their] legal proceedings with respect to such a difficult social question as marriage." Inveighing against the Tatars who made up the majority of these mullahs ("swindlers without exception"), he condemned the "dark reign" of a "people ignorant in the highest degree, hardly able to read and write, but infected with dark fanaticism and savage superstition." Appealing to the authority of one of the most renowned Russian Orientalists at midcentury, he noted that Professor Il'ia N. Berezin had shown, through study of the Qur'an and the hadith, that "Islam and education are incompatible, even hostile notions, one supplanting the other." Valikhanov dismissed the possibility of a "reformation in Islam," a religion formed on the "wild barbaric prejudices of nomadic Arabs of the sixth century, the traditions of spiritualists, Yids [*zhidy*], and the assorted hocus-pocus of Persian magicians of the same period."[46]

Worse than the Islam of Turks or Persians, he insisted, Tatar Islam was a form of "Puritanism." "Tatars reject poetry, history, mathematics, philosophy, and all natural sciences," Valikhanov alleged, "regarding them as temptations for the weak human mind, and confine themselves to Muslim scholastics and casuistry alone." From the Tatars, Kazakhs had learned to read books and poems written in the Tatar and Chagatay languages. In turn, this exposed the Kazakhs, Valikhanov speculated, to the teachings of Shamil, the formidable opponent of tsarist rule in the Caucasus, and other kinds of "fanatical chaos."[47]

Valikhanov urged the government to turn from concern with prosecuting cattle and horse theft and "generally disciplining the Kazakh people" to their education and to the scrutiny of the mullahs and dervishes corrupting them. He also proposed another means of re-forming Kazakh marital practices. To curb "the rude custom" of promising Kazakh girls in marriage from a very young age and with-out their consent, the government had assigned the regulation of marriage and divorce to the mullahs. He argued that this mistake could be corrected and the practice reformed even without the me-diation of Muslim clerics. The government could instead compel se-nior sultans and administrators to maintain "strict supervision," "un-der threat of responsibility," so that fathers did not marry off their sons and daughters before a certain age and without their approval. He warned that "police supervision and the spirit of the age" would require time to effect the desired changes and added that the large numbers of complaints and petitions about Kazakh marital disputes had demonstrated that even "the Muslim shari'a was completely powerless against the force of deeply rooted custom." In the interest of impeding the "harmful influence of any ultraclerical direction on the social development of peoples," and combating the mullahs and their "fanaticism," Valikhanov concluded that the state should re-move marriage from the control of Muslim authorities and, "in ac-cordance with the people's demand, leave cases concerning mar-riage and divorce as before to the court of biys, all the more so since for the Muhammadans marriage is not a sacrament."[48]

Valikhanov's goal of preserving the sway of "custom" against the encroachment of Islamic law called for a departure from imperial practice. In each confessional community, the state had reinforced the power of ecclesiastical authorities over family affairs. Among the Kazakhs, however, local clan elders maintained that cases involving marriage and divorce should belong to the court of biys. In antici-pation of a reorganization of law courts among the Cossacks and inorodtsy of western Siberia, the administration of the governor-gen-eralship had recruited Valikhanov to gauge opinion among local elites about possible reactions to the projected reforms. As their replies reveal, Valikhanov's efforts did as much to shape as to reflect the opinion that reached officials.

The Kazakh sultans and biys of the districts of Kokchetav, Akmolinsk, Atbasar, and Baian-Aul expressed the same demands, in nearly identical language, as Valikhanov had articulated in earlier memoranda on the reform of Kazakh customary law courts. All voiced their desire "to preserve intact the customs of our ancestors, which satisfy completely our kin-based way of life." They asked that the government leave their "court of biys and assemblies, which have existed among us since time immemorial, in all their force."[49] In the "spirit of the new statute on the organization of courts and judicial proceedings," however, these informants conceded that "some additions and changes" might be "useful." In each district, they insisted on the broadest jurisdiction for the judicial authority of biys and their application of "custom," though some deferred to the authority of imperial courts in judging many offenses enumerated in the tsarist criminal code.

Though advanced in the name of custom and a traditional "kin-based way of life," the informants' demands concerning marriage and divorce revealed widely varying practices. Elites in the district of Akmolinsk asserted that disputes involving marriage and divorce belonged to the court of biys, though they included the provision that licensed mullahs might participate in appeals. In Atbasar, by contrast, sultans and biys sought support for the displacement of mullahs and Islamic law altogether in language that betrays the imprint of their interviewer, Valikhanov: "Since marriage does not constitute a sacrament among us, but is a simple agreement, we ask then that disputes about marriage and divorce, now adjudicated by licensed mullahs, be left to the adjudication of biys according to [our] own steppe laws and customs." Respondents from Baian-Aul also requested that lawmakers intervene on their behalf. They requested that "disputes about marriage and divorce, which have been up to this time in the

hands of mullahs, be returned to the court of biys." Clan-based notables echoed Valikhanov in turning to the state to solicit assistance
against the mullahs' challenge to the fragile authority of the biys. Appealing to distant tradition, they sought to reverse contemporary
practices and check the power of the spokesmen for shari'a-based legal norms.[50]

Legislation of October 1868 initiated the formal integration of the steppe into the administrative structure of the empire.
It backed Valikhanov's claims about the predominance of Kazakh
custom and the authority of biys in administering legal norms in
family and other disputes. But contradictory principles animated
lawmakers in composing this provisional statute for the military administration of the territory. On the one hand, the division of the
area formerly ruled by the Kazakh hordes into four administrative regions—Ural'sk, Turgai, Akmolinsk, and Semipalatinsk—and their
further subdivision into districts, aimed at weakening the "clan principle" among the Kazakhs. As one Russian official and expert on
Kazakh customary law observed, the legislation divided the population into townships and settlements "with the goal of separating
Kazakh clans, because the unification of one large clan under the
power of one clan chieftain was recognized as harmful in the political sense." On the other hand, the customary law said to be rooted in
this same "clan principle" lay at the heart of the new policy orientation. The elders who interpreted and administered this law were to
serve as adjuncts to imperial rule in their role as the guardians of all
matters falling under the category of "civil affairs" as well as a large
number of those belonging to "criminal law" in the tsarist system.[51]

The 1868 statute assigned marital and family affairs to the court of
biys, where they would be adjudicated "according to popular customs," endorsing patriarchal customary law at the expense of the

shariʿa. Where marital disputes were concerned, the law instituted a unique mechanism of appeal that linked the practice of customary law to administrative authority. Like earlier legislation on other forms of customary law (as well as on the handling of Muslim inheritance disputes under the Orenburg Assembly), article 163 permitted the "side dissatisfied with the decision of the customary court" to turn with a complaint to the district chief, who then assumed the power to decide the case. Litigants who declined to accept this judgment could also present complaints to the governor. Appeals arising from marital and other disputes linked Kazakh custom to tsarist law. Ethnographers and administrators praised Kazakhs who turned to imperial law; and they lauded the influence of the general laws on customary law. Even so, the number of appeals never satisfied these officials.[52]

In the last decades of the century, there emerged from various locales evidence that proponents of Islamic law were gaining ground in the struggle between shariʿa and adat. The scholar Wilhelm Radloff found proof of this religious change in Kazakh songs. He termed the didactic songs that he collected "book songs" because Kazakh singers recited them from texts, whereas others were sung by heart. According to Radloff, the composers of these songs had been mullahs, and through these songs they had introduced Persian and Arabic words and grammatical constructions into the Kazakh language. Acting as the "messengers of Islam," these songs had spread the religion "like a slowly creeping poison." Through them, he charged, the small number of literate Kazakhs had become "alienated from the spirit of the people [*Volksgeist*]." The songs enjoined acceptance of the Prophet's message and emphasized ritual purity, the giving of alms, the centrality of prayer, recitation of the Qurʾan, and the avoidance of sin in a world where humans were mere "guests."[53]

In the late 1880s, N. I. Grodekov, an administrator and ethnogra-

pher, observed this "striving toward the shari'a" in many areas. Kazakhs such as the elder Umurbek of Aulieatinsk district told him that
"we are slaves of the shari'a, [and] we do not stand up for adat." Others had adapted elements from tsarist law, adat, and the shari'a.
Court registers examined by Grodekov listed rulings issued "according to adat," "according to full adat," "according to the shari'a," and
for a particularly weighty judgment, simply "according to the law."
He also reported the proliferation of mosques and the swearing of
oaths at the graves of Muslim saints and elsewhere "according to the
shari'a and the law." At the same time, he observed some variation
and selectivity in Kazakh appropriation of Islamic law. A notable
near Tashkent apparently made enemies when he demanded that
his wife wear a veil and occupy a separate space in their dwelling.
His opponents also criticized his ban on singing at his daughter's
wedding. They accused him of taking this practice from Muslims
(referred to here as "Sarts") in the neighboring city. Moreover, officials received more and more petitions from Kazakh communities
to permit the introduction of Islamic law among them.[54]

Tsarist authorities blamed Muslim missionaries. In the Volga and
Urals regions, Church and state officials had already marked Muslim men of religion as potential subversives. In their minds, the recurring episodes of apostasy from the Orthodox faith reflected the
work of the "Muhammadan clergy." Priests and police joined in
condemning itinerant as well as licensed mullahs when convert
communities coordinated mass renunciations of their baptismal rites
(or those of their eighteenth-century ancestors) and declared allegiance to Islam.[55]

Though St. Petersburg had long sent Tatar mullahs to the steppe
as missionaries, spies, merchants, and intermediaries, local officials
now viewed such figures as interlopers. Following Valikhanov, other
Russophone informants offered scholarly evidence supporting frontier officials' assertions about the predatory activities of Tatar mul-

lahs. The ethnographer Shakhimardan Miriasovich (Ivan Ivanovich) Ibragimov depicted itinerant mullahs from Kazan, as well as those from neighboring khanates, as exploiters of the credulous Kazakhs. The unlicensed "pretenders" had gained greater influence among them than the small numbers of official clerics permitted by the administration, Ibragimov suggested, because of their constant attentiveness to the ritual and other needs of the folk. He added that the Kazakhs had special regard for holy men whom they recognized as descendants of the Prophet, alongside sultans, as representatives of a hereditary elite.[56]

Imperial authorities and ethnographers also singled out Sufi guides (ishans) as particularly harmful agents of exploitation and deception whose selfish interests made them political adversaries of the state. In 1867 provincial officials identified the village of Sterlibashevo in Ufa Province as a "Muhammadan center" and the home of a charismatic "saint" who attracted followers from among Bashkirs and Tatars as well as Kazakhs. The tsarist conquest of much of Transoxiana, which the Russians called Turkestan, brought with it a Trojan horse, "Muslim clericalism." "This merging of the Kazakhs, who have long been indifferent to any faith, with Bashkir and Tatar clergy is very harmful," warned one official, "especially if one considers that in the recently acquired region of Turkestan fanaticism is even more developed among the people than among the Bashkirs and Tatars." Peter Pozdnev, too, argued that the Sufi guides of the Naqshbandi brotherhood in Orenburg Province exerted a dangerous influence on the Bashkirs, Kazakhs, and Turkestanis. Emphasizing tensions between mystics and more worldly Muslims, he charged that ishans "excite fanaticism in the people not only against Russians and non-Muslims generally, but also against Muslim rulers and clergy, when they regard it necessary for their own interests." As examples he cited episodes in 1868 when "dervishes" had supposedly turned Kazakhs in the Orenburg region against the imperial state. In the same year, he charged, they had discouraged Kazakhs in the district of Akmolinsk from accepting insignia distinguishing those assuming official posts.[57]

Pozdnev also referred to evidence gathered by "experts" on Kazakh life in the governor-generalship of Turkestan (established in 1867), who characterized ishans as "parasites" who not only caused great harm to the Kazakhs in "the economic sense" but also had an impact that was "disadvantageous in all respects for the successes of civilization." In the official newspaper of Turkestan, G. A. Arendarenko presented an alarming picture of Sufi influence on Kazakh followers *(murids)*.

> The influence of ishans on their murids is reflected on the whole cast of life of the latter: they wear turbans, perform prayers conscientiously, strictly observe fasts, establish mosques together in nomad encampments, send their children to town religious schools, where in a decade they cram them full with all the nonsense of Muslim learning, [and] turn them into sanctimonious hypocrites, and thus the Kazakh people degenerates generation after generation as a result of this ruinously perverted upbringing.

In language often used to describe Tatars—and in the western provinces, Jews—Arendarenko also accused Sufis from Central Asian towns (referred to here by the ethnonym "Sart") of combining their missionary activities with a vile form of predatory self-interest. With their "typical greediness, with the insatiability characteristic in such proportions only of the nature of a Sart," Arendarenko charged, the Sufi Sart "squeezes everything from his victim, beginning with domestic [items], naturally, [ranging from] the best animals to comely Kazakh girls, whom ishans either take for themselves as wives or give to relatives as calmly as [they would give] a horse."[58]

General N. A. Kryzhanovskii, the official entrusted with the Orenburg frontier region, reasoned that he could curb the "influence of the Muhammadan clergy on the Kazakhs" by removing them from the jurisdiction of the Orenburg Assembly, an institution that he and other provincial officials regarded as a serious rival to their authority. Already in October 1852, Count Perovskii, the governor of Orenburg and Samara Provinces, had instructed the Assembly not to involve itself in Kazakh affairs. The statute of 1868 also reiterated Kryzhanovskii's insistence on shielding Kazakhs from its grasp.[59]

But Kazakhs continued to appeal to Ufa for direction in religious matters. In 1866 Orenburg officials learned that Kazakhs still turned with marital disputes to the Assembly, which accepted their cases, citing a provision of the *Digest of Laws* that established the right of each "tribe" or "people" to enter into marriage according to its own laws and customs without the interference of Church or state officials.[60] Moreover, in September 1869 Kryzhanovskii complained to the minister of internal affairs that official mullahs from various areas had been sending denunciations to the Orenburg Assembly about Kazakhs who refused to perform religious rites. Besides clerics who asked the Assembly to help them discipline the irreligious in their charge, nonclerics also petitioned for the intervention of the Assembly. These Kazakhs insisted on the mediation of their disputes by Islamic scholars on the basis of the shariʿa.[61]

Tsarist authorities were forced to rely on threats prohibiting the mufti and officials in the Assembly from receiving such appeals or maintaining contact with the scholars and men of religion who served Kazakh communities. At the same time, critics of state policy argued that the advance of the shariʿa at the expense of the ostensibly secular patriarchy of adat furnished evidence for the need to abolish the Orenburg Assembly. In 1884 the missionary and Oriental studies scholar Nikolai I. Il'minskii wrote to the procurator of the Holy Synod, Konstantin P. Pobedonostsev, to alert him to the danger that he saw in the Assembly as a "Muslim cultural center in Russia."

Tatars used it to "unify and join" all the Muslims of the empire, he charged, citing recent German unification as a "model" for this kind of activity. Though Kazakhs had been removed from the jurisdiction of the Assembly, Il'minskii complained, "their heart is drawn to it by an old habit."[62]

Missionaries such as Il'minskii continued to insist that Islam had not truly sunk roots among the nomads, though it was only in the mid-1880s that the Imperial Orthodox Missionary Society extended its network into the steppe. To their disappointment, missionaries encountered competition from Tatars and other Muslim subjects whom the Orthodox suspected of pursuing their own missionary agenda. Robert Geraci has demonstrated that missionaries even suspected the Kazakhs of making Muslims out of the Russian colonists and Cossacks whose isolated settlements lacked churches. Faulting Russian officials, one of these missionaries, Father Nikol'skii, pointed to an administrator who, donning Kazakh clothes, promoted the performance of Islamic rites, though Kazakhs were in fact "not fully Islamicized." It was thus "a Russian *Orthodox* man," he complained, who "with a peaceful conscience, decides to teach the Kazakhs the correct fulfillment of religious, *Muslim* laws."[63]

An Islamic Restoration

Steppe policy came under fire from another angle as well. Some observers argued that official assumptions about Kazakh indifference to religion had led authorities to neglect the possibility of religious change. Believing that customary law would perform the disciplinary functions that religion fulfilled elsewhere in the empire, officials had failed to erect an institutional apparatus for state control of steppe religion. Shakhimardan Ibragimov and other critics of Tatar mullahs and Turkestani holy men pointed out that, contrary to the stated aim of steppe policy, the scarcity of licensed mullahs had made Kazakhs more reliant on itinerant prayer leaders whom the state could not monitor or control. Citing evidence from the district of Karakaralinsk, Ibragimov noted that state-approved religious leaders had taken to delegating ritual and other responsibilities to "private figures." This development in effect broke down the distinction, long esteemed by officials, between a "Muhammadan clergy" and a "laity." In turn, it had given rise to frequent complaints about marital disputes that ended up before tsarist authorities. Karakaralinsk officials complained that "illegal" marriages had proliferated. Performed without rites administered by the proper authority—and without the necessary registration in the official record—these unregulated marriages violated imperial law, as did unions between underage children or between older adults and young children. The court cases brought to light by Ibragimov suggested that the disputes that grew out of these arrangements sowed familial conflict and thus social discord and moral disorder in the steppe.[64]

Accounts like Ibragimov's provoked yet another policy shift. Lawmakers were forced to rethink their strategy of leaving Kazakh religion without hierarchical regulation. This reorientation brought steppe administration closer in line with the imperial practice of establishing hierarchical institutions in each confessional community in the empire. Indeed, in 1872 the tsarist state had created official Islamic hierarchies for the Sunnis and Shi'ites of Transcaucasia; and their efforts to form similar regulatory bodies in the Northern Caucasus continued.[65] At the same time, tsarist expansion deeper into Central Asia and the establishment of the governor-generalship of Turkestan brought several million more Muslims under tsarist rule and intensified official misgivings about the Islamic contamination of the steppe from this new territory.

Following the introduction of a new statute on the organization of Turkestan in 1886, the steppe nomads came under separate jurisdictions, including two governor-generalships, the Orenburg region, and western Siberia. Comparison of the state of "the religious affairs of the natives" in each territory revealed widely varying approaches to Kazakh religion.[66] Reasserting the prohibition against the involvement of the Orenburg Assembly, a commission of Akmolinsk and Omsk officials proposed to make local authorities arbiters of appointments to, and removals from, officially regulated clerical posts. Echoing Ibragimov, they maintained that

> supervision of the activity of mullahs officially confirmed in
> their own posts, and thus acting freely and openly, is much
> more convenient than supervision of the activity of persons
> not officially authorized for this and thus operating under
> the cover of secrecy and under the protection of figures who
> turn to them.[67]

The proposal permitted Kazakh communities to elect only one mullah per district, a unit encompassing several thousand tents stretching over hundreds of square kilometers. It also imposed numerous constraints on these candidates. Mullahs had to be chosen exclusively from among "Kazakhs, [who are] Russian subjects" and who had not been tried in court or placed under investigation. Moreover, the plan afforded imperial officials, from the local district chief to the governor, broad, though ill-defined, discretionary powers in confirming or rejecting appointments. Mullahs were not to enjoy any special privileges, such as a state salary or exemption from taxation, and communities that chose to assume their mullahs' obligations required the permission of the regional administration to do so. Governors also assumed the authority to make the construction of mosques, the establishment of religious schools, and monetary contributions to these institutions contingent upon their approval.

Clerical supervision of marriage stood out as an area of special concern. The commission of Akmolinsk and Omsk officials objected to inconsistencies in imperial law that in some locales left mullahs in charge of Kazakh marriages, including the keeping of official registers. They proposed that oversight of Kazakh marriages be transferred, along with record keeping, to Russian officials, citing a similar policy for Old Believers, dissidents from the Orthodox Church, as a precedent. Commissioners saw this measure as a necessary step toward the introduction of order to Kazakh marriage, but they noted that these goals did not include a defense of the indissolubility of Kazakh marriage. In their view, Kazakhs based the institution of marriage on coercion and violence rather than the consent of the bride, and this the commissioners condemned. Their aim, they noted, was "the protection of the woman in the Kazakh family" from her male relatives.[68]

Disregard for the woman's consent was the chief fault of Kazakh marriage, according to this commission. It concluded that "the majority of Kazakhs regard their own daughters and widows as valuable goods and trade them." Kazakhs did not acknowledge "that the law offers her the right of free choice of a husband."[69] The commission explained that Kazakh women rarely complained about their lot, though some took their cases to the customary law court. At the woman's insistence, these cases sometimes ended up before a Russian official, the district chief, who would then abrogate this type of marriage on the grounds that it had not been recorded in the official register.

Complaining that mullahs colluded in the practice of dismissing the rights of Kazakh women, and that this violated Islamic law, the commission backed officials who sought to compel mullahs to perform marriages only in cases where the bride offered her consent and witnesses certified to this. It also supported the demands voiced earlier by a number of elders in Valikhanov's survey of legal practices and institutions by severely curtailing the role of mullahs in administering marital affairs. In place of the mullahs, elders and township administrators were to maintain registers of births, marriages, and deaths.[70]

Despite the mediating role of Kazakh elders, the commission proposed provisions to make Kazakh marriage practices conform in a number of key points to imperial marriage law (based in its fundamentals on Orthodox canon law). The draft prohibited elders from concluding marital agreements on behalf of males younger than eighteen and females younger than sixteen, or in cases where both parties had not offered their consent, or when parents or others had attempted to coerce the bride and bridegroom. Finally, elders were obliged to confirm that a legal divorce or the death of a first husband had made previously married women eligible for remarriage. In the eyes of the commission, such marriages would take effect only when the necessary witnesses and participants had signed the agreement before the elder.

The proposal added that the marrying parties were permitted, if they so desired, to turn to a local mullah or other Kazakhs "for the reading of a prayer." Russian officials did not view this rite as obligatory, noting that "in and of itself [it] has no meaning for recognition of the legality of the marriage." The commission also threatened any non-Kazakhs who performed religious rites at marriages or any other occasions with criminal persecution for "the assumption of power not belonging to oneself." As with marriage, Kazakh divorce would belong to the realm of customary—not Islamic—law.[71]

Lawmakers remained divided on the role of the state, however. In 1887 a steppe administrator named Egorov elaborated on the recommendations made by Ibragimov and the commission of regional officials. He claimed that the Russian government had always maintained "the principles of religious toleration, to which the successful spread of Russian rule in Asia owed [so] much." Egorov's memorandum of 1887 identified "two main systems" in policy toward the religious affairs of inorodtsy. The first had prevailed in the European provinces, Siberia, and the Caucasus. According to this scheme, the government had assumed responsibility for naming and confirming "ecclesiastical figures" and for determining their rights, obligations, authority, and jurisdiction. In the second system, which the government had improvised more recently for the new imperial possession of Turkestan, the state had regarded the religious matters of inorodtsy as "their private relations." It did not confer upon the "clergy any official significance" or assign them any rights or duties.[72]

Criticism of the "first system," the policies in place in territories integrated into the empire in earlier periods, shaped the drafting of a new statute for the steppe under the conservative Alexander III (r. 1881–1894). Its authors had come to regard Islam as a generic foe of state interests. In lending the Muslim "clergy" an "official character," the government had enabled "the strengthening and intensification among the inorodtsy of dogmas tolerated in the Empire, among which Muhammadanism by its essence has an anti-state and hostile character in a Christian land."[73]

The influence of an official clergy had been particularly "unfavorable" on the Kazakhs, who had adopted only the few "Muhammadan rites and views" that did not conflict with "the immemorial customs of the Kazakh people, representing the product of its tribal, clan, and historical life." Immune to "fanaticism," they remained Muslims only "superficially and in name." The Kazakhs had no indigenous clergy, this memorandum asserted, and the state need not supply them with one, given that "any literate Kazakh" might bear the title *mullah* and recite the prayers that made up "almost all of the religious ritual among them." Egorov concluded that the appointment of official mullahs in the steppe would only strengthen Islam there and thus be "harmful for state interests."[74]

Unlike bureaucrats in Kazan, Samara, Orenburg, Ufa, Astrakhan, and elsewhere who had to contend with a century-old official Islamic hierarchy, steppe authorities made use of the broader latitude at their disposal to devise new institutions and policies. Critics seized on the institutionalization of Islam as the single greatest obstacle to the "Russification" of the steppe and the "removal [from it] of Muslim foundations." They claimed that only Islam stood in the way of the transformation promised by colonization and the closer integration of the steppe and its population into the administrative and cultural life of the empire.

> With the gradual penetration into the steppe of Russian settlements and the growth of the Russian population, under the influence of Russian administration, courts, trade, and industry, and with the spread of Russian schools and especially with the introduction of military service, the Kazakhs should without doubt, in time, become Russian, become imbued with Russian views and understandings, [and] turn in large part to a settled way of life and Christianity.[75]

The memorandum recommended that proposed legislation forego any regulation of Kazakh religious affairs, using as a model the 1867 statute for the Turkestan governor-generalship, which denied Kazakh mullahs any "official significance."

Contrary to the recommendations of this last memorandum, the statute that became law in 1891 made appointments of Muslim clerical figures on a uniform basis. The statute on the administration of Akmolinsk, Semipalatinsk, Semireche, Ural'sk, and Turgai reaffirmed the policy that limited inhabitants there to one mullah (chosen from among this same population) per township unit, a territory drawn to enclose between one and two thousand tents *(kibitki)*. As Kazakh critics pointed out, this policy often permitted only one mullah for a territory the size of France. Communities required permission from the governors to construct mosques, for whose upkeep only consenting members of the community were made responsible. Such support would have to come without the aid of Muslim endowments, because the statute prohibited them in these territories.[76]

The government thereby reasserted a measure of state supervision by making mullahs subject to the approval of local governors. However, the approach expounded in the internal memorandum of 1887 still had a meaningful, if indirect, impact. Its formulation of the problem of religious toleration accorded with the outlook of tsarist officials in the steppe governor-generalship: the local administration should deal with the religious affairs of "Asiatic inorodtsy" not "in the form of law, but by means of administrative orders, not to be openly promulgated in the manner established for laws." Secrecy was necessary, it explained, "because any restrictions on religious freedom and constraints on the clergy may easily be understood and interpreted as the persecution of Islam and religious intolerance, which [would be] awkward for our influence in neighboring Muslim countries of eastern and southern Asia."[77]

In the late nineteenth and early twentieth centuries, stealthy "administrative orders" played an increasingly important role. They became the primary means for closing mosques and Islamic schools and for taking clerics under police surveillance and arrest. Governors and local police claimed to leave intact the narrow legal basis for toleration, but they simultaneously used the cover of administrative fiat to restrict the practice of Islam without openly undermining the geopolitical goals that they associated with toleration.

Officials shifted toward a policy of close regulation and surveillance of a small number of state-approved mullahs among the Kazakhs in the 1890s, but debates continued about the relative weight of custom and religion. In 1890 the official *Kazakh Steppe Paper* ran an editorial that asked, "Is the court of elders necessary for the

Kazakhs?" The editorial answered in the affirmative, maintaining that the resolution of disputes before "a court of biys and senior men" was a natural extension of Kazakh domestic life, where "all quarrels, insults, fights, and other squabbles" were resolved by recourse to this institution. "Each biy and elder regards it as a sacred duty at the hearing of a case to render the litigants completely impartial justice," it argued. The editorial contrasted the calm and order of the court of biys to the raucous procedure of "our lowest police instances," which the Kazakhs regarded as "wild" and "feared . . . like fire," and argued that only this type of court was "thinkable" under such conditions, instructing its readers to "rejoice, that the Kazakhs are attached to their own popular customs to such an extent that for the adjudication and resolution of affairs they resort to them, and not to the shari'a." The editorial offered the optimistic assertion that members of the horde turned to the mullah and the shari'a only in cases involving inheritance and divorce, whereas they brought all other disputes and suits before "distinguished figures" who adjudicated these cases "according to popular customs."[78]

Other Russian observers rejected this portrait of the vitality of customary justice among the Kazakhs. In 1892 an expert on Muslim legal affairs who had worked a number of years in administration in the Caucasus pleaded in the *Journal of Civil and Criminal Law* against officials' tendency "to idealize the patriarchal charm of the customary court." N. A. Dingel'shtedt maintained that the "privilege" of living "according to adat" had left "the people and the Kazakhs in particular dissatisfied with their own court." Since 1867, he argued, the people had found neither impartial justice nor anything "customary" in these courts. In place of "ancient adat," Kazakhs confronted "some kind of mixture, where there are fragments of both the shari'a and Russian laws, but [where] the main element is represented by arbitrariness."[79]

Dingel'shtedt departed from received opinion among officials in the steppe and Turkestan governor-generalships when he declared that the "customary court had had its day" and that the court of the justice of the peace should at last replace it. Dingel'shtedt was among the few Russian authorities who viewed the period since the establishment of tsarist administration as a time of uncertainty and discord in which novel conflicts troubled Kazakh communities. Many Kazakhs had adapted to new forms of sedentary life, while regulations and administrative practice had unwittingly transformed their courts, which were now "customary in name alone." Where Kazakhs once invited a biy to resolve disputes among them, elections introduced by tsarist legislation produced "government biys confirmed by the governor and decorated with a special badge." Dingel'shtedt portrayed this change as "an almost total betrayal of custom." Much more important, he maintained, it had caused "the decline of justice," so that "several million people dream with melancholy of finding not so much the lost adat as a fair court and justice."[80]

By the end of the nineteenth century, growing numbers of Kazakhs sought permission to opt out of the "customary" justice criticized by Dingel'shtedt. Rejecting a form of customary law in which Russian bureaucrats played a dominant role, these demands also centered on changes in tsarist policy toward religion. Numerous Kazakhs called for a separate institution headed by a mufti in the steppe from at least 1888, when discussion of projected changes to the statute on the administration of the steppe regions provoked debate both within and outside the bureaucracy.

Petitioners calling themselves the "Ural and Orenburg Elders" demanded the right to apply a uniform and systematic Islamic law under a muftiate. These Kazakh elders imagined this institution explicitly as a guardian of the shari'a. It would also perform some functions related to ecclesiastical control, but its chief task would be to combat the reign of "custom" where it conflicted with the shari'a. The elders backed their request by appealing to immemorial tradition. "For ages, we, the Kazakh people of the Muhammadan faith," their petition explained, "had made use of the decisions of muftis and kadis of those khanates in whose vicinity we lived."[81] They had turned to the Islamic jurists and judges of Tashkent, Turkestan, Samarkand, Kokand, and Khiva for the resolution of religious questions. After the Kazakhs "became subjects of His Imperial Majesty," they no longer had a mufti of their own, though they had expected the regime to provide them with one. The absence of an Islamic jurisconsult had resulted in "defects in our shari'a matters." Though the temporary statute had permitted the selection of official mullahs for each administrative township, the petition complained, these mullahs "do not merit the appointment" because their educational preparation had not been certified by a mufti.

But it was the anarchic state of marriage and the family that chiefly concerned these petitioners. Widows used the permission of state authorities to remarry without regard for the waiting period established by Islamic law. Women had also been turning to these officials to receive divorce papers "without any inquiries on the basis of the shari'a." Similarly, they charged, individual family members were inserting officials in the middle of inheritance cases in order to secure sanction for the denial of inheritance shares to their brothers. The elders also challenged practices long defended by many Kazakhs and others as central to immemorial custom: they castigated the continuation of a controversial practice (often criticized in Russian official and public circles) whereby relatives compelled a widow to remarry into the family of her deceased husband and give up control of the inheritance left to her and her children.[82]

Their religious affairs suffered, the elders pointed out, because the decisions of the licensed mullah in each township had "no power, due to the mullah's lack of rights." The temporary statute had weakened "the power of his decisions," referred to here as "fatwas," by allowing cases to be transferred to a civil jurisdiction in the event that both litigants remained dissatisfied with the handling of their case according to the shari'a. Meanwhile, biys decided cases contrary to the shari'a, even though, their petition conceded, "cases decided by custom, but needing adjudication according to the shari'a, should be decided in agreement with the spirit of the one and the other." To resolve these difficulties, the petitioners called for a "single, learned person empowered to resolve controversies of every kind among our mullahs and to interpret the meaning of the shari'a," citing the examples of the early Islamic community, when the Prophet adjudicated all disputes among his followers, and of Abu Hanifa, the founder of the eponymous school of legal interpretation to which most Muslims of the empire belonged. Finally, the Ural and Orenburg Elders tried to support their case for their own muftiate by demonstrating that the condition of Islam among the Kazakhs had much improved. They enjoyed the services of "quite good mullahs, madrasas, [and] mosques," their children studied, and worthy ishans led followers in the Sufi path, "so that the fulfillment of religious rites is much better than before." "Charity and good works" on behalf of the poor deserved a place among this people as among others.[83]

        Officials dismissed this and similar demands from Kazakh notables for a steppe muftiate. As police resorted to administrative measures to close Kazakh mosques and arrest clerics, Kazakhs issued more frequent demands for a reevaluation of their legal status and mobilized petition campaigns in defense of mosques and madrasas. In the early twentieth century, Kazakhs pointed to assaults on laws guaranteeing "freedom of religion" as a violation of their "rights." In addition to the encroachment of Slavic settlers on their grazing lands, restrictions on Kazakh access to clerics and Islamic education increased tensions in the steppe.

In abandoning its search for allies among steppe Muslims in the 1850s and 1860s, the state had departed from established practice in the territory under the Orenburg Assembly, in the Crimea, and, from 1872, in Transcaucasia. At the same time, this new direction put tsarist practice more in tune with new policies in the Northern Caucasus and with nearly contemporary European strategies, such as those of the French toward the Kabyle in North Africa and of the British toward the Punjabis in British India. Like the Russians in the Northern Caucasus, the French and British tried, without much success, to reinforce the secular custom of the tribe with the aim of supplanting—and guarding against—Islamic law. In the second half of the nineteenth century, Russians, too, were affected by changing European ideas about the incompatibility of Islam and what contemporaries understood to be progress and civilization. Tsarist administrators came to see that state reliance on Islam clashed with a new objective in the steppe—the cultural assimilation of the Kazakhs, their transformation into Russian speakers and Orthodox Christians.

Steppe officials were partially constrained by the basic principles of religious toleration in the tsarist law code. As even the opponents of Kazakh mosques and Islamic schools admitted, the toleration of Islam (albeit limited) in the steppe remained a useful means to influence opinion in neighboring Islamic lands that might, with time, be persuaded to submit to the empire with the promise of protection for the Muslim faith. Moreover, officials remained bound to the practice of affirming orthodox Islam outside of the steppe. Steppe authorities denied Kazakhs full toleration as Muslims because their religion did not appear to correspond to the normative definition of Islam as these bureaucrats knew it: pastoralists could not be true Muslims because they lacked mosques and a clergy like Muslims in Kazan or Istanbul.

Through each of these policy shifts, official thinking remained flexible. When evidence emerged of growing Kazakh attachment to the shari'a, recourse to itinerant mullahs, and potential unrest due to restrictions on mullahs and Islamic law, the state fell back on an improvised policy of regulating Muslim institutions, though with the use of clandestine administrative tools. By the end of the nineteenth century, steppe police found themselves once again involved in monitoring appointments to mosques and schools and even in adjudicating disputes among Muslim Kazakhs.[84] Although these arrangements restored some continuity to tsarist policy toward Islam, they failed to achieve close ties to local communities like authorities had forged in other Muslim regions of the empire. Such measures weakened the ability of the regime to police the Kazakhs and direct the course of colonization there. In Kazakh communities that had only a single mullah, children could not study the fundamentals of religion, and the shari'a did not govern the Muslim family. There the state planted shallow roots, scattering seeds of volatility on the horizon.

5

CIVILIZING TURKESTAN

In mid-June 1865 the residents of the oasis city of Tashkent received alarming news about the approach of foreign troops. According to Muhammad Salih, an eyewitness in the town, the "Nazarenes" appeared suddenly from the north, unleashing fire on the city walls and causing panic among its hundred thousand inhabitants. As the Russian troops lay siege, in each quarter of the city the men of influence—the elders, religious scholars, and well-born notables—gathered at the mosques and other public places to decide how to respond to the unexpected arrival of the Christian forces. Salih, a religious scholar and historian, recalled that Russian envoys soon appeared on the scene as well. They initiated contact to negotiate the surrender of this trading and artisanal center, the largest city in Transoxiana.

The Russian commander, General Mikhail G. Cherniaev, quickly concluded separate treaties with the elites of each quarter. Agreements with the religious scholars followed. These treaties stipulated that as a condition of the submission of the city the new rulers would ensure that the people remained steadfast in religion. To safeguard the Muslims of Tashkent against "absolute injustice," the Russian authorities guaranteed that these newest subjects of the empire would continue to live according to the shariʻa. They would pay Islamic taxes, maintain charitable endowments, and guard the poor from oppression. In Salih's account, these accords made the transition of power in Tashkent less a matter of conquest than of negotiation. Russian rule was made conditional upon the new authorities' support for the preservation of the moral injunctions and rights granted by God's holy law.[1]

When the tsarist army advanced to the south and west of Tashkent into the territory of the amir of Bukhara, Russian officers initiated similar negotiations there. They pledged to defend the faith of all those who would submit to the tsar. To the residents of Samarkand, they promised "peace and tranquility" in exchange for surrender. Commanders like Major General A. K. Abramov vowed to restore a more just Islamic order, declaring an end to internecine warfare and the corrupt rule of despots who, he claimed, violated even the rules of their own faith.

As Russian forces moved on Karshi, a town to the southwest of Samarkand, Abramov employed this strategy again. Having reached an agreement with the Bukharan amir, the general still faced opposition from the governor of Karshi, the amir's son. In October 1868 he reminded the inhabitants of the besieged region that the defiant governor had forgotten "God and the teachings of his Great Prophet Muhammad" by challenging his father. Abramov appealed to the population to press the governor to submit to his father and the Russians without shedding more "Muslim blood." "Let the people remember," he warned, "that God does not offer blessings and happiness to people who have led themselves to the point where brother has raised his hand against brother, and son against father."[2]

Like Cherniaev's treaties with the religious scholars of Tashkent, Abramov's admonitions about the Prophet had a significance beyond diplomatic rhetoric. Muslim elites like Muhammad Salih expected the new rulers to live up to their pledges. This is demonstrated by the attention the chronicler of Tashkent paid to these negotiations. Russian accounts, by contrast, tended to cast these encounters in a different light, downplaying the promises of reciprocity in the Russian declarations.

This latter point of view has obscured the extent to which such religious commitments determined the contours of the Russian empire-building venture in Central Asia. The image of its preeminence enabling Russia to dictate the terms of conquest has largely prevailed in historical treatments of tsarist expansion. The participants in these military campaigns themselves believed in the historic inevitability of this undertaking, the extension of European "civilization" and "progress" to an Asia stagnating under the twin burdens of "barbarism" and "backwardness." Later accounts reproduced key features of this narrative. Soviet historians judged tsarist rule in the region alternately as a "progressive" or a "reactionary" phenomenon, depending upon shifting ideological currents. But like their counterparts in the West, they tended to focus on the social and economic transformations initiated by the imperial center. Integration into imperial markets, the appearance of European-style cities, the introduction of railroads, the expansion of cotton production, and state-sponsored colonization by Slavic settlers all figure prominently in these approaches.

Historians have nonetheless disagreed about the scope of these changes. Despite the arrival of the locomotive and the Russian school, historians have argued, the Russian state remained weak in Central Asia. Government institutions were mostly confined to the new urban centers that grew out of military settlements adjacent to indigenous cities. Beyond these administrative outposts, tsarist authorities were thinly spread across nearly 1.3 million square kilometers among a population of some 6 million subjects. At the turn of the century, this produced a ratio of more than 117 urban residents and 2,112 rural inhabitants to 1 state official, or nearly double the average urban ratio and three times the rural ratio in the empire as a whole. In 1910 the region of Ferghana had a population of almost 2 million inhabitants, administered by only 58 Russian officials, including two translators.[3]

Given the limited capacity of state institutions, historians have noted the modest impact of tsarist administration on the diverse communities of the region. To be sure, they concede, the state played a key, if indirect, role in initiating social and economic change. The regime affected settled and nomadic populations alike, especially by facilitating colonization and expanding trade and agricultural production. However, many of these same accounts conclude that beyond the growth of a small merchant elite, significant social and cultural change would take place only under the Soviets, and then only with the onslaught of Stalin's "revolution from above." In this view, these communities would continue to occupy, in effect, a "world apart" from that of imperial, and later Soviet, Russia. Avoidance and resistance would endure as the most consequential indigenous responses to Russian rule.[4]

Historians, like their tsarist informants, have focused on Islam as the chief impediment to the imperial integration of Central Asia.[5] After all, the khans and amirs had mobilized their forces against the "infidels" in the name of defending the faith. The first governor-general of Russian Turkestan, Konstantin von Kaufman, believed that the "problem" posed by Islam would ultimately resolve itself in the face of progress—left to their own devices, Muslims would gradually abandon their backward faith. To this end, he blocked the Church from proselytization and announced a break with the tsarist practice of sponsoring and overseeing official Islamic authorities, proclaiming a policy of "ignoring Islam." Historians have taken this proclamation at face value, utilizing Kaufman's avowals of noninterference to sustain two separate and largely autonomous perspectives on the history of Turkestan, one for the Russians and one for the Muslims. Treatments of Russian images of Central Asians and state policy dominate the first approach; the study of a reformist Muslim elite, the "Jadids," defines the second.

This chapter shows instead how realities on the ground built on significant continuities, both with imperial strategies elsewhere in the empire and, equally important, with local Muslim practice predating the Russians. Tsarist engagement with Islamic institutions in Central Asia was not as systematic as in the regions under the Orenburg Assembly. It was nonetheless transformative. Despite public pledges of noninterference, Russian officials recognized that to hold this territory in Asia the empire needed an Islam policy. And despite the logistical obstacles to governing this territory, the regime enjoyed success in penetrating local communities for the sake of policing and control. In the half century that separated the Russian seizure of Tashkent in 1865 from the First World War, only one incident, a rebellion localized to Andizhan (Andijan) in 1898, seriously interrupted the stability that the regime established in this vulnerable borderland. The presence of tsarist troops make up only part of this story. As in other regions of the empire, the tsarist state established itself by creating religious ties. The Russian approach to Islam served as a catalyst for religious change, not apart from imperial institutions but squarely within them.

The New Khans

Following the disastrous Crimean War and the unsettling Polish rebellion of 1863, the Russian army sought to regain its diminished prestige in the territory bordering its imperial rivals British India and China and its more vulnerable neighbors Iran and Afghanistan. For the military men who subjugated the khanate of Kokand and made protectorates of Bukhara (1868) and Khiva (1873), the Russian state labored under an obligation of world-historical significance. As a representative of European civilization, it undertook the mission to enlighten and transform the ostensibly crude and barbaric inhabitants of Asia. To these generals and their civilian backers in Russia, such as the writer Fyodor Dostoevsky, Russia's oft-challenged claim to full membership in the family of European nations would be redeemed, once and for all, in the deserts and oases of the East. Like other "Oriental" societies, the societies of Transoxiana appeared stagnant and isolated, their rulers corrupt, effete, and cruel. Climate and race played their part in setting these societies on a path toward decline and submission to superior European forces, but their evident zeal for religion, so often highlighted in travelers' accounts, struck Russians as the fundamental cause of their immobility. And nothing appeared more unyielding than the power of the Muslim "clergy."

Many accounts of Muslim "reform" have tended to replicate such views, pitting rigid "traditionalists" of the preconquest period against the progressive "reformers" produced by transformations under Russian rule.[6] The notion that the men of learning and piety enjoyed unquestioned authority in their communities derives from two suspect, if diametrically opposed, sources: the established 'ulama themselves and their reformist critics, the Jadids. Both camps represented the absolute power of the religious establishment as an indelible feature of the preconquest landscape.

Adeeb Khalid has claimed that reformers utilized printing and modernized schools—like the Qur'anic school in Samarkand pictured in Figure 6—to sweep aside an older generation of Muslim elites. In identifying this group of intellectuals as catalysts of change, Khalid has illuminated an important development in Muslim intellectual life. But other scholars have highlighted the extent to which these reformers remained isolated within their own communities.[7]

Figure 6 A Qur'anic school in Samarkand. Courtesy of Library of Congress, Prints & Photographs Division, Prokudin-Gorskii Collection, LC-DIG-prok-02304.

Moreover, in the absence of a history of reading practices in the region, we still do not know how a Muslim public responded to this press and engaged with its reformist ideas. In Central Asia, Muslim papers and journals found neither readers nor patrons on a scale that permitted them a life span of more than two years. Their critics nonetheless adopted printing as well. In the meantime, new research has shown that manuscript production persisted alongside printing well into the twentieth century; and many of the printed (or lithographed) works available in regional bazaars were editions associated with established modes for the transmission of Islamic knowledge.[8]

Muhammad Qasim Zaman reminds us that "print has not heralded a 'priesthood of all believers' in Muslim societies, as the printing of the Bible in the vernacular is supposed to have done in Protestant Europe." As a means to standardize devotional texts at the expense of localized traditions and controversial interpretations, print may have done more to reaffirm "orthodoxy" than to undermine it.[9] Just as printing alone did not entail a reformist agenda, it was not mastery of technology, but mastery of the new colonial state, that allowed Muslims to gain backing for claims of religious authority.

Recent scholarship on precolonial Transoxiana has challenged notions that it was a static pre-tsarist (or pre-reformist) backwater, revealing instead its dynamism and retracing connections to a wider world.[10] Historians have made similar discoveries in the area of religion and have traced dramatic changes in the seventeenth and eighteenth centuries.[11] The spread of a novel direction in Sufism, the Mujaddidi line of the Naqshbandi brotherhood, and the poetic works of Sufi Allahyar offered new models of religious authority. They also sparked new controversies. More rigorous attention to rooting out "innovations"—practices that ostensibly departed from the shari'a and the example of the Prophet—inspired some 'ulama and political figures to seek a purification of society. Their targets were not limited to popular entertainments such as fighting, the smoking of water pipes, and the public reading of Rumi. Conflicts centered, too, on one of the essential rites of the Sufi path, the remembrance of God (zikr). Mujaddidis who regarded any but silent practice of zikr as an innovation clashed with other brotherhoods, such as the Qadiriyya and Yasaviyya, who employed mystical chants and verses; they even feuded with other Naqshbandis. In pursuing this campaign of ritual discipline and moral purity, the Mujaddidis gained the backing of the Manghit dynasty of Bukhara. These amirs sometimes suppressed the Mujaddidis' foes and otherwise aided their cause by expanding the number of Qur'anic schools and madrasas, which in turn drew students from the Russian empire.[12]

Relations between the regional dynasties and the 'ulama kept religious authority in flux. The legitimacy of these rulers hinged on their ability to present themselves as guardians of Islamic orthodoxy. Thus in Kokand 'Alim Khan banned as polytheism the practice of saying prayers and making sacrifices at trees. Temporal authorities also administered a hierarchy of religious offices and reinforced the authority of their appointees. In 1832 Muhammad Ali elevated the Sufi guide (ishan) Muhammad Salih to the position of "great khoja" (*khwāja*), warning the inhabitants "from little to great" of the "God-protected region of Ura Tepe" to defer to him. When filling posts at madrasas, the authorities issued instructions to "the learned people and the 'ulama and well-born and the notables of the province" to treat these figures "with the appropriate honor and respect." The khan's decrees even reminded subjects of the superior qualities of the descendants of the Prophet, the sayyids, when they occupied offices on his behalf.[13]

The network of Islamic institutions that the tsarist authorities confronted was relatively new. In the Ferghana Valley, much of this infrastructure dated only to Khudoyar, the last khan of Kokand. As part of a broader program to strengthen his hold on Ferghana, Khudoyar sponsored vast building projects, including the construction of mosques, madrasas, mausoleums, and structures used for Qur'anic recitation and other devotional purposes. He converted large tracts of land and water into endowments (waqfs) to support these institutions. The khan and his family also expanded their patronage of the religious establishment. Khudoyar surrounded himself with figures like Ishan Sakhib-zade, whom he recruited together with a retinue of relatives and followers from the rival state of Bukhara and whose arrival in Kokand was greeted by "all of the 'ulama, the common people and notables." Religious figures received gifts of property and exemption from taxation. Endowments provided salaries for readers of the Qur'an at the tombs of deceased relatives and saints. They also took the form of rights to water, land, and human labor, making whole villages (qishlaqs) the dependents of the ishans and other clerics and notables whom the khan appointed as endowment managers. Symbols of the piety of the khan, foundations presented an opportunity for the khan to redistribute resources among competing elites whose backing he needed.[14]

The public display of piety also bore risks. Khudoyar faced an uprising in 1856, apparently because a notable criticized his meager plans to renovate a madrasa. Accusations suggesting love of wine, women, cards, and boys swirled around thrones that rested on claims of moral rectitude. In a climate where state-backed religious scholars leveled charges of "unbelief" against rival sovereigns, rulers could be vulnerable to accusations of straying from the shari'a. Scholars made such accusations when khans or amirs ignored their judicial rulings, insulted mullahs, or drove students out of the madrasas.[15] And yet the religious establishment was not a monolith. Throughout the nineteenth century, the 'ulama looked to the khans and amirs to judge controversies within scholarly circles about Islamic law and mediate competition for control of prestigious mosque and madrasa positions.

When the Russians formed the governor-generalship of Turkestan there between the 1860s and early 1880s, they encountered Muslim communities already divided by competing interpretations of the shari'a who had long made temporal authorities central actors in the mediation of these disputes. Tensions surrounding Sufi practices—like the pursuit of ecstatic states of devotion—intersected with struggles for the leadership of mosques, madrasas, endowments, and shrines. In a study of endowment documents and genealogical works related to a shrine associated with the founder of the Yasavi Sufi order, Devin DeWeese has shown how these texts served as "discursive weapons" in the hands of competing communities claiming descent from the saint. Rival groups compiled these accounts in the nineteenth century, DeWeese argues, to validate their claims on the shrine before each new regime—Bukharan, Kokandian, or Russian—that assumed control of the area.[16]

The Russians inherited the fruits of these struggles for power within Islamic institutions. In Kokand, the 'ulama had solicited state intervention against their opponents, and laymen and women turned to the bek or khan to challenge the judgments of Islamic law court judges (known in the region as kazis, or *qāżīs*). According to a Russian official, A. K. Geins, husbands and wives had enjoyed "the right to turn to the censor [*ra'īs*] concerning matters of a completely confidential character." Geins's Muslim informants told him that this state-appointed inspector of markets and public morals investigated wives' complaints against husbands who failed to perform their conjugal duties or who "maintain" them "badly." The official could then apply corporal punishment to the husband and establish the proper maintenance for the wife. Similarly, the ra'īs disciplined the "profligate woman."[17] Drawing on their experiences with frequent regime changes in regions like Ferghana, where eighteen different rulers governed between 1709 and 1865, local communities readily adapted their legal strategies to the new power in the region.[18]

Though the arrival of the "Nazarenes" came as a shock to many, the Russians were not total strangers. They had long maintained economic and diplomatic ties with Transoxiana through steppe intermediaries and the trading centers along the frontier. Tsarist officials highlighted their regard for Islam in dealing with representatives from the settled oases; appeals to a shared struggle against irreligion was a vital element of Russian strategy. A Kokandian chronicle relates how frontier officials shamed an ambassador of the khan.

When Hadji Qurban protested the detention of his embassy during a cholera epidemic in 1831, Russian authorities castigated him, calling him "neither Muslim, nor Christian, Jew, Gabr [Zoroastrian], Hindu, nor of any other religion." Devoted instead to "drinking vodka at night, getting drunk, losing [his] senses and engaging in debauchery," the ambassador was "a man who does not respect divine law, the authority of his own khan, nor feels gratitude to his benefactor."[19]

Familiar with the activities of the Muslim "clergy" in Russia and the steppe, tsarist officials nonetheless confronted distinctive personnel and institutions in the newly conquered towns. In Transoxiana the Russians encountered one of the global centers of Islamic piety and scholarship. The region had been producing converts to Islam since the seventh and eighth centuries. The renown of Bukhara reached far beyond Central Asia, and regional scholars left a deep imprint on both Islamic mysticism and Hanafi legal thought.

Russians contended with a dense network of Islamic institutions. In Tashkent alone, they faced a town with some four hundred mosques. In Kokand in the Ferghana Valley, the Russians found a religious center with some 360 mosques and 149 Qur'anic schools (maktabs) and madrasas. Osh, a regional center of the khanate, had some 147 mosques. The most imposing of its six madrasas, the Alymbek madrasa, occupied more than twenty-five hundred square meters. To the southwest of the town rose a mountain known as the "throne of Solomon" *(Takht-i Sulaiman)*, a site that attracted Muslim pilgrims from throughout the region because of its association with the ancient prophet and other holy men and artifacts. And given the proximity of Afghanistan, India, and the Muslim possessions of the Chinese empire, both the Ministry of War and the Ministry of Foreign Affairs advised caution with respect to Islam. Thus despite the Russians' lengthy experience with Muslims elsewhere, Transoxiana presented a novel challenge.[20]

Russians nonetheless sought out the familiar. Traveling from the Orenburg frontier to Tashkent in 1866, Peter I. Pashino found the clergy's influence on the people "enormous." He added that "centuries are needed to eradicate it, because town residents receive education through them, and 85 percent of them, thanks to the clergy, are literate and have listened since childhood to a multitude of sermons on the superiority of Islam to all other religions and on disrespect toward unbelievers." The author of a recent essay on the Volga Tatars, Pashino emphasized similarities between Russia's Tatars and the urban population of Russia's new territories. Although he identified the largest group, "Sarts," as Aryans, he nonetheless concluded that their lives were "very similar to that of any Volga or Siberian Tatar." The Sarts were distinguished from the Tatars, he claimed, only in their adherence to "certain prejudices," which had disappeared among the latter "as a result of historical circumstances."[21]

Confident of success, the regime translated the politics of religious patronage to this setting as well. Following the conquest of each town, military officials sought out ties with religious notables. After seizing the town of Turkestan, they granted permanent tax exemptions to the most senior cleric, the *shaykh al-islam,* and others who claimed descent from saintly lineages such as the Yasavi. In Tashkent, Cherniaev agreed to meet the requests of local 'ulama seeking his confirmation of new clerical appointments, though he also deported nine clerics as threats to Russian rule.[22]

For their part, Muslim elites frequently reminded the Russians of the contractual basis of the new order and pressed for official backing for the reconstruction of a society governed by the shari'a. In August 1866 an address submitted to the governor-general by seventy-seven of "the most esteemed" religious and other elites greeted him with "bread and salt according to popular tradition," which the Tashkent elites noted "has existed in Russia since ancient times." In the year since the town's residents had "recognized the authority of the powerful All-Russian Emperor," they "succeeded in grasping how great is the fortune already conveyed upon us." The notables emphasized that "our faith has remained inviolable; our madrasas (schools) are supported and are flourishing; a *makhama* (popular court) has been established, which, acting justly, neutrally, and impartially, decides our cases completely in accord with the rules of our religion and according to popular customs." Free from all "illegal extortion," "insults and oppression," they expressed gratitude for the defeat of the forces of the Bukharan amir, which inaugurated a period of "complete tranquility and order, which in past times did not exist." Requesting "the unification of our region with Russia" on the same basis as "other parts of the Empire," the notables asked that the "powerful and merciful White Tsar look upon us as his children alongside his other loyal subjects."[23]

In Samarkand, Muslim elites sought to turn their submission to Russian rule into an alliance against ostensibly common foes. Following the surrender of the town and the declaration of a tax amnesty in 1868, the mufti Mullah Kamaladdin responded with a story from the life of Muhammad. "Our Prophet," he explained, "out of fear of the unbelievers ordered the Arabs who had adopted the Muslim faith to migrate to Abyssinia," whose king was then a Christian, because "God had communicated about this in the Qur'an: 'You know that of all [people] the most brutal haters of the believers are the Jews; and you also know that those who love the believers more than all are those who call themselves Nazarenes." Three years later, a Muslim judge from the neighboring town of Katta Kurgan solicited the Russian governor's aid against local Jews who supposedly resisted his authority, recalling that "His Excellency Governor-General Kaufman said to me: apart from capital punishment and the cutting off of hands and feet and the like, you can do everything, you will be everything, and you will supervise the correctness of all [tax] collections and where you notice abuse of any kind, you can inform our authorities." Political losses could be remade into gains for the shari'a.[24]

But as in the precolonial period, the men of religious authority were not united in becoming clients of the imperial regime. For some intellectuals, the arrival of the Russians inaugurated a period of godless injustice. In acerbic poetry condemning the "Nazarenes," writers like Muhammad Amin Ho'qondiy condemned the new era as "the end time" *(okhir zamon).* Another poet warned that the "Godless unbelievers had filled the world." Similarly, the Kokandian poet Muqimiy lamented that his land had been seized by immorality. Under the rule of the depraved, the kazis' judgments had turned to "dust." "In place of enjoining good [*amri ma'ruf*], evil works have become evident," he complained. Tricked by "the works of Satan [*shaytonliq*]" the people no longer respected learning and turned instead to debauchery. In this grievous epoch, the people had been seduced by "liquor, wine, home-brew" and gambling and had forgotten justice, humanity, honor, and religious learning.[25]

Tashkent's notables responded in a variety of ways to the Russian advance. A few utilized the mobility and connections afforded by Sufi and family networks to pursue alternative careers beyond Russian-controlled Tashkent. Elites like Ya'qub Khan Tura never adapted to the new order. Born in 1823, he served as an emissary of the khan of Kokand to Istanbul, where, on the eve of the conquest, he sought the support of the sultan against the Bukharans and the Russians. Within two years after the tsarist occupation, Ya'qub Khan abandoned the town where his father had been governor and he himself had been a judge and head of one of the main madrasas. He departed for Kashgar, where another renegade émigré from Kokand had recently led Muslim rebels against Chinese rule. There he became the ambassador of the newly formed amirate of Kashgar, drawing on affiliations with Sufi brotherhoods in the lodges of Istanbul.[26]

Most elites remained in Russian-controlled territory, and the imperial pattern of reliance on religious authority as a tool of state building continued. Notables vied for patronage in contests for judgeships, professorships, and endowment administration posts. Though a number of tsarist officials distrusted Muslim clerics as intermediaries, broader geopolitical objectives limited the range of options available to them. Their initial experimentation with Islamic institutions in Tashkent seemed, moreover, to promise improved relations with neighboring states. According to General Dmitrii Romanovskii, a Muslim envoy of the khanate of Kokand spoke in 1866 "with special sympathy about the institutions recently introduced . . . in Tashkent." The Kokandians would "consider themselves lucky to be accepted as subjects of His Imperial Majesty, if only they were given the hope that the shari'a will be preserved among them." Two decades later, religious policy remained a central aspect of the "guarantees and conditions" that formalized the submission of the Transcaspian region. There, after accepting the surrender of Turkmen tribes, General Komarov announced, "Your religious confession will remain inviolable." The issue required "no explanation" because "it is known to the whole world that millions of Muslims, subjects of the GREAT SOVEREIGN, have never been constrained in the free exercise of the rites of their faith."[27]

As elsewhere in the empire, however, toleration did not spell noninterference; its particulars had to be negotiated with, and reshaped by, intermediaries. Speaking before an assembly of Tashkenti notables upon his arrival in January 1868, Kaufman declared that the tsarist regime would be a defender of tradition, castigating indigenous rulers who "out of avarice . . . sometimes violated Muslim laws and imposed illegal taxes." The governor-general nevertheless introduced changes from precolonial practices. The residents of Tashkent and "all other Sarts" would be permitted to elect elders (*aksakals*) and Islamic law court judges (kazis). With the exception of "only a few crimes," justice would be administered by elected kazis

"according to the shari'a and custom in such a way that Russian bureaucrats will not have the right to interfere." If both sides agreed to
take their dispute to a Russian court, they had the right to have it adjudicated there "according to conscience [*po sovesti*]." In this view,
"native" courts were to be only "transitory" in nature. Eventually, as
locals gained exposure to the Russian laws and learned the Russian
language, and as Russian settlers arrived to strengthen ties to the
center, these courts would give way to imperial statute. In the meantime, Kaufman explained, "the government proposes to transfer into
the hands of the people a large part of the administration." At the
same time, he warned his audience, "the best people of Tashkent,"
to communicate to other residents that the government expected cooperation in return. Governing in the interest of the people's "own
good," it did not want to rule by "terror" (*strakh*).[28]

Far from maintaining the status quo, the regime transformed the
functioning of religious institutions. In 1865 Cherniaev had confirmed the senior judge as head of the Islamic hierarchy appointed
by the last Kokandian khan. His successor, Romanovskii, had attempted to replace this post with a collegial body modeled after
courts established in the Caucasus and Algeria in which popularly
elected judges and colonial officials would both preside, but this
court lasted only a half year or so. Russian authorities soon rid themselves of both the senior judge and the censor.[29]

As in the Volga and Urals regions, officials looked for men of influence in the mosque communities of Turkestan; and like their co-
religionists in the empire, many Turkestani Muslims sought out allies who might aid them in struggles within their own communities
over the implementation of divine law. The regime did not support
an official Islamic hierarchy in Turkestan because officials feared
repetition of the negative aspects of the history of the Orenburg Assembly. They did not want to lend Islam an organizational structure
that might further contaminate the region's nomadic populations.

But the same bureaucrats who fought the spread of Islam among the Kazakhs acknowledged that the settled inhabitants of the region would have to be treated differently. They feared that any constraints on Islam in towns where the religion was deeply rooted would jeopardize the tsarist presence. Indeed, some believed that the ancient madrasas of Samarkand and Bukhara produced even more "fanatical" students than elsewhere in the empire. Tsarist officials thus moved cautiously in establishing laws and institutions for the new governor-generalship. On an ad hoc and informal basis, the tsarist authorities aligned themselves again with men of religious learning and laypeople whom they believed stood for Islamic orthodoxy.

Officials valued the stability that they presumed would come with the khan's inheritance, even though it clashed with their pronouncements about Russia's civilizing mission. Although the state lacked an extensive bureaucratic apparatus like in the Volga and Urals regions, police and officials nonetheless became critical actors in religious disputes, intervening in conflicts dividing neighborhoods in Tashkent, Samarkand, Kokand, and other cities. By mediating disputes among Muslims and acting on complaints from clerics as well as laypeople, their reach extended into rural settlements as well.

The task proved particularly complicated in Turkestan, because Russian officials had to reckon with the legacy of the khans in seeking out the representatives of "orthodox" Islam. They feared introducing institutional innovations that might provoke Muslim resistance, as that in turn might jeopardize their fragile hold on a territory contested by several powers. But before they could affirm traditional moral and judicial authority, they had to identify it. Many Turkestanis came forward to cooperate in this search for continuity with the heritage of the khan. Tsarist officials then had to ajudicate the competing claims made by these informants about the character of Islamic personnel and institutions under the khanate.[30]

As a result, recognition of indigenous elders and judges as bearers of imperial authority did not merely confirm or place a new stamp on personnel and institutions inherited from the preconquest past. Religious families had long dominated certain posts. Muhammad Salih, the historian met above, inherited the post of imam in Tashkent from his grandfather.[31] But many of the people who came forward to occupy these roles were not necessarily true heirs, even though their claims to that effect sometimes deceived Russian officials. Where Russians introduced the electoral principle in the selection of officeholders, they only intensified rivalries among Turkestanis.

The tsarist regime functioned in Turkestan as an arbiter of religious disputes. The state was weaker there than in other Muslim regions, its position more exposed because of both the size of the population and the region's proximity to competing imperial powers. However, the foundations of the regime lay less in the civilizing designs of imperial elites than in the tactical alliances that grew out of the mediation of grassroots conflicts among Muslims. Given the regime's vulnerability in Turkestan, these interactions may have been more important to its functioning there than elsewhere.

Rather than floating above what officials took to be traditional institutions, the state became deeply embedded in Turkestani communities through its involvement in the struggles it helped to unleash. The state rejected a single official Islamic hierarchy for the region, but district chiefs and police inserted themselves into the neighborhood and village fault lines produced by competition for official patronage. These communities differed from those in the Volga and Urals regions in that they lacked lengthy experience with tsarist law and institutions. Some Turkestanis may have remained hopeful that Muslim political rule would be restored. But many more in these communities quickly adapted to the institutions of the empire, using these new resources to arbitrate religious controversies with their kinfolk and neighbors, making the tsarist state central to disputes already under way in the local mosque and madrasa.

Despite the ever-present anxieties of colonial officials and experts, the deep interpenetration of Islamic controversies and tsarist administration account for the relative strength and durability of the imperial order in Central Asia. Townspeople rioted under extraordinary circumstances, as in the cholera riots of 1892 in Tashkent, and Kirghiz occasionally clashed with Russian settlers or troops, most notably in the Andizhan uprising of 1898. But the instigators of such violence did not simply target Russians. In the cholera riots, a local notable tied to the administration was the primary object of mob violence; in the 1898 Andizhan uprising, an armed crowd of some two thousand attacked a tsarist garrison, killing twenty-two soldiers.[32] Their leader, Dukchi Ishan, sought not only to rid the area of Russians but also to forge a society that submitted fully to the shari'a, sweeping aside what he saw as the corrupted religion of the established Sufis and scholars. Thus even on these exceptional occasions of upheaval, the focal points of popular antagonism were the indigenous actors who mediated between Muslim communities and the state.[33] Hostility toward these mediators was more an asset than a liability for the empire during the first half century of tsarist rule in Central Asia. For the most part, Muslims became more engaged in their everyday lives in fighting one another than in struggling against the regime. Local administrators stood ready to referee these contests.

Colonizing the State

Soon after the administrative machinery of the governor-generalship of Turkestan started functioning in late 1867 and early 1868, Muslims began drawing authorities into the mediation of the very disputes that state officials had identified with the inviolable realms of "religion" and "custom." These included legal matters relating to the family, even though officials had identified this area of the law as one in which state intervention might provoke the most opposition. Still, Muslim litigants appeared in the recently constructed chambers of local imperial bureaucracy to request aid in resolving family conflicts. In July 1868 Shakir Bikulov asked the commandant of Tashkent, Rossitskii, to help him secure the return of his wife, who had fled to her relatives, taking with her the five-hundred-ruble bride-price. In this case Rossitskii refused to involve himself directly in the dispute and forwarded it to the kazis of Tashkent. Word continued to spread that the new authorities could offer some satisfaction, however, and locals came forward in search of advantage against their opponents. Some sought a way around established legal institutions and networks of patronage and authority; many more sought out alternatives to individual Islamic law court rulings without giving up recourse to these courts altogether. Especially in the area of family law and the administration of endowments, Turkestanis looked to these new officials to fulfill the roles assumed by their former rulers.[34]

Though Russians viewed them as ignorant of "law," the Turkestanis quickly familiarized themselves with imperial administrative and judicial practice and made tsarist law a resource in disputes about the shariʻa. Muslim elites and laypeople recognized their new rulers as potential allies in the struggle to cultivate a society based on the shariʻa, responding to the generals' pronouncements about official regard for local custom and religion. Although regulations of 1867 permitted "natives" to appear before Russian courts upon the mutual agreement of both parties to a dispute, Muslims rarely took their affairs to these courts.[35] Rather, Muslims solicited intervention to correct injustices in their own courts, on the basis of the shariʻa.

Townspeople and villagers came forward to serve in the lowest ranks of administration, especially as policemen, tax collectors, and translators. The gradual expansion of a state apparatus and settler presence created opportunities for merchants and artisans to assume roles in an emergent colonial economy.[36] Some entrepreneurs had already become familiar with Russian life. Merchants had engaged in long-distance trade through Russian markets and drew on decades of experience earned by travel to and sometimes residence in Orenburg (and its environs) and other towns linked to eastern trade networks.[37] Tatar soldiers and translators serving in the tsarist army also established contacts among their local co-religionists (with whom they shared linguistic ties).[38]

For Muslims, establishing a relationship with the district chief (*uezdnyi nachal'nik*) could bring substantial benefits. Muslim critics complained that a "money aristocracy" or "'ulama aristocracy" had amassed personal fortunes through interaction with the machinery of imperial government.[39] Yet such opportunities were not restricted to an aristocracy, nor did they come solely in the form of financial gain. Striking an alliance with an official might ultimately yield material advantage for a Muslim merchant or entrepreneur, but much more was at stake for feuding scholars, neighbors, and husbands and wives. For judges in particular, ties to imperial authorities and access to police, including the capacity to imprison or exile opponents, amplified the coercive powers of religious and communal authority.

Notables expected the tsarist administration to confirm privileges they had formerly enjoyed. The presentation of a royal decree from a khan became the basis for claims ranging from the control of property, especially of endowments, to judgeships and other official posts. Locals who demanded recognition of institutions and practices associated with the khanate evoked conflicting responses from state officials, many of whom suspected that this arrangement gave license to machinations by claimants to these posts.

These misgivings haunted the authorities. Eugene Schuyler, an

American diplomat who visited the region in the 1870s, claimed that the elective system for judges, elders, and policemen had "turned out very badly, bribery and corruption having become prevalent in the elections, and direct pressure at times exerted by the authorities for their favorites, certain persons being excluded from the lists as fanatical, and the choice of certain candidates almost commanded." Schuyler also observed that tsarist reliance on figures despised in local society nourished intrigue among notables clamoring for state backing. He presented the well-connected Said Azim as a prime example of an intermediary who owed seemingly everything to imperial power. "In reality the Sarts hate him," Schuyler asserted, noting, "I more than once heard people say that should the Russians ever leave Tashkent the first thing that would be done would be to kill Said Azim. He meddles in every matter, and is said, in carrying on his numerous lawsuits, to hire witnesses and buy up the Kazis, and there are few affairs of importance among the natives in which he does not somehow manage to have a ruling voice." Russian oversight of appointments also had a real impact on the practice of customary law—including the shari'a—when, as Schuyler observed, "the decisions of inefficient and corrupt judges in the end necessarily caused distrust and complaint, and the Russians are obliged to interfere either to quash the decisions or to insist upon their being carried out, which excites discontent under the Russian rule."[40]

In Zarafshan, by contrast, the local administrator, Georgii A. Arendarenko, viewed competition for elected judgeships as an occasion to manipulate the outcome, the surplus of candidates providing an opportunity to fill the posts with figures "most loyal to our interests." A defender of the shari'a as an "ancient law" with "many progressive, many humane principles," Arendarenko argued that these judges "valued the positions and, for the most part, discharged their duties superbly, remaining in their posts for several years."[41]

Though some 'ulama avoided association with the Russians, many others came forward in search of a new patron. They managed to persuade tsarist authorities to honor what they represented as traditional practices established under the khans. In 1868 the four kazis of Tashkent petitioned the commandant requesting that jurisconsults and other legal experts be allowed to continue in their capacity as advisers and scribes and to receive a set income from civil cases. The commandant did not see anything "suspect" about the request and concluded that it did not violate Muslim "custom," adding that it might even make their handling of cases "fairer."[42]

Other members of the 'ulama convinced tsarist authorities to put them on the government payroll. Mullahs in Novyi Margelan apparently received 180 rubles a year by order of the governor-general in exchange for issuing oaths and performing other services. From the district of Osh, another mullah petitioned the district chief for payment (as a "family man"), citing his five years of service for the local court investigator, the local commander, the field hospital, and others for whom he issued oaths and buried minor Muslim officials.[43]

To the Islamic law court judges of the district of Namangan in the Ferghana region, the arrival of tsarist authorities seemed to offer a resource in a fight to claim their rightful place in their mosque communities. Within three years of the tsarist annexation of the area in 1876, several judges requested that an official assign them the exclusive right, "in accordance with the shari'a," to oversee appointments to positions attached to mosques, Islamic schools, pious endowments, and law courts. Prayer leaders, teachers, endowment managers, jurisconsults, and others would be under their authority. The kazis sought to enlist the Namangan district chief's support in countering the actions of laypeople, who, they claimed, "had taken into their hands the right to replace and name [candidates] for these positions at their own discretion, [by] carrying on elections among themselves."[44]

Investigation of these claims by governor Abramov revealed that district chiefs in the Ferghana region had devised inconsistent responses to the competing demands advanced by kazis and laypeople. Lieutenant Colonel Batyrev, the district chief of Kokand, reported that "parishioners" chose and maintained prayer leaders, teachers, and mosque functionaries by themselves, while he appointed jurisconsults and legal consuls, either on the recommendation of the kazis or at his own discretion. The district chief also named professors *(mudarrises)* of madrasas and overseers *(mutevalis)* of endowments. As these figures "should distinguish themselves [by possessing] a particular morality and certain knowledge," he explained, a commission of four city kazis and "four of the most learned and moral mudarrises" assisted him in making these appointments by testing candidates' knowledge and gathering information about them. Final consideration of the candidate depended ultimately on the district chief, however. Batyrev recommended this policy for application throughout the region, noting that the demands made by the kazis of Namangan would only result in "abuses, for the kazis will either sell posts or name only their relatives."[45]

Other district chiefs assumed a more modest role, largely confining themselves to the confirmation of candidates proposed by mosque communities or judges. In the district of Margelan, members of mosque communities elected prayer leaders and teachers, while kazis chose jurisconsults and legal experts. Though the Kokand district chief had insisted on naming madrasa professors and overseers of endowments, the official in Margelan granted this right to the founders of the endowments (which also maintained the madrasas). From Andizhan, the district chief reported that the "esteemed and elderly natives" of the district had informed him that the khans or their representatives had formerly made all of these appointments and kazis had never enjoyed this right. This lieutenant colonel concluded that the kazis' request was "contrary to the rules of the shari'a." He proposed instead that an examination process be established, as under the khans, to measure candidates' qualifications. The Andizhan district chief also pointed out that the same figures appointed by the khans remained in office under tsarist rule, adding that he had given them orders to present themselves for reconfirmation in their posts in 1876 and in each following year.[46]

The military governor's plan for addressing this chaos highlighted the need to establish a uniform policy for the entire region, one that "would not break too much from the procedures we have followed on this subject to date and would correspond to the goals pursued by our government in the territory and the good of the people." Abramov concluded that, contrary to their claims, the Namangan kazis never had the right to make appointments to these various posts. The district chief was to play a critical role in confirming all of these appointments to ensure that figures "distinguished by religious fanaticism" and "those unreliable in the political sense because of their convictions" did not gain access to these offices. Local officials were to collect as much information as possible about the occupants of these posts to guarantee the appointment of qualified candidates, those who "are not capable of counteracting the realization of our tasks in the region." Abramov harshly criticized the involvement of a commission composed of local scholars, like the one operating in Kokand, in examining the competency of candidates. He noted that "given the current, relatively low mental condition of the Muslim population, of which the commission would be composed, its members would not be in a position to relate to those being examined impartially and would act in their own personal interests." Advising the gradual abolition of the commission in Kokand, he cautioned district chiefs to perform these important functions "circumspectly and impartially, for only with these qualities can one teach the population to trust the fairness of [government] actions . . . and [inspire] respect for the persons governing the population."[47]

Islamic authorities found themselves treading a line between Russian officials and public opinion, a dilemma they had not confronted on the same scale in the khanates. In 1879, residents of Andizhan complained that Islamic law court judges had inflicted injustices upon them. Tsarist authorities' inquiries revealed mixed opinions about these kazis. Not all residents complained, but some cited episodes of unfair treatment. In November 1882 Masadyk Amanbaev filed a complaint with the governor against a kazi, Iusuf Ali Khodzha, who, he claimed, had struck him twice with a whip during court proceedings. Seven witnesses confirmed Amanbaev's accusation. Iusuf Ali countered that Amanbaev had meddled in the case and insulted him, calling him "insane." The judge admitted to driving the plaintiff away from the court but denied using a whip. The two parties apparently reconciled later, but tsarist authorities remained concerned about the case because the judge had committed the offense of "giving insults" while "in the fulfillment of official obligations," a violation of the criminal code. Judges in the district of Kokand faced similar difficulties; over a ten-year period, the authorities fired eleven of the thirty-three kazis and prosecuted seventeen of them.[48]

Lay challenges did not always succeed. In 1881, notables from Ul'tarminsk petitioned the district head of Kokand to remove their kazi, Mullah Khusein Magomet Rakhimbaev, whom they accused of "immoral behavior (pederasty)." The district chief, Batyrev, found the charges "inconclusive" because all of the accusers relied on the testimony of one local resident who could not be located. Batyrev judged Rakhimbaev's defense all the more plausible, he reported, because he had heard that his accusers regularly used their status as electors of township managers and judges to enrich themselves by selling their votes to prospective candidates. Despite his skepticism, Batyrev found charges made by other elders compelling in some cases. In 1882 he fired a judge after elders complained about his handling of at least one inheritance case.[49]

Like Muslim authorities elsewhere in the empire, however, Turkestani 'ulama often felt emboldened by the backing of a state whose police power far exceeded that of its predecessors in the region. Islamic law court judges in particular had gained new powers. The Russians had abolished a number of offices and outlawed the application of corporal and capital punishments by these courts; they subjected judges to popular elections, fixed three-year terms, and closely scrutinized judges and their rulings. At the same time, the 1886 statute on the administration of the territory offered these judges novel means to project their influence. Breaking with the fluid practice of precolonial times, by which litigants could choose the judges to whom they brought their suits, the new regime territorialized these jurisdictions. Litigants now had to appear before the judges of their town quarter. Moreover, these judges wielded expanded discretionary authority, including the power to fine litigants up to three hundred rubles for various offenses and, most important, to give prison sentences of up to eighteen months to Muslims who contravened the shari'a. Litigants still retained the possibility of appeal, both to an assembly of judges and to tsarist officials. But a wide range of penalties—including fines less than thirty rubles and jail terms of under seven days—were exempt from review. To the Islamic court system of Turkestan, the tsarist regime contributed not only new punishments but a police force to implement such rulings—and to compel litigants, including Jews, to appear before the kazis.[50]

Tsarist officials remained poorly informed about the functioning of these courts; only an early twentieth-century investigation began to suggest the extent to which Muslim judges had adapted the regime to their own pursuits. Investigators were shocked to discover that courts prosecuted acts deemed religious offenses. A judge in Tashkent issued four-month prison sentences to two men and a woman charged with "engaging in acts contrary to the shari'a":

drinking beer and playing a stringed instrument, the *dutar,* in one of their homes. Another Tashkent kazi reportedly sentenced card-players to jail for a month, while a kazi in the Ferghana Valley town of Margelan jailed two Sart women for three months because they "spent time in the company of strange men" and fined a male Muslim for associating with gamblers and drinkers. Sart women apparently received prison terms "sometimes for several months" for wearing Russian clothes or appearing on the streets with an unveiled face.[51]

Tsarist law empowered administrators to abrogate such rulings. The senator who headed the investigation, Count Konstantin K. Palen, concluded that "Russian state power, of course, cannot regard such violators of the shari'a and adat [custom] as criminals." Each time officials used the article to revoke the judgment or decision of such a court, Palen claimed, it demonstrated to these judges that "they are not the isolated and all-powerful guardians of the Muslim law and religion, but the representatives of a united Russian Supreme authority and the executors of the law that is universal for all Russia." Yet Palen's investigation conceded that neither current legislation nor local administrative practice clearly established how to respond to judgments that treated particular acts as crimes according to local law when tsarist statutes did not regard them as such. Although some district courts annulled such rulings, others refused to overturn them. Between 1905 and 1907, prosecutors reviewed sixty-one such cases on an appellate basis, canceling fifty-six of them. Palen's report objected to three of the five rulings left standing by various district courts: a three-month prison sentence "for the consumption of beer," a four-month term "for bad behavior," and another four months "for drunken behavior, as an example and lesson for others." The prosecutor of the district court of Samarkand annulled a fifteen-day prison sentence for a Muslim butcher who sold to other Muslims lamb prepared by Jews, but in 1908 another prosecutor backed the ruling of a kazi in the town of Aulieata in the Syr Darya region who imprisoned two butchers there for selling such meat to Muslims.[52]

The story of the Islamic courts in the region reveals some of the ways Muslims appropriated tsarist police and prisons to amplify particular visions of the shari'a, but the regime simultaneously adapted Islamic law to its own purposes. An example of Russian tolerance for Russia's Muslim neighbors, maintenance of the shari'a seemed to guarantee more than social discipline. Paradoxically, it also offered a means for the state to seize vast amounts of land for the Romanov treasury and for settler colonization.

Like colonial powers elsewhere, the tsarist regime confronted an obstacle to state appropriation of land in the Islamic legal institution of the pious endowment (waqf). At the time of the Russian conquest, endowments attached to shrines, mosques, madrasas, and other institutions controlled extensive tracts of arable land. In many locales, foundations managed community access to water.[53] Madrasas received sizable annual incomes from hundreds of stores, caravansaries, mills, bazaar stalls, orchards, gardens, and fields in rural settlements. In Tashkent, the Khoja Ahrar madrasa disposed of a caravansary, fifty-two stores, three hundred storehouses, and other properties, which together earned an annual income of more than six hundred rubles for the school. In the district of Ferghana alone, waqf lands exceeded twenty-seven thousand acres.[54] Established for pious purposes according to Islamic legal principles, these foundations sustained mosques, madrasas, schools, and soup kitchens and generated alms for mendicant mystics like those shown in Figure 7. At the same time, waqfs generated incomes for the descendants of their founders, including Sufi dynasties. In many locales, families of

Figure 7 Sufis near Samarkand. Courtesy of Library of Congress, Prints & Photographs Division, Prokudin-Gorskii Collection, LC-DIG-prok-02315.

khojas, who claimed saintly lineages, retained control over enormous endowments—and the dependents who lived on these lands—for over three hundred years. The descendants of the mystic Khoja Ahrar managed to control into the early twentieth century most of the endowments he had founded in the late fifteenth century.[55]

Russian administrators remained uncertain about the social and religious underpinnings of the endowments immediately following the conquest. Fearing opposition from the "fanatical" classes who would be harmed by confiscations, they promised to honor the inviolability of the endowments, while seizing the property of political foes. In Ferghana, the Russians claimed property owned by figures like Abdullabek, the last person to occupy the throne of the khanate who fled to Afghanistan. But they left intact the foundations Abdullabek had established for shrines and a madrasa in Osh, and his sons continued to manage the properties.[56] Disputes over the management of such endowments—and of the schools and mosques they supported—presented local administrators with an entry point for intervention.

These struggles proved especially contentious because they intersected with family politics: fights for control of endowments brought with them feuding kin groups, 'ulama factions, and madrasa students. In 1868 the Beklerbek brothers, two sons of the founder of an endowment, sent a letter to Rossitskii, the commandant of Tashkent, complaining about the state of "despotism" into which the large madrasa and several mosques founded by their father had fallen. They blamed a professor, Sharafutdin Mazzum, for this disarray. They charged that his enjoyment of opium prevented him from performing his obligations. The brothers also accused him of interfering in the affairs of the manager of the endowment and using its funds for his own gain while the buildings fell into disrepair and students suffered from inadequate instruction. The brothers asked the commandant to reveal the opium-using professor's "treachery" and remove him from his post so that they might appoint another in his place.[57]

Eighteen of Mazzum's students submitted a rebuttal of these charges. They expressed their satisfaction with him and added that he "worried day and night about their instruction." The brothers' complaint against him was nothing more, they maintained, than "a lie and slander." The commandant referred this case to an elder, and a report on the case reveals that it ended in reconciliation.[58]

Another case from Kokand illustrates the critical function that

tsarist authorities assumed in contests for control of religious communities and their resources. In 1881 Batyrev discovered irregulari-
ties in elections for the post of endowment manager of the madrasa
Chal'pak. Khal'kdzhan Kasymbaev had appeared for confirmation
before him, claiming the support of the professors of the madrasa.
After approving the appointment, Batyrev learned that Kasymbaev's
claim had been false and removed him from office.

The subsequent investigation revealed that a second manager associated with the madrasa, Mullah Akhmet, had devised the scheme.
He had arranged Kasymbaev's "election" in return for a cash payment. According to Batyrev, Kasymbaev reneged on the deal after assuming his post, and Mullah Akhmet led a campaign to remove
him. Batyrev identified Kasymbaev as the primary cause of this "intrigue" and sentenced him to ten-day arrest, asking his superiors to
punish him further. In numerous episodes of this type, officials intervened in the administration of waqf properties by appointing and dismissing their managers.[59]

In mediating conflicting claims surrounding these foundations,
tsarist officials increasingly focused on the documents that purported
to establish the intentions of the founders and ground them in
Islamic legal conventions. As with other institutions, the regime
sought out continuities with earlier practices. Exemption from taxation emerged as the most important "right" that waqf managers aspired to secure under the Russians. To verify such claims, the state
conducted a review of endowment charters and other documents to
prove their authenticity and establish their status under pre-tsarist
rulers. But the bureaucracy was overwhelmed by the review. It lacked
the linguistic and technical skills necessary for the task, some institutions failed to submit charters, many documents were never properly
reviewed, and regional administrative peculiarities persisted.

The governors-general nevertheless managed to impose an intellectual coherence on the project. Drawing on the Orientalist gloss

on the shari'a as a body of fixed texts, developed by Kazem-Bek and other scholars in Kazan and St. Petersburg, administrators read the endowment documents with an eye to measuring their conformity with the strict letter of Islamic law on waqf.[60] Beginning with Kaufman, tsarist officials saw in Central Asian endowments the corruption of Islamic legal principles by greedy elites who hid under the cover of religion. Like other European powers, tsarist authorities used a supposedly more "authentic" reading of Islamic law to delegitimize the contemporary state of Muslim endowments as deviations from textually based principles.[61] In the Russian case, officials could claim to be refuting distortions of the shari'a when confiscating "illegitimate" waqfs. Like the anticlerical Orientalism of Kazem-Bek, such a position allowed the regime to assume a populist guise. The rejection of waqf claims demonstrated the tsarist commitment to "orthodox" Islamic law while making these contested resources accessible to the treasury and "liberating" the dependents who labored on these projects.

Tsarist confiscations never reached the scale of the French in Algeria. The policy still provoked opposition, though not all institutions were equally affected. In Osh, the Alymbek madrasa drew income from more than four thousand acres of land in the rural settlement of Chin-Abad. Its property in Osh itself originally included as many as 161 shops, which paid taxes in support of the madrasa. This waqf proved resilient: at the turn of the century, the shops attached to it generated 1,350 rubles of income for the madrasa. In 1906–1907, some 120 shops still paid into this fund. Elsewhere, the contraction of endowments caused many madrasas to go under, offering further proof in some quarters of the decline of morals under Russian rule. In Andizhan, by contrast, waqf revenues in support of local madrasas nearly tripled between 1892 and 1908.[62]

Though officials like Kaufman had looked forward to the weakening of religious sentiments among the "natives," not everyone rejoiced at the impact of the uneven harassment of Muslim foundations. By the 1890s, travel literature and photographic accounts of the once-grand architectural ensembles of Samarkand, Bukhara, and other locales pointed to the long-awaited decline. Weathered, crumbling mosque and madrasa facades presented Russian observers with a picturesque narrative that seemingly proved the thesis of Muslim decay and consigned Muslim initiative to the distant past. But some observers concluded that the "pitiful condition" of monuments in Samarkand was related to contemporary politics. One scholar pointed out that the famed Bibi Khanym mosque lacked an endowment. The object of both Russian pilfering and preservation efforts, the aging structure was "not only not supported" but was "systematically going to ruins."[63]

By the turn of the century, administrators had grown alarmed at the apparent decay of Islamic institutions and, with them, the guardianship of religious discipline. Officials in Ferghana even proposed to intervene to shore up some of the poorer madrasas. In 1895 they recommended a 1 percent tax levy on endowment properties, with proceeds to be used to subsidize impoverished madrasas. Governor-General A. B. Vrevskii rejected the proposal, after consulting with 'ulama who resisted increased taxation on existing waqfs.[64]

Waqf confiscations were not the only strains on relations between the regime and its Muslim intermediaries. With the growth of a Slavic settler population in the towns constructed adjacent to the major urban centers of the region, increasing sanitation problems provoked conflict with urban residents. Quarantines and sanitary inspections—and the resort to police power that made these practices possible—occasioned periodic protests. Military officials and, later, civilian doctors viewed as sources of contagion the intricate networks of canals, narrow winding streets, dense covered spaces, and the Muslim cemeteries located within the town walls. Their calls for the closing or removal of these cemeteries in the indigenous towns accompanied settlement of the adjacent "Russian" or "new" cities. The most serious conflict occurred in 1892, when the handling of a cholera outbreak in Tashkent sparked a crisis. Rumors spread of a Russian-sponsored plot to poison the water supply, while Tashkentis resisted sanitary inspections and quarantine regulations. Muslim protesters chased an elder from Old Tashkent into the Russian city and gathered before the city commandant. Cossacks ordered to disperse the crowd were joined by Russian mobs, who killed more than a hundred Muslims. A handful of Tashkenti notables were sentenced to death for violating "public order," though their sentences were later commuted to exile.[65]

On behalf of urban Muslims, like those of the town of Chust' in the Ferghana region, kazis spoke out against the new sanitary measures that clashed with Islamic burial practices. In 1879, Muslims there turned to the kazis in nearby Kokand to seek the repeal of prohibitions against burying their deceased family members and neighbors in cemeteries in town. The judges composed a tract supporting residents who opposed the restrictions and submitted it to tsarist officials, who responded by firing the kazis. The officials reported that their decision had provoked "disturbances" among residents, who protested the kazis' removal and demanded their reinstatement, apparently without success.[66]

Appreciation of conflicts between an authoritarian tsarist officialdom and Muslim men of religion should not obscure moments when the latter could mobilize the coercive power of the imperial regime in the name of true religion. Islamic authorities repeatedly enlisted tsarist police to help them suppress behaviors that they judged contrary to the shari‘a. Their appeals often succeeded, though tsarist practice was inconsistent.

For many religious scholars, the trade in boys made up and dressed as women, who danced and sang for the entertainment of men in teahouses and bazaars, stood out as the chief evil—to be combated, if necessary, with the assistance of the Russians. In 1872 Tashkent scholars drew tsarist officials' attention to the practice. Judges and other learned Muslims requested that the new regime enforce their prohibition against dancing boys and "various other customs." The dancing persisted, however, and judges appealed to the commandant again in 1884. They condemned the practice as a "sin" whose suppression by the authorities would be rewarded by the "Mercy of God." Though the commandant shied away from issuing a direct order conforming to the kazis' demand, he did instruct officially recognized elders and their assistants to persuade the people that "every respectable person, in his free time from work, [should] find himself a diversion that is not contrary to the duty of honor and the shari'a."[67]

In a similar episode, the Tashkenti notable Said Azim appealed to the vice-governor to suppress "dancing and other amusements" planned for a feast to be hosted by one of his rivals (who had not extended an invitation to him). In his complaint to the Russians, Said Azim argued that such activities would offend religious sensibilities. The American diplomat Schuyler noted, however, that the thousand or so guests who attended disagreed with Said Azim's claim that "the strict letter of their religion" prohibited these performances.[68]

The policy of "ignoring Islam" proved all the more difficult when Muslims themselves insisted on state intervention. Besides charging others with immorality, Muslims accused their neighbors and kinfolk of heterodoxy and illicit innovation. In 1885 Mullah Babydzhan Khal'p Rakhmankulov wrote the Ferghana governor "on behalf of the residents" of the settlement of Sokh in the districts of Kokand and Margelan to draw attention to a Kirghiz named Dzhaparkul. He complained that Dzhaparkul had proclaimed himself a "holy man" and was gathering followers. Dzhaparkul had violated "the entire Muhammadan law" and wrongfully declared others "nonbelievers." Rakhmankulov had called him before the local kazi, but Dzhaparkul had not wanted "to obey the shari'a" and so did not appear. Rakhmankulov explained that he wanted the governor to order someone to "catch" Dzhaparkul and "bring him to account for tormenting the people . . . for blasphemy and arbitrariness and for the seizure of others' livestock." The authorities should also prosecute "the township head Ashar Ali," he insisted, "for complicity in [these] disorders and for extortion."[69]

The official sent to investigate had a different story to tell. The Russian lieutenant colonel learned that they were both Sufi guides (ishans), with devotees among Kirghiz of two local townships. Dzhaparkul had studied at a madrasa in Kokand and had been a follower of Khakhim Khal'f, "the chief ishan in Kokand." The investigator also gathered that Rakhmankulov had "studied nowhere and is even, so to say, illiterate." His interviews revealed, moreover, that Dzhaparkul was respected by the local nomadic and settled populations; informers regarded him as a "completely honest person leading a modest and quiet life." Rakhmankulov's accusations could not be substantiated, the lieutenant colonel concluded, adding that locals had filed no complaints or suits against Dzhaparkul. Muslims whom he interviewed replied that Dzhaparkul "propagates nothing against religion but on the contrary . . . strictly fulfills all rites and rules of the shari'a and does not shy away from openly teaching others who do not follow these rules."[70]

The Russian investigator identified Dzhaparkul's opposition to Rakhmankulov's own controversial religious activities as the underlying cause of the dispute. Locals accused Rakhmankulov of gathering his followers in the evenings. They met not in the mosque but in a private home where men and women prayed together in one room. After prayers, Rakhmankulov and his followers danced and played guitar until sleep found them lying on the floor beside one another in their bedclothes. The ishan had been conducting these mixed-sex prayer meetings in the open, and Dzhaparkul felt compelled to speak out against them. He claimed that these gatherings not only violated the rules of the shari'a but were "immoral in the highest degree."[71] The official added that some two weeks earlier Dzhaparkul's followers began to reproach Rakhmankulov's followers for their participation in these evening gatherings. The offended Rakhmankulov then set off for the town of Margelan to file a complaint against his rival.

The governor of the Ferghana region reacted with some trepidation to this news. In June 1885 he distributed a confidential circular to all district heads alerting them to the "presence among the population of the region of a religious sect." After describing the group's purported activities, including their evening prayer gatherings, dancing, guitar playing, and communal sleeping arrangements, the circular drew a parallel between Rakhmankulov's adherents and a well-known group of Russian dissenters who stood outside the laws of both the Orthodox Church and the state: "In its method and setup it recalls the Khlysty sect that is prosecuted by our laws."[72]

The governor's circular also acknowledged difficulties in applying the relevant laws. In previous correspondence with the governor-general, the governor had noted the danger of permitting an "open sect" to "deprave" the people, thereby "violating the more or less pure Muslim doctrine." At the same, he hesitated to recommend that the administration itself submit to "a call from the population" to "defend the purity of the Muhammadans' [faith] and prosecute those inclined to heresy," even though the rites of this group "violate the general principles of morality." He advised officials to work "through the native administration" but warned of the corruptibility of "native" officials. Ultimately the Ferghana governor gained the support of the governor-general in his conclusion that imperial authorities should mask their involvement in this religious controversy by once again relying on influential intermediaries. They were "officially to ignore the question of this sect." After studying this group "by degrees and secretly," the government was to "act on the population by means of good advice through religious figures and residents esteemed among the people."[73] Tsarist authorities would thus fight "heresy," but only under the cover of their Muslim clients.

Many other cases reveal that the invocation of tsarist authority became a crucial strategy not only among clerical elites and would-be spiritual guides. As in the mosque communities under the Orenburg Assembly, recourse to administrative or judicial intervention against Islamic authorities or neighbors became an indispensable—if often unpredictable—tool in the hands of laypeople arguing about the law. In January 1874 Said Makhmud Khan sent a petition to the St. Petersburg gendarmes seeking "Most August protection" against the designs of Said Azim (the opponent of "dancing and other amusements" met above). The petitioner claimed that Said Azim intended to marry his nine-year-old daughter by force and with the aid of Muslim authorities. Alim Khodzha Iunusov, who enjoyed the state-conferred honorific "honored citizen," also appealed to St. Petersburg against Said Azim, claiming the latter had manipulated the Tashkent kazis into approving the marriage. Iunusov, too, sought the intervention of the sovereign as the "protector of order and the law of the empire": his objections to the kazis' decision had landed him in prison, and he demanded to be released as "an innocent old man."[74]

A "hereditary honorable citizen" with many friends in Russian business and official circles, Said Azim had initiated state involvement by filing a complaint before Colonel Medinskii against Said Makhmud Khan. According to Said Azim, Said Makhmud Khan had consented to his marriage proposal on behalf of his daughter and had even arranged a viewing but then reneged on the deal. Medinskii ordered the case to be taken up by the kazis. They found in favor of Said Azim, with the condition that the marriage take place after the girl reached the age of maturity.[75]

Said Makhmud and his family then announced their rejection of the kazis' ruling and appealed to the governor, General Golovachev.

Medinskii gathered the parties to announce the governor's decision confirming the kazis' ruling (but also suggesting the possibility of filing suit again when the girl reached maturity). At this meeting Iunusov supposedly declared "loudly and with authority that the governor does not decide the shari'a." When Iunusov refused to sign a document proclaiming his assent on behalf of Said Makhmud, Medinskii warned that such an act committed by one who knows Russian well (as he apparently did) was tantamount to the crime of "impertinence" *(derzost')*, for which the colonel arrested him and exiled him to Siberia.[76]

Laypeople from less privileged strata also negotiated their way through these changing judicial arrangements and appeared before the bureaucracy to present their cases to imperial officials. In 1876 Fatima Magometova, a Tatar woman living in Tashkent, sought out Medinskii's "protection and assistance in divorce," complaining of her husband's "drunken and depraved life" and asserting that he beat her and neglected her financial needs. The husband, a Kirghiz residing in the district of Kuraminsk, also turned to Medinskii asking that he secure his wife's return. Instead of referring the case to the mediation of local judges (in accordance with imperial law), the commandant instructed an official under him to conduct an investigation of the husband and "his way of life." According to Medinskii, the inquiry corroborated the woman's allegations by gathering evidence that her husband had "treated her brutally and even inhumanely" and had also taken money and possessions from her. At the same time, district chiefs annulled kazis' decisions, allowing women to escape men whom they did not want to marry. Similarly, in 1880 a woman named Khal'bibi appealed to the commandant of Tashkent asking him "to order the kazis to speed the resolution of my case," pleading with him "to require the kazis to give me a final divorce from my husband." Residents of the district of Sabzar in Tashkent challenged their kazi as well, charging him with accepting bribes in property cases. A female litigant, Khalmuratova, and her son, Seid Akbarov, also accused a judge named Mukhutdin of "arbitrariness" in an inheritance dispute, though in this case the regional administration found these charges "unsubstantiated."[77]

Alongside such disputes that divided a litigious society, competition for positions and leadership in neighborhoods in Tashkent, Samarkand, Kokand, and other cities and settlements engaged entire communities in broader disputes about religious authority, which in turn reflected complex generational, social, and economic tensions. News of struggles for leadership in mosque communities in Tashkent spread far beyond Turkestan. In February 1889 a Muslim newspaper reported on a scandal surrounding a proposal by a local notable for the construction of a new mosque near the Chimkent gates. Although the governor-general and the city duma approved the proposal, the patron's plan stalled when he could not collect the two hundred signatures necessary to make the proposal legal. Informants pointed to an "influential mullah" whose "enmity" toward the patron turned the community against the new mosque. In other cases, petitioners defended judges and other religious notables by discrediting their accusers. In 1880 Mullah Shakir petitioned the commandant of Tashkent on behalf of the residents of the quarter of Bishagach, who had reelected "for good service" their kazi and elder, and thanked the official for confirming their choice. However, a few "bad people," "who disturb both us and the authorities," had been turning to the Russians with accusations against them, "in pursuit of their own goals." Though the authorities had discovered these charges to be false in the past, Mullah Shakir complained, these "bad people" continued to make false allegations. The petitioner asked on behalf of his quarter that the commandant of the city "warn [these] bad people not to do anything bad," advising him "not to believe their words."[78]

In petitioning the authorities, Turkestani Muslims cited imperial law less frequently than their co-religionists in the Volga and Urals regions who had a better understanding of tsarist bureaucratic procedure. However, contact with a growing settler population in the new towns presented opportunities to Muslims in search of means to advance their claims in religious disputes. From Russian and Tatar immigrants, Turkestanis learned new strategies for dealing with the imperial state. Just as native informants presented themselves and their knowledge of local societies to the regime, imperial informants appeared in the form of individuals who could translate valuable information about the workings of tsarist institutions for locals.

Tsarist administrators tried to prevent Russians and Tatars from manipulating bureaucratic procedure. In 1877 Governor-General Kaufman threatened to exile a merchant named Zauer for writing petitions on behalf of Turkestanis, and in 1882 he instructed lower officials to reject petitions not actually composed by those who submitted the documents. When the Ministry of Justice discovered Kaufman's attempts to stem the flow of petitions and complaints from Turkestanis to the state, it rescinded the governor-general's order as a violation of the general laws, and the practice resumed.[79]

A Russian settler, Aleksei Podgorbunskii, played this mediating role for a Sart woman in Kokand in 1889. In the petition that he crafted with her "because of her illiteracy and by her personal request," the woman asked the governor of the Ferghana region to help her gain release from her marriage and freedom from her husband. Urban life—in this case, a brothel—had exposed the woman to "many good Russian people who out of sympathy for me explained my rather lowly and dirty position and advised me to free myself from the brothel." Persuaded by her new counselors to abandon the life of prostitution that her husband had forced upon her, she turned to the local kazis, who provided her with a document (*rivayet*) certifying that "a woman whose husband allows her to be traded is no longer the legal wife of this man." She then submitted this certificate to the district chief and announced, "I no longer wish to be a prostitute and want to become an honest woman and accept Orthodoxy." Moreover, she requested that she be "freed from the brothel and from the hands of my husband." She made a similar proclamation before the kazis to whom the district chief referred the case. Yet this declaration only landed her in detention in the *kazy-khane* (the building that housed the law court) for four days, after which she followed the kazis' direction to "reconcile" with her husband and give up her thoughts of becoming a Christian.

Her husband, "the tyrant," then pressed her, along with three other wives, back into the brothel. She turned at last to the governor to liberate her from her husband, "so that I may accept Orthodoxy and become an honest and useful woman for society and the State." Colonel Batyrev, the district chief who forwarded on this petition, claimed, however, that Podgorbunskii had been the sole author of this text. He noted that the judges had forbidden the husband to compel his wife to live as a prostitute and that the couple had moved on to the town of Khodzhent, where local authorities reported that the husband had taken up a different "profession." The governor elected "to take no action" on what now appeared to be a highly suspect complaint.[80]

With time, Muslim litigants gained greater access, without the aid of intermediaries like Podgorbunskii, to imperial law in constructing arguments about religion. In 1891 Kaip Kurbaev, a Kazakh from the Ural'sk region, petitioned the Ministry of War to protest a kazi court decision that "deprived me of a wife." He likened this outcome to taking "a piece of my body, as well as property," referring to his loss of the bride-price (in the form of livestock). Kurbaev contested the judge's interpretation of the shariʻa and the false evidence on which he claimed it was based. Against the judge's opinion that the marriage had been illegal and thus invalid, he countered that the kazi's citations "from Arabic books" did not apply to "my case" and insisted that "according to the shari'a as well as other laws this marriage is recognized as completely legal and cannot be refuted."[81]

The petitioner simultaneously pursued a second strategy that contradicted his first claims. In the first part of his petition he had claimed enough knowledge about the shari'a to question the reasoning offered to free his wife from him. In the second part, he cited the temporary statute on the administration of the Ural'sk region that declared that Kazakhs must be exempted from the jurisdiction of the shari'a and made "exclusively subject to the court of the Kazakh people." Thus, he concluded, the judgments made by the kazis of Mangilak and Ashkabad "do not have material significance as orders concerning affairs not under their jurisdiction." He asked that the two judgments be set aside and that his case now be transferred to a Kazakh customary law court. Though Kurbaev's second strategy involving imperial law might have been effective in other districts, the local Russian official backed the Islamic law court judges in this case. On his recommendation, the Ministry of War rejected Kurbaev's attempt to seek out new venues for his frustrated legal struggles.

As litigants like Kurbaev discovered, appeals to imperial judicial and administrative organs often entailed substantial risks. Tsarist authorities did not always respond in the ways that litigants' limited familiarity with imperial administrative and judicial practice had led them to anticipate. Rumors and misunderstandings shaped expectations on both sides. Contact with tsarist authorities sometimes exposed them to arbitrary arrest, extortion, and removal from office.

Tsarist involvement also presented dangers for the regime. Although many litigants turned to the tsarist official with some hope of receiving justice and protection, parties who lost out in such disputes might fault the authorities who had intervened. Suiunduk

Argynbaev, a Kazakh from the Akmolinsk region, was one of the many residents who found new ways to earn a living under the Russians. He had worked as a translator for three months in the district of Andizhan when he was called to the town of Khodzhent to appear before a judge. He returned to find that his wife had fled and hidden herself from him in Kokand. Authorities in the town discovered her there (apparently at Argynbaev's insistence) and ordered her to appear with Argynbaev before the kazis of Kokand. There she proclaimed that she had never been his legal wife.

Argynbaev then had to travel to the town of Andizhan to request a certificate from the judges there to prove that he had been legally married. He received this documentation, which he presented to the district chief, Lieutenant Colonel Obolenskii. In the meantime his wife had turned to Obolenskii with a petition maintaining that she and Argynbaev had never legally wed but had only lived together. She claimed, moreover, that her former lover had stolen things from her. When Obolenskii ordered one of his subordinates to confiscate these things from Argynbaev, the ensuing confrontation (the details of which remain unclear in the latter's account) landed the Kazakh in jail.

Tsarist authorities, Argynbaev complained, had not shown due regard for the documents furnished by the Andizhan kazis testifying that an imam had legally married the couple. In 1881 he brought this injustice to the attention of the governor to protest the "extortion and unfair action" of Obolenskii, whom he also accused of insulting him by asking his wife to unveil her face in violation of the shari'a, and who had chosen to believe her "empty proclamations" while ignoring his documents and the hundreds of witnesses who had known of his wedding.[82] Argynbaev discovered the perils inherent in resorting to Russian officials to restore order to his family on the basis of Islamic law, but his continued appeals to Obolenskii's superiors reveal that he had not entirely rejected the mediating role of the state. Argynbaev now had no power to refuse it.

Russian officials ruled Andizhan and other locales in Turkestan by making themselves central to the resolution of disputes like Argynbaev's. They maintained their position by force of arms, of course, but they rarely needed to call in troops during the first three decades of tsarist rule in the territory. In proclaiming toleration, lawmakers relied on the legal fiction of noninterference in customary law, in this case the shari'a, but instead became integral actors—alongside Muslim religious authorities and laypeople—in its elaboration. The mechanisms of intervention remained informal and still largely dependent upon the invocation of Turkestanis, however. Deeply implicated in the everyday workings of customary law, lower officials were comfortable in roles that made them essential arbiters of much of local community life, even when these roles bore striking similarities to those of the khan's functionaries. Tsarist authorities remained beholden to these courts, as they were to native elders, policemen, tax collectors, translators, and other locals who dominated the lowest ranks of the imperial order.[83]

From the perspective of broad sectors of Turkestani society, the Russian authorities had become unavoidable partners in the everyday practice of their religious law, by dispensing patronage, manipulating appointments, and influencing the outcomes of court rulings. In the eyes of many, these measures likely ensured the corruption of these courts, as Schuyler suggested. They made the functioning of Islamic law courts more dependent upon tsarist police power, as officials compelled the execution of unpopular decisions or struck down others to safeguard "humane" principles. Yet it would be premature to conclude, as did many reform-minded contemporaries, that tsarist policies had completely deprived Turkestanis of re-course to justice, as the victims first of the despotism of the khan, then of the tsar. Turkestanis regularly turned authorities' ideas about "customary law" and universal justice to their advantage. This was leverage gained for use in struggles with their neighbors and kin-folk—not necessarily against the regime.

On the one hand, for many state functionaries the image of tsarist administration as the guardian of humanity and universal justice de-termined what kinds of appeals would gain official support; such officials typically intervened on behalf of women and Jews who ap-peared to be at a disadvantage in a system they criticized as patriar-chal, theocratic, and corrupt. But in cases overseen by administrators who looked to "native tradition" as an adjunct of tsarist rule, litigants could appeal to tradition and thereby assign these officials roles anal-ogous to those played by the beks and khans of the precolonial order.

An uprising led by a Sufi leader in Andizhan in the Ferghana Val-ley in 1898 met with official calls for a total rethinking of Russia's approach toward Islam in Turkestan and elsewhere. The event high-lighted the apparent threat of Sufi guides. In Tashkent the authori-ties learned that many of the ishans there each had hundreds of loyal followers within the city and even in neighboring settlements. Dukchi Ishan, the charismatic figure behind the revolt of 1898, had gained the loyalty of some two thousand followers, including a Mus-lim tsarist officer in south Andizhan. Warning that "Shamil showed us that Sufism is much more dangerous than orthodox Islam," Gov-ernor-General Sergei M. Dukhovskoi proposed a strict new regime of bureaucratic supervision, cautioning the government about fu-ture Shamils and Dukchi Ishans. As we shall see in Chapter 6, Dukhovskoi lost out to more influential ministers in St. Petersburg, and he failed to reorient the empire's Islam policy. In the meantime, tsarist development of Turkestan further loosened control over the region's Muslims. The railroad dramatically increased the number of Turkestani pilgrims who went abroad on the hajj. It also brought more non-Muslim settlers to Central Asia to compete with Muslims over diminishing resources.[84]

Though the bureaucracy and police, in particular, turned to looking for Turkish agents behind every local disturbance, seasoned local administrators continued to seek out Muslim intermediaries and to cloak imperial policy in Islamic terms. For their part, a number of Muslims condemned Dukchi Ishan in satirical poetry, often with the aim of securing Russian favor. And in the wake of 1898 one such administrator advocated renewed attention to old principles. He proposed to demonstrate that the administration respected fairness and "punishes that which is punishable from the point of view of the ethics of Islam." In meetings with locals, he drew attention to commonalities between Islam and Christianity to encourage reconciliation. Moreover, he recommended that the regime base its demands on the Qur'an and shari'a to win the sympathy of the people and persuade them that, though their rulers are foreign, "the administrators nevertheless know [the indigenous] law and value that the inhabitants be good people according to their [own] law."[85]

Despite increased attention to "Pan-Islam" and "Pan-Turkism" as challenges to Russian rule in Central Asia, Muslims still looked to the state to pursue backing in disputes with religious opponents. Thus in 1906 'ulama in Tashkent petitioned the administration to shut down a reformist newspaper after it published criticism of a Qur'anic school. Official management of intra-Muslim disputes, including those between the Jadids and their foes, extended to censorship of anticlerical articles in the reformist press. As Ingeborg Baldauf has noted, however, official defense of the Islamic establishment in Turkestan did not apply to Sufi mystics. In the Jadids, tsarist officials found allies willing to denounce as the purveyors of "illicit innovation" the Sufi brotherhoods that Russian authorities feared from Chechnya to the Ferghana Valley.[86]

In the early twentieth century, Muslims shared with their rulers a preoccupation with moral decline, though their prescriptions for addressing this crisis differed. A petition from "shaykhs, Muslim scholars and residents of the Amu Darya district" to Senator Palen, the official sent to investigate conditions in Turkestan in 1909, drew attention to the source of this anxiety. In the petitioners' view, the phenomenon of moral decline was of very recent origin. At the time of the conquest, the authorities had pledged not to alter the "old ways that had existed from time immemorial" for the appointment of religious offices, "for which we were very glad and prayed for their health." The "old order" continued, they alleged, and "kazis were appointed from figures who knew the shari'a well." Moreover, "muftis and ra'ises existed, thanks to which morality among the Muslims was elevated." But decline set in when the process for choosing judges changed. When elders gained the power to elect kazis, they chose candidates like themselves, "ignorant and immoral," without any knowledge of Islamic law. At the time the Russian administration had limited the authority of these courts. The petition complained that kazis were no longer permitted "to interfere in religious matters."[87]

Restrictions on the guardians of the shari'a had unleashed moral disorder. Women assumed the right to choose husbands freely. Court rulings ordering them to return to their husbands were "always annulled," and women received documents permitting them to live on their own. Husbands and wives were permitted to adjudicate marital disputes as merely civil suits. Even offenses like murder and robbery now went unpunished by the Muslim courts. Deprived by the new rules of the interpretive guidance of muftis, kazis issued judgments "contrary to the shari'a." And without police supervision of the censor, merchants cheated their customers and women flouted the law and "freely [carried] on with men on the streets." Such changes put these "poor inhabitants" in conflict with "the fundamental rules of the shari'a."

But the implications of standing outside of God's law for their own salvation were not their sole concern. Rather, they feared "for the consequences, which may befall us and the Russian Empire for non-observance of the law given to us by God, as is stated in the articles of the shari'a (written in the Arabic language)." To restore the moral order that was so critical for both true religion and the state, the petitioners requested "with tears in their eyes" that the offices of mufti and ra'is be restored. They also asked that judges be chosen only from among those who were "moral and who had studied the shari'a well" and whose knowledge of Islamic law had been examined. Finally, the petitioners requested that mosques and madrasas be permitted to make use of endowment properties.[88]

The tsarist state remained the indispensable foundation of a just moral order, and thus of the authority of the men of religion. Like Muslims elsewhere in the empire, these petitioners sought to shape toleration to suit their ends, all the while highlighting the value of the faith for the empire. At the same time, such intermediaries set boundaries on the Russians' penetration of their communities. More than elsewhere in the empire, the tsarist authorities remained dependent upon disaffected Muslims to initiate contact with the local administration by denouncing their foes.

Through its engagement with controversies among Turkestanis, the regime intruded into the everyday life of local communities while establishing alliances with Muslim men and women in neighborhoods and villages throughout the territory. Recourse to the shari'a had unintended consequences for both sides, however. Turkestanis' appeals to the contradictory principles that underlay tsarist policy often placed Russian officials in a position of dependence upon Islamic institutions and the guardianship of orthodoxy within them.

Initiating and placing constraints upon tsarist involvement in local disputes, laypeople and clerics alike unwittingly blunted the "civilizing mission" of imperial authorities by embroiling them in the mediation of communal and familial conflicts. But the practice of holding Muslims to the letter of their own "law" gave the regime a valuable lever that made the management of this population—and its resources—more effective.

Toleration of Islamic law and institutions served a variety of essential functions in Turkestan. It relieved the Ministry of Finance of the expense of erecting another court system for several million Turkestanis (in addition to the already costly apparatus of the governor-generalship). Moreover, sanctioning the continuation of Islamic law and the institutions that supported it enabled the state to defer the many promises of the civilizing mission, like extension to the region of the "rule of law" and the limited civil rights enjoyed by subjects of the empire in the European provinces.[89] Such policies kept alive visions of further expansion—at similarly low costs—in the Muslim East.

6

HERETICS, CITIZENS, AND REVOLUTIONARIES

In building empire in Central Asia, the tsarist agents of "civilization" had found it expedient to draw on Muslim intermediaries and their faith as a useful means of social control where more formal Russian state institutions remained weak. If the mantle of Islamic patronage rested uncomfortably on the shoulders of Russian administrators in Turkestan, it began to chafe officials even more in the European part of the empire. There the Crimean War and other developments prompted state and Church authorities not only to raise new questions about existing policies toward Islamic institutions, but also to express broader concerns about the character of the Russian empire and its relationship to Europe.

Since the Napoleonic invasion, the Russian tsars had tried to accommodate the contemporary European notion that the people—the "nation"—should participate in politics and that nations and states should coincide as much as possible. Under Nicholas I, the government had responded to the challenge of nationalism in this multiconfessional and multiethnic empire by struggling to co-opt the Russian nation as a support of the monarchy. But the dynasty's growing reliance on "Orthodoxy, Autocracy, and Nationality" as its legitimizing principles left unresolved how this triad related to the tsar's non-Orthodox and non-Russian subjects. The existence of Islamic endowments, mosques, law courts, and schools struck critics of tsarist religious policies as evidence of the backwardness of the state in relation to Europe, where new political entities like Germany, Italy, and the Balkan states were forming on the basis of a single "nationality" sharing a common history, language, culture, and religion. From the 1860s, bureaucrats in St. Petersburg faced their own nationalist movements among non-Russians within the empire. They also confronted challenges to the status quo in the form of revolutionary and constitutionalist ideologies. Diverse forms of dissent lent greater urgency to the search for political stability through the cultural and administrative integration of the heterogeneous populations of the empire.[1]

From the reign of Alexander II, the regime embraced its own image of a national monarchy as the distinctive expression of Orthodoxy and the will of the Russian people. From the western provinces, the Baltics, and Finland, tsarist officials joined conservative Russian nationalists in the capitals who called on the regime to counter separatism and revolution among non-Russians by introducing institutional and legal uniformity, the Russian language, and the Orthodox faith to shore up the state in the borderlands.[2] In May 1867, M. N. Katkov's nationalist daily, the *Moscow Gazette (Moskovskie vedomosti)*, directed the state to rely on "national, and not alien institutions" in this task. It contended that only the "national" Orthodox Church, not the Catholic Church, Judaism, Islam, or other confessions, "was present at the beginning of our historical life, at the birth of our state . . . All of our memories are connected with it, all of our history is filled with it."[3]

Conceding that a "civilized state" permitted different confessions to exist within its borders, the editorial argued that it was a "different matter" to "give force and power to all other religious institutions not having national significance." Just as the state erred in confusing toleration of Catholics with guarding the "purity" of Catholicism and compelling membership in, and submission to, the Church, imperial policy had mistakenly turned Kazan Province into a "flaming hearth of Muhammadanism." Islam was "flagging before Christian civilization in Muhammadan states," but "under Orthodox Russian rule . . . the powerful government of Russia has become Tatar and Muhammadan in these locales." The Russian government had taken on a "Polish and German character" on the western frontier and a "Tatar and Muhammadan character" on the Volga. The prevailing understanding of toleration undermined the government's "own nationality and state like only its most evil opponents could do."[4]

Nikolai Kryzhanovskii, the governor-general of Orenburg Province, envisioned strengthening the state by implementing these prescriptions on the ground. In 1866 he concluded that because the local "diversity of faiths has a harmful influence on the moral and political life of the people," "all activities of local officials should lean toward decreasing, by various measures, the very root of the evil, that is, diversity in faith, as well as the harmful results of this diversity." To combat this evil, he instructed officials to lead all to the "dominion of the Church" by "persuasion and enlightenment." But Kryzhanovskii did not interpret state assistance for the Church as a violation of the fundamental principles of toleration: "Observing completely the principle of religious toleration, it is nonetheless impossible to permit Muhammadanism and the schism [within the Church] to take the form of propaganda, at the manifest detriment of the predominant faith."[5]

In 1869 Kryzhanovskii challenged officials whose misunderstanding of toleration, he charged, led them to place the police at the dis-

posal of Islamic authorities in enforcing religious norms. "Not one of
the foreign confessions existing in the Empire, neither the Catholic,
nor the Lutheran," he noted

> has the right to seek the assistance of police power to re-
> proach its clergy and its parishioners in their religious du-
> ties. Such assistance would be even less appropriate and
> consistent with the views of the state interest in relation to
> the Muhammadan religion . . . one of whose main doctrines
> preaches hatred toward Christians.

Kryzhanovskii observed that it would "be strange and extremely impolitic if Russian police were charged with using the power given
them for the confirmation of Muhammadan mullahs in the rules
of the shariʻa . . . to instill in Muhammadan parishioners zeal toward
the Muhammadan faith." "To force Russian police to affirm and
spread the shariʻa in Russia," he argued, "to drive the people into
mosques and invite parishioners to monetary payments in support of
fanaticism [izuverstvo] may, in truth, be taken as a mockery of the
Russian authorities."[6]

Both Katkov and Kryzhanovskii appealed to historical images of
an ancient enmity between the native state Church and an ostensibly foreign Islam. But their seemingly conservative proposals entailed a more radical agenda. In demanding the disentanglement of
tsarist police power and Muslim religious institutions, they offered a
fundamentally new understanding of the role of the regime in local
life. Their critique called into question the shared moral universe of
Muslims and officials that had grown out of decades of administrative practice based on state patronage of Muslim scholars and selective guardianship of Islamic legal norms and doctrines.

A number of historians have commented on these anxieties surrounding a Muslim challenge to the integrity of the empire in the
late nineteenth and early twentieth centuries. Some accounts link

this development to the appearance of Pan-Islamic or Pan-Turkic sympathies among Tatar and other Muslim elites. Others view mistrust of Muslims through the lens of the struggle during this period between Muslim reformists, or "Jadids," and "traditionalists." Such studies of Muslim reform highlight Russian hostility toward the supposed agents of change in these communities, while underscoring instances of collusion between tsarist officials and "conservatives" aimed at undermining their common foes. Stalked and persecuted by the police agents of the regime, reformers, it is argued, struggled against both Muslim opponents and the state to enlighten their co-religionists in secular knowledge and national awareness and to secure autonomy for a reformed religion and modern nation. Seen in this light, the goals of reform-minded Muslims of the *fin de siècle* appeared to build on the earlier demands of Katkov and Kryzhanovskii for the separation of Islam from the intrusions of the state.

A wider examination of Muslim responses to these developments suggests a different picture, however. Shifting the focus of analysis from a narrow stratum of reformist elites to a broader range of actors, this chapter reveals the continued centrality of tsarist institutions to contests *within* Muslim communities for religious authority and the power to define Islamic orthodoxy in the last years of the empire. Accounts of reform and nationalism among Muslim elites have treated these movements largely outside the framework of imperial institutions. But the nexus of policing and Muslim activism decried by some Russian nationalists and Muslim elites alike persisted into the twentieth century, though in constantly evolving institutional and linguistic contexts.

Muslim agency was essential to this continuity. New research has shown how both Jadids and their opponents frequently looked to the state for assistance.[7] More importantly, recent studies have noted that the impact of the reform agenda on local mosque community life was quite limited. They have also questioned the extent to which differences of opinion between reformers and critics created deep fissures within these communities before the eve of the First World War.[8] This is not to argue, however, that Muslims formed a static and homogeneous monolith. Many older struggles for primacy in local mosques continued. Alongside Jadidism, enduring rivalries, unresolved controversies about the rites of the faith, and new currents of Islamic thought prompted intense debates and fierce conflicts throughout Muslim regions. In the state-directed reform era initiated by the emancipation of the Russian serfs under Alexander II, increased mobility, social stratification, urbanization, universal conscription, contact with Russian neighbors and bureaucrats—as well as the expansion of the book trade, printing, and literacy—made efforts to safeguard orthodoxy and guide the community to live in accord with the shari'a even more pressing.

As new voices claiming to speak for the tradition proliferated, the state's role as arbiter of disagreement and foe of heresy and the betrayal of God's law loomed larger than ever in the eyes of a wide range of Muslim men and women. Avoidance of all things Russian remained an option. But for a stratum of Muslim activists—who were a solid presence, male and female, clerical and lay, in mosque communities—the moral universe circumscribed by tsarist institutions proved very difficult to abandon, even as these bodies evolved. Russian critics' calls for the dismantling of the Orenburg Assembly did not succeed in St. Petersburg. But they did influence the government's choice of personnel. Though Professor Alexander Kazem-Bek backed Muslim selection of the mufti as being more consistent with Islamic law, the government opted to retain control; indeed, the bureaucracy's anticlerical spirit prevailed again when the Ministry of Internal Affairs chose for the post Salimgarei Tevkelev (in office 1865–1885) and Mukhamed'iar Sultanov (in office 1886–1915)—both of whom were Tatar landowners, not esteemed religious scholars.[9] These appointments diminished the authority of the Assembly in the minds of some Muslim critics, but one finds little evidence by the late nineteenth century of wholly autonomous communal mechanisms that such Muslims might have used to fulfill the religious obligation to "command right and forbid wrong" in the Volga and Urals regions. No doubt some forms of mediation existed beyond state institutions; but where consensus broke down, opportunities for the state opened up. The persistence of these interactions challenges the notion that Muslims lived in "a world apart" from the state or that ethnic or religious solidarities can be assumed as the essential and immutable foundations of these communities.

The world of the mosque community was the empire and beyond. Muslim men and women were embedded at once in a predominantly rural economy and in a legal culture and network of state institutions that shaped the local repertoire of Islamic debate and contention. Dependence on the enforcement mechanisms of the regime did not make Muslims powerless. A lengthy history of engagement with the bureaucracy, courts, laws, and administrative procedure placed Muslims in a position to adapt to new conditions, appropriate new languages for communication with the regime, and direct the course of state intervention in particular ways and block it in others.

Though Russian nationalists sought to marginalize the place of Islam in an empire increasingly dominated, they hoped, by a Russian nation, Muslims continued to adapt to and find religious refuge in the tsarist setting. In the early twentieth century, they claimed rights and aspired to become citizens within the limited civil rights regime of autocratic Russia; at they same time, they insisted on state backing for the "orthodoxy" of their competing visions of Islam. The rise of nationalist currents did not effect a parting of the ways between the tsarist regime and the mass of its Muslims subjects. To be sure, the number of those on the extremist fringes calling for confrontation and separation grew in the last three decades of the empire. But the din of their strident voices (often heard more loudly from outside Russia) should not drown out the majority that continued to seek accommodation and pursue integration. Muslims and tsarist elites alike struggled to cope with the many uncertainties of life at the tumultuous turn of the century in an empire undergoing rapid socioeconomic transformation and political upheaval. For many Muslims and state authorities, Islam was a much-needed anchor of stability. More than ever, mounting threats from abroad, especially in the form of Ottoman and European-backed Pan-Islamic movements, confirmed for more moderate Russian statesmen the value of toleration and the multiconfessional world of the Romanov empire. In this view, Islam remained a source of strength for the state and an asset that, if neglected, Russia's enemies—ranging from Germany and Japan to the Ottoman empire—would use to their advantage.

Confronting Islam

Following the Crimean War, local representatives of Church and state redrew the bounds of toleration, not by openly assaulting Islam but by claiming to protect Christians on the Volga and potential Christians among nomads in the steppe.[10] During the war, the government closed the organ of municipal self-administration *(Tatarskaia ratusha)* in the Tatar suburb of Kazan. The regime called on Muslim authorities to issue admonitions calling for sacrifice for the tsar and fatherland, though Muslims were also accused of shirking their duties.[11] Like other subjects, some resisted conscription or deserted. Small numbers of Muslims from the Volga and Urals regions may also have opted to emigrate to the Ottoman empire during or immediately after the Crimean War (or later in 1877–1878), even though the Orenburg mufti warned them against fleeing their fatherland.[12] In most cases, Muslims remained unsure about rumors of a government plan to convert conscripts to Orthodoxy and accepted the call to arms.[13]

Russian officials were self-conscious about harmonizing their policies with those of other imperial powers and meeting new challenges from the Islamic world. They watched as the British assigned primary responsibility for the rebellion of 1857 in India to Muslims and their supposed yearning for the restoration of Muslim sovereignty.[14] In Africa, too, Muslims were said to be the chief foe of European civilization, with Islam acting as both a source of opposition to French or British rule and a cultural alternative to their civilizing missions. Signs of Islamic reform and mobilization in the Ottoman empire, Egypt, China, and elsewhere provoked mixed responses of suspicion (and, less frequently, admiration, where it could be glossed as acceptance of the ideals of European reason). Russians followed the European press, which sounded the alarm about the threat of Pan-Islam, drawing attention to intellectuals like Jamaladin Afghani (1838–1897), who exhorted Muslims to unite against foreign domination. Russian commentators dwelled on dangers posed to European supremacy everywhere by a "fanatical" population emerging from a state of languor and stagnation. A French text distributed among tsarist officials, *Islam in the 19th Century,* laid particular stress on the dangers of "reformist tendencies" that fueled "popular movements on behalf of national and religious authority versus the secular power of usurpers or foreigners." It identified "renewal and propaganda" in Asia and Africa as a "serious danger" for "the actual interests of the civilized world."[15] Within the tsarist empire Shamil and Dukchi Ishan served as reminders of this peril, though the former was captured in 1859 and then allowed to emigrate, following a brief captivity as a celebrity of sorts, and the latter was hanged.[16]

Developments in the Ottoman empire appeared particularly menacing. Abdülhamid II (r. 1876–1908) attached renewed importance to the sultan's claim to the title of caliph, the political leader of the entire Muslim *umma* (the worldwide community of the faithful), as an instrument of both domestic and foreign policy.[17] Moreover, St. Petersburg suspected that Russian interest in the fate of Orthodox co-religionists and Slav "brothers" in the Balkans would be countered by the Turks and their sultan-caliph, who would make similar appeals for the loyalties of Muslims in the heartland of Russia as well. In 1877–1878, war against the Ottomans gave anti-Muslim commentators cause to identify the oppressors of the Orthodox Bulgarians and Serbs with Russian Muslims. While popular prints depicted the conflict as a war between Orthodoxy and Islam, a war to bring "the arrogant moon" of the Ottoman flag to its knees, the missionary Mikhail Mashanov warned that the Muslim knows no fatherland: "his fatherland is wherever there is Islam."[18]

The criteria of religion and language increasingly competed with devotion to the dynasty as the markers of allegiance to the imperial order. Where patriotism had once been measured by loyalty to the monarch alone, knowledge of the Russian language and membership in the Orthodox Church became more urgent priorities in an age when states reorganized along national lines appeared to define the future of Europe. Speculation about the subversive designs of Muslims, supposedly coordinated by political opponents within and beyond the borders of the empire, was rife in nationalist circles that encompassed Russian elites ranging from newspaper editors to the highest ranks of the Holy Synod and other ministries. Yet Muslim adversaries of the "state interest" never monopolized the attention of Russian rightist, Pan-Slav, and Orthodox elites in Moscow and St. Petersburg. They competed with Jews, Poles, Germans, Armenians, and other non-Orthodox Christians as well as with revolutionaries and unruly peasants and workers. Nor were Muslims the primary targets of rightists. In Kazan Province in 1905, for example, monarchist "Black Hundreds" even formed local branches designed to recruit a Muslim membership.[19] As scapegoats for various ills of the post-emancipation era, Muslims' attractiveness varied according to the vicissitudes in educated Russians' anxieties about these other groups.

Local experiences lent a distinctive color to the confrontation with Islam as perceived by bureaucrats in Samara, Ufa, Simbirsk, Orenburg, and Kazan. The composition of the Orthodox community was a central concern inherited from the Nicholaevan era. Church surveys had revealed that 109 of 213 parishes in the province of Kazan were mixed parishes that contained non-Russians *(inorodtsy)* whom the Church continued to classify as "converts." In the diocese of Kazan alone, the survey identified more than fourteen thousand "converted Tatars."[20] Converts unleashed scandals when they rejected Orthodoxy by the hundreds at the accessions of Alexander I and Nicholas I and again in 1866. Apostasy spread along paths prepared by activists (and their allies in the lowest ranks of the bureaucracy) who coordinated the campaigns and supplied copies of the same petitions to converts who sought the tsar's approval— and thus legal backing—for their reversion to the "faith of our ancestors." Frustrated by their inability to stem the flow of apostates in mixed settlements, churchmen secured central government approval for the revival of missions.

Under Nicholas I, the missions gave the Church a new foothold in local politics, and imperial law obligated temporal authorities to protect the privileged position of the tsar's faith. Indeed, the Church established itself as a powerful political force even on issues of provincial government not explicitly concerned with the condition of the missions. The guarding of the flock brought them into conflict with Muslims who maintained ties with baptized neighbors and kinfolk. Bishops initiated invasive police measures, as when they successfully lobbied governors to dispatch investigators and police to the scenes of "religious crimes."

Recourse to police power never completely stifled religious change and confessional mixing. But ecclesiastical initiative did have a profound effect upon the lives of people who had been counted, by either birth or personal conviction, as members of the Church. Those who had been baptized—or whose ancestors had received the sacrament—were subject to a range of punishments for shirking the obligations incumbent upon all whom this rite had initiated into the body of the Church. Penalties ranged from the admonition of the parish priest to penance in a monastery or reformatory. Church and state authorities exiled converts who failed to adopt "Russian ways." This involved the forced resettlement of converts to what officials believed to be a more firmly Orthodox environment, a Russian village in another district or province.[21] Tsarist authorities carried out population transfers in the 1840s and 1850s, breaking up and scattering families and whole villages across the region.

The Church also challenged Muslim book publishing, which the priest Malov called the "buttress of Muhammadanism" and a "weapon" wielded against Christianity. The Synod condemned the printing of Tatar, Persian, and Arabic books at the press attached to Kazan University, charging that it strengthened Muslim solidarity and served as an incitement to apostasy. The Ministry of Internal Affairs was sympathetic to this view. It argued that tsarist toleration could not permit the printing of the Qur'an, in particular, because Muslims themselves regarded it as a betrayal of their creed and thus "with the existence of religious toleration in Russia, no deviations from the ancient rules and customs of all confessions tolerated in Russia (as long as they are not counter to state laws) may be permitted, especially on behalf of private speculation." The response of the governor of Kazan, based on local Muslim informants, contradicted this claim, however. He pointed out that Muslims accepted printing, and that restrictions might prove harmful to the empire. Warning that the British and their agents might seize the book trade, the governor concluded, "The printing in Russia of the Qur'an and other books in Oriental languages should spread among neighboring Muslim peoples a trust in Russia's protection and religious toleration, which may not be useless." As a result, the printing of the Qur'an and other Islamic texts continued in private and university presses, and the Church failed to undo this aspect of toleration.[22]

From the second quarter of the century, clergymen and many state officials came to view their Muslim neighbors and subjects through the lens of confessional struggle. "The number of mosques staggers every Orthodox Russian Christian when he shows up in Kazan or its environs," Malov complained. Census reports revealed that Muslims formed large populations in a number of districts; in the province of Ufa, they made up an absolute majority. Nonconforming Christians seemed to amplify the menace of Muslim proselytizing among Christians and pagans. The bishop of Ufa alerted his flock to the presence of "95 thousand pagans, 16 thousand schismatics of various sects and one million 31 thousand Muslims." He warned that "they are all enemies of Orthodox Christians and Christ's Church." Moreover, the appearance of Ottoman subjects who traveled through the region as merchants, and who were often linked to Sufi gatherings, provoked anxieties of a Christian land under siege, of the making of a "Muhammadan territory."[23]

In the 1860s and 1870s, these communities confronted new challenges from Church and state. Aided by various lay organizations, the Church adopted a range of measures designed to deepen the non-Russian converts' commitment to Christianity. In 1863 Nikolai Il'minskii, a professor of the Kazan Theological Academy and an associate of Kazem-Bek, began to establish a network of schools in which non-Russians would receive Russian education, in part through their own native languages. He maintained that these "Russo-Tatar schools" offered "the most promising path to the future spread of the Russian language and Russian ways." They made up one element in a broader strategy aimed at shielding non-Russian Christians from the influence of Islam. Lay missionary societies joined the missionary section of the academy in combating Muslim "corruption" of non-Russian converts to Orthodoxy. They also supported the publication in the Tatar language of polemical tracts that refuted, they claimed, the errors of the Muslims.[24]

Provincial officials aided the Church in countering the spread of Islam. Governors denied communities permission to open new mosques in villages and towns where populations outgrew their parishes and the number of mullahs serving them. From the mid-1850s, they adopted the goal of reducing the numbers of the "Muhammadan clergy," whose books and "propaganda" they blamed for Orthodox converts' flight from the Church.[25]

Incidents like the desecration of an icon of the Mother of God with human feces in Kazan Province in 1867 became fodder for raw confessional conflict when suspicion fell on Tatars who had been working in the village. Anyone could be punished according to tsarist criminal law for desecrating an icon, but the authorities interpreted such acts in this region as evidence of a Muslim assault on Orthodoxy and the state. A justice of the peace in the district of Sviazhsk expressed this sentiment in light of "Muslim propaganda." The desecration struck him as particularly noteworthy because the suspects came from the only Tatar village on the right bank of the Sviiaga River. These Tatars lived surrounded by Russians and had never displayed "fanaticism." Sooner than others, he argued, they would be "capable of becoming Russian," adding the condition, "if only the necessary attention were turned toward this in a timely manner?" The embittered justice of the peace expressed his "readiness" to apply himself fully to this "good cause."[26]

The archbishop joined the police in reading the attack on the icon against the backdrop of the elemental struggle of Orthodox Christianity with Islam. The act of soiling a sacred object with feces was not committed out of "ignorance" or "incomprehension," concluded the village priest, Fyodor Lebedev. Rather, it showed "malicious contempt toward the Orthodox faith and its confessors, committed with the aim of shaking respect toward the sacred object and reverence for the icons, [which] cannot, [and] must not remain without investigation and strict punishment of the guilty." The desecration of the image of the Mother of God had been carried out "with contempt and blasphemy, offending in the extreme the religious feeling of all pious Christians of the village of Mamatkazin." Backing the suspicions of the residents about their Tatar neighbors, who had been present in large numbers the evening of the crime and "had drunk heavily" with a Russian villager, the archbishop demanded "the punishment of the guilty, or at least . . . the strict restraint of all Muhammadans of the village of Tatarskii Mamatkazin, so that henceforth they will not dare to mock a Christian sacred object." After police made inquiries, the investigator had a Tatar named Bikkulov arrested and jailed, though he admitted that he did not have "complete proof" of his guilt. Thus even where the fate of converts and confessional boundaries were not concerned, local representatives of the Church had the power to mobilize the coercive instruments of government to affirm the supremacy of the state religion over merely tolerated faiths.[27]

Although the Church limited the practice of toleration in many mixed locales, Muslims continued to appeal to the older images of religion, which from the late eighteenth century had sustained official backing for Islamic legal and ethical norms as foundations of a disciplined social order. When Simbirsk authorities learned in the 1870s that people in several villages of the district of Buinsk were abandoning Orthodoxy, it singled out a mosque in Trekh Boltaevo as the source of the "corruption." Although Church officials persuaded the Senate that the mosque had been built without permission (and without the minimum parish size of two hundred souls), an official of the Department of Religious Affairs of Foreign Confessions in the Ministry of Internal Affairs concluded that closing the mosque would "not be in agreement with article 45 of the *Fundamental Laws*, which awards Muhammadans freedom of religion, and thus I do not find it possible to agree with the present decision of the Ruling Senate."[28]

The residents of Trekh Boltaevo also protested the closing. The local mullah petitioned Alexander II, appealing to the utility of his religion for the tsar and of the general benefit of the proper interpretation of imperial law. In March 1874, Mullah Toktamish Abekeev pointed to the errors committed by the local administration. The mosque had not been built without permission, he claimed, or else he would not have received an official assignment there. Moreover, he had the license to prove it. The parish counted 214 members, putting it over the two-hundred-person minimum, which, he noted, applied only to *new* mosques, not to those already in existence. Thus the administration was acting "not completely judiciously," and its decision to close the mosque had placed a "constraint on our religion." In response to charges of corrupting nearby Christians, Abekeev noted that the local church was more than a *verst* (just over a kilometer) away. While the church was no more than thirty years old, the mullah added, the mosque was more than a hundred years old. Responsibility thus lay with those who allowed the church to be built so close to the already existing mosque in the first place.[29] Abekeev also rebutted the Church authorities' assertion that the presence of mosques threatened Christians, citing the example of towns like Simbirsk and Kazan, where only two hundred meters or less separated mosques and Orthodox churches. There Christians were not seduced by Islam.

The government order that the parishioners of Trekh Boltaevo attach themselves to another mosque more than six kilometers away, Abekeev argued, would deprive his people of religion—something the tsar could scarcely afford. According to the shari'a, Muslims must pray at appointed times throughout the day, he explained, so that "the closing of our mosque will be a death-blow to our lives." The mullah related the significance of the daily prayers: "Since we do not know when God will send us death, we must always be prepared at every hour and thus we are not entitled to put off the offering of these obligatory prayers . . . especially since the existence of our mosque is not contrary to Your Most Autocratic Law." The fulfillment of religious obligations was especially important because

> now the people have grown very weak, especially the young,
> who demand strict and edifying exhortations: first on knowl-
> edge of God, second on His Tsar and holy law and third on
> the offering of prayers to God for His Orthodox Tsar and the
> entire August Household! and finally for those near to him
> and for all who live in the land, since our law, the "shari'a,"
> strictly orders us to do this.

To respond to the conditions of the times, more, not fewer, mosques were needed. Through an increase in the number of mosques, "the edification of the Muhammadan people would also increase, so that they would understand: what is God? what is the Tsar? what is a human? and the aim of human life?" The people would learn by "reproof and exegesis of both the holy and Tsarist law." But when the mosques are closed, the mullah warned, no one "feels himself obligated to engage in such edification and when in our settlements there are almost no learned people, then the Muhammadan people must positively perish: for so few strive for good or the truth, and, without mentors, [we] quickly pave a broad path to all that is bad."[30]

Abekeev's entreaty to the emperor to "restore our path to the fulfillment of our sacred obligation" fell on deaf ears, even despite his promise to pray fervently for the tsar and his family. Count Emanuel Sievers, the director of the Department of Religious Affairs, reversed the earlier ruling of his department and sided with the Senate. His final report relied on an article of the imperial Building Statute to justify the closing of the mosque—and to uphold the protection of nearby Christians.[31]

Confessional differences also aggravated tensions among neighbors and kinfolk in Tatar communities. Those who had been baptized but did not separate themselves from the local Muslim community by attending church or observing the rites and holidays of the Orthodox calendar often remained on the margins of the Muslim community. Other converts sustained ties to Islam through the bonds of kinship and occupation. Still other converts appear to have broken off all connections to Muslim relatives and neighbors, or the latter may have made this break for them. In some communities, Muslims rejected entirely those who maintained even ephemeral association with the Church. Since the eighteenth century, Muslim notables had occasionally appealed to St. Petersburg for help in expelling apostates from their midst. It appears unlikely that men of learning and piety applied the penalty that many Islamic jurists had set for apostates: death. Though in 1879, police in the district of Spassk investigated a murder that may have been committed to punish apostasy. Five villagers stood accused of beating to death a woman who had supposedly voiced the desire to convert to Christianity and had received a sixty-ruble reward from provincial officials.[32]

The combined efforts of the Church, its lay affiliates, and provincial administrators spawned rumors of official plans for the forced conversion of Muslims. Tatars read about state-sanctioned missionary efforts in the press and in the Tatar-language pamphlets distributed by missionaries. News spread throughout villages and towns reporting on the pronouncements of bishops and priests who enjoined all Russians, from peasants to officials, to enlighten their non-Christian neighbors with the teachings of Christ. Rumors of conversion campaigns continued to unsettle members of mosque communities until the fall of the tsarist regime. This issue, more than any other, soured relations between Muslims and officialdom in the Volga and Urals regions.

Muslims thus interpreted administrative and educational reforms as veiled attempts to subject them to Christianization. In 1865 the state transferred the Bashkirs in the Urals region to civilian administration. In the 1870s it imposed new forms of taxation on peasants in the Volga provinces, sparking conflicts between rural Tatars and the authorities in several districts of Kazan Province. The announcement of plans to institute Russian-language training in non-Russian schools provoked broader Muslim opposition. In 1870 the Ministry of Education argued for the need to spread the Russian language and general education among Cheremis, Chuvash, Votiaks, and other peoples at risk of "becoming Tatar and Muhammadan . . . like the Kazakhs." The ministry aimed at countering Muslim "influence in the region" and achieving the "Russification" of the non-Russians and their "merging with the Russian people." Ministry of Education officials rejected assertions that this plan infringed upon religious toleration: "The teaching of the Russian language has nothing to do with the persecution of the Muhammadan religion."[33]

Many Muslims agreed. Hundreds of young men enrolled in the schools established by the Ministry of Education to train Tatar teachers of the Russian language. Kazan merchants and entrepreneurs also supported Russian language instruction in the Qur'anic schools (maktabs) and colleges (madrasas) they funded. Muslim elites enjoined their co-religionists to learn the language of the state so that they could compete more successfully with Russians in trade and commerce, defend themselves in Russian courts, and, according to reformers, gain access to superior European learning.

Although the ministry's plans for the promotion of Russian language instruction found both supporters and opponents among Muslims, two related measures announced in the ministry's resolutions of February 1870 gave rise to more uniformly hostile reactions. Formerly autonomous, maktabs and madrasas now fell under the jurisdiction of an educational inspectorate. To encourage Muslims to embrace the Russian language and education, the Council of Ministers decided to make Muslims demonstrate the ability to read and write Russian before the government would permit them to assume government appointments (including positions in the reform-era organs of local self-government, the *zemstva*).

More important in the eyes of mosque communities, the government also proposed to make Muslim clerics fulfill this obligation before receiving their licenses.[34] Fearing state intervention as a first step toward the eradication of Islamic education, Muslims protested both the extension of the inspectorate and the requirement that the 'ulama take time away from their pursuit of religious learning to study Russian. The proposal left the bureaucracy divided as well. The Ministry of Internal Affairs countered the Ministry of Education by pointing to the danger of disturbances in Tatar communities. As a result, the government postponed enforcement of the language requirement for Muslim clerics.[35]

Such measures formed part of a broader strategy aimed at the cultural integration of non-Russians into the institutional life of the empire. In 1874 the government introduced universal conscription. Although inhabitants of the governor-generalships of the steppe and Turkestan remained exempt, the Minister of War, Dmitrii Miliutin, placed particular emphasis on the cultural impact of military service on non-Russians. He maintained that it would strengthen the empire by further integrating its non-Russian peoples. "General obligatory participation in military service, uniting in the ranks of the army men of all estates and all parts of Russia," he argued, "presents the best means for the weakening of tribal differences among the people, the correct unification of all the forces of the state, and their direction towards a single, common goal." Although Muslims complied for the most part, communities feared that conscripts would be exposed to harmful influences, like Christianity and drink. Like many other officials, the vice-governor of Samara Province recognized that mistrust, unrest, and panic might jeopardize public order. In hopes of rebuilding a degree of trust, he enlisted the Orenburg mufti to quell such talk. In December 1878 he appealed to the mufti Salimgarei Tevkelev to distribute one thousand copies of a circular that would reassure Muslims of the baselessness of stories about the impending conversion of Muslims to Christianity and affirm the "inviolability of the Muhammadan religion."[36]

In this environment of confessional conflict, Muslims learned in 1888 of a plan to enforce the previously postponed law compelling Muslim clerics to learn the Russian language. The news provoked a petition campaign that linked villages across several provinces. Building on earlier efforts to secure permission for conversion from Orthodoxy to Islam, the movement politicized tens of thousands of villagers and townspeople. Throughout the region, laypeople and clerics appealed to tsarist law in defense of toleration, which, they argued, the language requirement violated. Although the regime had created an inspectorate for non-Russian schools in the 1870s, the language law would have a more far-reaching impact because its implementation would necessitate several years of Russian language instruction. Muslim critics pointed out that time spent away from the study of the languages and religious sciences necessary for training as learned Muslims would disrupt the transmission of religious knowledge. Such a burden, they argued, would leave mosque communities without qualified personnel to lead them in prayer, perform obligatory rituals, adjudicate disputes, or interpret the shari'a.

The coordination of a petition campaign against the law built on, and likely expanded, preexisting horizontal ties among disparate mosque communities. Trade, study, the veneration of local saints, and a growing interest in a shared past dating back to the ancient Bulghars on the Volga had long connected Muslims in the region. Earlier episodes involving the coordination of appeals on behalf of converts had offered lessons in communicating with the bureaucracy. Communities came together to secure a repeal of the measure by appealing to the regime's own laws on toleration. Elders in many villages preserved copies of laws related to the historical record of the locale, passing them on for generations. On the basis of such records, Muslim historians compiled accounts of legal landmarks affecting local communities.[37] An underworld of bilingual clerks, merchants, and retired soldiers flourished between the mosque and provincial chancellery. Informants helped compose and reproduce petitions for Muslim communities stretching from the Volga to the Amu Darya Rivers and assisted petitioners in framing their demands as "rights."

The market in imperial legal knowledge expanded with the commercial book trade. While Muslims may not always have printed such manuals and guides themselves, publishers targeted Muslims as consumers. One unofficial compilation published in Kazan in 1898 collected relevant laws concerning Muslim "clergy" and schools. Its editor advised readers to recall article 45 of the first volume of the *Digest of Laws*, which said that "all subjects of the Russian state enjoy in all parts free exercise of the faith and liturgy according to its rites." This collection was thus "essential" for akhunds, mullahs, and teachers in madrasas and maktabs because it "reveals the requirements of the law and explains the obligations and broad rights awarded by the Russian government, to which constant and boundless gratitude should be expressed on the part of Muslims."[38]

Copied and recirculated throughout the region, these petitions appealed to tsarist law and the "rights" and "privileges" protected by it. For many communities, the new language law represented a break with the rights and privileges of "freedom of religion" that they and their ancestors had enjoyed. In the three hundred years since the descendants of the village of Shugur in Samara Province had entered "under the protection of the Russian Empire," they had always "enjoyed freedom of religion, without the slightest constraint." The author of the petition, Khairetdin Mavliutov (whose spoken words were transcribed for him by a resident of his village), traced the beginning of infringements upon these ancient rights to the establishment of the "Anti-Muslim Missionary Section" of the Kazan Theological Academy, which devoted articles and whole books to attacks on "their peaceful and forever humble neighbors, the Muslim Tatars." Mavliutov cited its first *"Anti-Muslim Miscellany" (Protivo-musul'manskii sbornik)* of 1873, which had inflamed the Muslims, he claimed, by proposing instruction in Russian as a means to reveal the mullahs' errors. Mavliutov explained the anger of his co-religionists by quoting the third sura of the Qur'an against conversion from Islam, an act that condemned one to be "among the unfortunate in the next life." He also complained that similarities in the language used in the *Miscellany* and that in tsarist decrees, first in 1870 (on the expanded jurisdiction of the Ministry of Education) and most recently in 1888, had produced a "dispiriting impression" on Muslims. Mavliutov added that the new law clashed with the shari'a. Like thousands of other Muslims who feared apostasy and the decline of religion, Mavliutov denounced the language requirement as something that "alienated them from piety."[39]

The campaign politicized Muslim villages and neighborhoods everywhere, but one should not overestimate the consensus forged by wide-scale opposition to the language law, which placed Muslims who had already studied Russian or who advocated its study in an awkward position. In a letter to the governor of Kazan, a mullah from the district of Tetiush' requested protection from the "violent reprisal" of his mosque. His parishioners, whom he labeled a "fanatical society," had threatened to remove him from his position because he refused to sign their resolution against the law. The mullah explained that he had already completed a course for the preparation of teachers of Russian,

> knowing well the enormous significance of the Russian language, and even having in mind the necessity of it for us Russian Muhammadans from the point of view of general education, as well as for our everyday interactions with Russians, as the generally used and predominant national and . . . state language, having worldwide significance from the political point of view.[40]

Because he resisted, his parishioners had prevented him from visiting the mosque, so that he could not offer prayers for the tsar and imperial family. The villagers had even branded him "an apostate from the Muhammadan faith."[41]

Guarding the True Path in an Era of Sin

Such cries for preservation of the inviolability of Islam in the face of Russian language laws and other novel forms of state interference did not reflect a total reorientation of religious debate in mosque communities away from state institutions and imperial law. Rather, by invoking principles of toleration and the autonomy of religion, Muslims sought to negotiate a new role for the state in shaping and policing the boundaries of the Muslim community. Despite mosque closings, the harassment and surveillance of men of religion, the rejection of visa applications to make the hajj, and recurring rumors of a wide-scale conversion campaign, Muslims persisted in appealing to the state—and its police organs—in the pursuit of competing visions of God's command and the collective obligations of the community of Islam. For its part, the state continued to turn to Muslim clerics, both within and outside the official establishment, to offer religious legitimation for the day-to-day administration of the empire. It also continued to provide Muslims with venues for the mediation of religious disputes. Though St. Petersburg retreated from sponsorship of an official Islamic establishment in the steppe and Turkestan, it expanded on earlier efforts to erect such hierarchies elsewhere. In 1872 it established separate administrative bodies for the Sunnis and Shi'ites in Transcaucasia.[42]

Muslim clerics and laypeople, too, continued to view tsarist officials as instruments of Islamic orthodoxy. Local authorities still assumed this role, though they sometimes now did so with greater reluctance, and more covertly. The Orenburg Assembly received instructions to direct Muslims to approach the district police less frequently and with greater discretion. In 1861 it nonetheless petitioned the governor of Kazan to prohibit the celebration of a holiday *(jïen)* in the villages of the province as an un-Islamic occasion marked by immoral behavior and frivolous spending. The petition won the backing of the governor, who instructed local police to prevent such celebrations. When a Tatar peasant presented a similar complaint in 1884 to the governor about this "harmful" holiday, "which does not have anything to do with the shari'a," Governor N. Andreevskii again directed police to prohibit it on the grounds that it was "harmful in the moral sense," led to economic ruin, and because it was not "established by the shari'a." When imams in the district of Mamadysh in Kazan Province petitioned the Assembly in 1865 for help in preventing Muslim women from traveling to the nearby Russian bazaar with uncovered faces, however, the Assembly replied that the petitioners themselves should dissuade the women from acting against the shari'a. In the following year it instructed locals, in case of "acts contrary to the shari'a," to seek "the assistance of local authorities orally and not in writing."[43]

Despite some attempts to free the Russian bureaucracy from its Muslim supplicants, Muslim activists insisted that the state had a critical role to play in realizing God's plan, especially where interpreters of the tradition arrived at conclusions that their co-religionists regarded as beyond the pale of orthodoxy. For these champions of orthodoxy, such movements confirmed the intercession of the state as a necessary means to correct those who strayed from the true path of the shariʻa.

The centrality of the reform-era state to Islamic controversies is perhaps illustrated best by the story of a group that in the early 1860s began to identify itself as "God's Regiment of Muslim Old Believers" (*Bozhii polk starovercheskogo musul'manskogo obshchestva*).[44] Derdemend Dervish Bagautdin Vaisov proclaimed himself the thirty-second successor to a line of warriors imbued with the "spirit of Muhammad" and committed to "the strengthening of the faith and the correction of morality." A native of the village of Mal'vino in the district of Sviazhsk of Kazan Province and a member of the Naqshbandi Sufi brotherhood, he traced this line to Muhammad's lifetime, to a saint named Vais who transmitted the Prophet's teachings in its purest form. This line passed to the Volga region in the ninth century, when one of its "warriors" brought the "true faith" to the Bulghar kingdom.

After gathering followers in Kazan, Vaisov separated himself from the town's mosques, where mullahs and scholars challenged his claims. His opponents taunted him, subjected him to ridicule, and pelted him with rocks on the street. As a guardian of the old truth based on a more faithful transmission of the Prophet's teachings, Vaisov preached against the Muslim clerics in the region. He accused them of being "Wahhabis" and "heretics," deviants from the Qur'an who neglected the purity of the faith to cater to the powerful. Assuming the title of "head" (*sardar*) of "God's Regiment of Muslim Old Believers," Vaisov instructed his followers that the regiment was subject only to the shariʻa and rejected local authorities and imperial laws, including those governing taxation and conscription. He held the Orenburg Assembly in particular contempt, referring to its officials as "idol-worshippers," "schismatics," "swine," and the "dogs of Antichrist."[45] Vaisov nonetheless resolved that his movement should have the status of an imperial institution, accountable only to God and the emperor. In 1862 he founded a "state prayer-house" in Kazan with the permission, he maintained, of Alexander II.

His conflicts with the official hierarchy dated to the early 1860s, when the hierarchy had undermined his petitions to the government seeking state support (and funding) for a Sufi lodge *(tekke)* in Saratov on the site of the tomb of a blind mystic, Mukhammed-Seid Dzhafar, who had inducted Vaisov into the Sufi tradition. On the recommendation of official Muslim clerics, and Alexander Kazem-Bek, the government declined his appeal. In 1872 the Orenburg mufti also rejected his request to act as a legal specialist for the Assembly. Condemning his "ignorance" of the shari'a and warning the government that he was dangerous both "for society and the authorities," the mufti asked provincial officials to confine Vaisov to his place of residence to prevent him from contacting other Muslims in the region. After Vaisov's repeated conflicts with the Assembly, the judges unsuccessfully appealed to the Ministry of Internal Affairs to place him in a reformatory for four months for violating the shari'a as well as tsarist law prohibiting the "spreading of false rumors" (article 933 of the penal code), a provision commonly used to suppress behavior the Assembly branded as unorthodox.[46]

The movement was a distinctive product of the Russian imperial environment. Vaisov and his regiment faulted the Assembly for the decline of the faith and morality, rejected many imperial institutions and laws, but pledged loyalty to the emperor. Besides adopting the polemical language shared by the official Church and its dissenters, the Old Believers, Vaisov's group organized its "state prayer house" along the lines of the Assembly. Declaring itself an "autonomous clerical organization," the regiment maintained parish registers for its members. The house also ran a school and a treasury. Later the regiment used it as a kind of chancellery from which it printed its own letterhead and disseminated public announcements and declarations to state officials.[47]

In the early 1880s, relations worsened between Vaisov and local Muslims and state authorities. He continued to condemn the decline of religion, even warning, in November 1882, which corresponded to the beginning of the year 1300 in the Islamic calendar, of the end of the world and the punishment of the "unbelievers."[48] Two years later his followers' refusal to pay taxes—and continued denunciations from their opponents in Kazan mosque communities—led to a major clash with the police. After Vaisov and his followers barricaded themselves inside their prayer house, the police stormed the building, killing a number of the group.

In 1885 the survivors wrote to Alexander III seeking protection. They explained that they submitted only to "the superior authorities and not [lower] civil authorities" because "we are not Tatars or Orthodox peasants . . . but God's Regiment, loyal subjects of God [and] the Tsar." Thus, they lived only "on the basis of the holy shari'a and in accord with the holy fatherland, and not according to that foul and cursed law . . . written for the dogs of Antichrist." They sought help against local civil authorities who had destroyed their "Imperial Prayer House."[49]

Vaisov was committed by the authorities to a mental hospital, but he retained loyal followers, possibly numbering in the thousands. They included his wife, who called herself the "spiritual mother" of the movement and "the servant of the whole world." In the late 1880s she repeatedly appealed to the governor of Kazan Province to intercede on behalf of her family to provide them with an apartment and to protect them from the "faithless Tatars" and police. Other members of "God's Regiment" also turned to the tsar and governor to send armed guards to shield them from the stones and insults of their neighbors, "Antichrist's dogs." In July 1890, petitioners representing the eighteen households of the village of Karsham loyal to the "old belief" warned that their celebration of an upcoming holiday would be met by an uprising and begged for protection.[50]

In interactions with the state, like-minded activists drew on a language that simultaneously linked religious heterodoxy to disloyalty to the tsar and tied local controversies about Islamic identity to wider debates in the Muslim world. In 1881 a Muslim cleric from Simbirsk Province petitioned the minister of internal affairs, Mikhail Loris-Melikov, to warn him about a dangerous "sect" in his village. Abdullatif Khalitov sought out the minister's aid against this sect and the "ruinous consequences" of its teachings. Khalitov had completed his studies in the 1840s at one or more madrasas and passed an exam administered by the Orenburg Assembly, which granted him a license to lead prayers, teach, and administer justice according to the shari'a. Khalitov said in his petition, "[as mullah] I never deviated from the law [*zakon*] of the state and the shari'a; and in accordance with my training I never permitted any heretical teaching, keeping the faith of Muhammad in its purity." In 1862 he received the permission of the provincial authorities to build a mosque and madrasa. But in the mid-1870s, Khalitov had to turn to the Orenburg Assembly to restore orthodoxy in his village when a "Wahhabi sect" supposedly began to corrupt "not only simple peasants" but also "semiliterate mullahs."[51]

Life in Bedengi, a village of some 330 souls on the west bank of the Volga River, had been turned upside down by the followers of "Wahhabism." When Khalitov spoke out against them, they threw themselves on the imam, he explained, because he prayed for the tsar, which their teachings did not permit. During a confrontation in the mosque, followers of the Wahhabi sect not only insulted Khalitov but beat him and drove him from his position. The former

imam now appealed to the minister of internal affairs to demonstrate, in the name of "the just Russian law," that "goodness always
prevails." For Khalitov, "the just Russian law" meant police investigation of the teachings of the Wahhabis and his reinstatement as
imam, permitting him to offer prayers for "His Imperial Majesty"
and for "Your Highness," Loris-Melikov.

Even in an era when Alexander III sought to present the monarchy as the embodiment of Orthodoxy and ethnic Russianness, religious heterodoxy among the non-Orthodox remained a political issue. Despite a number of concessions to sectarian groups under
Alexander II, Khalitov's accusation was enough to prompt multiple
investigations of religious life—and political attitudes—in Bedengi.
He ensured that the authorities would associate false belief with disloyalty by claiming that his opponents attacked him for defending
prayers for the tsar. Khalitov, by contrast, demonstrated his devotion
to imperial law, the shari'a, and the tsar. He had defended the faith
against heresy and had engaged in useful scholarly work, including a
translation of an Arabic-language Islamic legal text prepared by Professor Kazem-Bek; he had also collaborated on the publications of a
scholar whom he identified simply as Vaisov.

Khalitov did not elaborate on the Wahhabi teachings that yielded
what he called "ruinous consequences," but he did add that the
mullah whom the Orenburg Assembly assigned to investigate his
charges in 1876 was his "personal enemy." Khalitov protested the appointment of this Mustaich, who, he said, was the "chief Wahhabi
follower" and had, despite Khalitov's opposition, collected money
for the Turks; Mustaich then traveled to Turkey on the hajj. He returned at the end of 1880, Khalitov charged, to collect more money
and spread the "heretical teaching." Due to his "libel" against
Khalitov, Mustaich, the author of only "one small brochure . . .
filled with the most diverse heretical teachings and crude blasphemy," had managed to remove the learned Khalitov from his post.

Such accusations concerning blasphemy and the rejection of the tsar's authority continued to prompt police intervention. Khalitov's strategy of casting religious controversy as political crime triggered an investigation but ultimately failed to deploy the police and "the just Russian law" to "command good, and forbid wrong." Others who succeeded managed to reframe the terms of Islamic debate and its provisions for the possibility of a spectrum of multiple outcomes. They translated them instead into the binary language of orthodoxy and heresy that would correspond to the preconceptions of the police. In this case, reference to Wahhabism, the movement founded by Muhammad Ibn 'Abd al-Wahhab in eighteenth-century Arabia to purify Islam of ostensibly polytheistic practices, appears to have been lost on these officials. To contemporary Muslims, however, it made an important statement about Islamic orthodoxy and its relationship to the Russian state. The charge of "Wahhabism" here seems to have been a defense of Sufi practices against a reformist critique of such devotions.

But Khalitov was not simply the defender of a static and insular Islam. At the conclusion of his last correspondence with St. Petersburg, he identified himself as a "Muslim Old Believer," revealing himself as an adherent of the pious protest movement that condemned the increasing social stratification of Russian Muslim society and the corruption of the official Islamic establishment. For "Wahhabis" and Old Believers, the Muslim community and true belief were to be formed with, not against, the state. The contest between good and evil required the police, tsarist law, and the shari'a.

Activists such as Vaisov and Khalitov were not the only Muslims to devote themselves to stemming the decline of religion. The acceleration of socioeconomic change in the last quarter of the nineteenth century heightened anxieties surrounding conflicting claims about true religion. New forces unleashed by industrialization transformed villages, towns, and cities. Far-reaching changes in labor markets and mobility created more varied roles for youth and women. The spread of the railroad and telegraph, mass migration to the cities, the swelling of the ranks of the newly employed in factories and mines and various commercial enterprises, as well as the emergence of a mass market in consumer goods, contributed to a sense of crisis among the representatives of established authority. Their dilemma was shared by the 'ulama and lay activists. At the same time, older controversies persisted. Even renowned scholars faced denunciations and discipline at the hands of foes for performing controversial rites. As for previous generations, the timing of prayers and fasts in the northern climes of Eurasia, with long days of darkness in winter and sunlit summer nights, remained particularly divisive. Shihabetdin Märjani, one of the most celebrated scholars of the Volga region, was suspended from his licensed position as imam and preacher for half a year in 1874 when others protested to the Orenburg Assembly that he had begun the Ramadan fast a day early.[52]

Officials sometimes hesitated to take on the mediation of religious conflicts among laypeople and clerics, but their concern with controlling the 'ulama increased under Alexander II and Alexander III. State intervention took the form of more careful surveillance and the occasional arrest of clerics suspected of Pan-Islamic and anti-government sentiment. Here, too, Muslims adapted to this shift in official priorities in their complaints and denunciations. In 1870 the administration in Ufa began to follow the activities of Zaynullah Rasulev (Zeinulla Khabibullin), a shaykh of the Naqshbandi Sufi brotherhood. Officials received reports that Muslims came from throughout the region to revere him as a "saint," even though he had introduced practices not sanctioned in the Qur'an, like the "innovation" of prayer with a rosary. On the day of the celebration of Muhammad's birth, some three thousand Bashkirs traveled to meet him for festivities that included the recitation of religious texts and a feast.[53]

In pursuit of Rasulev, the administration was aided by denunciations from local Muslims. In 1872 men of religious learning and piety in Sterlibashevo (Isterlibash) charged him with "heresy and distortion of Islam" in a denunciation to the Orenburg Assembly. They accused him of performing the ritual remembrance of God (zikr) orally, a practice condemned by most of the region's Naqshbandiyya adherents and proscribed by the official hierarchy. In 1862 the Assembly had labeled its practitioners "apostates from the shari'a" and barred them from mosques. Besides their objection to what they regarded as an unlawful innovation, Rasulev's detractors were hostile toward his affiliation with a new line of the Naqshbandiyya, the Khalidi branch. While in Istanbul on pilgrimage to Mecca recently, Zaynullah had been inducted into the Khalidiyya by Shaykh Ahmad Ziyauddin Gümüşhanevi, a figure with close ties to the sultan and the Ottoman bureaucracy. Rival shaykhs may also have opposed Zaynullah because he drew local Tatar, Bashkir, and Kazakh devotees away from them. Although Rasulev successfully defended his behavior before the Orenburg Assembly, provincial authorities arrested the shaykh and exiled him for nearly nine years. It seems that his opponents persuaded the administration that Rasulev's ties to Gümüşhanevi and his Istanbul Khalidiyya made him a harmful influence upon his large group of followers and a threat to the state. Elsewhere, officials apparently continued to suppress Sufi practices that ran afoul of the Orenburg Assembly. In Astrakhan Province, an imam persuaded a police superintendent to order a parishioner to desist from instructing others in the "shaykh's science" in his home.[54]

An Imperial Muslim Community

All of these developments, combined with the birth of a Muslim periodical press and the appearance of alternatives to the established maktab and madrasa education in the 1880s, sharpened tensions among competing spokesmen for the Islamic tradition. Viewing the school as an "organ of mental and moral training [*vospitanie*]," Ismail Bey Gasprinskii and a new generation of reformers in the Crimea, the Volga region, Siberia, and later Central Asia focused on Islamic schools as the key medium for the reform of Islam, a prescription borrowed in many respects from European Oriental studies literature on the "backwardness" and "stagnation" of Islam, which Muslim reformers contrasted to European "enlightenment" and "progress." Ahmed Zeki Velidi Togan described in his memoirs how his exposure to Oriental studies, popular scientific literature, and atheist tracts aimed at undermining the Orthodox Church led him to adopt the view that Islam, and Muslim education in particular, was in need of drastic "reform."[55] After the establishment of Gasprinskii's bilingual Turkic and Russian newspaper *The Translator (Tercüman / Perevodchik)* in 1883, reformers turned to the press and the theater to enjoin their co-religionists to pursue "knowledge and enlightenment." These "Jadids" earned their name from their innovations in education, including a new phonetic method *(usul-i jadid)* for teaching the Arabic alphabet, which they advocated in place of the syllabic method. They also campaigned for the introduction of new subjects, including math, science, geography, history, and, in some cases, the Russian language.[56]

Many traditionally educated Muslim scholars opposed these innovations. But reformers and their critics shared a focus on moral decline. Though differing in generational and socioeconomic profiles, as Stéphane Dudoignon has argued, competing elites held in common a concern about restoring the "moral rigor" of the Muslim community, which they believed had declined under Christian domination.[57] As in Russian peasant villages and the sprawling cities, public morality stood out as one of the most distressing casualties of the social and generational turmoil and dislocation brought about by rapid socioeconomic change. As we have seen in previous chapters, however, public drunkenness, brawling, sex outside of marriage, refusal to attend mosque prayers, and disrespectful behavior toward parents and elders predated the locomotive, the modern factory, and the anonymity of city life. Indeed, such conduct had long been the stuff of discord and strife that pulled at the fabric of mosque communities and divided quarreling village factions, kinship groups, mullahs, and laymen and women.

Many reformers now saw such behavior as the symptom of a broader crisis provoked by neglect of God's original design as exemplified in the early history of Islam, by Muhammad and his companions. Journals and newspapers in Kazan, Orenburg, Bakchisarai, Baku, and other cities called for a return to the example of the Prophet and the foundational principles of early Islamic legal interpretation and the transmission of religious knowledge, while insisting on the compatibility of Islam and modern science. Intellectuals resorted to the new periodical press to correct the straying of their co-religionists, while lay activists continued to fall back on the familiar channels established with local police organs.

The two spaces of contestation overlapped as well. The new Muslim press became another forum for the pursuit of mosque conflicts. From the Volga to Turkestan, Muslim readers followed accounts of intrigue in local communities. *Tercüman* reported on many of these disputes, but its editors also recognized that competing factions sought to use the paper to advance their own causes. After reporting on the Orenburg notable Khusainov's plans for a "new, transformed" madrasa, the editor noted, the paper received three letters challenging this account. *Tercüman* conceded that the story turned out to be less about the transformation of the school and more about a dispute within the community regarding the election of the teacher. Three hundred members of the community elected a mullah, but Khusainov rejected the choice. What followed next was "a story very common among Muslims when they have to elect someone": "complaints to the provincial administration, an inquiry into the figures who signed the decision, and so forth."[58]

The ancestors of these community activists had also made recourse to tsarist administrative and judicial bodies with the aim of imposing their visions of Islamic orthodoxy upon disagreeable mullahs and laypeople. While their forebearers had appropriated a vocabulary of moral decay from Sufi poetry and songs, many lay and clerical activists in the late nineteenth and early twentieth centuries drew upon a wider and more heterogeneous range of conceptual and rhetorical resources. They went beyond the internalist languages of Sufism and Islamic reformism, referring to a more general state of moral crisis born of contemporary economic disruption and social disorder. Their invocation of "tradition" made a prescriptive claim about conduct that *should* guide the community of Islam. Appeals to this broader context became a major extension of a proven strategy that relied on the translation of the terms of Islamic debate into the legal and religious categories of state officials. At the same time, reformers did not embrace secularism in the sense that many historians have claimed. *Tercüman* repeatedly argued that equality between Muslim and non-Muslim subjects meant that the decisions of Islamic law courts should gain the consistent backing of "temporal authority" in family matters. In 1891 Gasprinskii even argued that the principle of religious toleration prevented Muslims from opting out of their religious courts.[59]

Muslim activists denounced the putative breakdown of the family order—and sexual deviance outside it—as an illicit innovation punishable by both the shari'a and imperial law. They represented prostitution as an alien and heretofore unknown social evil visited upon Muslim communities in an increasingly decadent age. Though members of mosque communities had petitioned to shelter their prayer leaders and sons and daughters from the state when it intruded in the arena of Islamic education, self-appointed guardians of Islamic morality nonetheless sought out the coercive power of the police in suppressing the participation of Muslim women in the sex trade.

Muslims also resorted to justice of the peace courts on matters of morality. In late 1888 or early 1889, a young woman named Galiakbarova turned to the justice of the peace court in the city of Kazan to file a complaint against a Muslim townswoman, Khisamuddinova. Galiakbarova had accepted a job to work as a seamstress in Khisamuddinova's apartment. According to an account of the case in the newspaper *Tercüman*, the plaintiff arrived at the apartment to begin work one evening when she noticed that it was frequented by men "with very shameless manners." And when Khisamuddinova invited the young woman to join the "guests," Galiakbarova realized that she had become "the victim of a vile deceit" and turned to the court for satisfaction. For its part, *Tercüman* applauded the decision of the young woman, calling on "society" to aid the "gallant girl" and to exclude Khisamuddinova as an "amoral and harmful woman."[60]

Similarly, in 1889 thirty-two Muslims from the town of Chistopol' in Kazan Province petitioned Mufti Mukhamed'iar Sultanov, and through him the governor of the province, requesting action against Muslim prostitutes there. They appealed for "an order on the basis of both the shari'a and civil law" to bring an end to "such vile behavior among Muslim women," explaining that these women not only practiced the trade in their town but had corrupted others among the local poor women. Drawn from the ranks of those who could not earn a living, their numbers had grown, "such that without any inhibition they walk and roam all the streets, bazaars, and squares dressed up and with uncovered faces."[61]

Police authorities responded coolly to these charges, however. The officers sent to investigate the case reported that news of unveiled Muslim women in public had not reached them and that they had not encountered the phenomenon. They knew of only one

Muslim prostitute in the village of Kakmysh in Mamadysh district, adding that there had never been more than four prostitutes in Chistopol'. Moreover, they noted, local authorities had never taken measures against them. The officer in charge concluded his report on a skeptical note. From conversations with local Muslims he gathered that the appearance of these prostitutes had not scandalized Muslim society there. The initiative behind the protest lay rather with a single individual, Akhmet Abdulvakhitov Karimov, about whom this official had had occasion to report to his superiors in August of the previous year. Karimov had penned the petition on his own, he charged, and had lobbied local inhabitants to sign it.

Under the pious and conservative Nicholas II (r. 1894–1917), the police targeted interaction between Muslims in various parts of the empire and communication with co-religionists in Bukhara, Cairo, Delhi, and Istanbul as strands of a Pan-Islamic conspiracy orchestrated from the Ottoman capital. Increased pilgrimage and contact through the periodical press nonetheless strengthened these ties. At the same time, the regime's own policies paradoxically contributed to the emergence among the empire's scattered and varied Muslim communities of a common confessional and political identity. Like the British in colonial India, the regime increasingly treated diverse Muslim populations and social groups as a unified entity with its own particularist political interests defined, not by nationality or ethnicity, but by religion.[62]

The first empire-wide census in 1897 played a particularly important role in this process. Census takers renewed rumors of government-sponsored conversion and met with resistance from Vaisov's followers in Kazan. But the census also created the possibility of imagining a single Muslim collectivity in a new way in the Russian empire. Along with native tongue, estate, profession, and education, confession was one of the main categories of the census. In 1897 officials counted nearly 14 million Muslims out of a total population of 150 million tsarist subjects, although they conceded that they had undercounted Muslims, especially women, because local communities had frequently denied census takers access to the interior of their homes.[63]

When Nicholas II faced widespread opposition and calls for representative government at the beginning of the twentieth century, Muslim activists throughout the empire drew on the numerical weight revealed by the 1897 census to demand political representation—along confessional lines—proportionate to their demographic size. But Muslims also seized upon the census takers' own admissions to having undercounted their co-religionists. In petitions from the Volga and Urals regions, the Caucasus, the steppe, Siberia, and Turkestan, peasants, townspeople, merchants, Cossacks, and members of other social groups appealed to the tsar and his ministers for the recognition of political and civil rights for the "twenty million Muslims" of the empire. Some claimed that they belonged to a community of thirty or even forty million Muslims.[64]

After Russian defeat in the Russo-Japanese War of 1904–1905 and Bloody Sunday in January 1905, political opposition to the autocracy spread throughout imperial society. This wave of politicization affected Muslims across the empire, and they joined other tsarist subjects in petitioning Nicholas II for fundamental political changes. They shared as well in the loose consensus that held disparate opposition groups together through the spring and summer of 1905 around a core set of demands, including calls for the regime to broaden civil rights and establish representative institutions. During the revolutionary crisis of 1905, they joined Old Believers, Armenians, and others in demanding greater religious toleration. A decree of 26 February 1903 had announced the government's intent to "strengthen the strict observance by the authorities . . . of the ordinances of religious toleration." To placate opposition groups, the regime issued another decree on 12 December 1904 promising reforms in local government, factory legislation, censorship, and other areas. It promised to review legislation relating to "schismatics, as well as figures belonging to other Christian and non-Christian confessions," with the goal of "strengthening" the foundations of toleration in the empire. It pledged to remove "every form of constraint" not permitted by law. As critics noted, however, the law still did not allow "freedom of conscience" (svoboda sovesti), that is, the right to choose one's confession or freedom to proselytize. Thus the law prohibited conversion from Orthodox Christianity. The state also retained the right to regulate interconfessional marriages.

Although late nineteenth-century discriminatory legislation targeted Jews in particular, non-Christians in general faced restrictions. Laws prohibited marriages between non-Christians and Catholics or Orthodox. (Muslims and Protestants were permitted to marry, but Protestants were not allowed to marry "pagans".) Nor could Christians and non-Christians adopt each other's children. Moreover, non-Christians who did not enjoy the status "natives" (tuzemtsy) were not permitted to acquire real estate in Turkestan or the steppe. A law of 1889 had restricted non-Christians' right to act as jurors in jury trials or private attorneys without special permission from the ministers of Justice and Internal Affairs or to sit on district or provincial educational councils. In some provinces, the law did not permit non-Christians to serve as foremen of juries or work as domestic teachers or tutors.[65]

In April 1905 another decree addressed toleration directly and vowed to remove remaining discrimination against non-Christians and Old Believers. Finally, the Manifesto of 17 October 1905 established "freedom of conscience."[66] When the revolution forced Nicholas II to allow creation of a parliament, the Duma, as a concession to widespread opposition, Muslim politicians argued that their demographic weight should translate into political power, namely the right to redefine religious toleration and establish broader autonomy for Muslim schools, the press, and the official hierarchies in Ufa, the Crimea, and the Caucasus.

Muslims participated in politics in the Duma period principally as Muslims, rather than as merchants, peasants, or another social category reflecting their birth or occupation. Mirroring the institutional architecture of the empire, they acted through parties established along confessional lines. The Muslim fraction in the Duma initially allied itself on many issues with the liberal Constitutional Democrats, but other Muslims found common cause with the Socialist Revolutionaries on the left. Facilitated by the slackening of censorship laws after October, an expanded Muslim press brought Duma politics and debates about the reform of Muslim education and Islamic institutions to towns and villages.[67] Conflicts with the Orthodox Church, petition campaigns, and even subordination to the Orenburg Assembly contributed to a newly shared form of confessional consciousness among Muslims throughout the empire. The census and expanded networks of communication and transport linked Muslims in Kazan, Orenburg, Ufa, and elsewhere to other Muslim subjects in Siberia, the Caucasus, the steppe, and Turkestan as well as to an international Muslim community. As members of a cosmopolitan elite, many notables also drew on nineteenth- and early twentieth-century reformist currents in Islamic thought, including those that stressed the need for greater unity and cooperation among the world's Muslims.

Though brought together as the objects of an all-encompassing "Muslim question," communities continued to be marked by deep divides. International events like the Russo-Japanese War affected the rhetorical choices made by feuding clerics, who accused rivals of praying for the victory of the Japanese as "fellow Muslims." Theological disputes exacerbated older social and generational tensions. Regional and local identities and notions of religious authority remained strong. In Turkestan, some residents of Tashkent refused to admit immigrant Tatars into their mosque communities, while from the steppe Kazakhs lobbied for their own muftiate. Tensions were also pronounced among Muslim peoples on the Orenburg frontier.

One Muslim political activist, Zeki Velidi Togan, recalled that Bashkirs and Kazakhs disliked the Tatar scholar Märjani, who they thought wrote "disparaging remarks" about their knowledge of Islam; one mullah even burned a copy of his major compendium of the biographies of regional scholars because it associated the Bashkirs with shamanism.[68]

Muslim petitions during the revolution of 1905 reflected a range of political and religious viewpoints, but an emphasis on civil rights was a key common denominator; the petitions reflected a broad area of collective interest among Muslims, one held in common with other social, political, ethnic, and national groups in the empire. But certain issues set Muslims apart as they explored the possibilities of a new political order. Muslim demands reflected the particularistic concerns of confessional politics. They generated one of the fault lines along which the consensus uniting oppositional society splintered in October 1905 after the tsar granted a representative assembly.

Muslims from the village of Toiguzina in Viatka Province petitioned St. Petersburg in January 1905 asking that the Orenburg Assembly oversee mosques and schools without interference from provincial government. They sought the exemption of mullahs from military service as "unbefitting their place in society," adding that the conscription of mullahs in the last war had left them without prayer leaders. The Viatka petitioners also asked that the mufti be elected by the local clergy and those among "learned Muhammadans who are completely familiar with the rules of our religion, since they know better the figures who are capable and worthy of the office of mufti." They also requested that the clergy be allowed to resolve cases involving marriage and divorce "according to the shari'a, without submitting cases of this kind to the general civil laws," explaining that this last article was motivated by news that a draft of the civil code proposed placing Muslim marriage under the jurisdiction of the "civil court." These projected laws, the villagers noted, "are directly contrary to the rules of the Qur'an and the teachings of our faith, and thus in case of the confirmation of this draft in such a form the fulfillment of this law will entail our forced deviation from the rules of religion." Finally, the Viatka villagers asked that their mullahs be freed from study of the Russian language, a requirement that had made examination of candidates' knowledge of the religious sciences of "secondary importance, which we find abnormal."[69]

Tatars whom the Orthodox Church regarded as converts petitioned Prime Minister Sergei Witte, requesting recognition as Muslims. They denied ever being assigned Orthodox names and explained that, even though they constantly go the mosque to pray, the local mullahs "do not give us names at birth, do not marry us and do not even bury us, or record [our] births, marriages or deaths in the register of the local mosque." The petitioners complained that their status left them vulnerable to various hardships: "Young people are often taken [early] from our families for military service . . . and in other relations we find ourselves, with hands on our hearts, in a very difficult situation." Asserting that they had always been Muslims and belonged neither to the Orthodox nor to the "Old Believer sect," they asked that the authorities inform the local mullahs that they were not apostates from Islam (pointing out that "we ourselves do not understand why we are called this").[70]

A delegation of Muslim reformist notables from Kazan, including Said G. Alkin, Gabdulla G. Apanaev, Akhmetzian Ia. Saidatev, and Iusuf Akchurin, submitted a petition on behalf of the Muslim community as a whole. They expressed their loyalty and devotion to tsar and fatherland and lamented that their "sins" had visited on "our fatherland the gravest of evils—internal disorder [*smuta*]." As the government turned to the fulfillment of the tsar's manifesto of December 1904, they asked that the Committee of Ministers consider correcting the "deficiencies, gaps, and imperfections" of tsarist law on toleration, "which are not completely in accord with the spirit of the divine revelation given us through the Prophet." First, they asked that the three judges of the Orenburg Assembly, and especially its head, be a "clerical figure in the full sense of the term," given the institution's duty to oversee everything under the divine law. They proposed that the mufti as well as the three kadis of the Assembly be chosen exclusively from the ranks of clerics by the entire community of Muslims under the muftiate.

Noting that the "smallest nonobservance of any law of the shari'a places each orthodox Muslim in grave sin," the petitioners asked that all "temptation to this sin" be removed by legislation making all Muslim marital, family, and inheritance matters subject only to "our religious law." They wanted the Assembly alone to supervise Islamic education and pious endowments, as public property intended for charitable and religious purposes. The Kazan notables also sought freedom of the press and speech for Muslims and for the exemption of Islamic literature from any censorship besides the Assembly. The petitioners joined other Tatars in requesting that those who had been registered as Orthodox, but who remained Muslims, be given the right to register according to their true faith: "It is our holy obligation to take care of them, so that those illegally professing our holy Islam do not live a forced lie."[71]

The "relative freedom" of sexual relations, which had increased in recent years among all the peoples of the empire, had affected Muslim women as well. The Kazan notables pointed out that Muslims sometimes committed infanticide out of fear that the orphans left by such cases would be raised as Christians. They asked that Muslim communities be allowed to adopt and raise children who were abandoned in their midst or even outside their communities, when they displayed "all signs of Muslim racial origin."

Their clergy also lacked the prestige enjoyed by Christian confessions in Russia, the Kazan reformers pointed out. Remaining peasants and townspeople, they were indistinct from the "dark and ignorant villagers." Their lack of status harmed religion, because it encouraged parishioners to assume a "base familiarity" with their mullahs. The Kazan delegation asked that the state attract better people to official posts by providing them with the privileges and titles enjoyed by other clergies, making them equal to the "clergy of the predominant church in the state." They proposed that their clergy be assigned the hereditary title "honored citizens" (*pochetnye grazhdane*) with the same rights as the Orthodox clergy but without being required to learn the Russian language. Finally, the reformist notables asked that Muslims be allowed to enter into all ranks of state service and acquire property throughout the empire.[72]

Two issues dominated petitions from the steppe: land and religion. The state-sponsored migration of landless peasants from European Russia had driven Kazakhs from their grazing lands. But religion and the contest between customary law (adat) and the shari'a was of equal importance to many communities. In June 1905, Kazakhs from the Turgai region submitted a petition to the Ministry of Internal Affairs requesting state support for Islamic institutions among them. They maintained that their people had converted to Islam in 1262, citing "the historian of Islam, August Müller," the German Oriental studies scholar. They explained that their religion taught submission to "the Tsar in heaven" as well as the "Tsar on earth," a principle that "preserves our people from attraction toward liberalism and keeps us in total submission to and respect for the authorities and laws." Moreover, they observed, attempts to obstruct the ties between the Kazakhs and the Tatars had been fruitless. They likened the impact of official restrictions on the number of mullahs in the steppe to the phenomenon of "priestlessness" *(bezpopovshchina)* practiced by dissenters from the Orthodox Church who rejected the authority of priests. The practice of assigning one mullah per township, according to the steppe statute of 1891, left Muslims on a territory the size of France to search out a single cleric to perform essential duties for them. Without legal registration in official registers, "each Kazakh is deprived of his rights by this law to such an extent that he is deprived of the opportunity to prove the legality of his origin, age, and status."[73]

The Turgai Kazakhs pointed out that this provision also meant that the dead went without burials, while marriage, "not made sacred by religion, had to become a simple commercial agreement of buying and selling, which can be broken easily and arbitrarily by the contracting parties." Children resulting from these marriages were regarded as illegitimate. Since the 1868 shift in policy away from supporting Islam among the Kazakhs, the moral condition and political loyalty of the Kazakhs had suffered from the suppression of Islam.

> Forty years have passed since the people heard the word of
> God from the lips of their spiritual pastor or heard a single
> sermon about the obligations of each of them before God,
> the Reigning Sovereign-Emperor and the entire govern-
> ment, about which the co-religionists of the Kazakhs, the
> Tatars, Bashkirs, and Mishars, hear from their licensed mul-
> lahs every Friday in their mosques.

Kazakh children, in addition, were compelled to live in "total ignorance" of the rules of their religion. The petitioners cited the case of Baita Asanov, whom the state prosecuted in 1899 for providing children with religious education at his home. Asanov responded by asking "What am I being punished for? It's not a tavern or a whorehouse."[74]

This group of Turgai Kazakhs protested secret government measures to Christianize them. They disdained in particular governor-general Kryzhanovskii, who had boasted, they claimed, that converting the Kazakhs would be "as easy for him as putting his cap on his head." The petitioners also rejected attempts by Il'minskii and Minister of Education D. A. Tolstoi to render their language in the Russian script. The Turgai Kazakhs requested instead that the government provide the "five million Kazakhs" with their own "ecclesiastical administration," with a mufti and one judge (kadi) per region. A single hierarchy would guarantee that the shari'a be applied uniformly. They asked that the mufti be a person with a European education, elected by the people

> for life and confirmed by the tsar, who would direct the religious development of the people toward humanity [and] philanthropy without distinction of nationality or faith, destroy [and] dispel the harmful appearance of Muslim fanaticism, introduce the principle of the equality of the sexes and respect for the individuality and freedom of women.

The petitioners concluded by conceding that they would accept subordination to the Orenburg Assembly if Kazakhs were appointed to the muftiate as assistants or muftis.[75]

Elsewhere in the steppe, communities who identified themselves as Muslims asked the regime to grant them their own muftiates or attach them to the muftiate in Ufa. Petitioners like those of the Semireche region asked not only for a separate muftiate (in Pishpek) but also for the abolition of the customary law courts, whose resolutions "are not based on anything except for antiquated customs which do not conform to our cultural stage and the spirit of [our] religion." They joined other Kazakhs in asking for permission to open schools and mosques and to establish endowments to support them.[76]

An appeal from merchants and clerics from Orenburg and the nearby Tatar settlement of Kargala in the spring of 1905 reflected a complex mixture of pleas for equal rights for Muslims and other citizens and distinctly confessional demands. Two hundred years had passed, they pointed out, since they were given the right to settle in the Orenburg region. The provisions of this arrangement "proclaimed from the height of the Throne" included "recognition of us as citizens with full rights [*polnopravnye grazdane*], both in the legal [and] juridical sense and in the ecclesiastical, moral, and religious sense." Since then, they had sacrificed many lives and much labor to transform the Orenburg region into a "trade region." Yet their "rights diminished more and more and we have turned from citizens with full rights into some kind of separate people [*osobennaia narodnost'*], as though having nothing in common with the subjects of Russia."[77]

The supplicants from Kargala made clear that they understood this anomalous status to concern more than regional history. They lamented the lot of all Muslim subjects, calling for changes in policy that affected Muslims in general and the relationship between the Orenburg Assembly and other state institutions in particular. "In expectation of enlightenment and justice," they asked first that "all the Muslims' marriage, inheritance, and family matters and affairs concerning their religious education" come under the purview of the Assembly, which would enjoy the exclusive right to issue the "final resolution" of these cases. They requested permission to found endowments and to assign the Assembly the task of overseeing them. Muslims must also be allowed, they insisted, to elect the mufti and judges of the ecclesiastical assemblies through representatives. The petitioners envisioned an organization for 'ulama of the empire transcending the separate geographic jurisdictions of the four official hierarchies to achieve a consensus on religious interpretation. They sought permission for "annual congresses of mullahs for the uniform resolution of new questions that may arise."[78]

Besides making appeals for both the autonomy and standardization of Islamic institutions, these petitioners proposed ways to redefine their place, as Muslims, in the wider imperial polity. They called for an end to censorship of Muslims books and for "freedom of speech and the press." For their 'ulama, they requested repeal of the Russian language requirement as well as fulfillment of a longstanding demand (especially from this region) that the regime confer upon "our clergy equal rights with the Orthodox clergy." The desire for greater parity with the Church was reflected as well in their demand for state help in stopping conversion from Islam. Muslim authorities should enjoy the right to "admonish" persons "straying" from Islam for not less than six months. Permission to convert should be given, the petition maintained, only upon certification that this "admonition" had been delivered. It insisted, moreover, that no Muslims be allowed to convert while still in their minority. In another move aimed at redressing the balance between Muslims and Christians, the petitioners contended that they should not be forced by city authorities to stop trade on Christian holidays.[79]

For all of their demands for religious autonomy, this group of Muslims took for granted that integration of their co-religionists into imperial institutions such as state schools, the army, and the bureaucracy would and indeed should continue, though with new laws to guarantee both equality and the accommodation of religious difference. Recruits should be permitted to take their oaths in Tatar (instead of Russian) and should receive only food permitted by their faith. They requested that children studying in state schools at the lower and middle levels should spend the same number of hours per week studying "our scripture" (*zakon Bozhii*) as their Orthodox counterparts spent studying theirs. Besides seeking the right to open secular Tatar-language schools without interference, the supplicants called on state authorities to abandon the "Russificatory direction in Russian schools." They advised the repeal of "all restrictions connected with the practice of the Muslim religion," like limits on enrollment in institutions of higher learning and advancement in the bureaucracy as well as the prohibition against the acquisition of property in Turkestan.

Although there was much that was new in this and similar petitions, Muslims continued to fall back on the police power of the regime as an indispensable pillar of their vision of Islamic community. They retained this role for the state even as they and others imagined a thorough transformation of government institutions in so many other areas of life in the midst of revolutionary turmoil in 1905–1907. The plea for state interdiction of Muslim conversion (without a six-month period of "admonition" from a Muslim religious figure) stands out as a prime example. The rallying cry of "freedom of conscience and religion" united Old Believers and other dissenting branches of Orthodoxy as well as non-Christians like Jews, Buddhists, and, of course, Muslims. For this last community, in particular, the right to abandon Orthodox Christianity, especially when one's conversion had been coerced or linked to the conversion of one's ancestors, figured as one of the chief grievances against state officials who bowed too low before the cross.

By calling for state mediation of conversion from Islam, these Muslims sought parity with a powerful faction of the Church that insisted on state protection for its faith. They called on the state to restrict freedom of conscience for Muslims when such a right would have allowed Muslims to abandon Islam. Thus these petitioners were vulnerable to the same criticism leveled against Orthodox hierarchs who made police coercion a cornerstone of the Church. The symmetry appears all the more striking in this case when one considers the articles of this Orenburg petition that suggested an expanded role for the state in the disciplining of the Muslim community and the regulation of its morality. The article concerning provisions for Muslim recruits added that Muslims should be kept away from wine. Another echoed numerous other Muslim appeals to government officials under Nicholas II: "For the protection of the sanctity of the family hearth and the preservation of the purity of our families," it requested that state authorities "prohibit Muslims from opening brothels, and absolutely not permit Muslim women to engage in prostitution."[80]

In 1905 and 1906, Muslim political activity expanded broadly. Muslim elites, both men and women, like other educated Russians, established newspapers and periodicals and founded civic organizations for the promotion of education and philanthropy.[81] Notables convened three congresses and a fourth in 1914 to prepare political demands. Like Muslim petitioners throughout the empire in 1905, delegates called for a constitutional monarchy and parity with Christians and other tsarist subjects. Their demands included respect for Muslim holidays and public support for their schools and clergy.[82] They sought reorganization of the official Islamic hierarchies, including the establishment of a muftiate for Turkestani Muslims, and proposed that each of these muftis stand for election by the entire community every five years. A new supreme position (*rais al-ulama*) would oversee all of them as the highest representative of Russia's Muslims with the right to petition the tsar directly.[83]

Muslims failed to win support for these reforms in the Duma, which focused primarily on improving the status of Old Believers.[84] After 1909 the Church blocked government plans for the substantial reform of legislation concerning non-Orthodox confessions. Formerly a proponent of broader toleration, the prime minister, Peter Stolypin, proclaimed before the Duma in spring of 1909:

The monarch, according to our law, is the defender of the
Orthodox Church and the custodian of its dogmas . . . [and]
these religious laws will operate in the Russian state and will
be confirmed by the Russian Tsar, who for more than one
hundred million people was, is and will be an Orthodox
Tsar.[85]

Despite Muslim petitions, the government turned to combating "Pan-
Islam," which they believed was strengthened by defeat at the hands
of the Japanese. Representatives of the Ministries of Internal Affairs,
War, Justice and Education seized on Muslim political demands as
evidence of "separatism." They convened special commissions in
1910 and 1913 to discuss the "Muslim question" and review legislation concerning Islamic affairs. Missionaries from the Volga region
were invited to sit on these commissions, where they advocated
tighter state control over Muslim schools and the abolition of the official Islamic hierarchies.[86]

Despite these attacks, the Orenburg Assembly continued to fulfill
its function as an instrument of clerical discipline and center of
Islamic legal and doctrinal authority. As of 1889, it oversaw 4,254
parishes in which 7,203 clerics served a population of some 3.5
million Muslims. According to a survey published on its one hun-
dred-year anniversary, it had judged 13,927 men worthy of an official
license between 1836 and 1889 (making an average of roughly 263
per year). In the 1880s it handled some 1,200 cases per year. Most
dealt directly with the testing and certification of clerics and the mediation of conflicts among them, and between them and restive parishioners. But annually these also included between 200 and 250
disputes involving clerics and laypeople regarding inheritance and
some 150 divorce cases.[87]

Though Church and many provincial authorities had turned
against it, the Assembly in fact deepened its reach into local Muslim

life in the early twentieth century, drawing on a growing budget and improved means of communication, transportation, and bureaucratic record-keeping. Through printed tracts and a journal, clerics associated with the Assembly pressed the 'ulama and laypeople under them to recognize their subordinate roles and to respect the state-granted rights and duties of licensed authorities. Its increased capacity to discipline and intervene in mosque communities permitted the Assembly to guide the faithful in new directions, highlighting greater uniformity in the interpretation of Islamic law and the timing of prayers and holidays, even if it did not succeed fully in implementing its prescriptions.[88]

Muslim laypeople and clerics thus sought broader autonomy for the Assembly (and similar bodies) but could not break with the state entirely. Committed to state involvement in Islamic affairs, they tried to direct the form that such engagement might take. In addition to calls for government support for clergy and schools, reformers assigned the state a key role in the mediation of intracommunal and intrafamilial conflicts.[89] Although tensions between local Muslim communities and state authorities had dramatically increased in various regions, Muslims continued to rely on certain kinds of police intervention.

The splintering of communities along generational and ideological lines may have increased this reliance in some locales. Madrasa students rebelled against their teachers and were drawn to the radicalism of the left. As Dudoignon has shown, Muslim activists took new aim at folk tradition; they singled out holidays like "Ploughman's Day" (*Saban tuyi*) and extravagant weddings, sometimes arguing instead for the celebration of the Prophet's birthday, as a more frugal alternative. Lines between "reformers" and their opponents hardened when a new generation (*yashlar*) of Islamic scholars returned from abroad to challenge older prayer leaders (and their patrons) for positions at mosques in the Volga region. Intensified by the harsh tenor of the periodical press, these conflicts worsened after 1910 with Muslim political exclusion from the tsarist parliamentary system.[90]

Yet Muslims were unprepared to give up on the state as a potential ally in the imposition of Islamic orthodoxy and the disciplining of the community. Even activists like Gabiga Valiullina, the widow of a village mullah from Kazan Province, turned to the Russian authorities. In a petition of 1910 she pointed out that since her husband's death in 1897 she had offered free religious instruction for twenty-five to thirty Muslim girls in her home. However, the local licensed mullah had sent the police to issue an order to end her lessons because, she charged, her efforts deprived this cleric of the fees that the girls' parents would have to pay him to give lessons. Her petition requested that the state protect her services from the greed of this mullah.[91]

After 1905, moreover, tsarist authorities and Muslims had new grounds to seek out mutual accommodation. As minister of internal affairs and chairman of the State Council, Stolypin warned officials in 1910 to be on the lookout for Turkish emissaries seeking support for "the unity of the whole Muslim world," noting, in particular, the danger of the "Tatar Muslim movement" and its "center" on the Volga. Mullahs adapted to these concerns about revolution and Pan-Islam. Many branded their enemies revolutionaries, furnishing the police with denunciations that led to the harassment and closing of a handful of reformist madrasas.[92] Despite vague calls for a national foundation for the empire, neither the Church nor officials in a single ministry ever established total control over tsarist policy.

Geopolitical concerns constantly informed how tsarist elites managed domestic politics. Even war with the Ottomans in

1877, and a related uprising among Muslims in the Northern Caucasus, did not effect a reversal in the minds of officials who grasped the
broader problems of maintaining an empire in such an age. "The
fact of our victory over Turkey," Prince D. I. Sviatopolk-Mirskii
wrote from the perspective of the Caucasus in 1878, "should not
serve as an obstacle to the establishment of our friendship with Islam." In Asia, he added, "we should appear . . . as the protectors of
the native population from English domination." In response to proposals to curb Muslim rights further after the Andizhan rebellion in
the Ferghana Valley, Finance Minister Sergei Witte reminded his
colleagues in 1900 that "our domestic policy on the Muslim question represents an important factor of foreign policy." Highlighting
the cultural diversity of Muslim subjects as well as their geographic
diffusion, he called talk of any kind of "religious and political union
among them" unrealistic and added that the "Muslim East" had increasingly become an issue of concern—and competition—for "the
cultured peoples of Europe," especially the Germans.

From Istanbul, the Russian ambassador responded to interministerial debates about Islam in a similarly cautious fashion. Nikolai
V. Charykov pointed to the international implications of Russia's
policies. He drew attention to a kaleidoscope of conspiracies lurking
behind movements like Pan-Islam, which he saw as a Zionist-backed
phenomenon bringing together under Turkish aegis "Jewish hatred
of Russia and European socialism and anarchism."[93] A critic of the
"fanaticism" of Islam, Charykov nonetheless repeated the charge
that the Germans and Japanese also backed this force, which posed
a challenge not only to Russia, but to Britain and France. Adding
race to the mix, the ambassador proposed that "Christian states"
ward off this "yellow danger" from the East by securing "the assistance of its white, though Muslim colleagues, with whom they have
deep racial and confessional roots." Thus the tsarist state should con-

tinue to take care that new administrative measures "do not create irreconcilable enmity and an impassable abyss between Christians and Muslims."[94]

Such defenses were more than theoretical. For the Russian officials who supervised the acquisition of land and the resettlement of some three thousand colonists in northern Persia on the eve of the First World War, resort to religious authority was critical, as E. V. Sablin noted from Tehran, because "the single and natural law of the land, the shari'a is very advantageous for us, especially when all formalities demanded by the shari'a are observed at the completion of agreements." Muslims had similar incentives to pursue their fate within an empire at peace, even though a few had begun to look abroad for alternatives in Tokyo or Istanbul. As a young preacher instructed the faithful in a sermon that he committed to print in 1908, the obligation to migrate or perform the hijra could also be understood as a duty to be fulfilled internally, for "we are not compelled to migrate from these towns in the fatherland *(vatan)*." "For us another kind of migration is necessary," he added, "from jealousy and enmity to . . . loving affection, from deviation and wrong to faithfulness and justice, from neglectfulness and indolence to effort and striving . . . [and] from dispersion to unity." Even in the context of the Balkan wars of 1912–1913, Muslim elites, too, denied that there was "a war between 'cross' and 'crescent'."[95]

Loyalty to the empire did not mean giving up hopes on the possibility of full citizenship in a reformed Russia. Muslims continued to raise objections to changes in the penal and civil codes that conflicted with Muslim political demands. The question of whether or not Muslims, as future citizens, would have to trade the shari'a (governing inheritance, marriage, and divorce) for a uniform civil code proposed by liberals invited skepticism from Muslims. Muslims became socialists and liberal constitutionalists. But many more rejected secular alternatives to the established legal and institutional arrangements that maintained both Muslim communities and the hierarchies of empire. Muslims pushed the regime for equal rights and broader toleration, but the tsarist state lay at the heart of Islam for most communities of the empire. Though much divided Muslim activists and tsarist police, they nonetheless colluded to diminish the possibility of freedom of conscience in the last years of tsarism. The varied Muslim communities of the empire remained embedded in, and helped to sustain, an empire founded on religious discipline for all the tsar's children.

EPILOGUE

In 1913 Russia celebrated the three-hundredth anniversary of the Romanov dynasty. Official ceremonies honored the unity of tsar and people.[1] Although the symbols of seventeenth-century Orthodoxy dominated the celebrations, Muslims also commemorated the tercentenary, in mosques throughout the empire, on 21 February 1913. Muslims embraced the occasion as an opportunity to demonstrate their loyalty to the monarchy and patriotism for Russia but also to assert their rights as "citizens," which in the tsarist context meant entitlement to the same limited rights as other imperial subjects. In St. Petersburg, the amir of Bukhara and the khan of Khiva joined Muslim members of the Duma, a representative of the Orenburg mufti, and local Muslims, including a lieutenant colonel and major general, for prayers. After a reading from the Qur'an, the mufti's representative praised Catherine the Great and all of the Romanovs, who had been the first sovereigns to legalize the establishment of mosques in Russia. The number of mosques had reached six thousand under the Orenburg Assembly. After the sermon, Mukhammed Zarif Iunusov declared that "devotion to the throne and love for the motherland are ordered by God himself and his Prophet Muhammad." He reminded the faithful of the Qur'anic injunction to "Obey God and His Prophet and those in authority among you" and of a saying attributed to Muhammad, "Love of the motherland is a sign of faith."[2]

At the end of the prayers, Mukhametsafa Baiazitov, the head of the capital's Muslim community and the future Orenburg mufti (in office 1915–1917), gave a speech "in the Russian language," as the official account pointed out. He observed that Muslims, "together with all of our fatherland," were devoted to the dynasty. Baiazitov emphasized Muslim union—and parity—with Russians in laying the autocratic foundation of the state: "When 300 years ago Russian people called on the ancestor of our Sovereign, Michael Feodorovich Romanov, to rule, several Tatar princes signed the document." Pointing to these signatures alongside those of Russian clergymen and aristocrats, Baiazitov concluded that "the Orthodox Russian people as well as orthodox Muslims were committed in fraternal unity to this great matter of state, without regard for differences of faith, differences of blood, or differences of language, when it came to the organization of our common fatherland."[3]

The outbreak of the First World War put such sentiments to the test. Following the publication of a fatwa by the head of the Ottoman religious establishment directing Muslims to wage jihad against the Russians, the British, and the French, the Orenburg mufti Mukhamed'iar Sultanov issued his own call for Muslims to show their patriotism, arguing that "the Russian state is our fatherland, near and dear to our hearts, the hearts of Muslims, but also to the hearts of all peoples who live in it."[4] More than a million Muslims answered his call, declaring themselves "patriots" and "true sons of the fatherland." Fighting alongside Orthodox Christians, Jews, Buddhists, Catholics, Protestants, and others, they served in mixed units against the Ottoman, German, and Habsburg armies. At the front, mullahs led the faithful in prayer in improvised field mosques. Muslim combatants earned doubleheaded eagle medals in lieu of the crosses of St. George awarded to their Orthodox compatriots. Although Nicholas II stressed his Orthodox piety and sentimental bond with the Russian people during the war, he also staked his legitimacy on non-Russian support. On his travels along the home front in 1914, the tsar visited mosques as well as Orthodox cathedrals to demonstrate his role as the "father" of a multiconfessional imperial family.[5]

The emperor's mosque visits might seem out of place at a moment when numerous figures within the government and in society at large raised the banner of Russian nationalism as a rallying force for the empire. Like the mosque sermons of 1913, however, Nicholas II's tour demonstrated instead the persistence of strategies that had long been critical to the Romanov dynasty's successful maintenance of empire. The last tsar inherited a government that Catherine the Great had made into a patron of Islam. Informed by the ecumenical piety of Alexander I, the Ministry of Internal Affairs gave institutional form to Catherine's generic Enlightenment notion of toleration. In the second quarter of the nineteenth century, the militaristic discipline of Nicholas I elaborated a bureaucratic structure for non-Orthodox confessions, including a state-sponsored Islamic establishment to control a Muslim "clergy." Under Nicholas, the Orthodox Church reemerged as an actor in communities where it feared losing Christians to Islam. But this pressure did not divert his government from devising systematic legislation to regulate all of the tolerated faiths of the empire. The Nicholaevan state remained committed to the pursuit of Muslim intermediaries in ruling the empire even at the height of its war in the Northern Caucasus against Shamil. During the reign of Alexander II, the challenge to Russia's entanglement with Islamic institutions came not only from the Church but also from various Russian nationalist camps within both the bureaucracy and educated society. For nationalist thinkers, official backing for Islam was a betrayal of the historic mission of the state. Beginning in the 1860s they succeeded in limiting the reach of Islamic institutions when the eastern frontier stretched into the north Caspian steppe and Central Asia, where administrators confronted populations who seemed to differ from the Muslims that they had encountered on the Volga. In the late nineteenth century, Russian nationalist elites pushed the regime further toward more uniform administration—and tighter control—of the non-Russian borderlands. Yet despite the new emphasis on "nationality" as the unifying principle of modern European states during the reigns of Alexander III and Nicholas II, neither tsar dismantled the imperial architecture for the management of Islam in Russia. The particularistic order of confessional politics remained the foundation of the empire.

Catherine's successors built on and adapted the basic principles of her approach toward Islam as a force for social discipline and imperial loyalty. But not even the military's extraordinarily brutal campaigns against Muslims in the Northern Caucasus spelled a rejection of the Catherinian proposition that the state could use Islam to strengthen the stability of the empire. In the second half of the nineteenth century, the Church, the Ministries of War, Internal Affairs, Foreign Affairs, and Education, as well as ethnographers, Oriental studies scholars, and other experts disagreed about the particulars of policy toward the empire's varied Muslim populations. In the policy debates that resulted from these differences, two interlinking state priorities prevailed. Both were fundamentally conservative: concern for order and discipline among Muslim populations at home and attention to Russia's reputation in the eyes of Muslims abroad almost always trumped radical calls for a departure from the regime's commitment to the mode of toleration introduced by Catherine. The Ministry of Internal Affairs guarded the first principle, seeking stabil-

ity first of all in the family, then in the parish structure subordinated
to the official Islamic establishment. The Ministry of Foreign Affairs,
often joined by the Ministry of War, focused on the potential impact
of tsarist policies on Russia's neighbors. Thus tsarist toleration of Islam was an elaborate system for policing both the mosque and the
borders of the empire. This strategy, tsarist officials reasoned, would
enhance prospects for further expansion into the vulnerable Muslim
lands along its southern frontiers.

Between the late eighteenth and early twentieth centuries, repeated confrontations with the Ottomans meant that St. Petersburg
had to compete in an international arena for the loyalties of its Muslim subjects.[6] The legacy of a particular moment in Enlightenment
thought, Russia's treatment of Islam also formed part of a dynamic
imperial system that tied together the religious politics in the Habsburg, Ottoman, Hohenzollern, and Romanov empires. Catherine II
had been inspired by Joseph II's statist approach to religion in Habsburg lands, for example. And like Russia, the Habsburgs constructed
a domestic Islamic establishment to deflect Ottoman influence following Vienna's annexation of Bosnia-Herzegovina in 1878.[7] Alongside other European powers, Russia had a very direct impact on the
character of Ottoman rule over non-Muslims. Beginning in 1839 the
Ottoman state introduced a series of reforms aimed at shoring up its
authority in the face of European powers that increasingly lobbied
the Porte on behalf of its non-Muslim subjects. Promising equality
for non-Muslims, the reforms also expanded and institutionalized
the Ottoman system for the management of religious communities
(*millets*). State concessions and foreign pressure led to the proliferation of new millets whose lay and clerical elites exercised centralized
authority over community members. In many Jewish and Christian
communities, these reforms heightened the authority of clerics.[8] As
in Russia, the Ottoman state attempted to enhance its power by governing through the hierarchies constituted by these administrative

units. In both settings, the regimes sought to engage their subjects, not solely as members of the bounded ethnic or national groups that historians tend to study, but as the members of religious communities.

The Ottoman millet system and the Romanov's tolerated faiths formed the essential building blocks of empire. Wary of the development of nationalism among the subject peoples, both governments effectively instrumentalized religion in managing populations whose religions differed from that of the ruling dynasty. The state-sponsored confessionalization of these heterogeneous populations yielded a dense network of policing institutions. Both empires prospered on the promise of official support for elites who would discipline subordinate members of a given community in the name of religion. In neither context did "toleration" grant rights to individuals. Both regimes resorted to violence, especially in borderlands shared with contiguous empires. Yet the Ottoman and Romanov attention to confessional politics—and to the mediation of disputes arising from the fractious world within each millet or tolerated confession—also explains the relative cohesion and stability of imperial societies that endured until the First World War.

The Ottoman and Romanov systems were also striking in their differences. By the late nineteenth century, both had generated calls for greater autonomy from the imperial center. But the European patrons of these communities proved a greater threat to the Ottoman hold on non-Muslims. St. Petersburg, by contrast, never faced a concert of foreign powers demanding a vast array of special concessions for their co-religionists.

But the story of Russia's more successful management of its confessional politics at the heart of empire would be incomplete if we dwelled only on institutions and geopolitics. More than the product of raw coercion, the empire was also a product of imagination, not just of elites but of heterogeneous groups of subjects. Beginning in the late eighteenth and early nineteenth centuries, the state supplied the confessional lens on the empire. But such a strategy would not have achieved much, had it not tapped into the consciousness of so many imperial subjects. This approach worked in the case of Muslim communities in large measure because it promised a hierarchical structure for mediating the disputes that simmered in mosques and madrasas. The state offered the authority to resolve these disputes once and for all. The tsarist understanding of toleration promised peace—between rulers and ruled, and among the faithful. The system worked because Muslims, Jews, and others came forward to engage these mediating institutions. In the case of Islam, Muslims even managed to capture the state in many locales, turning its policing and judicial organs into partisan weapons wielded on behalf of contested readings of the faith. The guardian of "orthodoxy" among all faiths, the tsarist order rested on foundations of discord and conciliation. And for religious entrepreneurs committed to realizing the commands of the faith, the empire supplied powerful means of coercion.

These deep structures of thought and practice were not limited to Muslims. Anti-Muslim polemic had been a constant feature of this world; it continuously circulated and encouraged war with Russia's Muslim neighbors. But such calls were muted both by St. Petersburg's ambitions abroad and by concern for domestic order. Popular histories associated Tatars, Turks, and others with treachery and violence. In the early nineteenth century, the noblewoman Anna Labzina recalled that her mother feared nothing in this world but Tatars.[9] But the figure of the dangerous Tatar did not present the only model for intercommunal interaction.

The notion that all of the diverse peoples of the empire shared a divine master, professing a form of imperial monotheism, also endured, shaping Russian attitudes. Labzina recounted how her mother had an alarming confrontation with a group of some two hundred Bashkirs who appeared on horseback at her estate near Ekaterinburg to complain of a property dispute. In hopes of mollifying the horsemen, she offered them a dinner, "barrels of beer, wine, and liquers," and an appeal, "I have no other protector except God, whom you know as well. He alone is our father. He created both me and you, so don't you fear His authority? Whither would you drive me from my land? I shall stay here alongside you and devote myself to serving you. Among you, too, are those who love God, and I can live serenely anywhere." Moved by her kind words (and perhaps by the alcohol), the Bashkirs approached her "with tears in their eyes." "Be at ease, our kind neighbor and friend," they assured her, "now we are not your enemies, but your protectors."[10] Their meeting ended in embraces and warm pledges of friendship.

Muslims, too, adopted this image of a social order rooted in divine submission to a single God. In the eighteenth century, the shared bonds of monotheism became a familiar trope in petitions to imperial authorities. Even the rebel Pugachev, whom the Holy Synod of the Orthodox Church castigated as "the disciple of Antichrist Mahomet," played on a common religiosity in his communications with Muslims whom he recruited to his ranks.[11]

Between this image of the Prophet as a "disciple of Antichrist" and official fears of a Pan-Islamic fifth column in the twenty million Muslim subjects of Nicholas II, tsarist images of Islam continued to evolve. Indeed, the state was never merely a neutral patron of Islam. It supported only what its own experts—and their Muslim informants—identified as orthodox Islam. For Muslims of the Volga and Urals regions, Siberia, and the capitals, the establishment of a mufti as the single voice of religious orthodoxy had initiated a radical break with the past. Its bureaucratic apparatus and regulatory activities at the mosque level transformed local religious life, imposing greater uniformity and cultivating devotion to the monarchy and fatherland. Muslim reformers and Russian scholars of Oriental studies depicted these communities as the image of a stagnant and timeless Islam, but they overlooked the dramatic changes that had already taken place since the late eighteenth century. They downplayed the dynamism and vitality of religious debate that contact with tsarist institutions had unleashed and ignored the initiative of Muslim laypeople who challenged the authority of the 'ulama by adapting imperial law and bureaucratic procedure to Islamic controversies. To a greater extent than in other states, Russian Muslim commoners ('awamm), could strike alliances with police officials to aid them in shaping the tenor of local religious life, in disciplining husbands, wives, and children as well as 'ulama who had strayed from the true path.

The intermingling of tsarist legal and Muslim religious conceptions has a broader significance for understanding how the regime managed its Muslim populations and what these subjects had at stake in taking religious disagreements with relatives and neighbors to Russian officials. Throughout the modern Muslim world, nationalist and religious movements have located the defense of Islam in the domestic sphere. Deploying women and the family as the most authentic repositories of Islamic tradition and national culture, varied movements have pledged to guard domestic spaces against the encroachments of colonial states.[12] Subjects of other empires may have regarded the colonial state apparatus, as Ranajit Guha has suggested, as "an absolute externality," but in tsarist Russia, Muslim men and women continued to regard the regime as a guardian of the divine law where it mattered most: in their domestic lives.[13]

The tsarist regime took on a different guise in Muslim regions that lacked an extensive bureaucratic apparatus linking Islamic affairs to the state. By rejecting official Islamic hierarchies for Turkestan and the steppe, state officials deprived themselves of a mechanism for controlling Muslim intermediaries. Turkestanis quickly learned to mobilize state power against their opponents in religious disputes, but the regime remained almost completely dependent upon local 'ulama and laypeople to initiate these interactions. In the steppe, it lacked substantial institutions with the capacity to act on the Kazakh family or seek out congruences between customary and religious legal norms and imperial law. Full integration of the populations of the steppe and Turkestan was inhibited, not by the survival of customary law, but by the state's failure to establish more extensive ties to Muslim institutions and collaborators.

Where the tsarist state had erected officially sponsored Islamic structures, as in Transcaucasia, in the Crimea, and, for the longest period of time, in the territory under the Orenburg Assembly, the empire managed to integrate Muslim communities. The interdependence created by this policing of Islamic orthodoxy created access to villages and towns under these institutions. And during the war, it yielded manpower for the front. But in areas that fell under tsarist rule at moments when tsarist officialdom hesitated to seek such Islamic entanglements, tsarist state building never achieved the capacity to make a difference during the wartime crisis. Just as these subjects remained more loosely integrated into the empire, they never made the state the imaginative resource that so captivated the minds of the pious on the Volga and elsewhere under the Orenburg Assembly.

The legacy of this interpenetration of the state and Islamic institutions presented a formidable obstacle to the total disestablishment of state and religion after 1905. Russia's main Islamic establishment remained remarkably stable. Staffed by just five muftis from the late eighteenth century, the Orenburg Assembly in Ufa knew none of the intrigue, firings, and constant turnover of the Ottoman learned hierarchy.[14] The increasingly bureaucratized Assembly and muftiate in Ufa claimed monopoly control of Islamic interpretation for millions of tsarist subjects. Yet it did so only by leaning heavily on the tsarist police to enforce its writ. Although the Assembly never entirely displaced local competitors, Muslims protested calls for its dissolution.

Its tsar-appointed and unrepresentative leadership failed to satisfy a diverse population. Most Muslims nevertheless considered the alternative of oversight on the part of state officials more threatening still. Reformers and their opponents alike had habituated themselves to the notion that a single state institution should aim toward the uniform interpretation of Islamic tradition, although they disagreed about the form such learned exposition should take.

The heterogeneity and overlap of disparate legal institutions and practices strengthened the imperial order. The monarchy's rejection of a state based on liberal European understandings of the rule of law made it reliant on customary and religious law throughout the empire. These particularistic legal systems were in turn embedded in its broader legal framework.[15] The case of the Muslim subjects of the empire shows how imperial power and the shari'a might interact in ways that bolstered the tsarist regime and integrated these populations into imperial Russian society.

The successes—and limits—of the tsarist confessional system were revealed during the First World War. The conflict proved to be more than just another Russo-Turkish war pitting tsarist versus Ottoman Muslims. For elites exposed to the circulation of Pan-Islamic ideas, the war was an opportunity to realize anticolonial ambitions. More important, another European power challenged Russia's role as guardian of Islam. Allied with the Ottomans, Germany targeted the Muslim populations of its imperial rivals, Great Britain, France, and Russia. From Istanbul the sultan and caliph commanded Muslims to wage jihad against their enemies, while a German fight song (to which an Oriental studies scholar contributed) called "Muslim comrades" to battle: "I'm a Christian, and you're a Muslim, / But that doesn't harm a thing! Our victory is certain, / Our fortune is no dream!"[16] By 1915 the Germans had devised plans to establish prisoner-of-war camps to prepare Muslim prisoners from the allied armies for use against their former masters.[17]

A prayer leader at one of these prisoner-of-war camps in Germany knew Russian and other languages spoken by many prisoners who arrived from the eastern front. Indeed, the imam hailed from Siberia. Now in the employ of the Ottomans and Germans for whom he composed sermons and other texts, Abdürreşid Ibrahim had been a religious scholar in Russia. For four years he served as a judge attached to the Orenburg Assembly. When its head, Mufti Sultanov, went on the hajj in 1893, Ibrahim had acted as mufti for eight months. Ibrahim had been one of the mufti's detractors, claiming, "He knows neither religion, nor the shari'a, and is ignorant of reading and writing."[18] Ibrahim later put his criticism of Sultanov—and of tsarist policy in general—into print, and from the relative safety of Istanbul he called for Muslims to emigrate from Russia. His critical text was smuggled into Russia, however, and the Foreign Ministry exerted pressure on the Porte to return him. Ibrahim remained mobile and traveled widely, however. Despite a brief period of arrest in Odessa, Ibrahim joined the Muslim political movement that had emerged in 1905. He agitated on behalf of Muslim solidarity in Japan and even returned to Ufa in 1907, when he found the Orenburg Assembly "in the condition of a lifeless corpse."[19]

The geopolitical shifts of the First World War strained the tsarist regime's confessional system and opened up new possibilities for figures like Ibrahim. He looked first to the Ottomans and then to the Germans for assistance in securing rights for Russia's Muslims. By the end of the war, he had appealed to the American president, Woodrow Wilson, and to the pope, whom he entreated, "As leader of the Christian world please resist these inhumane acts [by the Russians]."[20] Ibrahim was by no means alone in charting this course beyond the tsarist empire. Other Muslim notables would throw their lot in with one of the states that emerged from the ashes of the Ottoman empire and would even become leading ideologues of Turkish nationalism; these included Iusuf Akchurin of Kazan, who became Yusuf Akçura, a nationalist icon in modern Turkey.[21]

With the support of Germany and the Ottoman state, elites such as Ibrahim and Akçura utilized the war to promote their Pan-Islamic and Pan-Turkic causes, but the conditions of wartime Russia dimmed their appeals for the empire's Muslims. Most continued to pursue survival within Russia, though each region experienced the war differently. Muslims in the European and Siberian provinces had supplied recruits, and the war brought fighting deep into the Caucasus; the populations of the steppe and Turkestan still enjoyed the exemption from conscription that had been granted, in most cases, at the time of conquest, and was preserved by Russian bureaucrats suspicious of their usefulness on the battlefield.

This changed in 1916. Desperate for labor, the government attempted to call up nearly a half million men from the steppe and Turkestan to serve in work units behind the front lines. Local populations responded to the conscription campaign with various forms of protest, ranging from avoidance to rebellion. The government lost control of vast swathes of territory as resistance spread from the towns to the steppe. Rebels attacked Russian settlers and officials. Tsarist forces distributed arms to Slavic colonists, and officially sponsored punitive expeditions killed and uprooted tens of thousands of men, women, and children. Historians have pointed to this violence as the culmination of decades of conflict over land and other resources. They have also seen it as a reflection of deep ethnic tensions below the surface of imperial society.[22]

A closer look at the forms that such violence took suggests yet another dimension. Though insurgents sometimes targeted Russian civilians and officials, the earliest stages of this violence focused on "native" officials, sometimes including clerical figures.[23] The uprising revealed the fragility of the indigenous elites, like the notable

Figure 8 Portrait of a Muslim elder (*aksakal*) in Samarkand, shown with medals awarded for service to the tsarist government. Courtesy of Library of Congress, Prints & Photographs Division, Prokudin-Gorskii Collection, LC-DIG-prok-02303.

pictured in Figure 8, through whom the government ruled these territories. The breakdown of the regime's reliance on intermediaries in the steppe and Turkestan highlights the volatility of the search for accommodation—and mutual advantage—between Muslims and Russian authorities. In the past, popular hostility toward these intermediaries had been more an asset than a liability for the empire. For the most part, Muslims became more engaged in their everyday lives in fighting one another than in struggling against the regime. But the risks for these individuals could become like those faced by similar figures who mediated between imperial rulers and indigenous constituencies elsewhere. As Ronald Robinson has observed, "Too drastic concessions in sensitive areas would undermine the basis of their authority and set their forced contracts with Europe at nought."[24]

The war had strained the empire's resort to indirect rule through such elites, but 1916 was not a total break with the imperial past. The revolts did not necessarily represent a repudiation of the empire's approach toward Islam. Both sides still appealed to Islam to legitimate their claims. While some 'ulama sanctioned acts of violence against the state and its local officials and settler populations, tsarist officials joined other mullahs in condemning the unrest as a violation of the shari'a.[25]

This interpenetration of state and Islamic institutions sustained, but also outlived, the tsarist regime. Its collapse did not spell the demise of older legal practices or interrupt conflicts among Muslims. The large Slavic settler population and local socialists aspired to continue Russian political domination of local Muslims. Violence, famine, and emigration followed the Bolshevik takeover, but the fighting was not only between Russians and Turkestanis. Local reformers—the Jadids, or as they were more frequently known, "the youth" (yashlar)—struck an alliance with elements of the Soviet leadership. For the Jadids, this meant a state on the basis of their reformist interpretation of the shari'a—and military strength against their more numerous opponents. Between 1920 and 1924, the Bukharan Republic ruled according to the Jadid vision of the shari'a, declaring equality of the sexes, the empowerment of youth, and a socialist future.

Though much had changed with the passing of the old order, geography had not. After 1917 the political actors who struggled to restore the empire had to contend with the fact that bordering states still identified in varying ways with Islam. Moreover, as prospects for socialist revolution seemed to fail in Europe, the Bolsheviks looked to the colonial East. Though "backward," the Muslim world in particular seemed ready for liberation with the aid of the Soviets.[26]

The Soviets inherited more than the geopolitical environment of the Romanov empire. The search for authoritative leaders, not to mention personnel to staff the growing Communist Party and state bureaucracies, renewed older possibilities for cooperation with the ʿulama. Soviets and Muslims continued the tsarist search for congruences, but in a new ideological context. Some Muslims had committed to the left under the old regime. Others saw in the vague slogans of the new regime some affinities with Islam and looked to cooperate with it on the basis of such principles.[27] The statism of tsarist society—what Peter Holquist has called its propensity "to idolize the state as an ideal in its own right and an instrument for achieving all its own fondest dreams"—shaped the mental horizons of Muslims as well. Moreover, Muslims had extensive experience in remaking state institutions as their own.[28]

Muslims and the Soviet state thus drew directly on the institutional inheritance of the tsar. Though the Bolshevik government carved up Central Asia into national republics within a federal system (putting an end to the Bukharan experiment), it revived many of imperial Russia's Islamic institutions, even staffing them with the old personnel.[29] It permitted the reestablishment of an official Islamic hierarchy in Ufa in 1923. A former judge of the Orenburg Assembly, Rizaeddin Fahreddinev (Ridāʾaddīn Fakhraddīn ōghlī), became its mufti. Renamed the Ecclesiastical Administration for the Muslims of Russia and Siberia, it revived many of the functions of its predecessor but assumed an even more important role in representing the Soviet state before foreign Muslims. Elsewhere, Islamic law courts and schools persisted—and in some locales, even thrived. The government restored pious endowments in Central Asia and, in a symbolic repudiation of the old regime, returned to religious leaders in Ufa an ancient copy of the Qurʾan that tsarist military authorities had captured in Tashkent. Local authorities targeted some Muslim communities in antireligious campaigns, but before 1929 persecution was not systematic. For the Bolsheviks, the Orthodox Church had been the linchpin of the old regime, while Islam represented a force to be overcome by more gradualist methods, especially when revolutionary fires might be kindled in Persia and Afghanistan, and Soviet control remained weak in Muslim regions of the old tsarist empire.

At the same time, the young Soviet state, like its imperial predecessor, continued to share much in common with other Muslim governments. In the name of modernization, numerous postwar states further curbed Islamic institutions and authorities, limiting their control over law and education and diminishing their material resources. In many respects, the new Turkish state was more severe than Lenin's government. Şerif Mardin has likened Republican Turkey's policies in the 1920s to "secular Jacobinism."[30] Under Kemal Atatürk, it did away with the caliphate, along with the office of the şeyhülislam and the Ministry of Religious Affairs and Pious Foundations. It closed Islamic law courts and madrasas and dispersed their personnel. Going beyond the outlawing of Sufi brotherhoods, who had been implicated in rebellions against the state, the Kemalist regime targeted devotional sites such as saints' tombs and shrines. Republican Turkey made secular elementary education compulsory, introduced secular law codes, and outlawed the use of religious titles like *mullah* in official life. While the Ministry of Education supervised the training of prayer leaders and preachers, a Department of the Affairs of Piety oversaw "all matters concerning the beliefs and rituals of Islam," and a Faculty of Divinity at the University of Istanbul elaborated various reformist positions, including the use of a Turkish translation of the Qur'an.[31] In the 1930s the Stalinist regime caught up with its neighbor and exceeded its disciplining of Muslim authorities by unleashing a murderous campaign of executions, mosque and madrasa closings, and deportations and re-settlements.

For the Turks, as for the Soviets, the Second World War confronted these governments with the need to return to more accommodationist policies. In Turkey it prompted a shift away from many restrictions on religious education, pilgrimage, and the veneration of saints' tombs. Seeking the support of the faithful during the war, the Soviet state shifted from its aggressive assault on Islamic institutions and personnel. In 1943 it established four regional Islamic hierarchies but submitted them all to centralized control from Moscow.[32]

This system of centralized bureaucratic organization of Islamic affairs and state support for official Islamic scholars broke down only in the late 1980s and early 1990s, when conflicts among Muslim activists splintered these bodies in the Russian Federation and other former Soviet states. With the collapse of the USSR in 1991, new forms of competition broke out among Muslims who, in seeking to return their people to the faith, have fought one another to gain the backing of the state in the process.

As in 1917, the contest for the post-Soviet order has focused on control of the state. Like earlier generations, Muslims who claim religious authority in the former Soviet Union have readily adapted to the symbolic resources at hand. Soviet Orientalism supplied most educated elites with a very narrow understanding of Islam. Endorsed by state-sponsored Muslim authorities, this conception of Islam, rooted in the privileging of a limited textual canon, has led the personnel of government institutions to conclude that much of what Muslims regard as Islam is inauthentic.[33] In the context of conflicts over state sovereignty in Chechnya and elsewhere, the suggestion that particular Muslim practices are "foreign" or are associated with violence has limited post-Soviet toleration. The elastic accusation of "Wahhabism" may have entered clerics' polemical vocabulary as early as the 1950s and persisted as a focus of concern for the

KGB. The charge has greater resonance today, though now it more directly conveys the suggestion that purported "Wahhabis" are Saudi drones bent on committing acts of violence, even in the many instances when no evidence—apart from a beard—supports these charges.[34]

Officially committed to toleration and the recognition of official Islamic authorities, each of the former Soviet states seeks legitimation through patronage of Islam. Each government also puts its police at the disposal of officially backed authorities—and thus of feuding Muslim communities. Muslim citizens of the Russian Federation outside of Chechnya have fared better on the whole than their co-religionists in former Soviet republics such as Turkmenistan and Uzbekistan, where Muslims are regularly imprisoned and even tortured for their beliefs.

Fear of Islamic radicalism and terrorism dominates public discourse in all of these states. But the specter of Islam has also been a very valuable tool in the hands of ruling elites.[35] In the 1990s the appearance of radical groups on Russia's frontiers, notably in Chechnya, Daghestan, and nearby Afghanistan, gave Moscow valuable leverage in international affairs. On the world stage, Islam could prove useful for the Kremlin, even when it animated oppositional movements. For both international and domestic audiences, governments have glossed conflicts with very heterogeneous origins as the fruits of "Islamic fundamentalism." To be sure, a small number of militants have taken up arms against these states in the name of the faith, but these governments have also resorted to such labels to conceal fighting over drug corridors, state resources, and political rights.[36] These dangers have since produced valuable opportunities for those in power in Moscow, Baku, Tashkent, Bishkek, Astana, Dushanbe, and elsewhere. Since 2001, solidarity in the "war on terror" has generated military and financial rewards from the West. Having dashed the democratic hopes born with communism's demise, these formerly Soviet regimes have seized upon Western anxieties about the threat of Islam to gain international backing for authoritarian rule at home. Security forces trained by the United States, which has also used not only an airbase but jails in Uzbekistan to house detainees without trial, have been implicated in the murder of civilians in Andijan in May 2004. Criticism of human rights abuses remains muted.

Although Muslims of the former Soviet Union have reestablished many ties to co-religionists elsewhere, the primary focus of Muslim politics in the region remains the capture of the institutions of the regime. They represent simultaneously the keys to political influence, religious authority, policing, and access to international funding. And like their imperial and Soviet predecessors, these states remain committed to trying to police the boundaries of orthodoxy— supporting "moderates" and repressing supposed "Wahhabis" and criminalizing groups such as the internationalist Hizb-ut-Tahrir who oppose established states as insufficiently "Islamic."[37]

In seeking to contain Islam for the nation-state, these policies extend beyond the former Soviet Union. In varying forms, they have assumed center stage in Western debates about immigration and the future of the nation. Long a model for civil rights activists within Russia, Europe is poised to adopt the restrictions that its eastern neighbors have placed on freedom of conscience. Europe might now look to Russia's past to learn about the broader consequences of the search for peace between Muslims and their non-Muslim rulers. European calls for the regulation of Islam and the recruitment of "moderate" intermediaries are an alternative to the violent and repressive conduct of militias in Chechnya or Bosnia. But some of these proposed controls also resemble the restrictive measures on religious liberties that lay, in part, behind recent violence in Uzbekistan.

In France, Germany, Great Britain, the Netherlands, and elsewhere, governments have struggled to create official Islamic institutions to receive state backing in exchange for disciplining clerics and severing their ties abroad. Like the Russians before them, these European states seek to recruit clients who will interpret Islam in ways that political elites find expedient. But these intermediaries are likely to face the same pressures as those in the tsarist empire and will be similarly beholden to the state to advance their interpretations. Religion and policing will become more closely intertwined.

This project, like similar ones pursued by European powers in the nineteenth century, conceives of Islam in an instrumental fashion. It seeks to use Islam for politics while admonishing Muslims to remain apolitical. Such strategies of co-optation, patronage, and policing made Islam an enduring pillar of the tsarist imperial order, but they are ill suited for democratic states that value democracy and human rights.

ABBREVIATIONS

NOTES

ACKNOWLEDGMENTS

INDEX

ABBREVIATIONS

AVPRI   Arkhiv vneshnei politiki Rossiiskoi imperii, Moscow

GA   *Gasïrlar avazï / Ekho vekov*

GAOO   Gosudarstvennyi arkhiv Orenburgskoi oblasti, Orenburg

ITBRI   *Islam na territorii byvshei Rossiiskoi imperii: Entsiklopedicheskii slovar'*, ed. S. M. Prozorov, 4 vols. (Moscow: "Vostochnaia literatura" RAN, 1998–2003)

IVAN RUz   Institut vostokovedeniia Akademii nauk Respubliki Uzbekistan, Tashkent

MIBASSR   *Materialy po istorii Bashkirskoi ASSR* (Moscow: Izdatel'stvo Akademii nauk SSSR, 1960)

NART   Natsional'nyi arkhiv Respubliki Tatarstan, Kazan

PSZ   *Polnoe sobranie zakonov Rossiiskoi Imperii*

RGIA   Rossiiskii gosudarstvennyi istoricheskii arkhiv, St. Petersburg

RGVIA   Rossiiskii gosudarstvennyi voenno-istoricheskii arkhiv, Moscow

SIRIO   *Sbornik Imperatorskogo russkogo istoricheskogo obshchestva*

STsOMDS   *Sbornik tsirkuliarov i inykh rukovodiashchikh*

*rasporiazhenii po okrugu Orenburgskogo
Magometanskogo Dukhovnogo Sobraniia 1836–1903 g.*
(Ufa: Gubernskaia tipografiia, 1905)

TsGARU Tsentral'nyi gosudarstvennyi arkhiv Respubliki
Uzbekistan, Tashkent

TsGIARB Tsentral'nyi gosudarstvennyi istoricheskii arkhiv
Respubliki Bashkortostan, Ufa

NOTES

Introduction

1. Natalie Zemon Davis, *Society and Culture in Early Modern France* (Stanford: Stanford University Press, 1975), 152–187. For Chechnya, see Anna Politkovskaya, *A Small Corner of Hell: Dispatches from Chechnya*, trans. Alexander Burry and Tatiana Tulchinsky (Chicago: University of Chicago Press, 2003), 91–94.

2. See, for example, Jörg Baberowski, *Der Feind ist überall: Stalinismus im Kaukasus* (Munich: Deutsche Verlags-Anstalt, 2003).

3. On perceptions of Central Asia, in particular, as the USSR's most vulnerable possession, see R. D. McChesney, *Central Asia: Foundations of Change* (Princeton, N.J.: Darwin Press, 1996), 3. Such views did not displace fears that the Soviets might come to some understanding with Muslim countries and turn Europe's former colonies against the capitalist world. See, for example, Alexandre Bennigsen, Paul B. Henze, George K. Tanham, and S. Enders Wimbush, *Soviet Strategy and Islam* (Houndsmills, UK: Macmillan, 1989); and more generally, Richard Bulliet, *The Case*

for Islamo-Christian Civilization (New York: Columbia University Press, 2004).

4. See Mariam Abou Zahab and Olivier Roy, *Réseaux islamiques: La connexion afghano-pakistanaise* (Paris: Autrement, 2002); Ahmed Rashid, *Jihad: The Rise of Militant Islam in Central Asia* (New Haven: Yale University Press, 2002); Aleksei Malashenko and Martha Brill Olcott, eds., *Islam na postsovetskom prostranstve: Vzgliad iznutri* (Moscow: Moskovskii Tsentr Karnegi, 2001); and, most recently, "Uzbekistan: The Andijon Uprising," International Crisis Group Asia Briefing, No. 38, 25 May 2005.

5. See Richard S. Wortman, *Scenarios of Power: Myth and Ceremony in Russian Monarchy*, 2 vols. (Princeton: Princeton University Press, 1995 and 2000).

6. See Andreas Kappeler, *Russland als Vielvölkerreich: Entstehung, Geschichte, Zerfall*, 2nd ed. (Munich: C. H. Beck, 1993); Dominic Lieven, *Empire: The Russian Empire and Its Rivals* (New Haven: Yale University Press, 2001); and John P. LeDonne, *The Russian Empire and the World, 1700–1917: The Geopolitics of Expansion and Containment* (Oxford: Oxford University Press, 1997).

7. For example, Ronald Grigor Suny, "The Empire Strikes Out: Imperial Russia, 'National' Identity, and Theories of Empire," in *A State of Nations: Empire and Nation-Making in the Age of Lenin and Stalin*, ed. Ronald Grigor Suny and Terry Martin (Oxford: Oxford University Press, 2001), 23–66; see also John W. Slocum, "Who, and When, Were the *Inorodtsy*? The Evolution of the Category of 'Aliens' in Imperial Russia," *Russian Review* 57, no. 2 (Apr. 1998): 173–190.

8. Richard Bulliet, *Islam: The View from the Edge* (New York: Columbia University Press, 1994), 194.

9. Author's interview with Farid Asadullin of the Council of Muftis in Moscow, November 2004.

10. See Devin DeWeese, *Islamization and Native Religion in the Golden Horde: Baba Tükles and Conversion to Islam in Historical*

and Epic Tradition (University Park: Pennsylvania State University Press, 1994); and Allen J. Frank, "Varieties of Islamization in Inner Asia: The Case of the Baraba Tatars, 1740–1917," *Cahiers du monde russe* 41, nos. 2–3 (Apr.–Sept. 2000): 245–262.

11. D. Iu. Arapov, ed., *Islam v Rossiiskoi imperii: zakonodatel'nye akty, opisaniia, statistika* (Moscow: IKTs "Akademkniga," 2001), 324–327.

12. See, for example, Willis Brooks, "Russia's Conquest and Pacification of the Caucasus: Relocation Becomes a Pogrom in the Post-Crimean War Period," *Nationalities Papers* 23, no. 4 (1995): 675–686.

13. Mark Mazower, "Violence and the State in the Twentieth Century," *American Historical Review* 107, no. 4 (Oct. 2002): 1158–1178, quotation at 1163. On Ottoman involvement and the Islamic legal debates, see Michael Kemper, "Khālidiyya Networks in Daghestan and the Question of Jihād," *Die Welt des Islams* 42, no. 1 (2002): 41–71; and Bedri Habiçoğlu, *Kafkasya'dan Anadolu'ya Göçler ve İskanları* (Istanbul: Nart Yayıncılık, 1993). Tadeusz Swietochowski points out that "the Russian consulate in Tabriz issued 312,000 visas between 1891 and 1904," in *Russia and Azerbaijan: A Borderland in Transition* (New York: Columbia University Press, 1991), 10–22. On Muslim emigration from neighboring states into Russian Central Asia, see, for example, RGVIA, f. 400, op. 1, d. 2329, d. 3692, and d. 4009; AVPRI, f. 187, op. 485, d. 684; and Jennifer Siegel, *Endgame: Britain, Russia and the Final Struggle for Central Asia* (London: Tauris, 2002).

14. In his collective biography of reformist intellectuals and their engagement with "politics," Adeed Khalid pays attention to economic changes brought about by the Russian conquest of Central Asia but largely ignores the state, except as an instrument of repression. See *The Politics of Muslim Cultural Reform: Jadidism in Central Asia* (Berkeley: University of California Press, 1998); for a fundamental reinterpretation of Islamic history in the Northern

Caucasus, see Michael Kemper, *Herrschaft, Recht und Islam in Daghestan: Von den Khanaten und Gemeindebünden zum ǧihād-Staat* (Wiesbaden: Reichert Verlag, 2005).

15. Edward Louis Kennan Jr., "Muscovy and Kazan: Some Introductory Remarks on the Patterns of Steppe Diplomacy," *Slavic Review* 26, no. 4 (Dec. 1967): 548–558; Richard White, *The Middle Ground: Indians, Empires, and Republics in the Great Lakes Region, 1650–1815* (Cambridge: Cambridge University Press, 1991), 52.

16. See Robert Tignor, ed., *Napoleon in Egypt: Al Jabarti's Chronicle of the First Seven Months of the French Occupation, 1798*, trans. Shmuel Moreh (Princeton, N.J.: Markus Wiener, 1993); and Erich Prokosch, trans. and ed., *Molla und Diplomat: Der Bericht des Ebû Sehil Nu'mân Efendi über die österreichisch-osmanische Grenzziehung nach dem Belgrader Frieden 1740/1741* (Graz: Verlag Styria, 1972), 91–92. On great power attempts to mobilize Muslims against rival empires, see Selçuk Esenbel, "Japan's Global Claim to Asia and the World of Islam," *American Historical Review* 109, no. 4 (Oct. 2004): 1140–1170; Naimur Rahman Farooqi, "Pan-Islamism in the Nineteenth Century," *Islamic Culture* 57, no. 4 (Oct. 1983): 283–296; and Fritz Fischer, *Germany's Aims in the First World War* (New York: W. W. Norton, 1967), quote at 121. On France as a *"puissance musulmane,"* see David Robinson, *Paths of Accommodation: Muslim Societies and French Colonial Authorities in Senegal and Mauritania, 1880–1920* (Athens: Ohio University Press, 2000); and on Habsburg patronage, see Robert J. Donia, *Islam under the Double Eagle: The Muslims of Bosnia and Hercegovina, 1878–1914* (New York: Columbia University Press, 1981).

17. For an overview of the tsarist confessional order and the regime's treatment of Jews, Buddhists, Catholics, Protestants, and Armenian Christians alongside Muslims, see Robert Crews, "Empire and the Confessional State: Islam and Religious Politics in Nineteenth-Century Russia," *American Historical Review* 108, no. 1 (Feb. 2003): 50–83.

18. Benjamin Nathans has challenged this view of Russia's Jews, show-
ing how many experienced "selective integration," gaining access
to higher education, the professions, and even the capital of the
empire. See *Beyond the Pale: The Jewish Encounter with Late Imperial Russia* (Berkeley: University of California Press, 2002). See
also Yuri Slezkine, *The Jewish Century* (Princeton: Princeton University Press, 2004).

19. See Shihabetdin Märjani, *Möstäfadel-äkhbar fi äkhvali Kazan
vä Bolgar (Kazan häm Bolgar khälläre turïnda faydalanïlgan
khäbärlär)*, ed. Ä. N. Khäyrullin (Kazan: Tatar. Kit. Näshr., 1989),
which appeared first in 1900; and Riḍā'addīn Fakhraddīn öghlï,
Āthār (Orenburg: Karimova, 1904–1909).

20. *Pis'ma o magometanstve* (St. Petersburg: V Tipografii III Otd.
Sobst. E. I. V. Kantseliarii, 1848), 91–92 and 144; F. M. Dostoevskii,
Dnevnik pisatelia, ed. V. N. Bunin (St. Petersburg: Lenizdat, 1999),
517; and on opera, see Richard Taruskin, "'Entoiling the Falconet':
Russian Musical Orientalism in Context," *Cambridge Opera Jour-
nal* 4, no. 3 (Nov. 1992): 253–280.

21. M. M. Speranskii, *Proekty i zapiski* (Moscow: Izdatel'stvo Akademii
nauk SSSR, 1961), 92–94; and E. A. Vishlenkova, *Zabotias' o
dushakh poddannykh: Religioznia politika v Rossii pervoi chetverti
XIX veka* (Saratov: Izdatel'stvo Saratovskogo universiteta, 2002).

22. For example, Lieven, *Empire*; on the reformist Ottoman state's
measures to compel piety and obedience to the shari'a, see, among
others, Kemal Çiçek, "Tanzimat ve Şer'iat: Namaz Kılmayanlar
ve İçki İçenlerin Takip ve Cezalandırılması Hakkında Kıbrıs
Muhassılı Mehmet Tal'at Efendi'nin İki Buyruldusu," *Toplumsal
Tarih* (Mar. 1995): 22–27.

23. Rudolph Peters, "State, Law and Society in Nineteenth-Century
Egypt: Introduction," *Die Welt des Islams* 39, no. 3 (1999): 267–272,
and the essays that follow.

24. Selim Deringil, *The Well-Protected Domains: Ideology and the Legitimation of Power in the Ottoman Empire, 1876–1909* (London:
Tauris, 1999); and Muhammad Qasim Zaman, *The Ulama in Con-*

temporary Islam: Guardians of Change (Princeton: Princeton University Press, 2002).

25. Martin Chanock, *Law, Custom, and Social Order: The Colonial Experience in Malawi and Zambia* (Cambridge: Cambridge University Press, 1985); and Richard Roberts and Kristin Mann, "Law in Colonial Africa," in *Law in Colonial Africa*, ed. Kristin Mann and Richard Roberts (Portsmouth, N.H.: Heinemann, 1991), 3–58. On the definition of "orthodoxy" as a function of power, see Talal Asad, "The Idea of an Anthropology of Islam," Center for Contemporary Arab Studies, Georgetown University, Occasional Paper Series (Mar. 1986), 15; and *Genealogies of Religion: Discipline and Reasons of Power in Christianity and Islam* (Baltimore: Johns Hopkins University Press, 1993), 27–54.

26. See, for example, Kemal H. Karpat, *The Politicization of Islam: Reconstructing Identity, State, Faith, and Community in the Late Ottoman State* (Oxford: Oxford University Press, 2001); Abdulvahap Kara, *Türkistan Ateşi: Mustafa Çokay'ın Hayatı ve Mücadelesi* (Istanbul: Da Yayıncılık, 2002); İbrahim Maraş, *Türk Dünyasında Dinî Yenileşme (1850–1917)* (Istanbul: Ötüken, 2002).

27. Zaman, *The Ulama in Contemporary Islam.*

28. Rogers Brubaker, *Ethnicity without Groups* (Cambridge, Mass.: Harvard University Press, 2004), esp. 7–27; I am very grateful to Benjamin Nathans for drawing my attention to this argument. On Muslim disagreements in the Caucasus, see Kemper, "Khālidiyya Networks."

29. For example, John Bowen, "Does French Islam Have Borders? Dilemmas of Domestication in a Global Religious Field," *American Anthropologist* 106, no. 1 (Mar. 2004): 43–55. See also Riva Kastoryano, *Negotiating Identities: States and Immigrants in France and Germany,* trans. Barbara Harshav (Princeton: Princeton University Press, 2002).

30. On American attempts to secure fatwas on behalf of the occupation of Iraq, see, for example, Rajiv Chandrasekaran, "How Cleric Trumped U.S. Plan for Iraq: Ayatollah's Call for Vote Forced Oc-

cupation Leader to Rewrite Transition Strategy," *Washington Post,* 26 Nov. 2003; and Patrick E. Tyler, "After the War: Baghdad," *New York Times,* 5 June 2003.

1. A Church for Islam

1. Yohanan Friedman, *Shaykh Ahmad Sirhindī: An Outline of His Thought and a Study of His Image in the Eyes of Posterity* (Montreal: McGill-Queen's University Press, 1971); Hamid Algar, "A Brief History of the Naqshbandī Order," in *Naqshbandis: Cheminements et situation actuelle d'un ordre mystique musulman / Historical Developments and Present Situation of a Muslim Mystical Order,* ed. Marc Gaborieau, Alexandre Popovic, and Thierry Zarcone (Istanbul: Isis Press, 1990), 3–44.

2. On these Sufi networks linking Russia and Central Asia, see Riḍā'addīn Fakhraddīn ōghlī, *Āthār,* vol. 6 (Orenburg: Karimova, 1904), esp. 276 and 317; Michael Kemper, *Sufis und Gelehrte in Tatarien und Baschkirien, 1789–1889: Der islamische Diskurs unter russischer Herrschaft* (Berlin: Klaus Schwarz Verlag, 1998), 82–212; Shihabetdin Märjani, *Möstäfadel-äkhbar fi äkhvali Kazan vä Bolgar (Kazan häm Bolgar khälläre turïnda faydalanïlgan khäbärlär),* ed. Ä. N. Khäyrullin (Kazan: Tatar. Kit. Näshr., 1989), 270; and Hamid Algar, "Shaykh Zaynullah Rasulev: The Last Great Naqshbandi Shaykh of the Volga-Urals Region," in *Muslims in Central Asia: Expressions of Identity and Change,* ed. Jo-Ann Gross (Durham, N.C.: Duke University Press, 1992), 113–114.

3. See, for example, Alexandra Merle, *Le miroir ottoman: Une image politique des hommes dans la littérature géographique espagnole et française (XVIe–XVIIe siècles)* (Paris: Presses de l'Université de Paris-Sorbonne, 2003).

4. Ibid., 197.

5. Andrei Lyzlov, *Skifskaia istoriia* (Moscow: Izdatel'stvo "Nauka," 1990), 157.

6. Ibid., 326 and 333.

7. B. H. Sumner, *Peter the Great and the Ottoman Empire* (Hamden,

Conn.: Archon Books, 1965); E. V. Chistiakova, "A. I. Lyzlov i ego 'Skifskaia istoriia,'" in Lyzlov, *Skifskaia istoriia*, 362.

8. E. A. Rezvan, "Koran v Rossii," *ITBRI*, 1:47–58; John P. LeDonne, *The Grand Strategy of the Russian Empire, 1650–1831* (Oxford: Oxford University Press, 2004), 74; *Alkoran o Magomete*, trans. P. Postnikov (Moscow: Sinodal'naia tip., 1716); *Sokrashchenie magometanskoi very* (Moscow: V Universitetskoi Tipografii u N. Novikova, 1784).

9. Michael Khodarkovsky, *Russia's Steppe Frontier: The Making of a Colonial Empire, 1500–1800* (Bloomington: Indiana University Press, 2002), 189–201; Hans-Heinrich Nolte, *Religiöse Toleranz in Russland 1600–1725* (Göttingen: Musterschmidt Verlag, 1969), 54–89; Andreas Kappeler, *Russlands erste Nationalitäten: Das Zarenreich und die Völker der Mittleren Wolga vom 16. bis 19. Jahrhundert* (Cologne: Böhlau Verlag, 1982). On violence and the destruction of mosques, *PSZ*, vol. 12, no. 8,978 (22 June 1744), 157–158.

10. *PSZ*, vol. 9, no. 6,890 (11 Feb. 1736), 743; *PSZ*, vol. 12, no. 8,978 (22 June 1744), 158–159.

11. Iskander Gilyazov, "Die Islampolitik von Staat und Kirche im Wolga-Ural Gebiet und der Batïršah-Aufstand von 1755," in *Muslim Culture in Russia and Central Asia from the 18th to the Early 20th Centuries*, vol. 1, ed. Michael Kemper, Anke von Kügelgen, and Dmitriy Yermakov (Berlin: Klaus Schwarz Verlag, 1996), 69–89; F. G. Islaev, *Islam i pravoslavie v Povolzh'e XVIII stoletiia: Ot konfrontatsii k terpimosti* (Kazan: Izdatel'stvo Kazanskogo universiteta, 2001); on the mosques at Sterlibashevo and Kargala, see Allen J. Frank, *Muslim Religious Institutions in Imperial Russia: The Islamic World of Novouzensk District and the Kazakh Inner Horde, 1780–1910* (Leiden: Brill, 2001), 165–173.

12. Richard S. Wortman, *Scenarios of Power: Myth and Ceremony in Russian Monarchy*, vol. 1 (Princeton: Princeton University Press, 1995), 110–146; and Alan W. Fisher, "Enlightened Despotism and Islam under Catherine II," *Slavic Review* 27, no. 4 (1968): 542–553.

13. Paul Dukes, ed. and trans., *Russia under Catherine the Great*, vol. 2 (Newtownville, Mass.: Oriental Research Partners, 1977), 104–105; Isabel de Madariaga, *Russia in the Age of Catherine the Great* (New Haven: Yale University Press, 1981), 151–163, 503–518.

14. Karl Schwarz, "Vom Nutzen einer Christlichen Toleranz für den Staat: Bemerkungen zum Stellenwert der Religion bei den Spätkameralisten Justi und Sonnenfels," in *Im Zeichen der Toleranz: Aufsätze zur Toleranzgesetzgebung des 18. Jahrhunderts im Reiche Josephe II, ihren Voraussetzungen und ihren Folgen*, ed. Peter F. Barton (Vienna: Institut für protestantische Kirchengeschichte, 1981), esp. 86–89; on cameralism and religion generally, see Marc Raeff, *The Well-Ordered Police State: Social and Institutional Change through Law in the Germanies and Russia, 1600–1800* (New Haven: Yale University Press, 1983), 56–69; I. G. G. Iusti [Justi], *Osnovanie sily i blagosostoianiia tsarstv, ili podrobnoe nachertanie vsekh znanii kasaiushchikhsia do gosudarstvennogo blagochiniia*, pt. 3 (St. Petersburg: pri Imperatorskoi Akademii nauk, 1777), 30–42.

15. On Kant, see Klaus Schreiner, "Toleranz," in *Geschichtliche Grundbegriffe: Historiches Lexikon zur politisch-sozialen Sprache in Deutschland*, vol. 6, ed. Otto Brunner, Werner Conze, and Reinhart Koselleck (Stuttgart: Klett-Cotta, 1990), 505.

16. See Gregory L. Freeze, "The Rechristianization of Russia: The Church and Popular Religion, 1750–1850," *Studia Slavica Finlandensia* 7 (1990): 101–136; on Catherine's plans, see Roger P. Bartlett, *Human Capital: The Settlement of Foreigners in Russia 1762–1804* (Cambridge: Cambridge University Press, 1979).

17. See Madariaga, *Russia*, esp. 510–515. Sonnenfels also emphasized the disciplining of the clergy as a key aspect of *Religionspolizei*. Unlike Justi, he also insisted that questions of dogma fell within the purview of the state. Schwarz, "Vom Nutzen," 89–90.

18. See John LeDonne, *The Russian Empire and the World, 1700–1917: The Geopolitics of Expansion and Containment* (New York: Oxford University Press, 1997); and Madariaga, *Russia*, 187–204.

19. A. Lentin, trans. and ed., *Voltaire and Catherine the Great: Selected Correspondence* (Cambridge: Oriental Research Partners, 1974), 124, 128; Andrei Zorin, *Kormia dvuglavogo orla . . . : Literatura i gosudarstvennaia ideologiia v Rossii v poslednei treti XVIII–pervoi treti XIX veka* (Moscow: Novoe literaturnoe obozrenie, 2001), 34, 102.

20. S. V. Soplenkov, *Doroga v Arzrum: Rossiiskaia obshchestvennaia mysl' o Vostoke (pervaia polovina XIX veka)* (Moscow: "Vostochnaia literatura" RAN, 2000), 12; A. A. Vigasin and S. G. Karpiuk, eds., *Puteshestviia po Vostoku v epokhu Ekateriny II* (Moscow: "Vostochnaia literatura" RAN, 1995), 101–133.

21. The decree was entitled "On the Toleration of All Confessions and on the Prohibition of Hierarchs from Entering into Affairs concerning Other Confessions and the Construction of Prayer Houses according to Their Law, Leaving All of That to Secular Authorities." *PSZ*, vol. 19, no. 13,996 (17 June 1773), 775–776.

22. M. M. Shcherbatov, "Statistika v razsuzhdenii Rossii," *Chteniia v Imperatorskom obshchestve istorii i drevnosti Rossiiskoi pri moskovskogo universiteta* 3 (1859): 61.

23. *Kniga Al'-Koran aravlianina Magometa, kotoryi, v shestom stoletii sydal onuiu za nizloslannuiu k nemu s nebes, sebia zhe poslednim i velichaishim iz Prorokov Bozhiikh* (St. Petersburg: V Tipografii Gornogo Uchilishcha, 1790), xiii–xv.

24. *Sokrashchenie,* 2–5.

25. *Russkii posol v Stambule: Petr Andreevich Tolstoi i ego opisanie Osmanskoi imperii nachala XVIII v.* (Moscow: Glavnaia redaktsiia vostochnoi literatury, 1985), 40–41.

26. F. A. Emin, *Kratkoe opisanie drevneishego i noveishogo sostoianiia Ottomanskoi Porty* (St. Petersburg: pri Morskom shliakhetnom kadetskom korpuse, 1769), 26, 36–37. See also Mouradgea D'Ohsson, *Tableau général de l'empire othoman,* vol. 4, pt. 1 (Paris: Firmin Didot, 1791), 495–530; Ivan Lepekhin, *Dnevye zapiski puteshestviia doktora i akademii nauk ad"iunkta Ivana Lepekhina po raznym provintsiiam rossiiskogo gosudarstva 1768 i 1769 godu,*

pt. 1 (St. Petersburg: Imperatorskoi Akademii Nauk, 1795), 179; Soplenkov, *Doroga*, 9.

27. Maksim Nevzorov, *Puteshestvie v Kazan', Viatku i Orenburg v 1800 godu*, pt. 1 (Moscow: V Universitetskoi Tipografii, 1802).

28. See Gregory L. Freeze, *The Russian Levites: Parish Clergy in the Eighteenth Century* (Cambridge, Mass.: Harvard University Press, 1977); idem, *The Parish Clergy in Nineteenth-Century Russia: Crisis, Reform, Counter-Reform* (Princeton: Princeton University Press, 1983).

29. Dzh. I. Meskidze, "Mansur," *ITBRI*, 1:68–69; G. L. Bondarevskii and G. N. Kolbaia, *Dokumental'naia istoriia obrazovaniia mnogonatsional'nogo gosudarstva Rossiiskogo*, vol. 1 (Moscow: Izdatel'stvo NORMA, 1998), 462–463.

30. Allen J. Frank, *Islamic Historiography and 'Bulghar' Identity among the Tatars and Bashkirs of Russia* (Leiden: Brill, 1998), 21–39; G. B. Khusainov, ed., *Pis'mo Batyrshi imperatritse Elizaveta Petrovne* (Ufa: Ufimskii nauchnyi tsentr RAN, 1993), 26 (transcription of original Turki text), 71 (Russian translation).

31. D. D. Azamatov, "Orenburgskoe magometanskoe dukhovnoe sobranie," *ITBRI*, 1:84–85. Idem, "Khusainov, Mukhamedzhan," *ITBRI*, 1:101–102; *MIBASSR*, 5:683; on Russian and Ottoman relations, see Norman Itzkowitz and Max Mote, eds. and trans., *Mubadele: An Ottoman-Russian Exchange of Ambassadors* (Chicago: University of Chicago Press, 1970); on frontier mosques, see Frank, *Muslim Religious Institutions*, 161–217; on the Qur'an under Catherine, see E. A. Rezvan, "Koran v Rossii," *ITBRI*, 1:50.

32. See Fisher, "Enlightened Despotism"; Akdes Nimet Kurat, "Rus hâkimiyeti altında İdil-Ural ülkesi," *Ankara Üniversitesi Dil ve Tarih Coğrafya Fakültesi Dergisi* 23, nos. 3–4 (1965): 124–125. Here I have translated *dukhovnoe* as "ecclesiastical" rather than "spiritual," which is the more common translation in English-language scholarship. This institution was devoted not to the cultivation of "spirituality," but to regulation and discipline, very much in the spirit of Peter the Great's *Ecclesiastical Regulation* of 1721. See

James Cracraft, *The Church Reform of Peter the Great* (Stanford: Stanford University Press, 1971); the decrees establishing this body are in *PSZ*, vol. 22, nos. 16,710 and 16,711 (22 Sept. 1788), 1107–1108.

33. Fisher, "Enlightened Despotism"; *MIBASSR*, 5:563–564. Though the exams were to be conducted in Tatar, all documents produced by the Assembly were to be in Russian with Tatar translations, but officials were never able to enforce this provision.

34. *MIBASSR*, 5:564–566, 565.

35. Ibid., 565.

36. Ibid., 566.

37. Azamatov, "Orenburgskoe magometanskoe dukhovnoe sobranie," *ITBRI*, 1:84. Known in Russian as the *Orenburgskoe Magometanskoe Dukhovnoe Sobranie,* Tatar sources referred to this institution variously as the *Orenburg idare-i shariyya* (Orenburg Shari'a Administration), *Orenburg mahkemesi* (Orenburg Court), or *Orenburg sobraniesi* (Orenburg Assembly); *MIBASSR*, 5:683.

38. *MIBASSR*, 5:559–560.

39. Danil' D. Azamatov, "The Muftis of the Orenburg Spiritual Assembly in the 18th and 19th Centuries: The Struggle for Power in Russia's Muslim Institution," in *Muslim Culture in Russian and Central Asia from the 18th to the Early 20th Centuries,* vol. 2, ed. Anke von Kügelgen, Michael Kemper, and Allen J. Frank (Berlin: Klaus Schwarz Verlag, 1998), 355–384; *MIBASSR*, 5:683–684.

40. GAOO, f. 6, op. 3, d. 2411, ll. 79–80.

41. Ibid., 85 ob., 82 ob., 75–76.

42. This Ottoman office undertook many of the same disciplining functions, including the appointment, dismissal, and regulation of Muslim authorities. See Murat Akgündüz, *XIX. Asır Başlarına Kadar Osmanlı Devleti'nde Şeyhülislâmlık* (Istanbul: Beyan, 2002).

43. See M. Khalid Masud, "*Ādāb al-muftī*: The Muslim Understanding of Values, Characteristics, and Role of a *Muftī*," in *Moral Conduct and Authority: The Place of Adab in South Asian Islam,* ed.

Barbara Daly Metcalf (Berkeley: University of California Press, 1984), 124–151.

44. GAOO, f. 6, op. 3, d. 2411, ll. 121–123 ob. and 126, 126 ob.

45. Ibid., 127–128.

46. PSZ, vol. 31, no. 24,819 (18 Oct. 1811), 872; GAOO, f. 6, op. 4, d. 8085, ll. 49–49 ob. and 69 ob.

47. PSZ, 2nd ser., vol. 7, no. 5,500 (14 July 1832), 498–505.

48. GAOO, f. 6, op. 3, d. 4744, ll. 1 ob.–2; E. A. Vishlenkova, "Idei mira i ekumenizma v politicheskoi zhizni Rossii pervoi chetevti XIX v.," in Mirotvorchestvo v Rossii: Tserkov', politiki, mysliteli, ed. E. L. Rudnitskaia (Moscow: Izdatel'stvo "Nauka," 2003), 195–223.

49. GAOO, f. 6, op. 2, d. 724, l. 135.

50. Ibid., ll. 135–135 ob. The mullah was known in Tatar as Khäbibulla b. äl-Khösäen b. Gabdelkärim äl-Orï (1767–1843); Märjani, Möstäfadel-äkhbar, 260; Riḍā'addīn Fakhraddīn ōghlī, Āthār (Orenburg: Tipografiia M.-F. G. Karimova, 1905), 9:7; Märjani, Möstäfadel-äkhbar, 232; Kappeler, Russlands erste Nationalitäten, 460.

51. Märjani, Möstäfadel-äkhbar, 260–261.

52. Fakhraddīn ōghlī, Āthār, 9:7.

53. Märjani, Möstäfadel-äkhbar, 261; Kemper, Sufis und Gelehrte, 59.

54. Märjani referred to this region as "Mishärstan," drawing attention to Khäbibulla's appeal among the Mishars, whom he and others (who identified themselves as "Bulgars" or "Tatars") regarded as a separate people with an inferior understanding of Islam.

55. Märjani, Möstäfadel-äkhbar, 261; Fakhraddīn ōghlī, Āthār, 9:7; Märjani, Möstäfadel-äkhbar, 262.

56. Michael Kemper, "Entre Boukhara et la Moyenne-Volga: 'Abd an-Nasir al-Qursawi (1776–1812) en conflit avec les oulémas traditionalistes," trans. Stéphane A. Dudoignon, Cahiers du Monde russe, nos. 1–2 (Jan.–June, 1996): 42; Kemper, Sufis und Gelehrte, 59.

57. Joseph Schacht, "Abu 'l-Layth al-Samarkandi," Encyclopaedia of

Islam, 1:137. This text was translated into Tatar and published in Kazan. J. G. Zäynullin, *XVIII yöz–XX yöz bashïnda tatar rukhani ädäbiyäti* (Kazan: "Mägarif" näshriatï, 1998), 121–123.

58. GAOO, f. 6, op. 2, d. 724, l. 135 ob.–136; f. 6, op. 2, d. 1026, ll. 5–5 ob.; Algar, "Shaykh Zaynullah," 113–114; and Kemper, *Sufis und Gelehrte*, 58–59.

59. GAOO, f. 6, op. 2, d. 1026, 4 ob; the original denunciation could not be located: the cleric who authored the document had supposedly misplaced it and taken ill in the meantime; ibid., ll. 9–9 ob. and 21–21 ob.

60. The mufti was also known as Gabdessälam b. Gabderräkhim b. Gabderrakhman b. Mökhämmäd äl-Bögelmävi äl-Gabderi. See Kemper, *Sufis und Gelehrte*, 70–73.

61. *PSZ*, 2nd ser., vol. 2, no. 893 (Feb. 1827), 168–169. On Sagitov (Gabdessatar b. Sägïyd' äsh-Shïrdani), see Märjani, *Möstäfadel-äkhbar*, 273; Radik Salikhov and Ramil' Khairutdinov, *Respublika Tatarstan: Pamiatniki istorii i kul'tury tatarskogo naroda (konets XVIII–nachalo XX vekov)* (Kazan: "Fest," 1995), 118; and Azamatov, "The Muftis," 364–365; Kazan authorities solicited the opinion of Sagitov (rather than the mufti) about burial laws, *PSZ*, 2nd ser., vol. 5, no. 3,659 (13 May 1830), 396.

62. TsGIARB, f. I-295, op. 3, d. 303, ll. 3 ob.–4. Sagitov cited "proclamations" of 7 June 1734, 22 June 1763, and 18 Mar. 1797, an *ukaz* of 17 June 1773, articles 494 and 496 of Catherine's *Instruction*, article 62 of the Statute on Decorum, and article 124 of the Statute on Towns; ibid., l. 5.

63. TsGIARB, f. I-295, op. 3, d. 303, ll. 1 ob., 7–7 ob. Gabdrakhimov rebuked his rival for replying to the government's request without consulting the Assembly, thereby "scorning its authority," ibid., l. 8.

64. *PSZ*, 2nd ser., vol. 5, no. 3,659 (13 May 1830), 396, 397.

65. Ibid.; and Michael S. Stanislawski, *Tsar Nicholas I and the Jews: The Transformation of Jewish Society in Russia, 1825–1855* (Philadelphia: Jewish Publication Society of America, 1983).

66. Karl Fuks [Fuchs], *Kazanskie Tatary v statisticheskom i*

etnograficheskom otnosheniiakh (Kazan: V Universitetskoi Tipografii, 1844), 72–73; Jane Idleman Smith and Yvonne Yazbeck Haddad, *The Islamic Understanding of Death and Resurrection* (Albany: State University of New York Press, 1981), 31–61.

67. See TsGIARB, f. I-295, op. 3, d. 303, ll. 13–13 ob and 20–23, 23–23 ob. The document referred to the fatwa as a "decree" *(ukaz)*: ibid., 15–16, 24 ob., 34, and 37–37 ob.

68. *Osmanlı devleti ile Azerbaycan Türk hanlıkları arasındaki münâsebetlere dâir arşiv belgeleri*, vol. 1 (Ankara: T. C. Başbakanlık Devlet Arşivleri Genel Müdurlügu, 1992), 191–200; and Austin Jersild, *Orientalism and Empire: North Caucasus Mountain Peoples and the Georgian Frontier, 1845–1917* (Montreal: McGill-Queen's University Press, 2002), quotation at 15.

69. *PSZ*, vol. 11, no. 8,881 (1836), 133–134.

70. D. Iu. Arapov, ed., "M. S. Vorontsov i musul'mane Kryma," *Sbornik Russkogo istoricheskogo obshchestva* 155, no. 7, (2003): 105–107; "Sovershenno zapretit' v"ezd v predely nashi," *Istochnik* 5 (2002): 18–19.

71. "Sovershenno zapretit'."

72. Marc Raeff, ed., *Russian Intellectual History: An Anthology* (New York: Humanities Press, 1966), 14–30, 23 (quotation), 16.

73. Bondarevskii and Kolbaia, *Dokumental'naia istoriia*, 464–465, 378.

74. Ibid., 471–474.

75. See Michael Cook, *Commanding Right and Forbidding Wrong in Islamic Thought* (Cambridge: Cambridge University Press, 2000).

76. Peter Hauptmann, *Die Katechismen der Russisch-orthodoxen Kirche: Entstehungsgeschichte und Lehrgehalt* (Göttingen: Vandenhoeck & Ruprecht, 1971), 253–255; *STsOMDS*, 3; L. Klimovich, *Islam v tsarskoi Rossii: Ocherki* (Moscow: Gosudarstvennoe antireligioznoe izdatel'stvo, 1936), 59–61.

77. *STsOMDS*, 3; recruitment officials suspected Tatars, Jews, and other non-Russian groups of avoiding service more than others by practicing self-mutilation on themselves and their children: Elise Kimerling Wirtschafter, *From Serf to Russian Soldier* (Princeton:

Princeton University Press, 1990), 7–8; *STsOMDS*, 3–4; Kemper, *Sufis und Gelehrte*, 71, 148–158.

78. *STsOMDS*, 4.

79. Wirtschafter, *From Serf to Russian Soldier*, 8.

80. TsGIARB, f. I-295, op. 3, d. 2615, ll. 2–3, 3 ob.–4.

81. Ibid., 4–4 ob.

82. Ibid., 9 ob., 10 ob.–11. Translations of these terms appeared in Nikolai Tornau, *Izlozhenie nachal musul'manskogo zakonovedeniia* (St. Petersburg: V Tipografii II Otdeleniia Sobstvennoi E. I. V. Kantseliarii, 1850), 8.

83. TsGIARB, f. I-295, op. 3, d. 2615, ll. 13–13 ob.

84. Ibid., 14–14 ob., 15.

85. Filaret called on the Orthodox to express "sadness and remorse of the heart and real tears because we serve the Lord imperfectly and unworthily or even earn His anger with our sins." Hauptmann, *Die Katechismen*, 228 and 300; for Obruchev's exchanges with the new mufti, see TsGIARB, f. I-295, op. 3, d. 2615, ll. 15–16 ob. (emphasis added).

86. *Kolonial'naia politika rossiiskogo tsarisma v Azerbaidzhane*, 310; *PSZ*, vol. 38, no. 28,891 (25 Jan. 1822), 36–37; on repentance, see Annemarie Schimmel, *Mystical Dimensions of Islam* (Chapel Hill: University of North Carolina Press, 1975), 109–110; M. S. Stern, *Al-Ghazzali on Repentance* (New Delhi: Sterling, 1990); *PSZ*, 2nd ser., vol. 20, no. 19,283 (15 Aug. 1845), 971–972.

87. TsGIARB, f. I-295, op. 3, d. 3977, l. 30 ob.

88. Ibid., 31 ob.–32, 36 ob.

89. Wortman, *Scenarios of Power*.

90. A. J. Wensinck, "Khutba," *Encyclopaedia of Islam*, new ed., 5:74–75; and Ira Marvin Lapidus, *Muslim Cities in the Later Middle Ages* (Cambridge, Mass.: Harvard University Press, 1967).

91. Petitions and government correspondence commonly made reference to a decree of 25 Feb. 1796 establishing prayers for the tsar, though it apparently was not published. See V. G. Gadzhiev, ed.,

Russko-Dagestanskie otnosheniia v XVIII–nachale XIX v.: Sbornik dokumentov (Moscow: "Nauka," 1988), 289–290. See, also, TsGIARB, f. I-295, op. 3, d. 35; *Kazakhsko-russkie otnosheniia v XVIII–XIX vekakh (1771–1867 gody): Sbornik dokumentov i materialov* (Alma-Ata: Izdatel'stvo "Nauka," 1964), 207; and John Shelton Curtiss, *The Russian Army under Nicholas I, 1825–1855* (Durham, N.C.: Duke University Press, 1965), 255–272.

92. Muhammad Khalid Masud, "The Obligation to Migrate: The Doctrine of *Hijra* in Islamic Law," in *Muslim Travellers: Pilgrimage, Migration and the Religious Imagination*, ed. Dale F. Eickelman and James Piscatori (Berkeley: University of California Press, 1990), 29–49, 36.

93. See Peter Hardy, *The Muslims of British India* (Cambridge: Cambridge University Press, 1972), esp. pp. 107–115; and Masud, "The Obligation to Migrate."

94. Kemper, "Entre Boukhara et la Moyenne-Volga," 45; idem, *Sufis und Gelehrte*, 290–299; Salikhov and Khairutdinov, *Respublika Tatarstan*, 234; Utiz Imani was also known as Gabderräkhim b. Gosman b. Särmäki b. Kïrïm äl-Utïz Imäni (1754–1834).

95. Kemper, *Sufis und Gelehrte*, 299–307.

96. Ibid., 147–171; for the case from Kargala, see TsGIARB, f. I-295, op. 3, d. 100–101 ob; TsGIARB, f. I-295, op. 2, d. 43, ll. 54 ob.–57 ob., 387 ob., 789–790.

2. The State in the Mosque

1. *MIBASSR*, 5:567–568.

2. On the activities of Muslim merchants and entrepreneurs, see Allen J. Frank, *Muslim Religious Institutions in Imperial Russia: The Islamic World of Novouzensk District and the Kazakh Inner Horde, 1780–1910* (Leiden: Brill, 2001), 174; Andreas Kappeler, *Russlands Erste Nationalitäten: Das Zarenreich und die Völker der Mittleren Wolga vom 16. bis 19. Jahrhundert* (Cologne: Böhlau Verlag, 1982), 455–481; Michael Kemper, *Sufis und Gelehrte in Tatarien und*

Baschkirien, 1789–1889: Der islamische Diskurs unter russischer Herrschaft (Berlin: Klaus Schwarz Verlag, 1998); and Christian Noack, *Muslimischer Nationalismus im Russischen Reich: Nationsbildung und Nationalbewegung bei Tataren und Baschkiren, 1861– 1917* (Stuttgart: Franz Steiner Verlag, 2000), 39–109.

3. For example, "Mökhämmätnajip khäzrat yäzmasï," *GA*, nos. 1–2 (2003): 49; and Allen J. Frank, "A Chronicle of Islamic Communities on the Imperial Russian Frontier: The *Tavārīx-i Ālṭī Ātā* of Muḥammad Fātiḥ al-Īmīnī," in *Muslim Culture in Russia and Central Asia*, vol. 3, ed. Anke von Kügelgen, Aširbek Muminov, and Michael Kemper (Berlin: Klaus Schwarz Verlag, 2000), 473.

4. See Dale F. Eickelman, "Changing Interpretations of Islamic Movements," *Islam and the Political Economy of Meaning: Comparative Studies of Muslim Discourse*, ed. William R. Roff (London: Croom Helm, 1987), esp. 20–27; and William R. Roff, "Islamic Movements: One or Many?," in Roff, *Political Economy of Meaning*, 31–52.

5. Friedhelm Berthold Kaiser, *Die russische Justizreform von 1864: Zur Geschichte der russischen Justiz von Katharina II. bis 1917* (Leiden: Brill, 1972), 1–89; and R. R. Khairutdinov, *Upravlenie gosudarstvennoi derevnei Kazanskoi gubernii (konets XVIII – pervaia tret' XIX v.)* (Kazan: Izdatel'stvo Instituta istorii AN RT, 2002); and Näjip Näkkash and Fäyzelkhak Islaev, eds., "Mulla saylau tamgalarï," *GA* 1–2 (1998): 108–113.

6. Michael M. J. Fischer, *Iran: From Religious Dispute to Revolution* (Cambridge, Mass.: Harvard University Press, 1980), 138; and Abdul-Karim Rafeq, "Public Morality in 18th-century Ottoman Damascus," *Revue du monde musulman et de la Méditerranée* 55–56, nos. 1–2 (1990): 180–196.

7. Soviet scholarship treated Muslim clerics as mere instruments of feudal interests and depicted the laity as the victims of their manipulation. See L. Klimovich, *Islam v tsarskoi Rossii* (Moscow: Gosudarstvennoe antireligioznoe izdatel'stvo, 1936); on the doc-

trinal background behind Muslim lay initiative, see Michael Cook, *Commanding Right and Forbidding Wrong in Islamic Thought* (Cambridge: Cambridge University Press, 2000).

8. See Gregory L. Freeze, "The *Soslovie* (Estate) Paradigm and Russian Social History," *American Historical Review* 91, no. 1 (Feb. 1986): 11–36.

9. Ira Marvin Lapidus, *Muslim Cities in the Later Middle Ages* (Cambridge, Mass.: Harvard University Press, 1967), 108; and Roy P. Mottahedeh, *Loyalty and Leadership in an Early Islamic Society* (Princeton: Princeton University Press, 1980), 136–150.

10. *Kazanskii vestnik* cited in *Istoriia Tatarii v materialakh i dokumentakh* (Moscow: Gosudarstvennoe sotsial'no-ekonomicheskoe izdatel'stvo, 1937), 259; "Mökhämmätnajip khäzrat yäzmasï," *GA*, nos. 1–2 (2003): 45–59; and Riḍā'addīn Fakhraddīn ōghlī, *Āthār*, vol. 10 (Orenburg: Tipografiia M.-F. G. Karimova, 1905), 102.

11. On Muslim women, see Nikolai Petrovich Rychkov, *Zhurnal, ili dnevyia zapiski puteshestviia Kapitana Rychkova po razynm provintsiiam Rossiiskogo gosudarstvo, 1769 i 1770 godu* (St. Petersburg: pri Imperatorskoi Akademii Nauk, 1770), 5; P. A. Shino [Pashino], "Volzhskie Tatary," *Sovremennik* 81 (1860): 269–270 and 281–284; Agnès Kefeli, "The Role of Tatar and Kriashen Women in the Transmission of Islamic Knowledge, 1800–1870," in *Of Religion and Empire: Missions, Conversion, and Tolerance in Tsarist Russia*, ed. Robert P. Geraci and Michael Khodarkovsky (Ithaca: Cornell University Press, 2001), 250–273; and *Kazanskie gubernskie vedomosti*, 22 May 1844, 321.

12. *PSZ*, vol. 26, no. 19,885 (22 May 1801), 655; unlike the 1822 ruling, in the recently annexed Crimea a decree of 17 December 1796 had exempted clerics there from corporal punishment as well as conscription and taxation (*PSZ*, vol. 38, no. 28,891 [25 Jan. 1822], 36–37).

13. Art. 1231, *Svod zakonov Rossiiskoi imperii, izd. 1857 g.*, vol. 11, pt. 1

(St. Petersburg: V Tipografii Vtorogo Otdeleniia Sobstvennoi Ego Imp. Velichestva Kantseliarii, 1857), 223; *PSZ*, vol. 31, no. 24,819 (18 Oct. 1811), 872.

14. *PSZ*, 2nd ser., vol. 1, no. 715 (1 Dec. 1826), 1264–1265; Ibid., vol. 24, no. 23,259 (21 May 1849), 284.

15. Ibid., vol. 1, no. 564 (31 Aug. 1826), 911–912; GAOO, f. 6, op. 4, d. 9958, ll. 8–8 ob.

16. TsGIARB, f. I-295, op. 3, d. 1096, ll. 1–1 ob.

17. Ibid., 26–26 ob.

18. Ibid., 27 ob.

19. Ibid., 28 ob.–29, 29–29 ob.

20. See Michael Stanislawski, *Tsar Nicholas I and the Jews: The Transformation of Jewish Society in Russia, 1825–1855* (Philadelphia: Jewish Publication Society of America, 1983), 133–134.

21. For example, Shihabetdin Märjani, *Möstäfadel-äkhbar fi äkhvali Kazan vä Bolgar (Kazan häm Bolgar khälläre turïnda faydalanïlgan khäbärlär)*, ed. Ä. N. Khäyrullin (Kazan: Tatar. Kit. Näshr., 1989), 278–279; and Kemper, *Sufis und Gelehrte*, 60; on regional pilgrimage, see Allen J. Frank, "Islamic Shrine Catalogues and Communal Geography in the Volga-Ural Region: 1788–1917," *Journal of Islamic Studies* 7, no. 2 (1996): 265–286.

22. Märjani, *Möstäfadel-äkhbar*, 283, 288.

23. Cited in D. D. Azamatov, *Orenburgskoe magometanskoe dukhovnoe sobranie v obshchestvennoi i dukhovnoi zhizni musul'manskogo naseleniia iuzhnogo Urala v kontse XVIII–XIX vv.*, Kandidatskaia dissertatsiia (Ufa, 1994), 34.

24. TsGIARB, f. I-295, op. 3, d. 1692, l. 1; when Nicholas I introduced the conscription of Jews in 1827, he exempted rabbis as well (Stanislawski, *Tsar Nicholas*, 19).

25. In fact, the decree stressed the voluntary character of such agreements (*PSZ*, 2nd ser., vol. 1, no. 564 [31 Aug. 1826], 911–912); TsGIARB, f. I-295, op. 3, d. 1692, ll. 1 ob.–2 ob., 14–15.

26. TsGIARB, f. I-295, op. 3, d. 1692, ll. 3 ob.–4.

27. *PSZ*, 2nd ser., vol. 25, no. 23,932 (20 Feb. 1850), 126.

28. For example, mullahs attached to Bashkir regiments received 150 rubles a year until 1833, when their salary increased to 300 rubles per year. *PSZ*, 2nd ser., vol. 8, no. 5,885 (4 Jan. 1833), 9. The senior akhund serving in the Guards' corps received a salary raise in 1843, from 400 rubles to 1,500 rubles. *PSZ*, vol. 18, no. 16,442 (9 Jan. 1843), 22. The Ministry of War compensated nonmilitary clerics who performed rites for Muslim troops quartered in their parishes. From 1844, the imam of the Ufa Cathedral mosque received 90 rubles a year and the azanchi earned 50 rubles. *PSZ*, vol. 19, no. 17,519 (14 Jan. 1844), 33. On the prohibition against trade, see *PSZ*, vol. 1, no. 564 (31 Aug. 1826), 911–912.

29. Quoted in Al-Ghazālī, *Inner Dimensions of Islamic Worship*, trans. Muhtar Holland (Leicester: Islamic Foundation, 1983), 31.

30. Karl Fuchs, *Kazanskie Tatary v statisticheskom i etnographicheskom otnosheniiakh* (Kazan: Universitetskaia Tipografiia, 1844), 92–93; Radik Salikhov and Ramil' Khairutdinov, *Respublika Tatarstan: Pamiatniki istorii i kul'tury tatarskogo naroda (konets XVIII–nachalo XX vekov)* (Kazan: "Fest," 1995), 25, 133–134.

31. Salikhov and Khairutdinov, *Respublika Tatarstan*, 81, 99.

32. Ibid., 181–182, 182.

33. A Russian observer emphasized the power of the bāy in the district of Kazan at midcentury: "In order to become a mullah in whatever village, it is necessary to collect from the residents their testimony [*prigovor*], whether they agree to have him as [their] mullah or not, but this is very simple: if only the *bāy* of this village agrees. The testimony is prepared and the signatures and markings [*tamgy*] of the illiterate population are affixed to it" (Shino, "Volzhskie Tatary," 269); the specification of such conditions in deeds is noted in Fakhraddīn ōghlī, *Āthār*, and Frank, *Muslim Religious Institutions*.

34. In his biography of Akhmed Khusainov (1837–1906), Fakhraddīn ōghlī acclaimed the merchant's role in the "revelation and restoration of waqf in Kazan and its environs, which had functioned from time immemorial, but had in recent times been discontinued." He credited Khusainov with leaving endowments worth a half-million

rubles. Rizaetdin ibn Fakhretdin [Fakhraddīn ōghlī], *Akhmed Bai*, trans. M. F. Rakhimkulova, 2nd ed. (Orenburg: n.p., 1991), 19–20. See also Danil' D. Azamatov, "The Muftis of the Orenburg Spiritual Assembly in the 18th and 19th Centuries: The Struggle for Power in Russia's Muslim Institution," in Kügelgen, Kemper, and Frank, *Muslim Culture in Russia*, 2:367, 379; and Frank, *Muslim Religious Institutions*.

35. TsGIARB, f. I-295, op. 3, d. 5802, ll. 1–10b.; in Ura, the Näzirs who founded the stone mosque there provided two thousand rubles for Ufa's first mosque under Mufti Gabdrakhimov in 1825 (Kemper, *Sufis und Gelehrte*, 68–69).

36. After midcentury, provincial officials began to emphasize the financial strain placed on small communities by the upkeep of mosques and argued for an increase in the two-hundred-soul minimum required for permission and, thus, for a decrease in the overall number of mosques and "clergy" (RGIA, f. 821, op. 8, d. 594, esp. ll. 8 ob.–9); see, also, the complaint from a mullah and muhtasib from a village in Orenburg Province to the Assembly in 1834, in which he pointed out that peasants had constructed a new mosque without his knowledge when he was away serving on the frontier in TsGIARB, f. I-295, op. 3, d. 1121 (and a similar charge in d. 4144, ll. 1–2).

37. Frank, "Chronicle," 452, 470.

38. Märjani, *Möstäfadel-äkhbar*, 239.

39. Riḍā'addīn Fakhraddīn ōghlī, *Āthār*, vol. 6 (Orenburg: Tipografiia M.-F. G. Karimova, 1904), 292.

40. Ibid., 317.

41. PSZ, 2nd ser., vol. 12, no. 10,594 (21 Oct. 1837), 801.

42. See, for example, Fakhraddīn ōghlī, *Āthār*, 6:284.

43. See the complaint about the role of an extended family in influencing elections in TsGIARB, f. I-295, op. 3, d. 35.

44. In 1819, residents of Chuvashskie Komaiury in Simbirsk addressed their supplications to the tsar, though they asked that the Orenburg Assembly also receive their request. The law directed local courts

and provincial offices to forward these matters to the "highest Muhammadan ecclesiastical authority" in Ufa. Ibid., l. 1 ob.

45. The critique of Sharafaddīn is quoted in Frank, "Chronicle," 464; the complaint against Fatkullin is in TsGIARB, f. I-295, op. 3, d. 910.

46. TsGIARB, f. I-295, op. 3, d. 910, l. 12.

47. Ibid., ll. 12 ob.–13. These petitioners were not alone in interpreting the outbreak of cholera as punishment sent from God to admonish those who rejected religion. The Orthodox Church instructed its members that "God's wrath" was the source of cholera, "which was merited by our sins." Nicholas I, too, is said to have warned residents of St. Petersburg who had joined in the Haymarket riots following the outbreak of cholera in 1831 that God had sent them their "burden." "Pouchenie k prikhozhanam po sluchaiu kholery," *Strannik* (Nov. 1866): 100–102; and Roderick E. McGrew, *Russia and the Cholera, 1823–1832* (Madison: University of Wisconsin Press, 1965), 112–113.

48. TsGIARB, f. I-295, op. 3, d. 910, ll. 41–41 ob., 45–46 ob.

49. Ibid., d. 46, ll. 8–9; d. 625, ll. 1–1 ob., 5, 13, 15, 21–22 ob.

50. Ibid., op. 2, d. 43, ll. 1215 ob.–17; op. 3, d. 5618, ll. 3, 13–13 ob., 31–32 ob.

51. Ibid., d. 5185, l. 1, ll. 2 ob.–3.

52. Shino, "Volzhskie Tatary," 288.

53. TsGIARB, f. I-295, op. 3, d. 11, l. 1.

54. Ibid., d. 6165, l. 19 (the Assembly attempted to reconcile them and requested that the police follow up on their feuding); op. 2, d. 43, ll. 130 ob.–132.

55. Ibid., op. 3, d. 5567, ll. 1–6 ob.

56. Ibid., 51–52 ob., 113 ob.–115 ob.

57. Mufti Gabdrakhimov intervened to veto the appointment of the son, raising questions about his youth and, given the neighborhood's dissatisfaction with his father, his own moral stature. The father appears to have returned to a position as imam in his native village of Yänga Kishet. Märjani, *Möstäfadel-äkhbar*, 301–302.

Elsewhere, 'ulama dynasties dominated prestigious positions. For example, Leon Carl Brown, "The Religious Establishment in Husainid Tunisia," *Scholars, Saints, and Sufis: Muslim Religious Institutions in the Middle East since 1500*, ed. Nikki R. Keddie (Berkeley: University of California Press, 1972), esp. 64–66. In other societies, "lineages of erudition" may have been more exceptional. Kenneth Brown has emphasized social mobility rather than hereditary or social exclusivity, arguing that learning "was the fief of no social group or groups" ("Profile of a Nineteenth-Century Moroccan Scholar," in *Scholars, Saints, and Sufis*, 127–148, citation at 132–133).

58. TsGIARB, f. I-295, op. 2, d. 43, ll. 1151 ob.–1152 ob.; ll. 1152 ob.–1153, 1157 ob.–1158 ob.

59. See an imam's complaint from the district of Tobol'sk in 1852, in ibid., op. 3, d. 3279. Shino, "Volzhskie Tatary," 257–264; Ildus Zahidullin, "Jiennar tarikhïnnan," *Kazan utlarï* no. 4 (1991): 174–176; Stéphane A. Dudoignon, "Qu'est-ce que la *'qadîmiya'*? Éléments pour une sociologie du traditionalisme musulman, en Islam de Russie et en Transoxiane (au tournant des XIXe et XXe siècles)," in *L'Islam de Russie: Conscience communautaire et autonomie politique chez les Tatars de la Volga et de l'Oural depuis le XVIIIe siècle*, ed. Stéphane A. Dudoignon, Dämir Is'haqov, and Räfyq Möhämmätshin (Paris: Maisonneuve et Larose, 1997), 213–214; and NART, f. 1, op. 3, d. 6030 and d. 7233. It became a subject of debate in organs of self-government as well. In 1885, Muslims from Kazan protested against a petition calling for the elimination of the festival. Boris Veselovskii, *Istoriia zemstva*, vol. 4 (St. Petersburg: Izdatel'stvo O. N. Popovoi, 1911), p. 421n2.

60. TsGIARB, f. I-295, op. 3, d. 6294, ll. 8–10, l. 13. Azamatov, *Orenburgskoe magometanskoe dukhovnoe sobranie*, 141. Danil' Azamatov describes the prosecution of two mullahs and two elders who disinterred the body of a Muslim who died in the cholera epidemic of 1848 and burned it in a field; they apparently viewed his death

as divine punishment for not attending prayers at the mosque; initially they were sentenced to exile in Siberia, but Nicholas I reduced their sentence to five months in jail, referring to their act as "a religious superstition extracted from the books of Islam [*islamizma*]" (Azamatov, *Orenburgskoe magometanskoe dukhovnoe sobranie*, 207).

61. TsGIARB, f. I-295, op. 3, d. 5789, ll. 1–1 ob.

62. Ibid., 5 ob.–6.

63. See, for example, Fätkhullah Khuseinov's letter to the mufti in Riḍā'addīn Fakhraddīn ōghlī, *Āthār*, vol. 3 (Orenburg: Tipografiia M.-F. G. Karimova, 1903), 109.

64. TsGIARB, f. I-295, op. 3, d. 5698, l. 3, 3–3 ob.

65. Ibid., l. 3 ob., 4 ob.

66. Ibid., d. 5048, l. 15.

67. Ibid., 15 ob.

68. Ibid., 17–17 ob.

69. Ibid., 34–34 ob.; Hamid Algar, "Silent and Vocal *dhikr* in the Naqsbandī Order," *Abhandlungen der Akademie der Wissenschaften in Göttingen* (Dritte Folge), no. 98 (1976): 39–46, citation at 43; B. M. Babadzhanov, "Zikr *dzhakhr* i *sama'*: Sakralizatsiia profannogo ili profanatsiia sakral'nogo," *Podvizhniki islama: Kul't sviatykh i sufizm v Srednei Azii i na Kavkaze*, ed. S. N. Abashin and V. O. Bobrovnikov (Moscow: Vostochnaia literatura, 2003), 237–250; and Annemarie Schimmel, *Mystical Dimensions of Islam* (Chapel Hill: University of North Carolina Press, 1975), 167–186. The new teaching may have derived from a member of the Qadiri or Yasavi order or from someone with simultaneous affiliations with one of these orders and the Naqshbandiyya, or Abdreshitov and his followers may have been performing melodic recitation of the Qur'an. See Kristina Nelson, *The Art of Reciting the Qur'an* (Austin: University of Texas Press, 1985), 32–51.

70. TsGIARB, f. I-295, op. 3, d. 1830, ll. 1–2 ob.

71. Ibid., l. 2 ob.

72. Ibid., 1.14, ll. 12 ob.–13, l. 16.
73. Ibid., d. 5048, ll. 9–9 ob. See Azamatov, *Orenburgskoe magome-tanskoe dukhovnoe sobranie*, 207.
74. RGIA, f. 821, op. 8, d. 995, l. 1–1 ob.
75. Ibid., ll. 2, 2 ob., 12.
76. See articles 1159–1164 of the criminal code in *PSZ*, vol. 20, no. 19,283 (15 Aug. 1845), 817–818.
77. RGIA, f. 821, op. 8, d. 995, ll. 2 ob.–3; on the state's approach to apostasy, see also Paul W. Werth, *At the Margins of Orthodoxy: Mission, Governance, and Confessional Politics in Russia's Volga-Kama Region, 1827–1905* (Ithaca: Cornell University Press, 2002).
78. RGIA, f. 821, op. 8, d. 995, ll. 3 ob.–4 ob.
79. Ibid., ll. 16–18, 36–37 ob., l. 40.
80. Ibid., ll. 40 ob.–41 ob.
81. Ibid., ll. 49–49 ob.

3. An Imperial Family

1. Quoted in William G. Wagner, *Marriage, Property and Law in Late Imperial Russia* (Oxford: Clarendon Press, 1994), 73. On this "family model of politics," see Lynn Hunt, *The Family Romance of the French Revolution* (Berkeley: University of California Press, 1992); Jacques Donzelot, *The Policing of Families*, trans. Robert Hurley (New York: Pantheon Books, 1979); and Richard S. Wortman, *Scenarios of Power: Myth and Ceremony in Russian Monarchy*, vol. 1 (Princeton: Princeton University Press, 1995).
2. Platon, *Kratkii katikhizis dlia obucheniia malykh detei* [1775], in *Pouchitel'nye slova*, vol. 6 (Moscow: U soderzhatelia Senatskoi Tipografii F. Gippiusa, 1780), 179; see also Gregory L. Freeze, "Bringing Order to the Russian Family: Marriage and Divorce in Imperial Russia, 1760–1860," *Journal of Modern History* 62, no. 4 (1990): 709–746.
3. K. D. . . . , *Opyt gosudarstvennogo prava Rossiiskoi imperii* (St. Petersburg: V Tipografii Imperatorskoi Rossiiskoi Akademii, 1833), 1–

2. European cameralists had highlighted religion's contribution to family discipline—and police interest in such regulation—as well. See Isabel V. Hull, *Sexuality, State, and Civil Society in Germany, 1700–1815* (Ithaca: Cornell University Press, 1996).

4. *Pis'ma o magometanstve* (St. Petersburg: V Tipografii III Otd. Sobst. E. I. V. Kantseliarii, 1848), 113. European cameralists were more ambivalent about polygamy, however. Many of them judged it natural for the "Orient," particularly as a means of population increase. See Hull, *Sexuality, State, and Civil Society,* 176–179.

5. Freeze, "Bringing Order," and ChaeRan Y. Freeze, *Jewish Marriage and Divorce in Imperial Russia* (Hanover, N.H.: Brandeis University Press, 2002), esp. 73–130; V. O. Bobrovnikov, *Musul'mane Severnogo Kavkaza: Obychai, pravo, nasilie* (Moscow: "Vostochnaia literatura" RAN, 2002), 171–175.

6. A. Z. Asfandiarov, *Bashkirskaia sem'ia v proshlom (XVIII–pervaia polovina XIX v.)* (Ufa: "Kitap," 1997), 51; and V. N. Vitevskii, *I. I. Nepliuev i Orenburgskii krai v prezhnem ego sostave do 1758 g.,* vol. 2 (Kazan: Tipo-Litografiia V. M. Kliuchnikova, 1897), 416.

7. Cited in Asfandiarov, *Bashkirskaia sem'ia,* 68; and MIBASSR, 5:402.

8. See Yuri Slezkine, *Arctic Mirrors: Russia and the Small Peoples of the North* (Ithaca: Cornell University Press, 1994), esp. 80–92.

9. Richard S. Wortman, *The Development of a Russian Legal Consciousness* (Chicago: University of Chicago Press, 1976); and idem, *Scenarios of Power; PSZ,* vol. 27, no. 20,231 (11 Apr. 1802), 106–107.

10. M. D. Chulkov described domestic Muslim marriage rituals in *Slovar' russkikh sueverii* (St. Petersburg: Shnor, 1782), 17–18, 25–27, 32–33; *Sokrashchenie Magometanskoi very: Perevedeno s Latinskogo* (Moscow: V Universitetskoi Tipografii u N. Novikova, 1784), 2–5, 7–10, 26–35, 38–53.

11. D. D. Azamatov, *Orenburgskoe magometanskoe dukhovnoe sobranie v kontse XVIII–XIX vv.* (Ufa: Izdatel'stvo "Gilem," 1999), 123–125.

12. MIBASSR, vol. 5, *Materialy po istorii*, 565.

13. *PSZ*, vol. 28, no. 21,634 (23 Feb. 1805), 843. The published decree did not mention that the government consulted with the Orenburg Assembly and other Muslim scholars; see *Opis' dokumentov i del, khraniashchikhsia v Senatskom arkhive. Otdel II, Tom III: Mart 1803 g.–Aprel' 1806 g.* (St. Petersburg: Senatskaia Tipografiia, 1915), 39. The State Council reaffirmed this decision in June 1826 (*PSZ*, 2nd ser., vol. 1, no. 386 [2 June 1826], 327–328).

14. See Gregory C. Kozlowski, *Muslim Endowments and Society in British India* (Cambridge: Cambridge University Press, 1985). Critics cited polygamy as an obstacle to population growth, claiming that the practice, "satisfying only sensibility, does not lead to an increase of the human race." *Orenburgskie gubernskie vedomosti*, 3 May 1847, 248–249; K. A. Nevolin, *Polnoe sobranie sochinenii K. A. Nevolina*, vol. 2 (Saint Petersburg: V tipografii Eduarda Pratsa, 1857), 152, 155; and Asfandiarov, *Bashkirskaia sem'ia*, 56–57. The French also supported the jurisdiction of the shari'a over inheritance, marriage, and other "civil" matters in Algeria. See Michael Brett, "Legislating for Inequality in Algeria: The Senatus-Consulte of 14 July 1865," *Bulletin of the School of Oriental and African Studies* 51, no. 3 (1998): 440–461.

15. A. Z. Asfandiarov provides numerous examples, like the case of one girl abducted from the fields in expensive clothes, in support of the conclusion that brides sometimes consented to their "abduction" to create a fait accompli in the face of parental opposition. Abduction may have been a strategy of poor males who could not afford the nuptial gift, which became more expensive in the nineteenth century. *Bashkirskaia sem'ia*, 64–68.

16. *MIBASSR*, 5:565.

17. N. V. Varadinov, *Istoriia Ministerstva vnutrennikh del*, pt. 2, book 2 (St. Petersburg: V tipografii Ministerstva vnutrennikh del, 1862), 99; GAOO, f. 6, op. 4, d. 8085, ll. 1–1 ob.

18. GAOO, f. 6, op. 4, d. 8085, ll. 54 ob., 68, 2–3 ob.

19. Ibid., ll. 46 ob. and 55 ob.; he added that decrees from the Ruling Senate of 28 May 1767 and 5 May 1811, which apparently remain unpublished, were supposed to discourage this practice. Ibid., l. 46 ob.

20. Officials in the capital pointed out that the Orthodox and Roman Catholic Churches forbade such marriages between Muslims and Christians. The Evangelical Church permitted such unions only when the wedding was performed by a Christian cleric. Golitsyn instructed the muftis to warn "Muhammadan ecclesiastical officials" against violating these rules, requesting that "they repeat this to their parishioners from time to time in their teachings at cathedral services." Skeptical of the muftis' capacity to relay these instructions, Golitsyn directed the police to exercise "supervision over the strict observation of the aforementioned rules." Ibid., d. 7601, ll. 1–2.

21. Ibid., d. 8085, ll. 46 and 55, emphasis added.

22. Ibid., ll. 46 ob.–47 ob., 71–71 ob. A note added that the Evangelical Church permitted marriages between Muslim men and Christian women on the condition that the children become Christians; however, it noted, "in St. Petersburg several children of Muhammadans [in state service] who married Christian women remain in the Muhammadan creed."

23. Ibid., ll. 47 ob., 75, 48, 59.

24. Ibid., ll. 48 ob.–50, 60 ob.–61, and 69 ob.

25. Ibid., ll. 50–50 ob., 57–57 ob., 72 ob. This mufti also proposed that those guilty of arranging and performing marriages without parental consent face prosecution by civil authorities.

26. Ibid., ll. 51–52. Like the mufti, judges reporting on offenses committed by figures below them were to "inform local civil authorities, if circumstances demand." The proposal issued similar directions to local officials, ordering them to observe "the execution of these rules" and to give "to whomever is appropriate information, commands, and . . . aid." Anyone who helped conceal such

women faced punishment as a "harborer" and escaped punishment only if a woman's charges against a husband's "cruel acts" were proved.

27. Ibid., ll. 195–203 ob.; *PSZ*, 2nd ser., vol. 1, no. 715 (1 Dec. 1826), 1264–65.

28. Azamatov, *Orenburgskoe magometanskoe dukhovnoe sobranie*, 125–126.

29. In 1835 the regime applied the minimum marrying age to Muslims as well as Catholics and Armenian Gregorians (*PSZ*, 2nd ser., vol. 10, nos. 7, 989 and 7,990 [22 Mar. 1835], 266); imams were to marry only those raised in their parish, utilize tax and parish registers to confirm that the parties had reached the required age, and verify that candidates were eligible according to the shari'a. On questioning by the imam, *STsOMDS*, 5–6.

30. *STsOMDS*, 5–6; on the issue of parity of birth, see Y. Linant De Bellefonds, "Kafā'a," *Encyclopaedia of Islam*, 4:404.

31. *STsOMDS*, 6–7. As in Orthodox parishes, soldiers' wives created complications. Suleimanov instructed imams to authenticate their divorce papers by comparing them with the register.

32. *PSZ*, 2nd ser., vol. 3, no. 2296 (21 Sept. 1828), 837–840; Freeze, "Bringing Order," 716–719; in 1832, the Ministry of Internal Affairs introduced registers to parishes under the Muslim administration in the Crimea, noting that it had received no reports of difficulties arising from this measure under the Orenburg Assembly (*PSZ*, 2nd ser., vol. 7, no. 5,770 [24 Nov. 1832], 859–860).

33. GAOO, f. 6, op. 4, d. 9184, ll. 1–4; *PSZ*, no. 2296, 838–839.

34. Azamatov, *Orenburgskoe magometanskoe dukhovnoe sobranie*, 128. In 1850 the Assembly intervened when a man wished to take a fifth wife. Ibid., 132, and Asfandiarov, *Bashkirskaia sem'ia*, 56–61.

35. *PSZ*, 2nd ser., vol. 5, no. 3559 (27 Mar. 1830), 236–237. The Senate left open the possibility that cases could be heard in "the appropriate judicial seats" when clerics failed to resolve them. In 1834 the State Council separated acts of disobedience in which other crimes were committed (to be taken up by civil authorities) from

those involving "moral disobedience to parents, as in marriages, verbal insult, and the like," which remained the jurisdiction of Muslim clerics. Ibid., vol. 9, no. 7,510 (30 Oct. 1834), 111–112, and vol. 10, no. 8,436 (30 Sept. 1835), 991–992.

36. Similarly, in 1846 the State Council allowed a dissatisfied party in a property dispute resulting from Muslim divorce to turn to civil courts, though it did not specify which laws were to be applied there. Ibid., vol. 8, no. 6591 (27 Nov. 1833), 697–698, and vol. 21, no. 19,582 (3 Jan. 1846), 13.

37. *MIBASSR*, 5:566.

38. *PSZ*, 2nd ser., vol. 7, no. 5500 (14 July 1832), 498–505.

39. As examples of such corrective punishment, he cited a Kazan criminal court that sentenced a Muslim found guilty of the offense to two weeks in a reformatory and the Orenburg mufti Khusainov's proposal that such offenders be sent to a work home. Ibid., 501 and 503.

40. Ibid., 502.

41. Ibid.

42. Azamatov, *Orenburgskoe magometanskoe dukhovnoe sobranie*, 139; *PSZ*, 2nd ser., vol. 12, no. 10,313 (8 June 1837), 526; ibid., vol. 20, no. 19,283 (15 Aug. 1845); article 2077 of the *Ulozhenie o nakazaniiakh ugolovnykh i ispravitel'nykh*, 971–972, which was reaffirmed in article 1211 of volume 11 of the *Svod zakonov Rossiiskoi Imperii* (1857).

43. P. A. Shino [Pashino], "Volzhskie tatary," *Sovremennik* 81 (1860): 281. See also M. Kazem-Bek, *Izbrannye proizvedeniia* (Baku: "Elm," 1985), 293–294; and Agnès Kefeli, "The Role of Tatar and Kriashen Women in the Transmission of Islamic Knowledge, 1800–1870," in *Of Religion and Empire: Missions, Conversion, and Tolerance in Tsarist Russia*, ed. Robert P. Geraci and Michael Khodarkovsky (Ithaca: Cornell University Press, 2001), 250–273.

44. The original correspondence of the mufti in Tatar and Persian is in Riḍā'addīn Fakhraddīn ōghlī, *Āthār*, vol. 4 (Orenburg: Karimova, 1903), 190–191. The document refers to the official by his first name and patronymic, Nikolai Fedorovich.

45. For example, Ronald C. Jennings, "Women in Early 17th Century Ottoman Judicial Records—The Sharia Court of Anatolian Kayseri," *Journal of the Economic and Social History of the Orient* 18 (1975): 53–114; and Leslie Peirce, *Morality Tales: Law and Gender in the Ottoman Court of Aintab* (Berkeley: University of California Press, 2003).

46. TsGIARB, f.I-295, op. 2, d. 173, l. 93 ob.; Fakhraddīn ōghlī, *Āthār*, 4:190–191; Azamatov, *Orenburgskoe magometanskoe dukhovnoe sobranie*, 143; on appeals to the mufti by women on the frontier, see, for example, TsGIARB, f. I-295, op. 2, d. 122, ll. 258–258 ob. and 166.

47. Azamatov, *Orenburgskoe magometanskoe dukhovnoe sobranie*, 130; TsGIARB, f. I-295, op. 3, d. 10, and op. 2, d. 173, l. 28 ob.

48. Though the Assembly ordered mullahs to mediate disputes arising from "insults" between spouses, it rejected petitions concerning "insult by words." Declining a woman's request in 1888, the Assembly ruled that "complaints about personal insults by persons of the Muhammadan confession do not concern investigation by their ecclesiastical authorities but belong to secular courts." It cited articles 224 and 225 of volume 10 of the *Digest of Laws*. TsGIARB, f. I-295, op. 2, d. 173, l. 831 ob., and op. 3, d. 1096, ll. 29–29 ob.

49. Ibid., d. 1749, ll. 1–1 ob.

50. Ibid., ll. 5, 9–11 ob.

51. Ibid., op. 2, d. 43, l. 492, 492 ob. Suleimanov issued the same instructions regarding a similar complaint against a husband from the town of Kazan (ibid., ll. 331–331 ob.).

52. It counted 11,596 marriages and 1,766 divorces in Orenburg Province; 6,311 marriages and 916 divorces in Kazan Province; 1,093 marriages and 67 divorces in Simbirsk Province; 3,341 marriages and 297 divorces in Samara Province; 921 marriages and 121 divorces in Viatka Province; and 682 divorces and 26 marriages in Saratov Province. In 1858 the Assembly recorded 25,975 marriages and 3,193 divorces (123 divorces per 1,000 marriages) (RGIA, f. 821, op. 8, d. 1095). Divorce rates among Jews averaged 145.2 per 1,000

marriages in 1860, while the Orthodox divorce rate (from 1858) was 0.1 per 1,000 marriages (Freeze, *Jewish Marriage*, 153).

53. A. Z. Asfandiiarov presents similar numbers for 1867, 1868, and 1876. *Sem'ia i brak u bashkir v XVIII–pervoi polovine XIX v.* (Ufa: Bashkirskii universitet, 1989), 73, and *Bashkirskaia sem'ia*, 72.

54. TsGIARB, f. I-295, op. 3, d. 3583, ll. 1–5.

55. The Assembly issued its ruling in 1888 and instructed the police to notify Temirneeva. Ibid., op. 2, d. 173, l. 111.

56. Ibid., d. 43, ll. 1215 ob.–1217, and d. 175, n.p. (journal entry of 25 Sept. 1889).

57. In August 1890 the Assembly sent instructions to the akhunds in the Inner Kazakh Horde repeating this prohibition, pointing out that valis who arranged such marriages would be punished in accordance with article 1563 of the 1885 edition of the penal code. It added that this "old habit" gave rise to conflicts, especially when a girl "is given away still in childhood to one [husband], and then marries another." *STsOMDS*, 39.

58. Azamatov, *Orenburgskoe magometanskoe dukhovnoe sobranie*, 131–132; TsGIARB, f. I-295, op. 2, d. 43, ll. 364 ob.–365, and d. 173, ll. 68–69.

59. TsGIARB, f. I-295, op. 2, d. 173, ll. 72 ob.–73. In 1903, Bashkir parents complained to the district court of Elabuga as well as to the Assembly about their twenty-year-old daughter, who had married a man from another village without their permission. They requested that the newlyweds both be punished. When the imam failed to reconcile parents and daughter, the Assembly ruled against the parents, citing Suleimanov's rules of 1841. The shari'a, it concluded, regarded a daughter's request for consent from her parents less as a legal requirement than "an act of decency and respect to them." Lacking other evidence to regard the marriage illegal, "for example, inequality in social position, [or] important corporal or mental insufficiency," the Assembly declined their request. *STsOMDS*, 202–204.

60. TsGIARB, f. I-295, op. 2, d. 173, ll. 587–588 ob. In another case, vil-

lagers in Astrakhan Province notified their imam that the wife of one of their neighbors could be found in the home of another man. The imam and six witnesses then entered the house and found the couple in the act of "indecent conduct." See the Assembly's journal for 13 Nov. 1889 in ibid., d. 175, n.p.

61. Ibid., d. 43, ll. 755–756 ob., and op. 3, d. 3510, ll. 23–24.

62. RGIA, f. 821, op. 8, d. 615, ll. 45–49 ob.; TsGIARB, f. I-295, op. 2, d. 122, l. 353. An akhund in the district of Ufa also reported to the Assembly in the same year about an imam who had accused a man of raping his daughter-in-law. In this case, an imam from a neighboring village was asked to investigate. See TsGIARB, f. I-295, op. 2, d. 122, ll. 245 and ob.

63. TsGIARB, f. I-295, op. 2, d. 122, ll. 59 ob.–60. Mufti Salimgarei Tevkelev referred this case to civil authorities, asserting that such an accusation did not fall under his jurisdiction.

64. Perevodchik / Tercüman, 5 Nov. 1889.

65. Michael R. Anderson, "Legal Scholarship and the Politics of Islam in British India," in Perspectives on Islamic Law, Justice, and Society, ed. R. S. Khare (Lanham, Md.: Rowman and Littlefield, 1999), 65–91.

66. E. A. Rezvan, "Koran v Rossii," ITBRI, 1:47–58; on Russia's investment in Oriental studies, see Robert Geraci, Window on the East: National and Imperial Identities in Late Tsarist Russia (Ithaca: Cornell University Press, 2001), esp. 158–194, and A. M. Kulikova, Vostokovedenie v Rossiiskikh zakonodatel'nykh aktakh (konets XVII v.–1917 g.) (St. Petersburg: Tsentr "Peterburgskoe Vostokovedenie," 1993). For an example of such texts, see N. Kolmogorov, "Ob osnovnykh postanovleniiakh islama," in Uchenye zapiski, izdavaemye Imperatorskim Kazanskim Universitetom, book 1 (Kazan: V Tipografii Imperatorskogo Kaz. Universiteta, 1848), 103–143.

67. "On the Appearance and Successes of Oriental Literature in Europe and Its Decline in Asia," in M. Kazem-Bek, Izbrannye proizvedeniia, 351 and 353. See, too, David Skhimmel'pennink van

der Oie [Schimmelpenninck van der Oye], "Mirza Kazem-Bek i Kazanskaia shkola vostokovedeniia," in *Novaia imperskaia istoriia postsovetskogo prostranstva*, ed. I. Gerasimov, S. Glebov, et al. (Kazan: Tsentr Issledovaniia Natsionalizma i Imperii, 2004), 243–270.

68. *Izlozhenie nachal musul'manskoe zakonovedenia* (St. Petersburg: V Tipografii II Otdeleniia Sobstvennoi E. I. V. Kantseliarii, 1850), iii–iv, viii; Tornau cited these local scholars in xi–xii.

69. Quoted in A. K. Rzaev, *Mukhammed Ali M. Kazem-Bek* (Moscow: "Nauka," 1989), 179. See also "Zapiska 'Ob ustroistve sudebnogo byta musul'man' (1863–1864 gg.) (Publikatsiia V. O. Bobrovnikova)," *Sbornik Russkogo istoricheskogo obshchestva* 155, no. 7, (Moscow: Russkaia panorama, 2003), 108–140.

70. See the introduction to the *Miukhteserul'-Vikaiet, ili sokrashchennyi vikaet: Kurs musul'manskogo zakonovedeniia* in Kazem-Bek, *Izbrannye proizvedeniia*, 244 and 294.

71. Cited in Rzaev, *Mukhammed Ali M. Kazem-Bek*, 184–185.

72. See the introduction to Kazem-Bek's *Sheraiul'-Islam, ili zakony musul'man shiitskogo veroispovedaniia: O nasledstve* of 1867 in his *Izbrannye proizvedeniia*, 299–300; Anderson, "Legal Scholarship," 74; see also Muhammad Qasim Zaman, *The Ulama in Contemporary Islam: Guardians of Change* (Princeton: Princeton University Press, 2002), 17–31.

73. Tornau cited with approval a German scholar who declared, "All of the Muslim empires are nothing but fractions of one and the same society, subject to the same law, to the same administrative and political code *(code administratif et politique)* and where everything is identical and common, down to the least important customs." *Izlozhenie nachal*, IX–X.

74. RGIA, f. 821, op. 8, d. 951, ll. 36–37 ob.

75. Ibid., ll. 30–30 ob.

76. Ibid., ll. 38 ob.–39.

77. The governor's records referred to Islamic commentaries: the *Kazy-Khan* confirmed that "a woman who has a husband is not

permitted to marry another one," and a citation from *Ali Efendi* seemed to support the kadi's ruling by calling for the divorce of the second husband (RGIA, f. 821, op. 8, d. 969, ll. 5 ob.–6). Used in the Ottoman empire and India, the *Kazy-Khan* was a collection of the legal opinions of a twelfth-century jurist. The *Ali Efendi* was a collection of legal opinions by a seventeenth-century Ottoman şeyhülislam. Th. W. Juynboll [Y. Linant De Bellefonds], "Kadi Khan," *Encyclopaedia of Islam*, 4:377; Ismail Hakkı Uzunçarşılı, *Osmanlı Devletinin Ilmiye Teşkilatı* (Ankara: Türk Tarih Kurumu Basımevi, 1965), 197; and Mehmet İpşirli, "Çatalcalı Ali Efendi," *Türkiye Diyanet Vakfı Islâm Ansiklopedisi* (Istanbul, 1993), 8:234–235.

78. RGIA, f. 821, op. 8, d. 969, ll. 3–3 ob. Emphasis in the original.

79. Kendzhe-khan was entitled, in Kazem-Bek's view, to maintenance *(nafaqa)* for the time of her first husband's absence (RGIA, f. 821, op. 8, d. 969, ll. 9–9 ob.); on Russian reformers' views of marriage, see Wagner, *Marriage, Property and Law*, chap. 3; and on British approaches, see Anderson, "Legal Scholarship," 74.

80. RGIA, f. 821, op. 8, d. 964, ll. 1, 4 ob.–9.

81. Ibid., ll. 11–11 ob.

82. Ibid., ll. 18 ob.–19. The sura reads in part, "Those who defame chaste women and do not bring four witnesses should be punished with eighty lashes, and their testimony should not be accepted afterward, for they are profligates" *(Al-Qur'ān*, 24:4).

83. See Geraci, *Window on the East.*

84. Danil' D. Azamatov, "The Muftis of the Orenburg Spiritual Assembly in the 18th and 19th Centuries: The Struggle for Power in Russia's Muslim Institution," in *Muslim Culture in Russia and Central Asia*, vol. 2, ed. Anke von Kügelgen, Michael Kemper, and Allen J. Frank (Berlin: Klaus Schwarz Verlag, 1998), 372–379.

4. Nomads into Muslims

1. After his trip to the steppe in 1769, Peter Simon Pallas declared, "Kazakhs are of the Muhammadan religion, which according to

them they already brought with them from Turkestan." For Pallas, polygamy and the payment of bride-price were the key markers of this identity. He noted that although Kazakhs were "enthusiastic enough in their belief," they remained "extremely inexperienced, because they have very few Muhammadan clergymen among themselves." Nonetheless, because the Kazakhs abstained from eating certain kinds of animals, Pallas concluded that the entire horde, not solely the khan around whom the "clergymen" concentrated, observed "the Muhammadan law quite precisely in their way of life." *Reise durch verschiedene Provinzen des Russischen Reiches*, vol. 1 (repr.; Graz: Akademische Druck- u. Verlagsanstalt, 1967), 392–393.

2. Richard Pierce, *Russian Central Asia, 1867–1917: A Study in Colonial Rule* (Berkeley: University of California Press, 1960), 9; Virginia Martin, *Law and Custom in the Steppe: The Kazakhs of the Middle Horde and Russian Colonialism in the Nineteenth Century* (Richmond, Surrey: Curzon, 2001).

3. See V. O. Bobrovnikov, *Musul'mane Severnogo Kavkaza: Obychai, pravo, nasilie* (Moscow: Vostochnaia literatura, 2002), esp. 142–175.

4. On these broader issues, see Daniel Brower, *Turkestan and the Fate of the Russian Empire* (London: Routledge Curzon, 2003).

5. Selim Deringil, *The Well-Protected Domains: Ideology and the Legitimation of Power in the Ottoman Empire, 1876–1909* (London: Tauris, 1998), 44–67, citation at 51; idem, "'They Live in a State of Nomadism and Savagery': The Late Ottoman Empire and the Post-Colonial Debate," *Comparative Studies in Society and History* 45, no. 2 (Apr. 2003): 311–342; Resat Kasaba, "L'Empire ottoman, ses nomades et ses frontiers aux XVIIIe et XIXe siècles," *Critique internationale*, no. 12 (July 2001): 111–127; and Ashraf Ghani, "Islam and State-Building in a Tribal Society: Afghanistan, 1880–1901," *Modern Asian Studies* 12, pt. 2 (1978): 269–284.

6. In some tribal societies, the maintenance of group boundaries proved as important as arguments about the correct interpretation of the Islamic tradition in shaping perceptions of hetero-

doxy. For example, Richard Tapper, "Holier Than Thou: Islam in Three Tribal Societies," in *Islam in Tribal Societies: From the Atlas to the Indus*, ed. Akbar S. Ahmed and David M. Hart (London: Routledge and Kegan Paul, 1984), 244–265. For analysis and critique of the oft-repeated claim that Kazakhs are "superficial" Muslims, see Bruce G. Privratsky, *Muslim Turkistan: Kazak Religion and Collective Memory* (Richmond, Surrey: Curzon, 2001); and Allen J. Frank, *Muslim Religious Institutions in Imperial Russia: The Islamic World of Novouzensk District and the Kazakh Inner Horde, 1780–1910* (Leiden: Brill, 2001), 274–313.

7. Patricia M. E. Lorcin, *Imperial Identities: Stereotyping, Prejudice and Race in Colonial Algeria* (London: Tauris, 1995); and David Gilmartin, "Customary Law and *Sharī'at* in British Punjab," in *Sharī'at and Ambiguity in South Asian Islam*, ed. Katherine P. Ewing (Berkeley: University of California Press, 1988), 43–62.

8. Allen Frank, "Islamic Transformation on the Kazakh Steppe, 1742–1917: Toward an Islamic History of Kazakhstan under Russian Rule," in *The Construction and Deconstruction of National Histories in Slavic Eurasia*, ed. Tadayuki Hayashi (Sapporo: Slavic Research Center, 2003), 261–289. See also Allen J. Frank and Mirkasyim A. Usmanov, eds., *An Islamic Biographical Dictionary of the Eastern Kazakh Steppe, 1770–1912: Qurbān-'Alī Khālidī* (Brill: Leiden, 2005).

9. Gul'mira Sultangalieva, "'Tatarskaia' diaspora v konfessional'nykh sviaziiakh kazakhskhoi stepi (XVIII–XIX vv.)," *Vestnik Evrazii*, no. 4 (2000): 20–36. On eighteenth-century imperial policies generally, see Michael Khodarkovsky, *Russia's Steppe Frontier: The Making of a Colonial Empire, 1500–1800* (Bloomington: Indiana University Press, 2002); Dov B. Yaroshevskii, "Imperial Strategy in the Kirghiz Steppe in the Eighteenth Century," *Jahrbücher für Geschichte Osteuropas* 39, no. 2 (1991): 221–224; and Dov B. Yaroshevskii, "Attitudes toward the Nomads of the Russian Empire under Catherine the Great," in *Literature, Lives, and Legality in*

Catherine's Russia, ed. A. G. Cross and G. S. Smith (Nottingham: Astra Press, 1994), 15–24.

10. Quoted in A. Dobrosmyslov, "Zaboty imperatritsy Ekateriny II o prosveshchenii kirgizov," in *Trudy Orenburgskoi uchenoi arkhivnoi kommissi*, vol. 11 (Orenburg: Gubernskaia tipografiia, 1902), 51.

11. Governor Osip Igel'strom recruited the future mufti Khusainov for 150 rubles a year to persuade Kazakhs to accept Islam and become Russian subjects. "Arkhiv Grafa Igel'stroma," *Russkii arkhiv*, book 3 (1886): 346. From the late 1780s through at least the first quarter of the nineteenth century, the Orenburg Frontier Commission made salaried appointments to mosques and schools "founded for the instruction of Kazakh children" in borderland settlements. See TsGIARB, f. I-295, op. 4, d. 498, ll. 18–20. On 'ulama in the steppe, see Shihabetdin Märjani, *Möstäfadel-äkhbar fi äkhvali Kazan vä Bolgar (Kazan häm Bolgar khälläre turïnda faydalanïlgan khäbärlär)*, ed. Ä. N. Khäyrullin (Kazan: Tatar. Kit. Näshr., 1989); Sultangalieva, "'Tatarskaia' diaspora"; Allen Frank, "Tatarskie mully sredi kazakhov i kirgizov v XVII–XIX vekakh," *Kul'tura, iskusstvo tatarskogo naroda: Istoki, traditsii, vzaimosviazi* (Kazan: Institut iazyka, literatury i istorii im G. Ibragimova, 1993), 124–128; and Frank, *Muslim Religious Institutions*, 275.

12. "Arkhiv Grafa Igel'stroma," 348, 349, 353; and Dobrosmyslov, "Zaboty imperatritsy Ekateriny II," 54–55.

13. The government also sent Muslim subjects from the Orenburg territory across the steppe to the khanates of Central Asia on diplomatic missions to negotiate trade and gather intelligence. See V. N. Shkunov, "Missii poruchika Abdulnasyra Subkhankulova v Bukharu i Khivu v 1810 i 1818 gg.," *Vostok*, no. 4 (1997): 17–23.

14. Sultangalieva, "'Tatarskaia' diaspora," 28–29; *Kazakhsko-russkie otnosheniia v XVIII–XIX vekakh (1771–1867 godu): Sbornik dokumentov i materialov* (Alma-Ata: Izdatel'stvo "Nauka", 1964), 199, 203–207, 212; and Märjani, *Möstäfadel-äkhbar.*

15. B. T. Zhanaev, V. A. Inochkin, and S. Kh. Sagnaeva, eds., *Istoriia*

Bukeeskogo khanstva. 1801–1852 gg.: Sbornik dokumentov i materialov (Almaty: "Daik-Press," 2002), 170–171; A. Evreinov, "Vnutrennaia ili Bukeevskaia Kirgiz-Kazach'ia Orda," *Sovremennik* (Oct. 1851): 73.

16. Contemporaries apparently attributed Dzhangir's propagation of sedentarization and the establishment of a permanent administrative seat *(stavka)* to the influence of his wife, Fatima. See S. Z. Zimanov, *Rossiia i Bukeevskoe khanstvo* (Alma-Ata: Izdatel'stvo "Nauka" Kazakhskoi SSR, 1982), 47. However, Allen Frank cites a Turkic manuscript that refers to "some semblance of a Tatar religious establishment" that had already been established under Dzhangir's father, Bukei. On some of the figures surrounding Dzhangir, see Frank's "Islam and Ethnic Relations in the Kazakh Inner Horde," in *Muslim Culture in Russia and Central Asia*, vol. 2, ed. Anke von Kügelgen, Michael Kemper, and Allen J. Frank (Berlin: Klaus Schwarz Verlag, 1998), 232–233.

17. Evreinov, "Vnutrennaia . . . Orda," 72.

18. Zhanaev et al., *Istoriia Bukeeskogo khanstva*, 242–244, 363, 398–399.

19. Ibid., 390, 403, 413–414, 431–437, 576.

20. Evreinov, "Vnutrennaia . . . Orda," 71.

21. On the emergence of these schemes as part of a distinct secular discipline in Europe, see Eric J. Sharpe, *Comparative Religion: A History* (London: Duckworth, 1975); and in Russia, see Yuri Slezkine, *Arctic Mirrors: Russia and the Small Peoples of the North* (Ithaca: Cornell University Press, 1994), 11–92; Yuri Slezkine, "Naturalists versus Nations: Eighteenth-Century Russian Scholars Confront Ethnic Diversity," in *Russia's Orient: Imperial Borderlands and Peoples, 1700–1917*, ed. Daniel R. Brower and Edward J. Lazzerini (Bloomington: Indiana University Press, 1997), 27–57; and T. V. Artem'eva, *Istoriia metafiziki v Rossii XVIII veka* (St. Petersburg: Izdatel'stvo "Aleteiia," 1996), esp. 289–292.

22. See Paul W. Werth, *At the Margins of Orthodoxy: Mission, Gover-

nance, and Confessional Politics in Russia's Volga-Kama Region, 1827–1905 (Ithaca: Cornell University Press, 2002).

23. Pis'ma Nikolaia Ivanovicha Il'minskogo (Kazan: Tipo-Litografiia Imperatorskogo Universiteta, 1895), esp. 65–66; and V. I. Ovsiannikov, Vostok v obshchestvenno-politicheskoi mysli Rossii (seredina XIX v.) (Moscow: Institut nauchnoi informatsii po obshchestvennym naukam Akademii nauk SSSR, 1990).

24. See, for example, Statisticheskoe opisanie Zakavkazskogo kraia (St. Petersburg: Tipografiia Shtaba Otdel'nogo Korpusa Vnutrennei Strazhi, 1835).

25. The work also earned international acclaim. It appeared in French in 1840 as Description des hordes et des steppes des Kirgiz-Kazakhs ou Kirgiz-Kaïssaks. Aleksei Levshin, Opisanie kirgiz-kazach'ikh, ili kirgiz kaisatskikh ord i stepei (St. Petersburg: V Tipografii Karla Kraiia, 1832), pt. 3, 52–53.

26. Pallas, Reise durch verschiedene Provinzen, 393–395.

27. Levshin, Opisanie kirgiz-kazach'ikh, 54–55.

28. "Zametki kirgiza o kirgizakh," Severnaia pchela, 5 Jan. 1861. Babadzhanov held mixed opinions of the mediating role assumed by Tatars. He shared the stereotypes disseminated in the Russian press about their "cunning" and "predatory" nature. Like Kazakh Muslim activists of the late nineteenth and early twentieth centuries, he insisted on an Islamic religious style among the Kazakhs that remained distinct from Tatar influence.

29. N. I. Veselovskii, Vasilii Vasil'evich Grigor'ev po ego pis'mam i trudam 1816–1881 (St. Petersburg: Tipografiia i Khromolitografiia A. Transhelia, 1887). On Grigor'ev's role in the Geographical Society, see Nathaniel Knight, "Science, Empire, and Nationality: Ethnography in the Russian Geographical Society, 1845–1855," in Imperial Russia: New Histories for the Empire, ed. Jane Burbank and David L. Ransel (Bloomington: Indiana University Press, 1998), 108–141; and on his frustration at having his expert knowledge ignored by the administration, see Nathaniel Knight, "Grigor'ev in

Orenburg, 1851–1862: Russian Orientalism in the Service of Empire?" *Slavic Review* 59, no. 1 (Spring 2000): 74–100.

30. Veselovskii, *Vasilii Vasil'evich Grigor'ev*, 124–125.

31. Ibid., 125.

32. Ch. Ch. Valikhanov, *Sobranie sochinenii v piati tomakh* (Alma-Ata: Glavnaia redaktsiia Kazakhskoi Sovetskoi Entsiklopedii, 1985), 5:178–179, 212.

33. "O musul'manstve v stepi," in ibid., 71. See also "Sledy shamanstva u kirgizov," in the same volume, 48–70.

34. See Jörg Baberowski, *Autokratie und Justiz: Zum Verhältnis von Rechtsstaatlichkeit und Rückständigkeit im ausgehenden Zarenreich 1864–1914* (Frankfurt am Main: Vittorio Klostermann, 1996).

35. Similarly, an 1803 law declared that tribute payers should be left "to their own laws and customs, according to which they will settle all of their minor affairs, without bringing suit against them [and subjecting them to] the red tape of court procedure." Quoted in M. M. Fedorov, *Pravovoe polozhenie narodov vostochnoi Sibiri (XVII–nachalo XIX veka)* (Iakutsk: Iakutskoe knizhnoe izdatel'stvo, 1978), 145–146. See also Slezkine, *Arctic Mirrors*.

36. See Rosane Rocher, "British Orientalism in the Eighteenth Century: The Dialectics of Knowledge and Government," in *Orientalism and the Post-Colonial Predicament: Perspectives on South Asia*, ed. Carol A. Breckenridge and Peter van der Veer (Philadelphia: University of Pennsylvania Press, 1993), 215–249; Michael R. Anderson, "Islamic Law and the Colonial Encounter in British India," *Institutions and Ideologies: A SOAS South Asia Reader*, ed. David Arnold and Peter Robb (Richmond, Surrey: Curzon Press, 1993), 165–185.

37. See Fedorov, *Pravovoe polozhenie*, 146–149.

38. This paragraph relies on the summary of the statute in Fedorov, *Pravovoe polozhenie*.

39. Valikhanov, *Sobranie sochinenii*, 4:78–79.

40. Ibid., 79.

41. Ibid., 80.

42. Ibid., 84–85.

43. Ibid., 80–82, 89–90, 90–91.

44. Ibid., 91, 92–96.

45. Ibid., 99.

46. Ibid., 99–100. Here Valikhanov wondered "whether there are such greedy extortioners anywhere on the earth like our Russian Muslim clergy," adding that the mufti in Orenburg also demanded bribes. Ibid., 100–101.

47. Ibid., 102.

48. Ibid., 103.

49. Valikhanov, *Sobranie sochinenii*, 5:121–130.

50. Ibid., 125, 127, 129. The document submitted by the sultans and biys of Kokchetav did not explicitly address the jurisdictional conflict between biys and mullahs in the mediation of disputes concerning marriage and divorce. See ibid., 121–123.

51. N. I. Grodekov, *Kirgizy i karakirgizy Syr-Dar'inskoi oblasti*, vol. 1 (Tashkent: Tipo-Litografiia S. I. Lakhtina, 1889), 13–16.

52. The relevant articles of the 1868 statute are reproduced in A. I. Dobrosmyslov, *Sud u kirgiz Turgaiskoi oblasti v XVIII i XIX vekakh* (Kazan: Tipo-Litografiia Imperatorskogo Kazanskogo Universiteta, 1904), 79.

53. See W. Radloff, *Die Sprachen der türkischen Stämme Süd-Sibiriens und der dsungarischen Steppe, III. Theil: Kirgisische Mundarten* (St. Petersburg: Kaiserliche Akademie der Wissenschaften, 1870). Radloff "rewrote" many of these texts with the aim of eliminating "non-Kazakh grammatical forms" and replacing "Arabic and Persian intruders." Ibid., xix.

54. Grodekov, *Kirgizy i karakirgizy*, 22–24, 215–216. For Muslim sources on Islamicization, see Aširbek K. Muminov, "Die Erzählung eines Qo as über die Islamisierung der Länder, die dem Kokander Khanat unterstehen," in *Muslim Culture in Russia and Central Asia*, vol. 3, ed. Anke von Kügelgen, Aširbek Muminov, and Michael Kemper (Berlin: Klaus Schwarz Verlag, 2000); and Allen J.

Frank, "A Chronicle of Islamic Communities on the Imperial Russian Frontier: The *Tavārīkh-i Ālṭī Āṭā* of Muhammad Fātih al-Īlmīnī," in Kügelgen, Muminov, and Kemper, *Muslim Culture in Russia and Central Asia*, vol. 3; and Frank, *Muslim Religious Institutions*.

55. See Werth, *At the Margins*.

56. The official press accused Tatar merchants and settlers of corrupting Kazakhs. In language resembling contemporary characterizations of Jews as swindlers of credulous Orthodox peasants, the press pointed to the predatory role of Tatars in peddling hashish and opium in the steppe (U. Subkhanberdina, ed., *"Kirgizskaia stepnaia gazeta": Chelovek, obshchestvo, priroda 1888–1902* [Almaty: "Gylym," 1994], 739–741); Sh. Ibragimov, "O mullakh v kirgizskoi stepi," in *Materialy dlia statistiki Turkestanskogo kraia*, ed. N. A. Maev (St. Petersburg: Tipografiia K. V. Trubnikova, 1874), 353.

57. Valikhanov, *Sobranie sochinenii*, 5:329–330; RGIA, f. 821, op. 8, d. 594, l. 31 ob.; Wilhelm Radloff, *Aus Sibirien: Lose Blätter aus dem Tagebuche eines reisenden Linguisten* (Leipzig: T. O. Weigel, 1884), 472. Muslim sources also identified the village as a center of Sufi activity that drew heterogeneous followers to its schools and lodges. See Babadzhanov, "Zametki kirgiza," 14–15; Frank, "Islam and Ethnic Relations," 240; and Petr Pozdnev, *Dervishi v musul'manskom mire* (Orenburg: Tipografiia B. Breslina, 1886), 76, 321–322.

58. *Turkestanskie vedomosti*, 15 Jan. 1880, cited in Pozdnev, *Dervishi v musul'manskom mire*, 324.

59. The law prohibiting the Orenburg Assembly from taking on cases involving Kazakhs appeared again in the "steppe statute" of 1891 (articles 97–98). Muslims nonetheless continued to challenge it, as in cases from 1880 (resulting in the repeat of a ban on ties between Ufa and Muslims in the governor-generalship of Turkestan) and 1892 (from Ural'sk). See *STsOMDS*, 16, 60–61.

60. RGIA, f. 821, op. 8, d. 602, ll. 6–6 ob. Notwithstanding Perovskii's

instructions, the Orenburg mufti remained engaged in Kazakh affairs and continued to direct the mediation of marital disputes according to Islamic law, as in a case brought by a Kazakh woman
against her husband in the town of Troitsk in 1854. See TsGIARB,
f. I-295, op. 3, d. 3583.

61. RGIA, f. 821, op. 8, d. 608, l. 1.

62. *Pis'ma Nikolaia Ivanovicha Il'minskogo*, 63–64.

63. Robert P. Geraci, "Going Abroad or Going to Russia? Orthodox
Missionaries in the Kazakh Steppe, 1881–1917," in *Of Religion and
Empire: Missions, Conversion, and Tolerance in Tsarist Russia*, ed.
Robert P. Geraci and Michael Khodarkovsky (Ithaca: Cornell Uni-
versity Press, 2001), 274–310, citations at 297–303.

64. Ibragimov, "O mullakh v kirgizskoi stepi," 356, 357–358. See also
Virginia Martin, "Kazakh Oath-Taking in Colonial Courtrooms:
Legal Culture and Russian Empire-Building," *Kritika* 5, no. 3
(Summer 2004): 483–514.

65. In the 1860s the Kazakh Steppe Commission explored the possibility of spreading Christianity among the nomads. Christianization
became an acknowledged goal of steppe policy, though one projected into some uncertain date in the future. The commission permitted only evangelization pursued "without inciting discontent
and unrest thereby." Moreover, the commission questioned the
Church policy of removing new converts from unbaptized Kazakh
communities. They suggested that the continued presence of individual Christians among Kazakhs would encourage others to convert as well. In 1869 the Holy Synod approved the commission's
proposal to allow mixed marriages between baptized and unbaptized spouses to remain in effect (RGIA, f. 821, op. 8, d. 602, ll. 15–
15 ob.). On contemporary attempts to establish official Islamic
bodies in the Caucasus, see D. Iu. Arapov, "Imperskaia politika
v oblasti gosudarstvennogo regulirovaniia islama na Severnom
Kavkaze v XIX–nachale XX vv.," in *Islam i pravo v Rossii: Materialy
nauchno-prakticheskogo seminara*, vol. 1, ed. I. L. Babich and L. T.

Solov'eva (Moscow: Izdatel'stvo Rossiiskogo universiteta druzhby narodov, 2004), 21–34.

66. RGIA, f. 821, op. 8, d. 602, ll. 40–40 ob.

67. Ibid., l. 42 ob.

68. Ibid., l. 43. The committee cited the work of officials in western Siberia who had taken up the "defense" of Kazakh women in 1875.

69. Ibid.

70. Ibid., l. 43 ob. These district chiefs also asked that the bride-price (kalym) be recorded there. Elders and township administrators were to preside over the arrangement of marriages in the *aul* of the bride in the presence of at least four witnesses (two from each party).

71. Ibid., l. 40 ob. The proposal noted that imperial courts might also annul marriages in cases where criminal offenses resulted in the exile of one of the spouses.

72. Ibid., ll. 77–77 ob.

73. Ibid., ll. 77 ob.–78.

74. Ibid., ll. 78–79.

75. Ibid., ll. 82 ob.–83; on the theme of colonization generally, see Willard Sunderland, *Taming the Wild Field: Colonization and Empire on the Russian Steppe* (Ithaca: Cornell University Press, 2004).

76. PSZ, 3rd ser., vol. 11, no. 7,574 (25 Mar. 1891), 142. Article 289 of the 1885 version of the criminal code assigned prison sentences ranging from four to eight months for mullahs who handled the mediation of marital and family conflicts in the Semireche, Urals, and Turgai regions. See Herman Koch, *Die Russische Gesetzgebung über den Islam bis zum Ausbruch des Weltkrieges* (Berlin: "Der Neue Orient," 1918), 118; for Kazakh criticism, see, for example, RGIA, f. 821, op. 10, d. 29, l. 7.

77. RGIA, f. 821, op. 8, d. 602, ll. 83–84.

78. Subkhanberdina, *Kirgizskaia stepnaia gazeta*, 104, 105. See also Tomohiko Uyama, "A Strategic Alliance between Kazakh Intellectuals and Russian Administrators: Imagined Communities in *Dala Walayatïnïng Gazetï* (1888–1902)," in *The Construction and De-*

construction of National Histories in Slavic Eurasia, ed. Tadayuki Hayashi (Sapporo: Slavic Research Center, 2003), 237–259.

79. N. Dingel'shtedt, "Zametki: Odno iz otzhivaiushchikh uchrezhdenii," *Zhurnal grazhdanskogo i ugolovnogo prava*, book 1 (1892): 2, 1–2.

80. Ibid., 3–4.

81. RGIA, f. 821, op. 8, d. 602, l. 103.

82. Ibid., ll. 103 ob.–104, 105.

83. Ibid., ll. 104–105 ob.

84. See, for example, Frank, "Islam and Ethnic Relations," 237–238.

5. Civilizing Turkestan

1. Muhammad Sālih Khwāja Tāshkendi, *Tārikh-i jadid-ayi Tāshkend*, IVAN RUz, 11073/II, a1/b1–3a/2b, available at zerrspiegel.orientphil .uni-halle.de/t386.html.

2. E. T. Smirnov, ed., *Sredniaia Aziia: Nauchno-literaturnyi sbornik statei po Srednei Azii* (Tashkent: Tipo-Litografiia torg. Doma "F. i G. Br. Kamenskie", 1896), 168–172.

3. Svat Soucek, *A History of Inner Asia* (Cambridge: Cambridge University Press, 2000), 204; Al'bert Kaganovich, "Nekotorye problemy tsarskoi kolonizatsii Turkestana," *Tsentral'naia Aziia*, no. 11 (1997), available at www.ca-c.org/journal/11–1997/st_13_kaganovich.shtml; *Otchet po revizii Turkestanskogo kraia, proizvedennoi po Vysochaishemu poveleniiu Senatorom Gofmeisterom Grafom K. K. Palenom: Oblastnoe upravlenie* (St. Petersburg: Senatskaia tipografiia, 1910), 38, 47.

4. See, for example, Douglas Northrop, "Subaltern Dialogues: Subversion and Resistance in Soviet Uzbek Family Law," *Slavic Review* 60, no. 1 (Spring 2001): 115–139.

5. An important exception is Daniel Brower, *Turkestan and the Fate of the Russian Empire* (London: Routledge Curzon, 2003).

6. See the valuable study by Adeeb Khalid, *The Politics of Muslim Cultural Reform: Jadidism in Central Asia* (Berkeley: University of California Press, 1998).

7. Khalid, *Politics of Muslim Cultural Reform*; Ingeborg Baldauf, "Jadidism in Central Asia within Reformism and Modernism in the Muslim World," *Die Welt des Islams* 41, no. 1 (2001): 72–88.

8. See Bakhtiyar Babadjanov et al., *Katalog Sufischer Handschriften aus der Bibliothek des Instituts für Orientalistik der Akademie der Wissenschaften, Republik Usbekistan* (Stuttgart: Franz Steiner Verlag, 2002); Martin Hartmann, "Das Buchwesen in Turkestan und die türkischen Drucke der Sammlung Hartmann," *Mitteilungen des Seminars für Orientalische Sprachen an der Königlichen Friedrich-Wilhelms-Universität zu Berlin* 7 (1904): 69–103; and Aftandil Ėrkinov, "The Perception of Works by Classical Authors in Eighteenth and Nineteenth Century Central Asia: The Example of the Khamsa of 'Ali Šīr Nawāī," in *Muslim Culture in Russia and Central Asia from the 18th to the Early 20th Centuries*, vol. 2, ed. Anke von Kügelgen, Michael Kemper, and Allen J. Frank (Berlin: Klaus Schwarz Verlag, 1998), 513–526.

9. *The Ulama in Contemporary Islam: Custodians of Change* (Princeton: Princeton University Press, 2002), 58; regarding the role that print might have played in reaffirming orthodoxy, in the late nineteenth century, for example, women gathered for ritual readings of a lithographed edition of tales from the life of the aunt of the Sufi Bahā' al-Dīn Naqshband, the *Kissa-ii* of Bibi Seshanba (see Annett Kremer [Annette Krämer], "Bibi Seshanba," *ITBRI*, 4:17).

10. See the pioneering work of Scott C. Levi, *The Indian Diaspora in Central Asia and Its Trade, 1550–1900* (Leiden: Brill, 2001); and idem, "The Farghana Valley at the Crossroads of World History: The Tyrant 'Alim Khan, 1798–1810," paper presented at the Fifth Annual Conference of the Central Eurasian Studies Society, Bloomington, Indiana, October 2004.

11. See Baxtiyor M. Babadžanov [Babadzhanov], "On the History of the Naqšbandīya Muġaddīdīya in Central Māwarā'annahr in the Late 18th and Early 19th Centuries," in *Muslim Culture in Russia and Central Asia*, vol. 1, ed. Michael Kemper, Anke von Kügelgen,

and Dmitriy Yermakov (Berlin: Klaus Schwarz Verlag, 1996), 385–413; idem, "Zikr *dzhakhr* i *sama*': Sakralizatsiia profannogo ili profanatsiia sakral'nogo," in *Podvizhniki islama: Kul't sviatykh i sufizm v Srednei Azii i na Kavkaze*, ed. S. N. Abashin and V. O. Bobrovnikov (Moscow: Vostochnaia literatura RAN, 2003), 237–250; and Anke von Kügelgen, "Die Entfaltung der Naqšbandīya Muğaddidīya im mittleren Transoxanien vom 18. bis zum Beginn des 19. Jahrhunderts: Ein Stück Detektivarbeit," in Kügelgen, Kemper, and Frank, *Muslim Culture in Russia and Central Asia*, 2:101–151.

12. Kügelgen, "Die Entfaltung"; and Babadzhanov, "History of the Naqšbandīya Muğaddīdīya."

13. Anke von Kügelgen, *Die Legitimierung der mittelasiatischen Mangitendynastie in den Werker ihrer Historiker (18.–19. Jahrhundert)* (Istanbul: Orient-Institut, 2002); V. Nalivkin, *Kratkaia istoriia Kokandskogo khanstva* (Kazan: Tipografiia Imperatorskogo Universiteta, 1886), 16; A. Mukhtarov, ed., *Materialy po istorii Ura-Tiube: Sbornik aktov XVII–XIX vv.* (Moscow: Izdatel'stvo Vostochnoi literatury, 1963), 62–63, 42, 52–53.

14. R. N. Nabiev, *Iz istorii Kokandskogo khanstva (feodal'noe khoziaistvo Khudoiar-khana)* (Tashkent: Izdatel'stvo "FAN" Uzbeksoi SSR, 1973), 222–223, 99–104, 223–225.

15. Nalivkin, *Kratkaia istoriia*, 133–135, 185–186; and R. N. Nabiev, *Tashkentskoe vosstanie 1847 g. i ego sotsial'no-ekonomicheskie predposylki* (Tashkent: Izdatel'stvo "FAN" Uzbekskoi SSR, 1960), 21.

16. Devin DeWeese, "The Politics of Sacred Lineages in 19th-Century Central Asia: Descent Groups Linked to Khwaja Ahmad Yasavi in Shrine Documents and Genealogical Charters," *International Journal of Middle East Studies* 31, no. 3 (Nov. 1999): 507–530. See also idem, "Khojagānī Origins and the Critique of Sufism: The Rhetoric of Communal Uniqueness in the *Manāqib* of Khoja 'Alī 'Azīzān Rāmītanī," in *Islamic Mysticism Contested: Thirteen*

Centuries of Controversies and Polemics, ed. Frederick De Jong and Bernd Radtke (Leiden: Brill, 1999), 492–519; and Babadzhanov, "History of the Naqšbandīya Muğaddīdīya."

17. A. L. Troitskaia, *Katalog arkhiva kokandskikh khanov XIX veka* (Moscow: Izdatel'stvo "Nauka," 1968), 66–72; A. K. Geins, *Sobranie literaturnykh trudov,* vol. 2 (St. Petersburg: Tip. M. M. Stasiulevicha, 1898), 463.

18. Beatrice Forbes Manz, "Central Asian Uprisings in the Nineteenth Century: Ferghana under the Russians," *Russian Review* 46, no. 3 (July 1987): 267–281.

19. Timur K. Beisembiev, ed. and trans., *The Life of 'Alimqul: A Native Chronicle of Nineteenth Century Central Asia* (London: Routledge Curzon, 2003), 33–34.

20. Geins, *Sobranie literaturnykh trudov,* 494; *Istoriia Kokanda (s momenta prisoedineniia Srednei Azii k Rossii do nastoiashchego vremeni)* (Tashkent: Izdatel'stvo "FAN" Uzbekskoi SSR, 1984), 25; V. Galitskii and V. Ploskikh, *Starinnyi Osh: Ocherk istorii* (Frunze: "Ilim," 1987), 80–81; V. L. Ogudin and S. N. Abashin, "Takht-i Sulaiman," *ITBRI,* 4:76–79.

21. Pashino, *Turkestanskii krai v 1866 godu,* 165–166, 169.

22. Geins, *Sobranie literaturnykh trudov,* 2:493; P. P. Litvinov, *Gosudarstvo i islam v Russkom Turkestane (1865–1917) (po arkhivnym materialam)* (Elets: EGPI, 1998), 53.

23. D. I. Romanovskii, *Zametki po Sredne-Aziiatskomu voprosu* (St. Petersburg: V Tipografii Vtorogo Otdeleniia Sobstvennoi E. I. V. Kantseliarii, 1868), 268–269.

24. Mirza 'Abdal 'Azim Sami, *Ta'rikh-i salatin-i mangitiia (Istoriia Mangitskikh gosudarei),* ed. and trans. A. M. Epifanova (Moscow: Izdatel'stvo vostochnoi literatury, 1962), 78; F. F. Pospelov, "Materialy k istorii Samarkandskoi oblasti," in *Spravochnaia knizhka Samarkandskoi oblasti,* vol. 10 (Samarkand: Tipo-litografiia T-va I. K. Sliianov, 1912), 124; and Robert D. Crews, "Islamic Law, Imperial Order: Muslims, Jews, and the Russian State," *Ab Imperio,* no. 3 (2004): 467–490.

25. *O'zbekistonning iangi tarikhi*, vol. 1, *Turkiston chor Rossiiasi mustamlakachiligi davrida* (Tashkent: "Sharq," 2000), 186–187; Mukimi, "Darig'o mulkimiz," available at zerrspiegel.orientphil .uni-halle.de/t341.html.

26. Hodong Kim, *Holy War in China: The Muslim Rebellion and State in Chinese Central Asia, 1864–1877* (Stanford: Stanford University Press, 2004); Thierry Zarcone, "Political Sufism and the Emirate of Kashgaria (End of the 19th Century): The Role of the Ambassador Ya'qūb Xān Tūra," in Kügelgen, Kemper, and Frank, *Muslim Culture in Russia and Central Asia*, 2:153–165. Similarly, after the Russians seized Karshi in 1866, the local governor, the oldest son of the Bukharan amir, elected to leave Russian-ruled territory. Despite receiving an amnesty from General Abramov, he fled to Khiva, Kashgar, Istanbul, and finally Peshawar. H. F. Hofman, *Turkish Literature: A Biobibliographical Survey* (Utrecht: Library of the University of Utrecht, 1969), 2:2–3.

27. Romanovskii, *Zametki*, 271; Palen, *Otchet po revizii Turkestanskogo kraia*, 31.

28. Palen, *Otchet po revizii Turkestanskogo kraia*, 13; see RGVIA, f. 400, op. 1, d. 613; RGVIA, f. 400, op. 1, d. 613, ll. 15–18.

29. V. V. Bartol'd, *Istoriia kul'turnoi zhizni Turkestana* (Leningrad: Izdatel'stvo Akademii nauk SSSR, 1927), 175–180.

30. On the political institution of the khanate, see R. D. McChesney, *Central Asia: Foundations of Change* (Princeton, N.J.: Darwin Press, 1996), 117–147. On official efforts to mobilize sermons on behalf of tsarist rule, see, also, Aftandil Erkinov, *Praying for and against the Tsar: Prayers and Sermons in Russian-Dominated Khiva and Tsarist Russia*, trans. Isabel Förster (Berlin: Klaus Schwarz Verlag, 2004).

31. Ä. Orinbaev and A. Boriev, *Tashkent Muhämmäd Salih Tävsifidä (XIX äsr)* (Tashkent: Ozbekiston SSR "Fän" näshriyati, 1983), 9.

32. Jeff Sahadeo, "Epidemic and Empire: Ethnicity, Class, and 'Civilization' in the 1892 Tashkent Cholera Riot," *Slavic Review* 64, no. 1 (2005): 117–139; B. M. Babadzhanov, "Dukchi Ishan i

Andizhanskoe vosstanie 1898 g.," in Abashin and Bobrovnikov, *Podvizhniki Islama*, 251–277; and Komatsu Hisao, "The Andijan Uprising Reconsidered," in *Muslim Societies: Historical and Comparative Aspects*, ed. Sato Tsugitaka (London: Routledge Curzon, 2004), 29–61.

33. See, for example, V. Ia. Galitskii et al., *Vozniknovenie i razvitie revoliutsionnogo dvizheniia v Kirgizii v kontse XIX–nachale XX vv.* (Frunze: Izdatel'stvo "Ilim", 1973), 30–50.

34. Richard A. Pierce, *Russian Central Asia 1867–1917: A Study in Colonial Rule* (Berkeley: University of California Press, 1960), 48–49; TsGARU, f. 36, op. 1, d. 432; an inventory of kazi court records under Kokandian rule reveals that women played active roles as litigants contesting the division of inheritance in the form of land, property, and money—women and men sued each other, their relatives, and others, and kazis and male and female litigants turned to secular authority, in this case the *bek*, to file complaints and petitions about their cases, a pattern continued under the tsars (Troitskaia, *Katalog arkhiva kokandskikh khanov*).

35. Between 1880 and 1882, district chiefs received 641 appeals from customary law courts in the Syr Darya region alone; see F. K. Girs, *Otchet revizuiushchego, po Vysochaisehumu poveleniiu, Turkestanskii krai tainogo sovetnika F. K. Girsa* (St. Petersburg: n.p., 1884), 29. Girs called the phenomenon of Muslims taking their complaints to Russian courts "very rare," having observed it only three times during his three-year investigation (ibid., 328).

36. See Brower, *Turkestan*.

37. See A. Zeki Velidi Togan, *Bugünkü Türkili (Türkistan) ve Yakın Tarihi* (Istanbul: Arkadaş, İbrahim Horoz ve Güven Basımevleri, 1942–1947), 272–273; Eugene Schuyler, *Turkistan: Notes of a Journey in Russian Turkistan, Khokand, Bukhara, and Kuldja*, vol. 1 (New York: Scribner, Armstrong and Co., 1876), 98.

38. Bartol'd, *Istoriia kul'turnoi zhizni Turkestana*, 175.

39. Togan, *Bugünkü Türkili (Türkistan)*, 272–274.

40. Schuyler, *Turkistan*, 1:168, 98–99, 2:237.

41. G. A. Arendarenko, *Dosugi v Turkestane 1874–1889* (St. Petersburg: Tipografiia M. M. Stasiulevicha, 1889), 169, 231–234.
42. TsGARU, f. 36, op. 1, d. 452, ll. 1–3.
43. Ibid., d. 979, ll. 1–1 ob.
44. Ibid., f. 19, op. 1, d. 398, l. 1.
45. Ibid., ll. 3–5 ob.
46. Ibid., ll. 8–9.
47. Ibid., ll. 11, 14–15, 16–16 ob. See also ibid., f. I-1, op. 22, d. 115, available at zerrspiegel.orientphil.uni-halle.de/t521.html.
48. See TsGARU, f. 36, op. 1, d. 339; ibid., f. 19, op. 1, d. 826, ll. 3–3 ob.; officials were not forced to conclude, at least from this case, whether or not a kazi might be punished for such an offense under imperial law because the case ended with the judge's death in 1883 (ibid., ll. 3 ob.–4); on the firing of kazis in Kokand, see *Istoriia Kokanda (s momenta prisoedineniia Srednei Azii k Rossii do nastoiashchego vremeni)* (Tashkent: Izdatel'stvo "FAN" Uzbekskoi SSR, 1984), 10.
49. TsGARU, f. 19, op. 1, d. 811, ll. 1–2 ob.; ibid., d. 747.
50. Crews, "Islamic Law, Imperial Order."
51. Palen, *Otchet po revizii Turkestanskogo kraia*, 121–122.
52. Ibid., 122–123, 116, 116–117.
53. Akhror Mukhtorov, *Istoriia Ura-Tiube (konets XV–nachalo XX vv.)* (Moscow: Institut istorii, arkheologii i etnografii imeni Akhmada Donisha AN Respubliki Tadzhikistan, 1998), 133; I. Usmanov, "Novye dokumenty po istorii Ura-Tiube XVII–XIX vekov," *Obshchestvennye nauki v Uzbekistane*, no. 6 (1986): 45–47.
54. V. P. Nalivkin, "Polozhenie vakufnogo dela v Turkestanskom krae do i posle ego zavoevaniia," in *Ezhegodnik Ferganskoi oblasti*, vol. 3 (Novyi Margelan: Tipografiia Ferganskogo Oblastnogo Pravleniia, 1904), 1–56, citation at 42; and Litvinov, *Gosudarstvo i Islam*, 166.
55. A. Mukhtarov, ed., *Materialy po istorii Ura-Tiube: Sbornik aktov XVII–XIX vv.* (Moscow: Izdatel'stvo Vostochnoi literatury, 1963), 34; R. N. Nabiev, "O kollektsii Ferganskikh dokumentov," *Obshchestvennye nauki v Uzbekistane*, no. 4 (1977): 61; Geins,

Sobranie literaturnykh trudov, 496; Galitskii and Ploskikh, *Starinnyi Osh*, 74–79; and Jo-Ann Gross, "The *Waqf* of Khoja 'Ubayd Allāh Aḥrār in Nineteenth Century Central Asia: A Preliminary Study of the Tsarist Record," in *Naqshbandis in Western and Central Asia*, ed. Elisabeth Özdalga (Richmond, Surrey: Curzon, 1999), 47–60.

56. Galitskii and Ploskikh, *Starinnyi Osh*, 78.

57. Girs, *Otchet revizuiushchego*, 353–354; TsGARU, f. 36, op. 1, d. 39, ll. 1–1 ob., 8–8 ob.

58. TsGARU, f. 36, op. 1, d. 39, ll. 4–4 ob.

59. Ibid., f. 19, op. 1, d. 642, ll. 5–6; Abduvalī Qushmatov, *Vaqf (Namudhoi zamindorii vaqf dar Shimoli Tojikiston dar solhoi 1870–1917)* (Dushanbe: "Irfon," 1990), esp. 55–56, 99–109.

60. See S. N. Abashin, "Islam v biurokraticheskoi praktike tsarskoi administratsii Turkestana (Vakufnoe delo dakhbitskogo medrese 1892–1900)," *Sbornik russkogo istoricheskogo obshchestva* 155, no. 7 (Moscow: Russkaia panorama, 2003), 163–191; and Nalivkin, "Polozhenie vakufnogo dela."

61. David S. Powers, "Orientalism, Colonialism, and Legal History: The Attack on Muslim Family Endowments in Algeria and India," *Comparative Studies in Society and History* 31, no. 3 (1989): 535–571.

62. Galitskii and Ploskikh, *Starinnyi Osh*, 73–79; A. Sharafiddinov, "XIX asr okhiri–XX asr boshlarida Farg'ona oblastida madaniy hayot tarikhidan," *Obshchestvennye nauki v Uzbekistane*, no. 2 (1978): 26, 27.

63. N. Shcherbiny-Kramarenko, "Po musul'manskim sviatyniam Srednei Azii (Putevye zametki i vpechatleniia)," in *Spravochnaia knizhka Samarkandskoi oblasti na 1896 g.*, ed. M. Virskii (Samarkand: Tipografiia Shtaba voisk Smarkandskoi oblasti, 1896), 4:56–60.

64. Litvinov, *Gosudarstvo i Islam*, 170.

65. Robert D. Crews, "Civilization in the City: Architecture, Urban-

ism, and the Colonization of Tashkent," in *Architectures of Identity in Russia, 1500–2000*, ed. James Cracraft and Daniel Rowland (Ithaca: Cornell University Press, 2003), 117–132; Sahadeo, "Epidemic and Empire."

66. See TsGARU, f. 19, op. 1, d. 332.

67. The petition also requested that tsarist officials help "compel attendance at the mosques," a request that officials did not meet, though they did enforce a ban on dancing, ostensibly as a measure to prevent the gathering of large crowds during a cholera outbreak (Schuyler, *Turkistan*, 1:162); TsGARU, f. 36, op. 1, d. 2419, ll. 2–2 ob., 4–4 ob.

68. Schuyler went on to argue that "the sincerity of Said Azim in this matter is shown by the fact that after the return of the Russians from the Khivan expedition he himself gave a large feast, at which he had all the amusements and dancing which had so offended his religion and morality on the previous occasion" (*Turkistan*, 1:99).

69. TsGARU, f. 19, op. 1, d. 1632, ll. 2, 2 ob.–3 ob., 3 ob.

70. Ibid., ll. 5–5 ob.

71. Ibid., ll. 5 ob.–6.

72. Ibid., ll. 12–12 ob.

73. Ibid., ll. 12 ob.–13. For more clerical denunciations, see A. P. Savitskii, *Sattarkhan Abdulgafarov—prosvetitel'-demokrat* (Tashkent: Izdatel'stvo "Uzbekistan", 1965), 11–13.

74. RGVIA, f. 400, op. 1, d. 365, l. 3 ob.

75. Kaufman and other Russian officials interpreted Said Makhmud Khan's refusal of Said Azim as a conflict between a "caste" of Sufi guides who objected to the marriage not because of Said Azim's age or because of the girl's youth but out of "intolerance" of his close ties to Russians. Ibid., ll. 10–12. For more on these characters, see Togan, *Bugünkü Türkili (Türkistan)*, 172–174, 178; and Schuyler, *Turkistan*, 1:89–91, 98–100.

76. RGVIA, f. 400, op. 1, d. 365, ll. 7 ob.–10; and Girs, *Otchet revizuiushchego*, 236–237. See also Brower, *Turkestan*, 73–74.

77. TsGARU, f. 36, op. 1, d. 1281, ll. 4-4 ob.; ibid., ll. 9 ob.-10, and Girs, *Otchet revizuiushchego*, 165; TsGARU, f. 36, op. 1, d. 1807, ll. 4-5 ob.; TsGARU, f. 1, op. 18, d. 33, ll. 4-6.

78. *Perevodchik*, Feb. 7, 1889; TsGARU, f. 36, op. 1, d. 1807, ll. 33-33 ob.

79. Girs, *Otchet revizuiushchego*, 219.

80. TsGARU, f. 19, op. 1, d. 2815, ll. 3-4 ob., 2.

81. Ibid., f. 36, op. 1, d. 452, l. 4 ob.

82. Ibid., f. 19, op. 1, d. 664, ll. 6-7 ob.

83. On their dominance of the Transcaspian region in particular, see V. V. Korneev, "Upravlenie Turkestanskim kraem: Real'nost' i 'pravovye mechtaniia' (60-e gody XIX v.-fevral' 1917 goda)," *Voprosy istorii*, no. 7 (2001): 56-70.

84. "Les Ichâns de Tachkent," *Revue du monde musulman* 13, no. 1 (Jan. 1911): 128-146, and Hisao, "The Andijan Uprising Reconsidered"; Dukhovskoi quoted in Hisao, "The Andijan Uprising Reconsidered," 47; on Slavic colonization, see Brower, *Turkestan*.

85. Aftandil Erkinov, "Andizhanskoe vosstanie i ego predvoditel' v otsenkakh poetov epokhi," *Vestnik Evrazii*, no. 1 (2003): 111-137; A. I. Termen, *Vospominaniia administratora: Opyt izsledovaniia printsipov upravleniia inorodtsev* (Petrograd: Tipografiia L. Saper, 1914), 4.

86. On this 'ulama petition, see Adeeb Khalid, "Printing, Publishing, and Reform in Tsarist Central Asia," *International Journal of Middle East Studies* 26, no. 2 (May 1994): 187-200, citation at 197; and on this alliance between Jadids and Russian authorities, see Baldauf, "Jadidism," 77-81.

87. RGIA, f. 1396, op. 1, d. 264, ll. 213-213 ob., reproduced at zerrspiegel.orientphil.uni-halle.de/t908.html.

88. Ibid.

89. Jean-Robert Henry has made a similar argument about the exclusionary implications of the maintenance of Muslim personal status law under French rule in Algeria. See "Droit musulman et struc-

ture d'Etat moderne en Algérie: L'héritage colonial," in *Islam et politique au Maghreb,* ed. Ernest Gellner and Jean-Claude Vatin (Paris: Éditions du centre national de la recherche scientifique, 1981), 305–313.

6. Heretics, Citizens, and Revolutionaries

1. See Raymond Pearson, "Privileges, Rights, and Russification," *Civil Rights in Imperial Russia,* ed. Olga Crisp and Linda Edmonson (New York: Oxford University Press, 1989), 85–102.

2. See Richard S. Wortman, *Scenarios of Power: Myth and Ceremony in Russian Monarchy,* vol. 2 (Princeton: Princeton University Press, 2000); Edward C. Thaden, ed., *Russification in the Baltic Provinces and Finland, 1855–1914* (Princeton: Princeton University Press, 1981); Theodore R. Weeks, *Nation and State in Late Imperial Russia: Nationalism and Russification on the Western Frontier, 1863–1914* (Dekalb: Northern Illinois University Press, 1996); and Andreas Renner, *Russischer Nationalismus und Öffentlichkeit im Zarenreich 1855–1875* (Cologne: Böhlau Verlag, 2000).

3. *Moskovskie vedomosti,* 9 May 1867.

4. Ibid.

5. RGIA, f. 821, op. 8, d. 609, ll. 28 ob.–29 ob.

6. Ibid., ll. 2 ob.–3.

7. See Christian Noack, *Muslimischer Nationalismus im Russischen Reich: Nationsbildung und Nationalbewegung bei Tataren und Baschkiren, 1861–1917* (Stuttgart: Franz Steiner Verlag, 2000), 207–209, 329–330.

8. See Stéphane Dudoignon, "Qu'est-ce que la '*qadîmiya*'? Éléments pour une sociologie du traditionalisme musulman, en Islam de Russie et en Transoxiane (au tournant des XIXe et XXe siècles)," *L'Islam de Russie: Conscience communautaire et autonomie politique chez les Tatars de la Volga et de l'Oural depuis le XVIIIe siècle,* ed. Stéphane Dudoignon, Dämir Is'haqov, and Räfyq Möhämmätshin (Paris: Maisonneuve et Larose, 1997), 207–225;

and Allen J. Frank, *Muslim Religious Institutions in Imperial Russia: The Islamic World of Novouzensk District and the Kazakh Inner Horde, 1780–1910* (Leiden: Brill, 2001).

9. See Danil D. Azamatov, "The Muftis of the Orenburg Spiritual Assembly in the 18th and 19th Centuries: The Struggle for Power in Russia's Muslim Institution," in *Muslim Culture in Russia and Central Asia*, vol. 2, ed. Anke von Kügelgen, Michael Kemper, and Allen J. Frank (Berlin: Klaus Schwarz Verlag, 1998), 355–384.

10. On this broader context, see Charles R. Steinwedel, "Invisible Threads of Empire: State, Religion, and Ethnicity in Tsarist Bashkiriia, 1773–1917" (Ph.D. diss., Columbia University, 1999); Robert P. Geraci, *Window on the East: National and Imperial Identities in Late Tsarist Russia* (Ithaca: Cornell University Press, 2001); and Paul W. Werth, *At the Margins of Orthodoxy: Mission, Governance, and Confessional Politics in Russia's Volga-Kama Region, 1827–1905* (Ithaca: Cornell University Press, 2002).

11. From the Crimean mufti, see *Sbornik izvestii, otnosiashchikhsia do nastoiashchei voiny*, ed. N. Putilov, book 5 (St. Petersburg: V Tipografii Eduarda Veimara, 1855), 200–203.

12. Serge A. Zenkovsky, *Pan-Turkism and Islam in Russia* (Cambridge, Mass.: Harvard University Press, 1960), 27. Despite these accusations, Muslim migration from the Russian empire during the war seems to have come nearly exclusively from the Caucasus and the Crimea. In some locales, the authorities encouraged Muslim flight. Most of the seven hundred thousand to nine hundred thousand Crimean and Caucasian Muslims who emigrated left after the war, from 1856 to 1860. A second mass exodus from these two regions occurred during and immediately following the Russo-Turkish War of 1877–1878. The government also forcibly relocated these populations within the empire. See Willis Brooks, "Russia's Conquest and Pacification of the Caucasus: Relocation Becomes a Pogrom in the Post–Crimean War Period," *Nationalities Papers* 23, no. 4 (1995): 675–686; Alan Fisher, "Emigration of Muslims from the Russian Empire in the Years after the Crimean War,"

Jahrbücher für Geschichte Osteuropas 35, no. 3 (1987): 356–371; and Peter Holquist, "To Count, to Extract, and to Exterminate: Population Statistics and Population Politics in Late Imperial and Soviet Russia," in *A State of Nations: Empire and Nation-Making in the Age of Lenin and Stalin*, ed. Ronald Grigor Suny and Terry Martin (Oxford: Oxford University Press, 2001), 111–144. But Ottomans encouraged Muslim emigration from Russia as a religious duty; see Bedri Habiçoğlu, *Kafkasya'dan Anadolu'ya Göçler ve İskanları* (Istanbul: Nart Yayıncılık, 1993).

13. See police reports on supposedly subversive activities among Muslims during the war in *Materialy po istorii Tatarii vtoroi poloviny XIX veka: Agrarnyi vopros i krest'ianskoe dvizhenie 50–70-kh godov XIX v.* (Moscow: Izdatel'stvo Akademii nauk SSSR, 1936), 156–164.

14. Peter Hardy, *The Muslims of British India* (Cambridge: Cambridge University Press, 1972), 61–91.

15. A. Shatel'e, *Islam v XIX veke*, trans. A. A. Kaltykovoi (Tashkent: Tipo-Litografiia Br. Portsevakh, 1900), 31 and 105. See also A. Krymskii, *Musul'manstvo i ego budushchnost'* (Moscow: Izdanie magazina "Knizhnoe delo", 1899); and V. P. Cherevanskii, *Mir islama i ego probuzhdenie: Istoricheskaia monografiia* (St. Petersburg: Gosudarstvennaia Tipografiia, 1901).

16. See Thomas M. Bartlett, "The Remaking of the Lion of Daghestan: Shamil in Captivity," *Russian Review* 53, no. 3 (1994): 353–367.

17. Selim Deringil, *The Well-Protected Domains: Ideology and the Legitimation of Power in the Ottoman Empire, 1876–1909* (London: Tauris, 1998).

18. See Mikhail Mashanov, *Verkhovnaia vlast' v islame* (Kazan: Univ. Tipografiia, 1878), 22; Stephen M. Norris, "Depicting the Holy War: The Images of the Russo-Turkish War, 1877–1878," *Ab Imperio*, no. 4 (2001): 141–168; Seymour Becker, "The Muslim East in Nineteenth-Century Russian Popular Historiography," *Central Asian Survey* 5, nos. 3–4 (1986): 25–47; and Geraci, *Window on the East*.

19. Peter Waldron, "Religious Toleration in Late Imperial Russia," in Crisp and Edmonson, *Civil Rights in Imperial Russia*, 114–116; and I. E. Alekseev, *Chernaia sotnia v Kazanskoi gubernii* (Kazan: Izdatel'stvo "DAS", 2001).

20. E. Malov, *Prikhody starokreshchenykh i novokreshchenykh tatar v Kazanskoi eparkhii* (Moscow: V universitetskoi tipografii, 1866), 7–8.

21. Rumors promised that the new tsar had granted converts permission to "return" to their original faith. See Andreas Kappeler, *Russlands erste Nationalitäten: Das Zarenreich und die Völker der Mittleren Wolga vom 16. bis 19. Jahrhundert* (Cologne: Böhlau Verlag, 1982). Such talk was rife at the accession of a new tsar and continued throughout the reigns of Nicholas I and Alexander II. Tsarist authorities quoted one such piece of news from Kazan Province in 1842: "The mullahs among the unconverted Tatars have some kind of decree [*ukaz*], or order about permission for all inhabitants of the Russian state to maintain that religion, which they choose of their own will." Malov, *Prikhody*, 22, 13–16.

22. Ibid.; NART, f. 1, op. 2, d. 483, ll. 1 ob.–2, 46 ob.–47; this ruling entrusted "a separate censor made up of professors of Oriental literature" with carefully scrutinizing Muslim religious texts before publication "so that nothing against the government and the ruling Church is printed in them" (NART, f. op. 2, d. 483, ll. 50–51).

23. E. Malov, *O tatarskikh mechetiakh v Rossii* (Kazan: V Universitetskoi Tipografii, n.d.), 68, which appeared in *Pravoslavnyi sobesednik* in late 1867 and early 1868; the diocesan journal likened local Christians who suffered at the hands of Muslims to "the martyrs of the first centuries of Christianity" (*Ufimskie eparkhial'nye vedomosti*, 1 Jan. 1891, 17 and 19).

24. Quoted in Zenkovsky, *Pan-Turkism*, 29; for an example of such a tract, see Mikhail Mashanov, *Mukhammedanskii brak v sravnenii s khristianskim brakom, v otnoshenii ikh vliianiia na semeinuiu i obshchestvennuiu zhizn' cheloveka* (Kazan: Tipo-litografiia K. A. Tilli, 1876).

25. RGIA, f. 821, op. 8, d. 594.

26. NART, f. 1, op. 3, d. 869, l. 1.

27. Ibid., 3–3 ob., 5–5 ob.; the bishop of Ufa would later accuse Muslims of wrecking and dismantling churches (*Ufimskie eparkhial'nye vedomosti*, 1 Jan. 1891, 19).

28. RGIA, f. 821, op. 8, d. 775, ll. 1–2 ob.

29. Ibid., 6–7.

30. Ibid., 7 ob.–8.

31. Ibid., 27 ob.–28.

32. See *SIRIO*, 115 (1903), 311–312, 400; NART, f. 1, op. 3, d. 4469, ll. 13–14.

33. "Postanovleniia Soveta Ministra narodnogo prosveshcheniia," *Zhurnal Ministerstva narodnogo prosveshcheniia* 148 (1870): 50–51, 52–53.

34. Ibid., 62. See *Mir Islama* 2, no. 4 (1913): 260–278; and, more generally, Robert Geraci, "Russian Orientalism at an Impasse: Tsarist Education Policy and the 1910 Conference on Islam," in *Russia's Orient: Imperial Borderlands and Peoples, 1700–1917*, ed. Daniel R. Brower and Edward J. Lazzerini (Bloomington: Indiana University Press, 1997), 138–161.

35. Wayne Dowler, *Classroom and Empire: The Politics of Schooling Russia's Eastern Nationalities, 1860–1917* (Montreal: McGill-Queen's University Press, 2001), 126–136.

36. Robert F. Baumann, "Universal Service Reform and Russia's Imperial Dilemma," *War and Society* 4, no. 2 (Sept. 1986): 31–49; NART, f. 1, op. 3, d. 4469, ll. 4–4 ob.

37. On regional and local histories, see Allen J. Frank, *Islamic Historiography and "Bulghar" Identity among the Tatars and Bashkirs of Russia* (Leiden: Brill, 1998); and R. A. Shaikhiev, *Tatarskaia narodno-kraevedcheskaia literatura XIX–XX vv.* (Kazan: Izdatel'stvo Kazanskogo Universiteta, 1990).

38. In the case of the language law first discussed openly in 1888, Muslims learned of the measure in the Russian-language and bilingual Tatar press as well as in Tatar-language almanacs published

by Russian publishers. *Sbornik zakonov o musul'manskom dukhovenstve v Tavricheskom i Orenburgskom okrugakh i o magometanskikh uchebnykh zavedeniiakh* (Kazan: Tipografiia P. I. Kidalinskogo, 1898); petitions frequently cited *Pravitel'stvennyi vestnik, Birzhevoi listok,* and *Perevodchik.* See also RGIA, f. 821, op. 8, d. 1078, l. 377 ob.

39. RGIA, f. 821, op. 8, d. 1078, ll. 445–445 ob., 446, 446 ob.–447.

40. NART, f. 1, op. 3, d. 7798, ll. 100–100 ob.

41. Ibid., 101.

42. For example, on official solicitation of clerical backing for state directives regarding the handling of animals, see Aidar Iuzeev, "Avtobiografiia Shikhabaddina Mardzhani," *GA,* nos. 3–4 (2000): 120; and Gul'nara Rafikova, "'Volnenie vozniklo iz zabluzhdenii i oshibok . . .' (Suleevskoe vosstanie 1885 g.)," *GA,* no. 2 (2004): 105–109; and on the Sunni and Shi'ite hierarchies in Transcaucasia, see D. Iu. Arapov, ed., *Islam v Rossiiskoi imperii (zakonodatel'nye akty, opisaniia, statistika)* (Moscow: IKTs "Akademikniga," 2001), 210–247; and Firouzeh Mostashari, "Colonial Dilemmas: Russian Policies in the Muslim Caucasus," in *Of Religion and Empire: Missions, Conversion, and Tolerance in Tsarist Russia,* ed. Robert P. Geraci and Michael Khodarkovsky (Ithaca: Cornell University Press, 2001), 229–249

43. On petitioning against this un-Islamic holiday, see "'Obychai, kotoryi ne otnositsia k shariatu,'" *Istoricheskii arkhiv,* no. 1 (2005): 203–206; for the imam's petition against unveiled women, see TsGIARB, f. I-295, op. 3, d. 6310, l. 6 ob.

44. E. V. Molostvova, "Vaisov Bozhii polk," *Mir Islama* 1, no. 2 (1912): 143–152; Chantal Quelquejay, "Le 'Vaïsisme' à Kazan: Contribution à l'étude des confréries musulmanes chez les tatars de la Volga," *Die Welt des Islams* 6, nos. 1–2 (1959): 91–112; M. Sagidullin, *K istorii Vaisovskogo dvizheniia* (Kazan: Tatpoligraf, 1930); K. F. Katanov, *Novye dannye o musul'manskoi sekte Vaisovtsev* (Kazan: Tsentral'naia tipografiia, 1909); and Michael Kemper, *Sufis und Gelehrte in Tatarien und Baschkirien, 1789–1889: Der*

islamische Diskurs unter russischer Herrschaft (Berlin: Klaus Schwarz Verlag, 1998), 393–429.

45. See RGIA, f. 821, op. 133, d. 508, l. 14, 15 ob.

46. Kazem-Bek advised the Ministry of Internal Affairs against approving the "adventurer's" request; see RGIA, f. 821, op. 8, d. 1170, ll. 10–12 ob.; ibid., f. 821, op. 8, d. 842, ll. 2 ob.–3, 57–57 ob., 58–59, and RGIA, f. 821, op. 8, d. 1170, l. 25 ob.

47. He continued to send denunciations of the Assembly to St. Petersburg in the 1870s. See RGIA, f. 821, op. 8, d. 1170, ll. 31–32.

48. Kemper, *Sufis und Gelehrte*, 414–423.

49. RGIA, f. 821, op. 133, d. 508, 14 ob.–15, 16–16 ob.

50. NART, f. 1, op. 3, d. 7629, ll. 13–14, 34–34 ob., 71–79 ob.

51. This case is drawn from RGIA, f. 821, op. 8, d. 615, ll. 81–91.

52. Iuzeev, "Avtobiografiia," 121.

53. TsGIARB, f. I-11, op. 1, d. 1533, ll. 5–6.

54. On the controversy surrounding Rasulev, see Hamid Algar, "Shaykh Zaynullah Rasulev: The Last Great Naqshbandi Shaykh of the Volga-Urals Region," in *Muslims in Central Asia: Expressions of Identity and Change*, ed. Jo-Ann Gross (Durham, N.C.: Duke University Press, 1992), 120; TsGIARB, f. I-295, op. 3, d. 5048, ll. 9–9 ob., 117–120, 120–121; Z. A. Ishmukhametov, *Sotsial'naia rol' i evoliutsiia Islama v Tatarii* (Kazan: Tatarskoe knizhnoe izdatel'stvo, 1979), 58–59; and on the imam in Astrakhan, see TsGIARB, f. I-295, op. 3, d. 1800.

55. Ismail Bey Gasprinskii, *Russkoe musul'manstvo: Mysli, zametki i nabliudeniia musul'manina* (1881; Oxford: Center for Central Asian Studies, 1985), 65; Ahmed Zeki Velidi Togan, *Vospominaniia*, trans G. Shafikov and A. Iuldashbaev (Ufa: "Kitap," 1994), 96–103 for example. For their relationship to other reformist currents, see Thierry Zarcone, "Philosophie et théologie chez les djadids: La question du raisonnement indépendant *(iğtihâd)*," *Cahiers du monde russe* 37, nos. 1–2 (1996): 53–64.

56. On the Jadids and the Muslim press, see Alexandre Bennigsen and Chantal Lemercier-Quelquejay, *La presse et le Mouvement Na-*

tional chez les musulmans de Russie avant 1920 (Paris: Mouton, 1964), 21–46; Adeeb Khalid, *The Politics of Muslim Cultural Reform: Jadidism in Central Asia* (Berkeley: University of California Press, 1998); Edward J. Lazzerini, "Beyond Renewal: The Jadīd Response to Pressure for Change in the Modern Era," in Gross, *Muslims in Central Asia*, 151–166; on debates about Muslim education, see Stéphane A. Dudoignon, "La question scolaire à Boukhara et au Turkestan russe, du 'premier renouveau' à la soviétisation (fin du XVIIIe siècle–1937)," *Cahiers du monde russe* 37, nos. 1–2 (1996): 133–210.

57. For a portrait of the "traditionalists" *(Qadimists)* that adopts the point of view of the Jadids, see Khalid, *Politics of Muslim Cultural Reform.*

58. *Tercüman / Perevodchik*, Apr. 21, 1889.

59. On Sufi poetry in the region, see Kemper, *Sufis und Gelehrte;* on Gasprinskii's view of family issues, see *Tercüman / Perevodchik*, 23 Mar. 1884, 21 Aug. 1891.

60. *Tercüman / Perevodchik*, Jan. 8, 1889.

61. NART, f. 1, op. 3, d. 7615, ll. 12–12 ob.

62. On officials' anxieties about interimperial ties among Muslims, see Daniel Brower, "Russian Roads to Mecca: Religious Tolerance and Muslim Pilgrimage in the Russian Empire," *Slavic Review* 55, no. 3 (1996): 567–584, and Adeeb Khalid, "Pan-Islamism in Practice: The Rhetoric of Muslim Unity and Its Uses," *Late Ottoman Society: The Intellectual Legacy*, ed. Elisabeth Özdalga (London: Routledge Curzon, 2005), 201–224; on the British tendency to see heterogeneous populations through the homogenizing lens of a Muslim confession, see Hardy, *Muslims of British India*, and Farzana Shaikh, *Community and Consensus in Islam: Muslim Representation in Colonial India, 1860–1947* (Cambridge: Cambridge University Press, 1989).

63. Brigitte Roth, "Religionen/Konfessionen," in *Die Nationalitäten des Russischen Reiches in der Volkszählung von 1897*, ed. Henning

Bauer, Andreas Kappeler, and Brigitte Roth, vol. A (Stuttgart: Franz Steiner Verlag, 1991), 319, 318–320.

64. See, for example, S. Rybakov, "Statistika musul'man v Rossii," *Mir Islama* 2, no. 11 (1913): 757–763.

65. Linda Edmonson, "Was There a Movement for Civil Rights in 1905?" in Crisp and Edmonson, *Civil Rights in Imperial Russia*, 263–285; Waldron, "Religious Toleration," 110–111; G. Blosfel'dt, "Polozhenie inovertsev i raskol'nikov soglasno Svodu zakonov," *Zhurnal Ministerstva Iustitsii*, no. 3 (1905): 177–204. See also N. P. Solov'ev, ed., *Polnyi krug dukhovnykh zakonov* (Moscow: Tipografiia A. P. Poplavskii, 1907).

66. Waldron, "Religious Toleration," 112–113.

67. See the exhaustive account of Muslim politicization in Noack, *Muslimischer Nationalismus*.

68. TsGIARB, f. I-11, op. 2, d. 73 and d. 84; Togan, *Vospominaniia*, 21.

69. *Petitions presented to Russian Government by Tatars in behalf of the Mohammedan Religion* [Columbia University Library Collection] (n.p., n.d.), 3–4, 4–5, 5. (Each petition in this collection is paginated individually.) This petition was rewritten on behalf of the Tatar villagers by Ivan Grakhov, a Russian peasant from a village of the same district of Elabuzh'.

70. Ibid., 1–2.

71. Ibid., 1–7.

72. Ibid., 8–12. See also Stéphane Dudoignon, "Status, Strategies and Discourses of a Muslim 'Clergy' under a Christian Law: Polemics about the Collection of the *Zakât* in Late Imperial Russia," in *Islam in Politics in Russia and Central Asia (Early Eighteenth to Late Twentieth Centuries)*, ed. Stéphane Dudoignon and Komatsu Hisao (London: Kegan Paul, 2001), 43–73.

73. RGIA, f. 821, op. 10, d. 29, ll. 5–7.

74. Ibid., l. 7.

75. Ibid., ll. 7 ob.–9, 10–13 ob.

76. Ibid., ll. 400–401. See also the March 1906 telegram from Muslims

of the Turgai region protesting a State Council member's reference to their religion as "Shamanism." RGIA, f. 821, op. 10, d. 29, l. 1.

77. A retired clerk named Ivan Turkin recorded the appeal for them. RGIA, f. 821, op. 8, d. 632, ll. 3–3 ob.

78. Another article related to state regulation of 'ulama requested repeal of the prohibition against mullahs, teachers, and others who received religious instruction abroad. Ibid., l. 4 and 5 ob.–6.

79. Ibid., ll. 4–5.

80. Ibid., 5.

81. See, for example, Ustav musul'manskogo obshchestva v Orenburge (Orenburg: Tipolitografiia F. G. Karimova, 1906); Ustav Orenburgskogo musul'mankogo zhenskogo obshchestva (Orenburg: Tovarishchestvo "Karimov, Khusainov i Ko", 1912); and Ustav Orenburgskogo musul'manskogo obshchestva potrebitelei (Orenburg: Tip. Mukhamedvaliia Abdulganievicha Khusainova, 1913). Muslims published 166 periodicals in twenty-six cities of the empire between April 1905 and February 1917. Musul'manskaia pechat' Rossii v 1910 godu (Oxford: Society for Central Asian Studies, 1987), 9.

82. See Radik Salihov, "L'implication des tatars musulmans dans les institutions électives d'auto-administration de la ville et de la province de Qazan, au tournant des XIXe et XXe siècles," in Dudoignon, Is'haqov, and Möhämmätshin, L'Islam de Russie, 155–174; "V zashchitu nashego dukhovenstva," Musul'manin, no. 2 (20 Jan. 1911): 53–55; and "Mysli vslukh," Musul'manin (15 Feb. 1911): 105–107.

83. See Politicheskaia zhizn' russkikh musul'man do fevral'skoi revoliutsii (Oxford: Society for Central Asian Studies, 1987); Necip Hablemitoğlu, Çarlık Rusya'sında Türk Kongreleri (1905–1917) (Ankara: Ankara Üniversitesi Basımevi, 1997); "Reforma musul'manskikh dukhovnykh pravlenii," Mir Islama 2, no. 11 (1913): 729–756; and Dilara Usmanova, "L'Assemblée spirituelle

musulmane au début due XXe siècle: Les projets de réforme face au pouvoir Russe," in Dudoignon, Is'haqov, and Möhämmätshin, *L'Islam de Russie*, 175–191.

84. Twenty-five Muslim deputies were elected to the first Duma (of 478 total) and 36 Muslim deputies to the second (of 518). The electoral law for the third Duma restricted Muslim participation, however. Only 10 sat in the third Duma and 7 in the fourth. Usmanova, "L'Assemblée spirituelle," and idem, "The Activity of the Muslim Faction of the State Duma and Its Significance in the Formation of a Political Culture among the Muslim Peoples of Russia (1906–1917)," in Kügelgen, Kemper, and Frank, *Muslim Culture in Russia and Central Asia*, 2:417–455.

85. Waldron, "Religious Toleration," 107, 112; and Geoffrey A. Hosking, *The Russian Constitutional Experiment: Government and Duma, 1907–1914* (Cambridge: Cambridge University Press, 1973), 97–100, quotation at 117.

86. In 1906 Nicholas approved a controversial set of laws for new primary schools "to spread knowledge of the Russian language . . . on the basis of love for [our] common fatherland." "Otdel spravochnyi," *Mir Islama* 2, no. 4 (1913): 269–278; and *Akt chastnogo soveshchaniia dukhovnykh lits okruga Orenburgskogo magometanskogo dukhovnogo sobraniia na 14 i 15 dekabria 1913 goda* (Ufa: Elektrich. Gubernsk. Tipografiia, 1914). See also Geraci, *Window on the East*, 266–308. On the interministerial review of the empire's policies toward Islam, see RGIA, f. 821, op. 133, d. 573; Usmanova, "L'Assemblée spirituelle," 182–186; and Geraci, "Russian Orientalism at an Impasse." On espionage organized by the Ministry of War to gauge the "contemporary mood of the Muslim world" and its operations in Turkestan, see RGVIA, f. 400, op. 1, d. 3772; and Iu. Arapov, ed., "Musul'manskoe dvizhenie v Srednei Azii v 1910 g. (Po arkhivnym materialam Departamenta politsii Ministerstva vnutrennikh del Rossiiskoi imperii)," *Sbornik Russkogo istoricheskogo obshchestva* 153, no. 5 (2002): 127–134.

87. It turned away an unknown number of would-be prayer leaders and teachers whom local mosque communities sent to Ufa for examination. *V pamiat' stoletiia orenburgskogo magometanskogo dukhovnogo sobraniia uchrezhdennogo v gorode Ufe* (Ufa: Tipografiia Gubernskogo Pravleniia, 1891), 31–32, 35–36. The same official source counted 2,527 successful examinees between 1804 and 1836, though it expressed doubt that this figure took account of all of those who passed exams and assumed positions as licensed clerics. If this number is roughly accurate, the Assembly would have more than tripled its licensing activities during the fifty years separating the early reign of Nicholas I and Alexander III, from an average of roughly 79 per year in the period 1804–1836 to 263 a year in 1836–1889.

88. For examples of Muslim authorities' attempts to define the exclusive rights of licensed 'ulama and to standardize ritual practices and legal interpretation through print, see Riḍā'addīn Fakhraddīn ōghlī, *Menasib-i diniye* (Orenburg: Karimov, 1910); Ramil Mingnullin, "Mäg'lümate Mäkhkämäi shärgïyä Orenburgiyä zhurnalï," *GA*, nos. 3–4 (2000): 227–235; and Michael Kemper, "Šihābaddīn al-Marğanī als Religionsgelehrter," in *Muslim Culture in Russia and Central Asia*, vol. 1, ed. Michael Kemper, Anke von Kügelgen, and Dmitriy Yermakov (Berlin: Klaus Schwarz Verlag, 1996), 129–165.

89. See the demands written at the 1914 Muslim congress, including one requesting official health certificates for men entering into marriage. Hablemitoğlu, *Çarlık Rusya'sında Türk Kongreleri*, 88.

90. Dudoignon, "Qu'est-ce que la *'qadîmiya'*?" and "Status, Strategies and Discourses." See, too, Noack, *Muslimischer Nationalismus*.

91. TsGIARB, f. I-295, op. 11, d. 348, ll. 132–132 ob.

92. "Turetskie emissary v Rossii," *Istoricheskii arkhiv*, no. 4 (2004): 87; and "Zapiski P. A. Stolypina po 'musul'manskomu voprosu' 1911 g.," *Vostok*, no. 2 (2003): 124–144; on clerical denunciations, see A. Arsharuni and Kh. Gabidullin, *Ocherki panislamizma i*

pantiurkizma v Rossii (Moscow: Izdatel'stvo "Bezbozhnik," 1931), 18–20; A. Battal-Taymas, *Alimcan Barudı* (Istanbul: M. Sıralar matbaası, 1958), 15–23; and Radik Salikhov and Ramil' Khairutdinov, "Vernopoddanicheskoiu pravdoiu podtverzhdaiu ... (Ishmukhamet Dinmukhametov)," *GA*, no. 2 (2004): 152–155.

93. T. N. Zagorodnikova, ed., "Bolshaia igra" v Tsentral'noi Azii: "Indiiskii pokhod" russkoi armii; Sbornik arkhivnykh dokumentov (Moscow: Institut vostokovedeniia, 2005), 52; "'Nasha vnutrenniaia politika po musul'manskomu voprosu iavliaetsia vazhnym faktorom politiki vneshei': S. Iu. Vitte i ego pozitsiia v musul'manskom voprose," *Istochnik* 2 (2003): 24–26; Dmitrii Arapov, "Russkii posol v Turtsii N. V. Charykov i ego 'zakliuchenie' po 'musul'manskomu voprosu'," *Vestnik Evrazii*, no. 2 (2002): 148–163, citation at 160.

94. Ibid., 155.

95. Cited in Vladimir Genis, *Vitse-konsul Vvedenskii: Sluzhba v Persii i Bukharskom khanstve (1906–1920 gg.); Rossiiskaia diplomatiia v sud'bakh* (Moscow: "Sotsial'no-politicheskaia MYSL'," 2003), 17; 'Abd al-Rahman Niyazi Nur-Muhammadzada al-Hajitarkhani, *Khutbalar majmu'asi* (Astrakhan: Tipografiia A. I. Umerova i Ko., 1908), 7–8; "Islam ve Khristiyanlik," *Yulduz*, 4 Dec. 1912.

Epilogue

1. Richard S. Wortman, "'Invisible Threads': The Historical Imagery of the Romanov Tercentenary," *Russian History* 16, nos. 2–4 (1989): 389–408.

2. "Torzhestva po sluchaiiu 300-letiia tsarstvovaniia Doma Romanovykh," *Mir Islama* 2, no. 1 (1913): 44.

3. Ibid., 45.

4. S. M. Iskhakov, "Pervaia mirovaia voina glazami rossiiskikh musul'man," in *Rossiia i pervaia mirovaia voina*, ed. N. N. Smirnov et al. (St. Petersburg: Izdatel'stvo "Dmitrii Bulanin," 1999), 419–431, citation at 420; and Akdes Nimet Kurat, "Kazan Türklerinin

'medeni uyanış' devri (1917 yılını kadar)," *Ankara Üniversitesi Dil ve Tarih-Coğrafya Fakültesi Dergisi*, nos. 3–4 (1966): 191–192.

5. Ego Imperatorskoe Velichestvo Gosudar' Imperator Nikolai Aleksandrovich v deistvuiushchei armii noiabr'-dekabr' 1914 g. (Petrograd: Tovarishchestvo R. Golike i A. Vil'borg, 1915).

6. Aleksei Miller, "Between Local and Inter-Imperial: Russian Imperial History in Search of Scope and Paradigm," *Kritika* 5, no. 1 (Winter 2004): 7–26.

7. Ferdinand Hauptmann, "Die Mohammedaner in Bosnien-Hercegovina," in *Die Habsburgermonarchie 1848–1918*, ed. Adam Wandruszka and Peter Urbanitsch, vol. 4 (Vienna: Verlag der Österreichischen Akademie der Wissenschaften, 1995), 670–701.

8. See, for example, Mark Mazower, *Salonica, City of Ghosts: Christians, Muslims and Jews, 1430–1950* (New York: Knopf, 2005), 153–155; and more generally, Ariel Salzmann, "Citizens in Search of a State: The Limits of Political Participation in the Late Ottoman Empire," in *Extending Citizenship, Reconfiguring States*, ed. Michael Hanagan and Charles Tilly (Lanham, Md.: Rowman and Littlefield, 1999), 37–66.

9. Gary Marker and Rachel May, trans. and ed., *Days of a Russian Noblewoman: The Memories of Anna Labzina 1758–1821* (Dekalb: Northern Illinois University Press, 2001), 13–14. On popular images hostile to Muslim peoples, see, also, Jeffrey Brooks, *When Russia Learned to Read: Literacy and Popular Literature, 1861–1917* (Princeton: Princeton University Press, 1985).

10. Marker and May, *Days of a Russian Noblewoman*.

11. Paul Avrich, *Russian Rebels 1600–1800* (New York: Norton, 1976), 217.

12. Afsaneh Najmabadi, "Hazards of Modernity and Morality: Women, State and Ideology in Contemporary Iran," in *The Modern Middle East: A Reader*, ed. Albert Hourani, Philip S. Khoury, and Mary C. Wilson (Berkeley: University of California Press, 1993), 663–687; and Deniz Kandiyoti, "Women, Islam, and the

State," in *Political Islam: Essays from Middle East Report*, ed. Joel Beinin and Joe Stork (Berkeley: University of California Press, 1997), 185–193.

13. Ranajit Guha, "Dominance without Hegemony and Its Historiography," in *Subaltern Studies VI*, ed. Ranajit Guha (Delhi: Oxford University Press, 1989), 272.

14. On volatility within this institution, see Murat Akgündüz, *XIX. Asır Başlarına Kadar Osmanlı Devleti'nde Şeyhülislâmlık* (Istanbul: Beyan, 2002).

15. Jane Burbank, "Legal Culture, Citizenship, and Peasant Jurisprudence: Perspectives from the Early Twentieth Century," in *Reforming Justice in Russia, 1864–1996: Power, Culture and the Limits of Legal Order*, ed. Peter H. Solomon Jr. (Armonk, N.Y.: Sharpe, 1997), 82–106.

16. Gerhard Höpp, *Muslime in der Mark: Als Kriegsgefangene und Internierte in Wünsdorf und Zossen, 1914–1924* (Berlin: Das Arabische Buch, 1997), 20–21.

17. See also Mark von Hagen, "The Limits of Reform: The Multiethnic Imperial Army Confronts Nationalism, 1874–1917," in *Reforming the Tsar's Army: Military Innovation in Imperial Russia from Peter the Great to the Revolution*, ed. David Schimmelpenninck van der Oye and Bruce W. Menning (Washington, D.C. and Cambridge: Woodrow Wilson Center Press and Cambridge University Press, 2004), 34–55.

18. Abdürreşid İbrahim, 20. *Asrın Başlarında İslâm Dünyası ve Japonya'da İslâmiyet*, ed. Mehmed Paksu, vol. 1 (Istanbul: Yeni Asya Yayınları, 1987), 82.

19. Ibid., 79.

20. İsmail Türkoğlu, *Sibiryalı Meşhur Seyyah Abdürreşid İbrahim* (Ankara: Türkiye Diyanet Vakfı, 1997), 20–87, citation at 78.

21. For example, François Georgeon, *Aux origines du nationalisme turc: Yusuf Akçura (1876–1935)* (Paris: Éditions ADPF, 1980).

22. See Edward Dennis Sokol, *The Revolt of 1916 in Russian Central*

Asia (Baltimore: Johns Hopkins University Press, 1954); and Daniel Brower, *Turkestan and the Fate of the Russian Empire* (London: Routledge Curzon, 2003).

23. P. G. Galuzo, ed., *Vosstanie 1916 goda v Srednei Azii: Sbornik dokumentov* (Tashkent: Gosizdat UzSSR, 1932).

24. Ronald Robinson, "Non-European Foundations of European Imperialism: Sketch for a Theory of Collaboration," in *Studies in the Theory of Imperialism*, ed. Roger Owen and Bob Sutcliffe (London: Longman, 1972), 117–140, citation at 121.

25. For example, "Gubernator v roli propovednika Korana," *Krasnyi arkhiv* 75, no. 2 (1936): 188–191.

26. See Xenia Joukoff Eudin and Robert C. North, eds., *Soviet Russia and the East 1920–1927: A Documentary Survey* (Stanford: Stanford University Press, 1957).

27. For example, "'Evropeiskii sotsializm imeet svoim pervoistochnikom tot zhe samyi islam . . .'," *Istoricheskii arkhiv*, no. 2 (2004): 172–182; S. M. Iskhakov, *Rossiiskie musul'mane i revoliutsiia (vesna 1917 g.–leto 1918 g.)*, rev. ed. (Moscow: Izdatel'stvo "Sotsial'no-politicheskaia MYSL'," 2004); and Iu. A. Poliakov and A. I. Chugunov, *Konets Basmachestva* (Moscow: "Nauka," 1976), 112.

28. Peter Holquist, *Making War, Forging Revolution: Russia's Continuum of Crisis, 1914–1921* (Cambridge, Mass.: Harvard University Press, 2002), 383–384.

29. See Yuri Slezkine, "The USSR as a Communal Apartment, or How a Socialist State Promoted Ethnic Particularism," *Slavic Review* 53 (Summer 1994): 414–452; Adrienne Lynn Edgar, *Tribal Nation: The Making of Soviet Turkmenistan* (Princeton: Princeton University Press, 2004); and Francine Hirsch, *Empire of Nations: Ethnographic Knowledge and the Making of the Soviet Union* (Ithaca: Cornell University Press, 2005).

30. Şerif Mardin, "Religion and Politics in Modern Turkey," in *Islam in the Political Process*, ed. James P. Piscatori (Cambridge: Cambridge University Press, 1983), 143.

31. See Niyazi Berkes, *The Development of Secularism in Turkey* (New York: Routledge, 1998), 461–503.

32. Mardin, "Religion and Politics," 144. For the USSR, see Yaacov Ro'i, *Islam in the Soviet Union: From the Second World War to Gorbachev* (New York: Columbia University Press, 2001); and Galina M. Yemelianova, *Russia and Islam: A Historical Survey* (New York: Palgrave, 2002).

33. See Devin DeWeese, "Islam and the Legacy of Sovietology: A Review Essay on Yaccov Ro'i's *Islam in the Soviet Union*," *Journal of Islamic Studies* 13, no. 3 (2002): 298–330.

34. See, for example, Alexander Knysh, "A Clear and Present Danger: 'Wahhabism' as a Rhetorical Foil," *Die Welt des Islams* 44, no. 1 (2004): 3–26; and A. A. Iarlykapov, "Narusheniia prav veruiushchikh-musul'man na territorii Stavropol'skogo kraia," in *Islam i pravo v Rossii: Materialy nauchno-prakticheskogo seminara*, vol. 1, ed. I. L. Babich and L. T. Solov'eva (Moscow: Izdatel'stvo Rossiiskogo universiteta druzhby narodov, 2004), 120–127. See also Bakhtyar Babadjanov, "Islam officiel contre Islam politique en Ouzbékistan aujourd'hui: La direction des Musulmans et les groupes non-Hanafi," *Revue d'études comparatives Est-Ouest* 31 (2000): 151–164; and Adeeb Khalid, "A Secular Islam: Nation, State, and Religion in Uzbekistan," *International Journal of Middle East Studies* 35, no. 4 (Nov. 2003): 573–598. See, too, Igor Rotar, "Kazakhstan: Attempts to Suppress Independent Muslims Continue," Forum 18 News Service, 23 Aug. 2005, available at www.forum18.org.

35. See, especially, Sanobar Shermatova, "Islamskii faktor v rukakh politicheskikh elit," in *Islam na postsovetskom prostranstve: Vzgliad iznutri*, ed. Aleksei Malashenko and Martha Brill Olcott (Moscow: Moskovskii Tsentr Karnegi, 2001), 205–232.

36. See, for example, Stéphane A. Dudoignon, "Political Parties and Forces in Tajikistan, 1989–1993," in *Tajikistan: The Trials of Independence*, ed. Mohammad-Reza Djalili, Frédéric Grare, and Shirin Akiner (Richmond, Surrey: Curzon, 1998), 52–85; and

Tamara Makarenko, "Drugs in Central Asia: Security Implications and Political Manipulations," *Cahiers d'études sur la Méditerranée orientale et le monde turco-iranien*, no. 32 (July–Dec. 2001): 87–115.

37. On transnational groups active in these states, see Peter Mandaville, "Sufis and Salafis: The Political Discourse of Transnational Islam," in *Remaking Muslim Politics: Pluralism, Contestation, Democratization*, ed. Robert W. Hefner (Princeton: Princeton University Press, 2005), 302–325; Mariam Abou Zahab and Olivier Roy, *Réseaux islamiques: La connexion afghano-pakistanaise* (Paris: Autrement, 2002); Bayram Balci, *Missionaires de l'Islam en Asie centrale: Les écoles turques de Fethullah Gülen* (Paris: Maisonneuve et Larose, 2003); Thierry Zarcone, "L'Islam d'Asie centrale et le monde musulman: Restructuration et interferences," *Herodote*, no. 84 (1997): 68–71; and Bakhtiiar Babadzhanov, "Vozrozhdenie deiatel'nosti sufiiskikh grupp v Uzbekistane," in *Sufizm v Tsentral'noi Azii (zarubezhnye issledovaniia)*, ed. A. A. Khismatulin (St. Petersburg: Filologicheskii fakul'tet Sankt-Peterburgskogo Gosudarstvennogo Universiteta, 2001), 331–351.

ACKNOWLEDGMENTS

The writing of this book took me on a long journey across Russia and Central Asia. When I began this research in the late 1990s, Chechnya remained in flames and ash, but life in other Muslim regions resembled that of Russian citizens elsewhere. Relative stability barely masked a generic sense of malaise and decline. Still, Tatarstan and Bashkortostan were worlds away from the war-torn Caucasus, where conflicts between Armenians and Azeris, Georgians and Abkhazians, Russians and Chechens, and many other tensions brought misery to the disoriented citizens who had abruptly lost their country, the Soviet Union, in 1991.

The prospect of studying Islam in the region was a new one. In recently opened archives, my hosts greeted me with hospitable curiosity. They offered help even when my research struck some of them as not quite "Russian" enough (my focus was Islam)—and not sufficiently "Tatar," "Bashkir," "Kazakh," or "Uzbek"—because I was interested in investigating how the empire had shaped Islam and the history of these peoples, a proposition that runs counter to the nationalist dictates that color the writing of history in the region. Despite their occasional disappointment, often amplified by the suspicion that the Americans had not sent a scholar to the region to study Islam for nothing, officials gave me access to these archives, a privilege that may have already expired for scholars today. This book would not have been possible without the able assistance of archivists at the Russian State Historical Archive, the Russian State Military History Archive, the Orenburg State Regional Archive, the Archive of the Foreign Affairs of the Russian Empire, the National Archive of the Republic of Tatarstan, the Central State Archive of the Republic of Bashkortostan, and the Central State Historical Archive of the Republic of Uzbekistan.

I am most grateful to a number of institutions that supported my research and, in the process, helped me fend off more than one scavenging dog and test fate with two flights on Bashkir Air. The Fulbright-Hays fellowship program enabled me to travel widely; its representatives at the American consulate in Tashkent remained unflappable—even indifferent—when I faced deportation there. The Council on Regional Studies and the Department of History at Princeton University funded language training and exploratory forays into the archives. The very generous support of the Mrs. Giles Whiting Foundation, the Princeton Society of Fellows of the Woodrow Wilson Foundation, the Kennan Institute of the Woodrow Wilson International Center for Scholars, the Working Group Modernity and Islam of the Institute for Advanced Study in Berlin, the American Council of Learned Societies, and the John W. Kluge Center at the Library of Congress allowed me to write up this research under wonderful conditions. For their expertise, hospitality, and generosity, I am particularly indebted to David Redman, Stanley Katz, Ingeborg Baldauf, Lutz Rzehak, Prosser Gifford, Blair Ruble, and Atiq Sarwari. Librarians at Princeton University, Columbia University, the New York Public Library, the Wilson Center, the Library of Congress, the University of California at Berkeley, American University, Stanford University, Indiana University, the British Library, the Staatsbibliothek in Berlin, as well as at libraries in Russia and Uzbekistan were always helpful.

The origins of this book probably lay somewhere on the inspiring campus of the University of North Carolina at Chapel Hill, where Donald Raleigh, David Griffiths, E. Willis Brooks, and Vasa Mihailovich in-

troduced me to the Russian past and the discipline of history and motivated me to pursue them further. At Columbia University, Leopold
Haimson's legendary creativity and expansive encouragement drew me
back to the nineteenth century, Mark von Hagen launched my interest
in empire, and Robert Crummey offered intellectual stimulation and
guidance beyond the call of duty. The example of Richard Wortman
solidified my decision to study imperial Russia. I learned a great deal
from his courses, which combined originality, rigor, and open-minded-
ness in an extraordinary way, and from his insightful reading of an earlier version of this book.

I had the unusual luck to begin this book as a dissertation at Princeton University, where my fellow students and faculty mentors created
an exciting environment. I am most grateful to Tom Papademetriou,
Mustafa Aksakal, Amy Randall, Gen Liang, David Gordon, Ignacio Gal-
lup-Diaz, Brian Cowan, Victoria Klein, Francine Hirsch, Chris Stone,
Cynthia Hooper, Greg Lyon, Sandra Bronfman, Amanda Wunder, and
Eileen Kane. Erika Gilson and Kamran Talattof gave generously of their
knowledge, time, patience, and humor—despite my tendency to be
tardy and tongue-tied. For introducing me to the study of colonialism, I
thank Gyan Prakash and Robert Tignor. Molly Greene opened up the
Ottoman world to me, a revelation that helped me formulate my approach to this book. An endless source of encouragement and ideas, she
endured multiple drafts of my work.

I owe a special debt of gratitude to Laura Engelstein (now at Yale) and
Stephen Kotkin, who brought their unrivaled intellectual talents, energy, learning, and generosity to the task of assisting me in innumerable
ways. They have been much more than dissertation advisers. In the
classroom, they shared their extraordinary insights into the discipline of
history and forcefully conveyed the masterful interpretive schemes that
have shaped my understanding of Russia. Steve has always posed the
right questions, probed for alternatives, suggested novel approaches, and
offered sound advice and encouragement—especially in the final stages
of this book, when he supplied key ideas. Laura has supported this book
from beginning to end, going beyond what any adviser should have to

do. She patiently read and edited draft after draft, pushed me in new directions, saved me from many of my own mistakes, and engaged tirelessly with my ideas. Her confidence in this project has meant a great deal to me.

This book has been much improved by scholars in various fields who graciously took time from their own work to help me. Aron Rodrigue, Richard Roberts, and Philippe Buc offered original insights from their respective fields outside of Russian history. Jonathan Berkey, David Powers, and members of the Working Group Modernity and Islam assisted me in understanding how my work relates to debates within Islamic history. I was fortunate to be able to receive feedback from participants of a stimulating reading group and seminar at the University of California at Berkeley, for which I would like to thank especially Yuri Slezkine, Nicholas Riasanovsky, Daniel Brower, and the late Reginald Zelnik. In numerous conversations and seminars, Nancy Shields Kollmann, Norman Naimark, and Amir Weiner have generously contributed a great deal toward reshaping the final contours of this book. Their close reading of the text sharpened the argument, improved the prose, and encouraged me to see my work in a new light. Margaret Anderson and James Sheehan, both historians of Europe, deserve special thanks—not only due to the spirit of generosity that they represent—but because their remarkable insights did so much to clarify what a book about the Russian empire should look like. For invaluable mentoring in the writing process, I thank Albert Camarillo, Paul Robinson, and Eileen Findley.

Joyce Seltzer of Harvard University Press demonstrated her characteristic patience and, at a very crucial juncture, inimitable judgment. I am in her debt. Don Pirius drew outstanding maps. Wendy Nelson, who edited the manuscript, did a brilliant job of making sense of my writing. Three reviewers who read the book for the press performed similarly Herculean tasks. Their criticism, praise, and queries were enormously helpful in clarifying what this book is about. They suggested new angles and sources, doubted others, and saved me from mistakes. It is a pleasure to thank the two anonymous reviewers and Mark Mazower, the third reader, for sharing their immense learning and sacrificing their time and energy to make this book much better than it otherwise would have been.

Finally, an expression of special thanks to friends and family is both long overdue and hopelessly inadequate. Olga Litvak, Deborah Cohen, and J. P. Daughton did more than is required of friends: they read my work and offered valuable feedback. For warm friendship throughout, I thank Travis Penland, Robert Martin, Mark Romine, Eric Bachmann, Shawn Rogers, Scott Levi, Ken Petersen, Christopher Cox, Marty Roupe, Patrick Mbajekwe, David Como, and Frank and Lumpi Trentmann. My greatest debts are to my parents, sisters, and Clifford, for their example, encouragement, and humor. For her wit, ideas, tolerance, kindness, conscience, and the joy that she radiates in immeasurable ways, I thank Margaret Sena, the truly talented historian in the family. It is to her that I dedicate this book in gratitude and love.

INDEX